D0709496

# The Collaborative Enterprise

# The Collaborative Enterprise

## Managing Speed
## and Complexity in
## Knowledge-Based Businesses

**Charles Heckscher**

Yale University Press

New Haven and London

Library of Congress Cataloging-in-Publication Data

Heckscher, Charles C., 1949–
    The collaborative enterprise : managing speed and complexity in
knowledge-based businesses / Charles Heckscher.
        p.  cm.
    Includes bibliographical references and index.
    ISBN 978-0-300-11464-5 (cloth : alk. paper)
        1.  Organizational change.    2.  Decentralization in management.
    3.  Cooperativeness.    I.  Title.
    HD58.8.H43   2007
    658.4'06—dc22        2006039444

A catalogue record for this book is available from the British Library.

The paper in this book meets the guidelines for permanence and durability of
the Committee on Production Guidelines for Book Longevity of the Council on
Library Resources.

To Lavinia, with love and gratitude for her help and support.

# Contents

Acknowledgments, ix

Introduction, 1

**Part I: The System**

1 From Bureaucracy to Collaborative Enterprise, 25

2 Strategies and Structures: Varieties
of Collaborative Enterprise, 54

3 Citibank e-Solutions, 85

4 The Culture of Contribution, 108

5 Collaborative Infrastructure, 135

6 Two Unresolved Problems, 170

**Part II: The Transformation**

7 Crossing the Collaborative Frontier, 195

**8** Journeys: Winding Paths to Collaboration, 211

**9** Leadership: The Interactive Approach to Change, 226

**10** Recapitulation, 246

**11** But Is It Good? 252

Appendix: The Research Base *By Charles Heckscher, Carlos Martin, and Boniface Michael*, 277

Notes, 289

Bibliography, 311

Index, 329

Acknowledgments

This discussion of collaboration is itself based on many collaborative efforts. I owe here a particular debt to Nathaniel Foote, who organized a group under the auspices of McKinsey & Co. between 1999 and 2001 to study the development of new forms of organization; and to the other members of that group, especially Russ Eisenstat, Jay Galbraith, Danny Miller, and Quentin Hope. Many of the ideas discussed in this book emerged from the concepts and data shared so freely and generously within this team.

Other collaborations that have greatly shaped my thinking include work with Paul Adler on the nature of collaborative community; with Michael Maccoby, Rafael Ramirez, and Pierre-Eric Tixier on the problem of changing systems; and with Anne Donnellon and others in my original foray into "post-bureaucratic" organization theory. Michael Maccoby has been a mentor and colleague through all these evolutions. And even farther back, my work with Talcott Parsons and his student, Mark Gould, gave me a set of general categories and rules of thought that I use constantly.

Carlos Martin and Boniface Michael contributed invaluable help in analyzing and coding cases and arguing with me about the fit between the data and the theory. I also wish to thank some of the patient readers who have helped me with extensive comments, including many of those mentioned above plus Sue Schurman, Frank Domurad, Lavinia Hall, and of course my editor, Michael O'Malley.

# The Collaborative Enterprise

# Introduction

The frontier of human productive capacity today is the power of extended collaboration—the ability to work together beyond the scope of small groups. This is the latest of a series of historical expansions of human abilities through an increase in the scope and richness of interactions. When people learned in the eighteenth century to extend the range of markets, social progress leaped forward. When, about a century ago, companies mastered the techniques of bureaucratic organization, they made possible the creation of products on a scale and a level of efficiency hitherto undreamed of. Now the problem at the leading edge of production is to combine knowledge and skills flexibly around changing tasks. For this purpose neither markets nor bureaucracies are optimal: the task requires new processes of collaborative communication, understanding, mutual adjustment, and shared problem solving.

This is of course a large assertion, as most business leaders would say that their key challenge is not collaboration but something else—globalization, or technological development, or sustaining innovation, or managing costs, or any of a hundred other issues that produce headlines in the management journals. Each of these requires intense attention on its own, but in the end all depend on the general capacity to mobilize people with widely diverse skills and views to work together. Increasingly, indeed, collaboration must extend beyond the firm, including allies and partners and subcontractors around the world. No single leader, no matter how brilliant, can keep a business moving for long simply through personal involvement; no system of rules and procedures, no matter how well worked out, can keep ahead of the curve of change. The underlying challenge of continuous adaptation to a changing environment requires the combined intelligence of many people with differentiated knowledge, and the business that can best draw on combined intelligence will best be able to do the more particular tasks that come to the foreground.

Alfred Chandler's magisterial historical studies have shown convincingly, with a century's hindsight, that the key challenge in the early twentieth century was the mastery of scale and scope; organizations that mastered that capability, through the development of integrated bureaucratic systems, were the ones that dominated the twentieth-century economy.[1] For them the problem was to mobilize effort on a scale never before seen. Today those techniques have become routine, and many companies that try to survive on this basis alone fall into the quicksand of commodity production. Now the challenge is mobilizing not effort but *intelligence*: to get people to use their particular knowledge and capacities in ways that continuously contribute to the success of the whole.

## WHAT IS COLLABORATION AND WHY IS IT IMPORTANT?

Collaboration means "working together." It implies much more than "living together," involving as it does a shared objective that cannot be reached without the contribution of all. Thus it necessarily implies processes of dialogue and negotiation, of exchanges of views and sharing of information, of building from individual views toward a shared consensus.

In a collaborative relationship the parties deliberately pursue a common purpose. This is not the case in the main alternative forms of organization, markets and hierarchies. In markets, participants seek to maximize their own benefit, and any collective good emerges without intention, through the action (as Adam Smith put it) of an "invisible hand." As for bureaucracy, one of its core principles is that only the top leaders should worry about the overall goals, and the rest should worry only about their own pieces. Until quite recently—not more than twenty years ago—it was in fact rare for companies to share strategic thinking with their employees. The overall goal was left not to the invisible hand of market interaction but to what Chandler famously called the "visible hand" of corporate leadership. Each part was supposed to stick to its own focus and to leave the big picture to the top.[2]

The concept of collaboration is not entirely new for business or for society: long before the dawn of recorded history, humans collaborated to hunt the mastodon or saber-toothed tiger. But until rather recently collaboration occurred only under rather specific, and now increasingly marginal, conditions: it required *sharply bounded* groups with *enduring* and *homogeneous* membership. Thus in classic literature collaboration was often thought of as grounded in fraternal groups, or "bands of brothers," though it also characterized some emergent religious movements such as the early Christian sects.[3] Under those narrow conditions people could *sometimes* work together, at least for a time, in flexible and interactive forms of problem solving.

Even under such conditions, collaboration has tended to be fragile, vulnerable to internal battles and factional splits. The biblical story of Jacob and Esau is the first record of the tensions that can divide even brothers. That is why all human societies, especially as they have grown beyond the hunter-gatherer phase, have moved rapidly toward systems of defined roles organized in hierarchies. There is a wide range of such systems, some formal and rule-based, some traditional and status-based, but they share basic elements: when people have defined roles they know what each is supposed to do, and when they nevertheless have conflicts a higher power can intervene to resolve them. These mechanisms work, in effect, because they do not require flexible collaboration: they shield people from the difficult, cumbersome, back-and-forth process of negotiation among equals. Though collaboration still exists in complex societies, it has retreated to the margins.

In the business world this pattern was played out in the late nineteenth and early twentieth centuries. Before that time production occurred mainly in small shops. Then bureaucracy began to emerge as a principle of organization, spreading from railroads to steel to automobiles and other industries; and as Max Weber, the great theorist of bureaucracy, pointed out even before 1900, "where the bureaucratization of administration has been completely carried through, a form of power relation is established that is practically unshatterable."[4] Large corporations quickly dominated small shops in most economic domains, through a combination of increased efficiency and increased financial leverage. By the mid-1930s, management theory converged toward a system of highly structured formal organization with clear job definitions, tight supervisory control, and consistent impersonal administration of rules.[5] A long line of critiques, starting with Weber and running through *The Organization Man* and *The Lonely Crowd*, expressed the fear that human beings would become irreversibly locked in the "iron cage" of bureaucracy.[6]

But then, about thirty years ago, something surprising happened: many companies began to reverse this long trend by encouraging the formation of egalitarian teams in the workplace. This trend was slow at first and difficult to implement, with a high rate of failure; but after the mid-1980s it gained momentum and spread widely. Managers learned reliably to establish "semi-autonomous teams" that worked with relatively little supervision and shared responsibility for issues like scheduling, quality management, and sometimes even hiring and discipline. Such teams are now the norm in most automobile factories and a key element of the famous Japanese system of "lean production" that has already transformed much of the manufacturing landscape.[7] This innovation has involved the development of a large array of new techniques and processes: brainstorming, consensual prioritization, the public use of easel pads and other record-keeping mechanisms—all these are ubiquitous today but were virtually unknown in the 1960s.[8]

This kind of "team," though important, is not a major breakthrough. It stays within the traditional boundaries I have cited: the teams are still bounded, homogeneous, and stable. They are composed of employees who in traditional bureaucracies work side by side—the group of subordinates under a single boss; they do not cross the familiar boundaries of unit or level. The "participation" movement has in effect brought informal teamwork, which has always existed beyond the reach of management control, into the light of day and into the reach of managerial systems. Its accomplishments are similarly limited. It enables groups to respond somewhat more flexibly than before to changing needs—people are able to cover for others in their group, to adjust the pace of their work to the level of demand, and to respond more easily to normal breakdowns and fluctuations in work from other parts of the system that impact them. It also allows workers to make small improvements more easily than before. As a result, most research on these efforts has shown some growth in productivity in the form of increases in product quality.[9]

## EXTENDED COLLABORATION

More recently, starting mainly in the 1990s, the problem of collaboration moved to another, far more challenging and unfamiliar level: to settings in which people come together from very different bases of knowledge and experience, for relatively brief periods, with no guarantees or even expectations of ongoing relationships. Task forces within a single multinational company, for instance, may be drawn from different countries, from different divisions and functions, even—perhaps most difficult of all—from different levels of the hierarchy. They often have not known each other before, or at least not well; and to an increasing extent even their tenure within the larger company is uncertain.

This *extended* form of collaboration, unlike local autonomous teams, represents a quantum shift and creates much bigger problems. Most theories of cooperation depend on the idea that the relationship will endure, at least long enough so that defectors will be punished by their counterparts. They also assume that people basically know the same things and understand the task in the same way. These baseline conditions do not apply in the situation of extended collaboration: people may come and go; they may contribute knowledge or experience that others lack and are not able to assess. Even among those at the core, roles are diffuse and shifting as the project evolves and changes; accountabilities are blurred, since it is difficult to pin results to any one individual or even a stable group; and lines of authority are confused, since people from multiple levels and parts of the organization may be involved and working as peers.

I use the term "collaborative *enterprise*" to refer to this collaboration that extends beyond the limits of permanent teams, units, or firms. In particular, the enterprise is not the same as the firm. On the contrary, companies in our collaborative sample are quite aware that they exist in broader "ecosystems," consisting of actual and potential allies and partners—that they cannot do everything themselves within one organization, but must rely on others with special knowledge to provide key components. Firms increasingly pay careful attention to their relationships to this wider environment. At Intel, for example, compensation throughout the company includes a focus not only on expanding its own business, but also on expanding the computer industry and the business environment as a whole, on the assumption that what is good for the industry is good for Intel.[10]

The "enterprise" is here conceived of as an interdependent collaborative network of diverse contributors. I use the term "cooperation" to refer to local, stable teams and relations and "collaboration" to refer to the core problem I am examining: the operation of extended, dynamic, and diverse systems of interaction (Table 1).

The failure to distinguish these two levels of collaboration leads to crucial errors. It is quite possible to have highly cooperative relations in stable units,

Table 1  Local and Extended Collaboration

| Local Collaboration | Extended Collaboration |
| --- | --- |
| Stable membership | Fluid, changing membership |
| Bounded (closed) | Open (porous boundaries) |
| Homogeneous skills | Diverse skills and capabilities |

including formally bureaucratic firms with strong loyalty-based "family" cultures; the classic successes of the last centuries, such as IBM and General Motors, achieved this communal warmth. Many writers have lamented the decline of such cooperation and advocated a return to greater stability. In doing so, however, they ignore the weaknesses of this form: its restrictiveness, pressure for conformity, hierarchical deference, and resistance to outside influences. They also miss the emerging possibility, which is the core topic of this volume, of a more open and diverse form of collaborative association.

## THE VALUE OF EXTENDED COLLABORATION

Why would businesses encourage such difficult and discomfiting types of activity? Because cross-boundary teams can do certain things that the traditional processes of bureaucracy cannot do, at least not well.

In general, systems of extended collaboration are particularly good for a core problem of the current economy: the utilization of complex knowledge. For the past century knowledge has become an increasingly interdependent and collaborative phenomenon, requiring the contributions of many specialists.[11] It is for this reason that the one system in our society that is dedicated to the creation of knowledge—the system of scientific research—is profoundly collaborative, governed through peer review and systematically open to innovation. A company that could achieve such innovative capability, without sacrificing the capability for normal production, would have an enormous advantage in today's economy.[12]

Many have suggested that the growth of knowledge value is not just an incremental change, but a more fundamental shift to a new stage or mode of production. As early as the 1970s Daniel Bell sketched a notion of "postindustrial society" based on information processing and "intellectual technology"; Manuel Castells has argued that we are passing into an "Information Age."[13] I do not need for my purposes to sustain quite such a broad societal diagnosis, but there seems little doubt that large sectors of industry are shifting their strategies. A century ago Frederick Taylor explicitly tried to remove knowledge from the daily production process and to center it in a few managers and engineers; his goal was to maximize value by making most organizational behavior entirely routine. The major thrust of the changes in work over the last few decades has been to bring knowledge back in—to encourage production workers to think about improvements in their work, to bring development labs into the core of business activity, to encourage salespeople to take initiative and responsibility in dealing with customers. Most radical of all, there have been growing efforts to overcome the strict division of labor and tasks built into bureaucracy, and to achieve more flexible ways of combining different forms of knowledge and expertise.

Consider, for instance, a knowledge-centered problem that has been extensively studied: the development of new automobile designs. At least three major skills are involved in this process: design, manufacturing, and marketing. In the pure bureaucratic approach these skills are organized in divisions with high and fixed walls dividing the parts. Design engineers produce the initial specifications based on their own sense of what is beautiful and important, then toss it "over the wall" to manufacturing. Manufacturing determines whether the design can actually be made efficiently; if not, it tosses it back. At the end of the chain, marketing tests it out on consumers and pushes it back up the chain if it doesn't work. At periodic meetings a higher executive who spans the three functions looks at emerging designs and may try to integrate the concerns of all three, but these are sporadic interventions.

This bureaucratic way of managing the process ensures that each of the component skills is developed to a high level and operates with strict accountability. But in the last few decades, as competition has increased and consumer tastes have grown more sophisticated, pressure has grown to produce new designs faster and at a higher level of innovation, integrating new technologies and responding to segmented markets. Gradually the weaknesses of the bureaucratic mode of organization have become apparent: though it is excellent for control and the development of expertise, it is cumbersome and full of friction at the interfaces.

So about twenty years ago companies began trying a new model: to put representatives of design, manufacturing, and marketing in one room and have them work things out together. The Japanese, with a cultural history of cooperation, were the initiators of this radical shift, and demonstrated fairly quickly that they could cut product development times by half or even more through the reduction of back-and-forth arguing.[14] Highly compartmentalized American auto companies adapted somewhat more slowly, but by the mid-1990s all had moved to some version of multifunctional engineering and at least narrowed the gap with their Japanese rivals. This experience has shown that if marketers, designers, and manufacturers combine their knowledge collaboratively they can come up with something far better for the business than if any one function dominates or controls the process.

Extended collaboration also increases organizational responsiveness—the capacity to sense and react to the external environment. Bureaucracies are, to the point of caricature, poor at responsiveness because they are structured to focus inward: each employee looks to a boss for direction. Those who are on the outer "skin" of the organization, generally salespeople, are separated off as a specific function with cultures and work lives very different from those of their fellows. If they spot something—a new customer need, a frequent complaint about a product, a swing toward a competitor—they can relay the information upward, but they cannot initiate changes and are not further involved in seeking solutions. Most of the organization, meanwhile, is completely cut off from the outside, focused on performing internal routines.

Collaboration makes it possible to connect responses directly to environmental stimuli. The salesperson can initiate discussions and participate in meetings with the design engineers, bringing the "outside" view directly into contact with those on the inside. Anyone, indeed, may be able to spot an opportunity and develop a response. In a well-documented case, IBM's nascent culture of collaboration in the mid-1990s enabled middle-level managers, who had spotted the power and potential of the Internet, to develop networks of exploration and support that gradually penetrated upward and throughout the system and led to action that was significantly faster than that of rivals.[15]

Finally, extended collaboration can increase organizations' ability to learn, that is, to continually improve their processes and routines. Again, bureaucracies are rather poor at this because of their emphasis on regularity and predictability. Frederick Taylor, the architect of "Scientific Management" in the early twentieth century, put it with characteristic unapologetic clarity: "Under our system, a worker is told just what he is to do and how he is to do it. Any 'improvement' he makes upon the orders given to him is fatal to his success."[16] Given bureaucracy's stress on vertical rather than horizontal communication, people are blocked from seeing the consequences of changes in their own jobs; only their bosses have a wide enough view to evaluate changes. Learning can in theory happen through suggestions from below that percolate upward, leading to structural changes that are pushed back down; but the difficulty of this process is such that reform is greatly hindered. Change happens in great bursts of "restructuring" rather than through constant evaluation and revision, and when it happens it benefits from neither the direct input nor from the commitment of those who have to carry it out.

Thus the value of knowledge and learning extends even to the heart of the traditional bureaucracy, in the assembly line and the semiskilled workers who repeat simple routines over and over. On the face of it, collaboration would seem of no use there; and yet it is there that lean production methods have shown that if you get workers to talk to each others and to their superiors, they regularly come up with significant improvements. This is not just a matter of motivation, of making them "feel" better about their work; it is far more importantly a matter of knowledge, of combining what the assembly-line workers know from their daily experience with the models of the engineers. Thus factories like the GM–Toyota NUMMI plant in California now build in regular periods in which people from all ends and levels of the production process meet to study what is going on and to work—collaboratively—to find ways of doing things better.[17]

The learning capability of extended collaboration has been further developed in some versions of Total Quality Management that bring people from multiple parts of organizations together in task forces to review processes and to develop improvements. In the best cases this becomes a continuous part of the way of operating, with many connections throughout the system, and leads to a reliably increased capability for identifying new opportunities and pushing the system to new heights.[18]

## LOYALTY, AUTONOMY, AND INTERDEPENDENCE

Collaboration contrasts with two long-standing "ways of seeing" the social order. The older one, still very strong, centers on loyalty, the valuing of long-term, stable relationships and diffuse commitments. Most human societies have been built on this foundation, with social relationships established by tradition and sustained by requirements of honor and duty. In complex societies, loyalty acquired a strong hierarchical aspect of dependence, in which loyalty by lower orders to their lords or groups was reciprocated by the higher orders' responsibility for protection and care.

The vision of loyalty is potent because it provides a sense of stability, security, and trust in the future. In periods of turbulence people often retreat even more to this sense of dependence. Shakespeare, writing during the vertiginous transition to modernity, sometimes portrayed challenges to kingly authority as threats to order on the deepest level—as in Richard's lament on being deposed by Bolingbroke:

> Revolt our subjects? That we cannot mend;
> They break their faith to God as well as us:
> Cry woe, destruction, ruin, loss, decay . . .[19]

Though this may seem a long way from the corporate world, the themes of diffuse obligations of loyalty to superiors and caring for inferiors, and the dangers resulting from violation of those duties, echo through corporate cultures to the present day. Chester Barnard, the former CEO of New Jersey Bell, articulated this core expectation in the 1930s:

> The most important single contribution required of the executive, certainly the most universal qualification, is loyalty, domination by the organization personality.[20]

Many studies of corporate life have emphasized this theme of dependence: that criticism of the boss, or any assertion of independence from the demands of the company, are taboo and "career killers." At one level this is just a matter of calculation based on the superior's power over subordinates; at another level, however, I have sometimes heard from middle managers undertones of a kind of moral terror that echoes Shakespeare's—not just worry about retaliation, but a fear that the decline of the pattern of loyalty may bring the whole system crashing down and take everything with it.

> Loyalty comes with trust and believing and this has been cast out across the whole company as being not the way to run a company. And then when you look around you see takeovers and the crumbling of everything in the whole economy. (Pitney-Bowes)

Many of these managers, even today, look back nostalgically to a time when the reciprocal bond of loyalty was taken for granted; and many critics of corporate layoffs and downsizing have explicitly or implicitly called for a return to that view of the world.

Collaboration is incompatible to this concept of loyalty and dependence because it requires genuine dialogue across levels as well as across units. The linchpin of the collaborative enterprise, the base of its increased power, is that it enables people to use their knowledge and capability to advance the common mission. Where subordinates know more than their bosses about certain problems, where they are working on multiple teams that give them different perspectives, where they understand in depth the changing needs of customers, it is essential for the success of the system that they feel able to challenge their bosses, to propose new ideas, to criticize and argue when necessary. The sense of security provided by the tradition of loyalty presents major obstacle to this kind of open dialogue.

The second competing world-view centers on individualism and autonomy: the notion that the individual should have a zone of independent judgment not subject to social or moral criticism, that should in fact be held to firmly as a sign of personal integrity. This view claims rights for individuals prior to society and any claims of traditional order. Historically, the moral stance of individualism was central to the modern era's break with feudalism and traditional society: it justified rejection of conformity to tradition and subservience to masters. The Renaissance challenged the medieval world-view in asserting the moral right of artists or merchants to pursue their own interests and visions independent of the encompassing body of the Church. Martin Luther went still further: his central assertion of the power of faith, based on personal study of the Bible, was in its essence a declaration of freedom of individual conscience from the moral authority of priests and Church. It is a central characteristic of almost every major evolution of the modern ethos, from the rationalism of the eighteenth century to Romanticism and twentieth-century "modernism."

Both markets and bureaucracies, core institutions of modernity, respect personal autonomy in this sense. In the market the individual stands supreme, making free choices to "truck and barter"[21] with other independent actors. In bureaucracy, a central principle is that experts should be left alone, within given parameters, to do the job as they see fit. Max Weber's original studies of bureaucracy emphasized the importance of building a wall of independence around officials so that they could exercise their expertise without irrational or personally motivated interference. The "over-the-wall" process described earlier in effect implements this vision, allowing designers and manufacturing engineers and marketers to remain true to their own training and vision, subjecting them only to impersonal rules from the organization as a whole. Herbert Simon, perhaps the most important postwar thinker on bureaucratic management, also emphasizes the value of autonomy: he shows the enormous gain in efficiency that comes from modularity, the breaking of tasks into separate hierarchically ordered "chunks" that can be pursued independently.[22] Robert Merton's famous study of bureaucratic character outlined the personality characteristics appropriate to this modular view: a good bureaucrat was characterized by "devotion to one's duties, a keen sense of the limitations of one's authority and competence, and methodical performance of routine activities."[23]

With such a history one would not expect it to be easy to ask people to give up their claims to moral and technical autonomy. Yet that is exactly what a collaborative organization does ask. It requires that people abandon the familiar ethic of "you do your job and I'll do mine," and that they give up trying to protect a zone of independence; instead, it asks that they enter into each other's ways of seeing. The marketer must become something of an engineer, and the engineer must be willing to take criticism from a marketer (and vice versa). At the most fundamental level, all participants must accept that they depend on each other to get done something that is important to each of them.

Thus at the most profound level the shift toward collaboration—the simple idea that "we should work together"—involves a modification of five centuries of Western tradition. The identifying impulse of modernity is the freeing of the individual from the pressures of the group. The collaborative ethos rejects both the subordination and deference of traditional society and the autonomy so central to modernity; it requires that individuals accept that they are intertwined with others and can succeed only through deliberate sharing of understanding and intention.

Such a shift would be impossible, of course, if there were not also a long history of collaboration to draw on. Human action is fortunately never uniform. Efforts to move from bureaucratic principles to collaborative ones have been under way for at least thirty years in business, dating from the development of worker participation and quality circle programs in the 1970s (though one might trace the origins even farther back to the job enrichment of the 1950s). Outside of business, many knowledge enterprises have worked in collaborative ways for a century or even more; the working of science, as a web of researchers sharing experimental results and subject to peer review, is probably the most developed form of extended collaboration we have.[24] Science indeed continued to develop in astonishing ways, such as the quite recent phenomenon in physics of research projects involving hundreds of co-authors, all operating as formal equals and sharing credit for the results.

Innovation in collaborative systems has recently been astonishing beyond the core "business" arena that is the focus of this volume. Open-source software development, for instance, has succeeded in coordinating large numbers of independent coders around very large, complex, and interdependent projects like the Firefox browser. And the early 2000s have brought the beginnings of "Web 2.0," which promises to facilitate distributed interaction on an unprecedented scale.

Business has been cautious about embracing these innovations, fearing a loss of efficiency and control; indeed, these radical forms of collaboration, from science to open source, have been to a greater or lesser degree insulated from the heavy pressures of market competition. Yet the achievements that can come from such flexible processes are attracting attention and seeding learning even in tough competitive sectors.

## PROBLEMS AND OBSTACLES

If collaboration is so smart, why isn't it rich? Why does bureaucracy remain so stubbornly in place? The answer is that collaboration—especially of the extended type—is extremely difficult. Hierarchies and markets are simpler because they are highly restricted and simplified patterns of interaction. Markets have many connections but carry very limited information—mainly price.[25] Communication in bureaucracies can carry much more information, but at the cost of greatly restricting the number of links: formally people communicate only with one boss and a small number of direct subordinates. Collaborative enterprise eliminates both restrictions. As with markets, the number of links is potentially infinite—anyone can contact anyone else; as with bureaucracies, the content of the communication can be "thick." The difficulty is in keeping this potential richness from devolving into chaos.[26]

In addition to multiplying the number of links, collaboration demands a great deal in each relationship; that is, links are not only numerous but also rich in information. In the market I have to worry only about getting what I want, while in a bureaucracy I have to worry only about doing what someone else wants. But if two people are both worrying about how they can make a result happen that they both want, the complexity intensifies enormously. They need to agree on the goal; they need to agree on a division of labor; and they need to readjust the goal and the division of labor as circumstances change and the project advances. This requires a lot of arguments, or at least of negotiations. It raises the danger of irreconcilable conflict, where people just see it differently and cannot come to agreement. It risks degenerating into long debates or polarized splits. If it isn't done well it may be worse than the bureaucratic disease.

From the business perspective, this is a double-edged and nearly paradoxical argument: collaboration is good *because* it is difficult; businesses can draw profits from it *because* it so often fails. It represents a competitive advantage that is not easily imitated.

The example of automobile design shows not only the power but also the risks of the concept. The seemingly sensible idea of getting everyone involved in the design process to sit down in a single room together has turned out to be very difficult to implement. The allegiances, accountability, and cultures of each party tend to remain oriented to their separate divisions and functions rather than to the group process that they are working on, and their trust in each other is often low. Though the details vary from company to company, design engineers often have viewed marketers as short-term and shallow in their thinking, unaware of the vital continuity of identity that distinguishes car companies from each other; marketers have viewed the designers as isolated in their own aesthetic and technical world, out of touch with the consumer. The bosses of the representatives on the team are even more suspicious, uneasy that their own people are making decisions outside their hierarchical control; they have sometimes tried to micromanage the process from outside the team. Given this suspicion and lack of understanding from their bosses, team members have often suffered in their careers.

Thus even though collaboration has advanced considerably in the arena of automobile design, the shift generally remains vulnerable to resistance and only partially realized. Rather than full dialogue among all parties with something to say, the process has developed more like a series of overlapping problem-solving discussions—tighter and more integrated than before, but still a long way from direct multiparty collaboration.[27] Tensions persist at the interfaces between the cross-functional processes and the functional/bureaucratic organization.

This small example, in short, contains in miniature a large set of problems faced by managers in most industries, and that is the focus of this book. If we look more broadly we see the story repeated on many scales and in many domains. AOL and Time Warner thought they could gain competitive advantage by combining creative production with media distribution; despite the compelling strategic logic, the merger essentially failed because the two organizations and kinds of employees could not work together. Technology companies like Digital Equipment and Wang failed because they were unable to connect the technical expertise of their hacker employees to the actual needs of consumers. Even the positive examples demonstrate the magnitude of the task.

Starting in the late 1990s, IBM made an enormous bet that it could win by combining the expertise of business consultants with the technical knowledge of their traditional base; they speak about it as a twenty-year process. Citibank realized in the 1970s that it could create compelling products by bringing together its expertise in particular countries and regions to shape broader, cross-national financing mechanisms; after twenty years of bruising internal struggles it began to actually demonstrate this capability. The major problem for those who sought to decode the human genome was to get the computer coders to talk with the biochemical experts. Beyond the business arena, we find the Department of Homeland Security confronted by the same essential problem of building relationships across the walls of bureaucratic agencies. Examples can be multiplied endlessly: newspapers are filled almost every day with stories that revolve around such efforts to create new knowledge synergies, the problems that often dog them, and the occasional successes that create enormous new value.

## THE GROWING CHALLENGE

Over the past decade the pace of experimentation has quickened in corporations. This means, on the one hand, that the outlines of the answers to some of the questions are beginning to take shape. On the other, it is becoming ever clearer that the capability for collaboration involves not just a local team, a company, or an industry, but society and indeed the world at large.

The widening scope of economic activity, aided to a large extent by collaborations in the form of supply-chain networks and alliances, has increased the number of distinct perspectives that are relevant to the production process. To stay with the example of automobile design: since both markets and processes are now international in scope, products need to appeal to more diverse constituencies and to draw on manufacturing capability in many countries. These points of view need somehow to be incorporated in the design process. It is not just that marketers need to communicate with engineers; Chinese marketers (for example) need to come to some shared vision with American marketers (and many others) so that the eventual product can appeal across borders; they also need to talk to Chinese and American manufacturing managers (and many others) so that local adaptations can be made as needed within a consistent overall design. Somewhere along the line legal representatives from many countries will need to weigh in to make sure that local regulations and sourcing requirements are met, and HR managers will need to consider how skills and labor capacity can best be allocated. Nor are national differences the only important ones: within countries, appeal to particular identity groups, such as women, has grown more important. If women are not part of the production process, a result may emerge that leaves them out of the buying process.

And this is not the end of it: the changes involved in the increasing scope of collaboration ripple out to social institutions beyond the economy. Since businesses are deeply interdependent with other parts of society—on educational systems, workforce attitudes and motivations, regulatory climates, and so on—the complexity of the decision web touches all these domains. Collaboration cannot become a normal way of doing business until these consequences have been worked through; and so far we are only at the very start of the process.

These larger interdependencies have been most visible so far in terms of careers. The bureaucratic career focused within a stable functional hierarchy: the middle tier came to expect to spend their working lives in one company and, if they were managers, working upward through a hierarchy; to anticipate gradual salary increases with seniority; and to count on company-based pensions for their retirement. The collaborative career is conceptually broader, carrying an individual with particular skills and interests across varying companies and projects. This has added to other forces in disrupting long-established expectations. The growing assumption of young workers, encouraged not only by business schools and managerial publications but also in the popular press, is that they will need to shape their own training and job searching. There is also an increased acceptance of the notion that people must "take responsibility for" their own retirements rather than counting on company plans. Yet there is also tremendous human cost as many people get caught in the transition without the traditional mechanisms of security, with a resultant backlash most strongly seen in the strength of anti-globalization sentiment.

The implications reach even to the core of the personality. Analysts of bureaucracy in the 1950s described the rise of a bureaucratic character, focused on expert performance and clear autonomy; some noted the ways in which this character was grounded in the mass education system of the time and in the single-earner family structure that also developed with the bureaucratic corporation. Today such a personality is no longer valued in most workplaces: companies seek risk-takers, creative types, highly flexible people who can learn new skills and work with diverse co-workers.[28] Schools, it may be noted, have begun to adjust their curricula to suit this ideal, using many team-based projects and stressing skills in negotiation and dealing with diversity. Families have widely evolved to encourage internal debate and negotiation rather than deference to parents and conformity to authority.

Thus it is evident that this is a large transition, and that it will be lengthy. As old institutions are threatened—the authority of managers, along with that of teachers and parents; the central value of corporate loyalty; the traditional protective role of bureaucracies—the change process encounters fear and resistance. As new problems are encountered—how to maintain accountability without a clear reporting line; how to maintain overall strategic consistency while encouraging flexibility—new experiments must be tried and new systems developed.

The danger in all this is a loss of coherence and clarity as new initiatives multiply and the pace of change accelerates. The opportunity that justifies these risks is the potential to use human knowledge more powerfully than ever before to solve complex problems.

## THE RESEARCH

The problem of collaboration has drawn a great deal of attention in the past decade—both from managers, who have struggled with a succession of "team-based" innovations and fads, and from academics, who have grown increasingly interested in networks as well as chaos, complexity, and other novel theoretical frameworks. On the whole, however, both the theory and practice of such "post-bureaucratic" organizations are in their infancy. Despite exciting stories that load down bookstore shelves, few companies have made more than small steps toward being able to coordinate flexible teams successfully, and scholarly work has thrown light only into a few corners of the darkness.

The challenge of understanding collaboration is partly methodological and partly theoretical. The theoretical problem is to move beyond the Weberian concept of bureaucracy. Over the past century a substantial edifice has been built on Weber's foundation, creating a rich and reasonably consistent view. Alfred Sloan and Pierre du Pont added the notion of a decentralized bureaucracy, with divisions serving as profit centers rather than being closely controlled by the organization; Barnard and others added an understanding of shared culture as a necessary component of successful organization; many writers (including Weber) have analyzed typical dysfunctions and limitations of the structure.[29] All of this holds together. But the wave of teams, task forces, processes, and restructurings of the past twenty years has challenged many of the basic assumptions and the theoretical models without so far generating a new foundation. In particular, the study of teamwork, networks, and other peer-to-peer systems has for the most part been divorced from the understanding of the hierarchy, as if they were incompatible. This has severely hampered the understanding of what organizations are doing.

The methodological problem is that it is extremely difficult to tell what is "really" going on in organizations, especially in a period of rapid change and experimentation. The rhetoric of cooperation and teamwork has certainly grown, but practice does not necessarily match it; therefore simply asking top managers or HR leaders what they think is happening—the most common methodological approach—can be quite inaccurate. Further, in this early period of change, there are far more failures than successes; so the effort that looks like a shining beacon one year often disappears the next. For these reasons the usual research approaches risk serious misunderstanding. I have frequently visited organizations that have been used as models by one writer or another, only to find that the reality does not, or does no longer, approximate the description.

A good understanding of what is going on therefore requires close knowledge, based on interviews or observations at multiple levels, over time. This is understandably rare: problems of access and feasible patience are overwhelming. I have tried, however, over the last decade, to approximate it as closely as possible. The analysis in this volume is based on a diverse set of data and experience, with many collaborators, including:

- A group of leaders wrestling with the problem of organization change that met every nine months for four years, sharing in-depth their stories as they evolved. In some cases colleagues and I conducted extensive interviews with middle managers around particular change problems.
- An extensive project, coordinated by Nathaniel Foote at McKinsey and Company from 1999 to 2001, to explore the organizational requirements for managing complex solutions organizations. In that context detailed cases were developed on more than a dozen companies.
- Further interviews I have done in about forty-five organizations, with varying degrees of detail. Fourteen of these, focused on middle management downsizing and restructuring around 1990, formed the basis of *White-Collar Blues*[30]; others since then have been part of various research projects.
- Knowledge gained from my involvement as a consultant in some major, long-term organization change processes, especially at AT&T and Lucent. This is supplemented by close analysis of change processes involving three of my colleagues at EDF (France), FS (Italy), and AT&T.[31]

• Research conducted at Citibank in 2001–2002 under a grant from the Citigroup Behavioral Sciences Research Council. This included a set of interviews and surveys focused on process improvement teams; interviews of customer relationships managers and their internal clients; and a detailed study over time of the Alliance group within e-Solutions. Together with extensive historical material developed by the McKinsey team, this has created the most complete case example that I have.

• A database built from secondary sources over the last decade.

I drew from these projects twenty-one case studies of which I, or one of the members of the groups with which I have closely worked, have extensive knowledge based on primary research and experience, usually with interviews at various organizational levels. Two Ph.D. students (Carlos Martin and Boniface Michael) and I coded the cases according to the categories and propositions of the theory of collaborative enterprise. This labor-intensive process resulted in a large spreadsheet with numerical codes, along with qualitative comments and data sources. (For details, see the Appendix at the end of this book.)

This systematic case analysis tests the core dimensions of the theory against as wide a range of examples as possible, while retaining the richness of understanding that comes only with case material. It can help to spot patterns that would not appear clearly in a smaller number but may emerge from the larger sample. More important, it highlights cases that don't fit in order to force reassessment of the theory.

Thus we can say with some confidence that the arguments made here hold across a range of companies, in several industries and countries. But this is evidently not just an empirical exercise: the patterns I sketch come out of a general point of view drawing on social and organizational theory. If it works, with the evidence and with readers, it is because it "makes sense" of large changes under way and experienced in different ways by large numbers of employees at all levels. To the extent that it does so, the patterns identified here should only grow stronger and clearer with time. The aim is, through understanding the present, to get a feel for the future.

## THE STRUCTURE OF THE BOOK

The fundamental point of view underlying this investigation is that organizations are going through a fundamental and long-term shift driven primarily by strategic requirements and choices, but deeply affecting organizational structure, culture, and infrastructure. These dimensions—strategy, structure, culture, and infrastructure—are closely linked but are rarely analyzed together: strategic theorists look outward and tend to assume that the organization can carry out whatever (in their view) the environment demands, while organizational theorists generally look inward and assume they are working with immutable principles of structure. But it is the ability to match organizational capabilities with conditions for success that determines the long-term success of organizations.

Strategy, structure, and culture are familiar terms but used in widely disparate ways; infrastructure is less familiar. For our purposes:

- Strategy is the determination of the organization's purposes and goals, generally over a three- to five-year time period—that is to say, longer-term than the immediate objectives, but less grand than visions of the next decade or more.
- Structure is the set of formalized responsibilities, roles, and rules that define the organization.
- Culture is a pattern of expectations shared by members of a group— expectations about how others will act and react to situations—that enable them to respond flexibly to adaptive challenges.
- Infrastructure is a set of "background" roles and systems that are not directly involved in the work process, but that help define and maintain the culture and structure. These typically include career systems, training, rewards, voice, and various kinds of communication and meetings that enable people to understand each other and the organization.

These vary in terms of how easily they can be set and modified by top management. Strategy is—at least on the surface—most easily established from the top; structure is harder, because it involves far-flung webs of responsibilities, but it can be monitored and sanctioned by management; infrastructure is still harder, because of its indirect relationship to the work product; culture is most difficult of all, and can in fact rarely be approached directly.

The linkage among these dimensions means, moreover, that the worlds interpenetrate. Top managers who believe they can focus on strategy without understanding and adapting the other dimensions will rapidly find themselves in trouble. As Winston Churchill once noted, "However beautiful the strategy, you should occasionally look at the results."

The essential division we will explore is between a familiar complex of strategy, structure, culture, and infrastructure of large twentieth-century organizations,

Table 2  Dimensions of the Emerging Enterprise

|  | Twentieth-Century Firm | Emerging Enterprise |
|---|---|---|
| Strategy | Mass production | Solutions |
| Structure | Bureaucracy | Collaborative enterprise |
| Culture | Paternalism | Contribution |

and the new, half-formed, untried complex that is emerging today to try to increase productive capability (Table 2).

• The key strategic driver is the need for increased flexibility in order to respond to market changes and to take advantage of technological innovation; broadly speaking, it is a move from "push" strategies focused on product excellence to interactive strategies that aim to understand and provide solutions for customer needs.
• To achieve that goal, structure must move from bureaucracy, which we know well, to a far less understood form that we are here calling collaborative, involving much use of fluid and far-flung teams.
• Beneath that, a web of cultural expectations built around notions of loyalty and caring must give way to something else. What this will be is not only uncertain but highly controversial, involving conflicting ideas of essential moral duties and differing conceptions of human nature. I will argue that the core of the new culture is a notion of contribution.
• Finally, there is an entire infrastructural base—new systems of careers, rewards, communication, and so on—that helps to sustain the system.

Such changes at best take a long time to accomplish; and in a large transformation like the one under discussion, they go beyond what any single organization can do. If families and schools teach paternalistic and bureaucratic values, as they largely did fifty years ago—values like deference to authority and avoidance of conflict—then it will be hard to staff organizations that want to be entrepreneurial and innovative. If retirement and children's educations and other major life challenges are structured on the expectation that they will be funded by a long-term single wage-earner, then the move to more uncertain careers will be deeply threatening on many levels no matter how management handles it.

This is just a first cut, and it is the task of the rest of this book to elaborate it. I have so far oversimplified things in some crucial ways. First, though the collaborative dimension is the key innovation now, hierarchy remains crucial to organization, and much of the practical task now is to work out how it relates to teamwork and involvement. Second, collaboration is not one thing; it has many variants appropriate to different conditions. Above all, it is not simple.

The patterns I describe are abstracted from a world in motion: to my knowledge, no company or system has achieved a stable collaborative state, and few remain in a stable bureaucratic one. All except a few niche companies, protected by some fluke of the market, are to some degree in transition—trying out new systems of accountability, figuring out what kinds of teams are needed where, exploring new kinds of career commitments, experimenting with ways of selecting employees. All this presents a very difficult terrain to cross in the journey toward greater flexibility, and produces many false turns. The issue of change management is partly having a clear picture of where you are heading—of the nature of collaboration, and the kind that is needed—and partly a matter of sequencing steps so as to avoid rebellions and vicious circles.

In the following chapters, I take up in sequence the issues of strategy, structure, culture, infrastructure, and the dynamics of change. Finally, I consider a question not often asked in this context: Is this change good? For most of the book I argue that it is clearly good, in most situations, for the particular value of economic performance; but there are values in society other than this. It is worth understanding, as we move on a trajectory that I believe will dominate the next half century or more, what effects it will have on other aspects of our lives, short- and long-term.

# Part I  The System

# Chapter 1 From Bureaucracy to
## Collaborative Enterprise

Since collaborative systems dismantle certain aspects of bureaucratic structure—reducing rules, levels, and job boundaries—people may assume that they are simply *less* structured. When asked about control, systems managers frequently respond, like one of my interviewees at DuPont, "Well, you know, we just do the right thing." The truth, however, is that collaborative enterprises need a great deal of structure to organize specialists around complex and fast-moving activities without descending into chaos—but it is a new *kind* of structure and discipline.

### ANALYZING CORPORATE STRUCTURES

#### Two Dimensions of Organization

All corporations, as well as other purposive organizations, must sustain two sets of relationships. The most familiar and most studied is a *hierarchical* set—that involving superiors and subordinates. Starting with Max Weber's[1] seminal analysis of bureaucracy in the late nineteenth century, the central concern has been how authority is legitimated and how it is applied: why people obey, and under what conditions; how authority can be most effectively exercised; and what kinds of pathologies result from excessive control and excessive deference. We learned during the past century, for example, that it is important to allow a certain degree of autonomy to subordinates in order to give them "room" to innovate and respond to new challenges; that the span of control in a classic bureaucracy should generally be between five and ten subordinates to each superior; and that a degree of generalized loyalty from the bottom toward the top helps hold things together.

But hierarchy is never enough either as a description or as a prescription for effective organization. Even the most structured bureaucracy cannot deal with everything through hierarchies: the stacked boxes of accountability must be supplemented by an ability to communicate horizontally across boundaries of function and level when necessary. I call this the *associational* dimension of organization.[2]

Associational relations are most easily recognized by the absence of power—though some people may have more influence and better connections than others, they cannot tell others what to do. The shift is very visible when bosses and subordinates shift into an associational mode: they engage in all kinds of equalizing symbolic activities, from sitting more informally to taking off jackets, swapping personal stories, and going out for drinks together.

These two dimensions—vertical and horizontal, or command and association—are common to all purposive organizations. The formal structure, composed of the familiar hierarchy of offices, forms the stable skeleton. The associational system, less well understood, cuts across the formal lines in more fluid and flexible ways. Thus formal hierarchy and association are in effect cross-cutting "layers" within every organization; and an accurate map of relationships must treat them both (Figure 1).

The most familiar way of treating these two dimensions has been to say that the hierarchical one is "formal" and the horizontal one is "informal." In bureaucracies, associational relations are indeed structured by informal ties—watercooler conversations, personal relationships, peer pressure. In such settings formal and informal relationships may conflict, as when workers band together to restrict output and outwit their managers; or they may harmonize, as when employees exchange valuable information across formal lines that helps all to do their own jobs better.

The informal organization was discovered—at least in the mainstream scholarly literature—by the researchers who conducted the "Hawthorne studies" at Western Electric around 1930, who were astonished to find that unrecognized

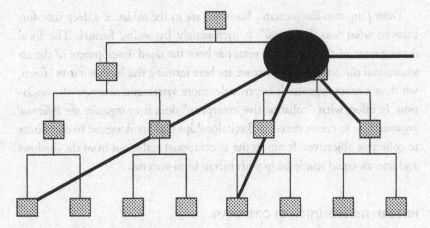

Figure 1: Hierarchical and associational relations (in gray and black, respectively)

networks among workers were distorting and shaping the effects of management systems. Elton Mayo and Chester Barnard followed with theories of how to mobilize this informal set of relationships for the good of the company through a "Human Relations" approach, giving rise to the modern personnel function.[3] Periodically others have rediscovered the phenomenon. Henry Mintzberg, reviewing research from the 1950s and 1960s, found that managers spent most of their time in lateral rather than vertical communication. Melville Dalton keenly observed the power struggles and cliques that constituted the world of managerial "politics," subverting rational organizational functioning. Peter Blau showed how informal consultations could sometimes improve and sometimes degrade output.[4]

The two ways of viewing organizations have remained largely separate, scarcely acknowledging each other as they move on parallel tracks. Those who study informal organizations have generally used anthropological approaches, relying on detailed observations of an area "hidden" from public view; their interest has been particularly in the way these underground relationships alter and subvert espoused policy. Those who study formal organizations are more likely to use models based on the assumption that employees will respond as rational individuals to formal incentives; for them the informal world is a nuisance, noise in the data, something to be controlled for. There is some convergence on the terrain of "leadership" studies, which essentially involves trying to understand how those in power can turn the informal system in the harmonizing rather than conflicting direction; this has always been seen as a delicate and uncertain art, quite distinct from the more scientific rules of "management."

These long-familiar patterns, however, are in the midst of a deep transformation: what was "informal" is increasingly becoming formal. The focal development of the past thirty years has been the rapid development of the associational dimension into what we are here terming the "collaborative" form, which is a more organized, larger-scale, more systematic *structure* of association. In effect what "collaborative enterprise" does is to *organize the informal organization:* to create peer-based relationships that are designed to contribute to collective objectives. It moves the associational realm out from the shadows and into an equal relationship with hierarchical systems.

## HISTORY: THE EVOLUTION OF CORPORATE STRUCTURES

The history of corporate organization can be told in terms of the emphasis and organization of the hierarchical and associational dimensions, and of the relationship between them.

### Level 0: Professional and Craft Associations

Until the Industrial Revolution, most organized economic activity was carried out through associations, dating back to medieval guilds; these generally functioned as self-governing associations of independent workers, with weak or nonexistent hierarchies. Because they were associational rather than hierarchical, they are seen today by many writers as precursors and even models for the current organizational changes, and the term "professional" is often used as a key value in collaborative enterprises.

But these associational systems were quite far from collaborative in our sense: the members operated for the most part very independently. They were linked primarily through traditional values and codes of conduct, learned in apprenticeships or schools, but not by ongoing collaboration. Until the past few decades there were, for instance, virtually no mechanisms by which doctors could come together to restructure their approach to a disease. Change came, when it came, through an infiltration of new knowledge into medical schools, which might then affect the practice of individuals over a few generations. Governance systems were aimed primarily at maintaining boundaries against the outside world and protecting the monopoly power of the membership. Internal discipline among professionals and crafts workers—sanctioning poor performance or even immoral actions—was weak, because the degree of interdependence was low; it didn't really hurt lawyers much if some of their fellows performed badly, because they could just avoid them.[5]

These are among the reasons that hierarchical organization, when it began to move into the economic sphere, was overwhelmingly successful; and, as Max Weber noted, as it became gradually more systematic and bureaucratized, it was able to drive out virtually all forms of "communal" action.[6]

### Level 1: Personal Control

The first major step in the development of hierarchical dimension, starting in the late eighteenth century, was hardly what we would today call "organization." Firms were almost entirely small, generally family-based, and managed through the personal authority of the owner. Relationships were sometimes informal and cooperative, at other times very oppressive, but always within the framework of a traditional community with a strong hierarchical shape. Such organizations could support only relatively small-scale production and low levels of complexity.

### Level 2: Simple Bureaucracy

As markets expanded, opportunities emerged to take advantage of scale. The railroads were the first organizations that really had to move beyond personal control in order to manage far-flung operations; they developed simple forms of bureaucracy soon after the Civil War. From then to the late twentieth century, the main strategic emphasis in more and more industries was on increasing the scale and efficiency of operations, to create and serve mass markets that were in their early stages.

The story told by Weber in the late nineteenth century was centrally about the coming of formal hierarchy—and the destruction of the communal and associational networks that stood in its way. In the realm of work the structure of the existing occupational communities had been relatively communal.[7] As these communities faced the growing power of capitalists, especially capitalist bureaucracies, they generally resisted, sometimes in explosive and highly conflictual ways. But they were unable to sustain that opposition, in large part because no one was "directing" or managing it.[8]

Weber, like many of the authors of current network literature, treated bureaucracy and associational communities as largely exclusive. His "ideal-type" definition of bureaucracy was all formal hierarchy with no association: each individual was theoretically responsible for doing a job, and not for outcomes beyond that job. In this view of the world,[9] if any officeholder has an issue with a peer, he refers the problem up the chain to someone who has authority over both of them. Attempts to "work things out" directly, or otherwise to transcend the boundaries of the office, are viewed as threats to the order of things.

The conception of pure hierarchy was probably never close to a description of reality, but it does seem to have been close to the *ideas* of many of the leaders who created the modern corporation. Frederick Taylor was perhaps the purest proponent of the view that association (at least among workers) was always an evil. He, like many managers whose names have been forgotten, was explicitly engaged in *breaking* the associational communities that resisted productivity-enhancing innovations. He did this by applying something close to Weber's purely rational conception of organization, forcing behavior into this mold through extremely tight control. The concept of peer relations was absent from theory partly because organizational leaders wanted it to disappear in practice.

Taylor, and corporate leaders at the beginning of the twentieth century, faced heavy resistance from supervisors used to the highly personalized relationships of power that had governed the early phases of large corporations. Supervisors generally ran little empires within which they were for the most part free to do whatever they wanted: they played favorites and used arbitrary, sometimes violent, means of control. They, as much as their workers, were fierce opponents of the new rationalizing trend.

So this early phase of corporation-building, in the terms introduced earlier, had two aspects. On the one hand, it was a matter of destroying existing associational networks—the communities and guilds that predated the emerging rationalized power structure. On the other, it involved the gradual development of the new power structure itself, moving from arbitrary and personalized use of power to a "scientific method" that constrained supervisors as well as the supervised.[10]

## Level 3: Decentralized Paternalist Bureaucracy

As markets matured further, gaining a larger and more sophisticated consumer base, pressure grew for more complex and differentiated products. The bellwether automobile industry evolved from the single-product Model T to the sophisticated generational sequencing of models and brands in General Motors. These pressures led to evolutions of the bureaucratic model—in particular, to greater decentralization and stronger informal association.

The "one-dimensional" view of the corporation, focusing only on the development of consistent and rational hierarchy, was inadequate on many levels. Two insights emerged clearly. First, to the extent that employees did adopt the pure rationalistic bureaucratic point of view, organizations became rigid, unresponsive, and inward-focused—what we mean today by the pejorative interpretation of "bureaucratic." Second, the informal peer relations did not vanish—they simply became disconnected from, and usually harmful to, the organization's goals. At the blue-collar level, workers formed new peer groupings that sometimes emerged in open conflict or unionization, but even more often remained hidden as "restriction of output" or collective "soldiering."[11] At the managerial level, truly bureaucratic organizations were classically riven by fierce "political" clashes among powerful subempires.[12]

Corporate leaders adopted two reforms to combat these dysfunctions. On the *hierarchical* dimension they decentralized: Alfred Sloan and Pierre du Pont famously invented during the 1920s the divisionalized structure in which units gained wider autonomy within the overall hierarchy. On the *associational* dimension they became aware that they needed more than formal structure: they needed a healthy culture to promote positive relations and cooperation. They therefore developed a culture of paternalistic caring and loyalty. Chester Barnard was one of the first systematizers of the idea in the late 1930s: "Informal organizations," he wrote, "are necessary to the operation of formal organizations as a means of communication, of cohesion, and of protecting the dignity of the individual."[13] This is very far from the pure rationalism and formalism of the early organization theorists. The emerging culture of loyalty was fostered and buttressed in many ways: through compensation and benefit systems that tied people to single firms; through corporate acts of "caring," including promises of lifetime security; through the development of explicit corporate values; through a new common language of "family"; through a set of supervisory orientations, pushed by personnel departments and embodied in the "Human Relations" movement, that strengthened the bonds between employees and the corporate group; and by many other systems and habits.

From at least the 1930s until the 1980s, this "hybrid" characterized all large successful companies: they were not merely bureaucracies but *paternalist* bureaucracies. There were cultural variations, to be sure, with some companies more successful and systematic than others in building this sense of loyalty, but I know of no significant exception to the pattern. This is a cross-cultural phenomenon as well: the vaunted Japanese system of lifetime employment and company loyalty is not essentially different, at the managerial levels, from that of U.S. companies in that time, or European ones either.[14]

While there have been many studies of formal structures, much less analysis has been conducted of the informal associational networks framed by paternalist cultures. But from a few observational studies one can extract common themes:

- There was a great deal of lateral communication unmapped by organization charts. My own interviews in many corporations, as well as those of others, consistently document informal cooperation among managers outside their range of accountability, sometimes quite elaborate and long-term.[15] The ability to build a network of relationships that could provide information and influence outside the normal channels has been one of the primary skills of successful managers in traditional firms.
- These paths of communication were heavily concentrated within the boundaries of the formal hierarchy—within divisions, and among the subordinates of powerful leaders. Cross-boundary communications did occur, but far more rarely.
- Lateral communications had no direct accountability or connection to the formal hierarchy. People engaged in them because they were necessary to the accomplishment of their jobs, but they were not managed or directly rewarded.

From the point of view of organizational effectiveness this kind of informal associational system was successful in "lubricating" bureaucracy and preventing undue rigidity. We know from a few studies that organizations that failed to create a culture of loyalty had counterproductive informal relationships: they became consumed with internal "politics," highly unresponsive to outside demands, and unable to combine to meet new challenges.[16] In organizations with a good paternalist culture, by contrast, the informal organization was positive: crises generally led to "heroic" responses in which the broad loyalty to the company came to the forefront and people pulled together to save it. In more normal times, moreover, there was considerable problem solving outside the formal structure.[17]

## THE DECLINE OF PATERNALISM

The system of paternalist bureaucracy enabled corporations to balance a certain level of efficiency, complexity, and adaptiveness, but the continued development of markets strained their capabilities. Compared to earlier forms of personal control, bureaucracy was enormously efficient; but at a certain point, traceable in polls to the 1960s,[18] it became seen as not efficient *enough* to meet the needs of increasingly demanding consumers. More exactly, in the framework we have been using, bureaucracy can be enormously efficient when pressures for complexity and adaptiveness are low—when products are fairly simple and changes in demand are slow. As these other pressures grow, however, it has to make compromises: the culture of loyalty helps to maintain some flexibility, but at the cost of diminished control and efficiency.

The paternalist culture of loyalty supported only a crude form of association, disconnected from organizational purposes. Its limitations are fundamental:

- The fact that informal links stay largely within the boundaries of formal structures merely reinforces those boundaries, encouraging the carving up of organizations into distinct "empires." Marketers and manufacturing people, for example, not only have different jobs but have different values and cultures, reinforced through their constant in-group interactions and frequently leading to scorn for each other.
- Efforts to bring groups together in task teams, to overcome the inefficiencies caused by these internal divisions, generate resistance. Members are more concerned with protecting their own "turf" than with achieving common objectives. They are both unable and unwilling to enter into real dialogue with other parts of the organization, since a crucial norm within bureaucracies is that each part should "respect" the expertise of others in their own areas.
- Because they are "hidden" and unregulated, lateral interactions rely heavily on direct exchanges of favors—I'll do something for you because I expect you'll do something for me sometime. This is a clumsy type of exchange, similar to economic barter, that is not conducive to pulling together around a difficult task and working through differences.
- The few communications links that cross formal boundaries have an accidental quality—that is, they usually originate not from the needs of the business but from some unrelated connections, such as membership in the same clubs or residence in the same neighborhoods or children's enrollment in the same schools. $X$ in production may know $Y$ in marketing, which might lead to some useful exchanges of information, but this relationship is not generated by the needs of the organization itself. The probability of making the *right* connections (from the organizational perspective) is low.

The bedrock of this kind of association is the expectation of long-term employment, which in the past created both emotional and self-interested bases for trust. The emotional base was a widely shared sense of loyalty; the self-interested base was the knowledge that one's dealings with fellow employees were likely to recur, so good and bad acts would not be forgotten. As the expectation of long-term employment in large companies declined, however, people's identity and self-interest both became disconnected from the company, reducing the effectiveness of this kind of collaboration.

For all these reasons, association in traditional firms has been inadequate for many of the demands of a knowledge economy and is becoming even more inadequate as the pace of mobility and change increases. Successful organizations increasingly need to be able to count on the fact that, for a given task, the right people will come together—no matter where they reside in the formal structure—and that they will be able to work successfully together. This demand requires a great deal more than the clumsy mechanisms of long-term loyalty and personal contacts.

### The Move to "Level 4": Collaborative Enterprise

The long-term trend, therefore, for at least the past thirty years, has been toward a *formalization* of the mechanisms of association. What used to be done by the "informal organization" is now to a substantial degree done by organized systems managed outside the hierarchical structure. This is the significance of the tremendous growth of innovative organizational forms: task teams, simultaneous development, quality circles, process management, and the rest of the panoply of techniques and fads that have swept the corporate world in that period. Companies are struggling in many ways to bring people in a coherent and planned way together around tasks, without losing control of the organization.[19]

This turns out to be a hard transition. Collaborative relationships have very different dynamics and rules from those of bureaucratic hierarchy, and attempts to combine them lead to multiple clashes. When teams are composed of people who are also peers in the formal organization, they must overcome the common tendency to avoid public confrontation and the resistance to peer discipline expressed in the deep abhorrence of "ratting," as well as superiors' tendencies to want to control and manage individuals. When teams also involve people who are at different organizational levels, things get even harder: the very same people who in one arena are expected to act in superior-subordinate relations—on one side projecting certainty and authority, on the other deference and loyalty—must now in another put aside the insignia of rank, respect each other as equals, and be willing to challenge each other's views.

The hierarchical structure has also changed in this period to some degree: spans of control have tended to increase, and responsibilities have been more decentralized;[20] but the real action has been in this creation of organized systems of collaboration. It is at the moment a very incomplete movement, with a high rate of failure and frequent retreats toward the safety of more traditional organizations. Yet few managers in the field would deny that the pressure for more complex and organized collaboration is growing.

This historical sequence is schematized in Table 3. In this account the center of activity today is around the move between "level 3"—the evolved corporate bureaucracy as described by Chandler and others[21]—and "level 4," a still-nascent form that incorporates more organized collaboration.[22]

## THE STRUCTURE OF COLLABORATION

The distinguishing mark of level 4 is the importance of formalized horizontal work relationships, in which people are connected by interdependence rather than by authority.

These horizontal relationships are often called "teams," but the ordinary use of that term can cause confusion: there are forms of teams in bureaucracy as well as in collaborative enterprise. Bureaucratic managers, for instance, may talk about "my team," but they mean a set of people linked by their relation to a person in authority, and usually homogeneous in skills. Other uses of the term "teamwork" refer to informal cooperation based on generalized loyalty and trust or personal friendships.

For collaborative systems, I will use instead the term "task team" or "task force" (though the latter has bad connotations in some organizations). A task team brings together people with varied skills from multiple organizational units and levels. They work together because they depend on each other: each is necessary to the quality of the overall result. A task team is not a permanent structure but is created for a purpose, and it exists only as long as it is needed for that purpose. Its membership is not fixed but varies according to the needs of different stages of the task.[23]

A collaborative system can be defined as one that *has the capacity to create effective task teams as needed.* It may operate for many purposes in a relatively traditional way, with people focused on their own jobs and reporting in a line of authority; but when they need to, people can cut across these lines and

**Table 3  Historical Evolution of Enterprises**

| | Economic Eras | Primary Strategy | Structure | |
| | | | Hierarchical Aspect | Associational Aspect |
|---|---|---|---|---|
| level 0 | Pre-industrial era (1800) | | Tradition- and value-based hierarchy (guilds, professions) | Occupational communities and self-governance |
| level 1 | Early industrial (to late 1800s) | | Personal control | Occupational community |
| level 2 | Early corporate (mid-1800s–early 1900s) | Scale and efficiency | Simple bureaucracy | Breaking down traditional occupational communities |
| level 3 | High corporate (late 1800s–1970s)—early phase | | Decentralized bureaucracy | Development of bureaucratic ethic, norms of interaction; Culture of paternalism and loyalty; Informal organization |
| level 4 | Post-industrial | Complexity and adaptiveness (solutions) | Front-back/matrixed hierarchy; interdependent teams | Breaking down community of loyalty; Development of "professional" culture and norms (contribution); Development of formalized collaborative processes |

Bureaucratic

Collaborative

quickly form working relationships. It does not supplant the hierarchy, but it supplements it with an organized system of peer connections.

Formalization means that these tasks are not taken on informally and out of sight of the regular accountability system but are part of the management of the overall strategy. Traditional bureaucracies, as described earlier, can create relationships or even groups that operate informally and under the radar to pursue purposes they see as important, but these relationships are catch-as-catch-can and limited at best. The formalization of task teams through process management and new accountability systems means that they can be constituted and managed as systematic parts of the overall strategic purpose.

Collaborative teams are created through organized processes. "Process management" becomes a central feature of organization: that is, there are systems and methods and accountabilities for creating teams and relations as needed. Task teams are fluid, and they cross boundaries: in their most effective forms, at least, they are not merely set up with a fixed membership and charge; rather, they evolve and bring in capabilities as needed. For that to happen without chaos, there is a need for a new type of complex rules of the game.

Thus, to make the basic contrast: in the bureaucratic or "vertical" dimension of organization, tasks are done by people in jobs, and the jobs are organized in chains of authority. In the collaborative or "horizontal" dimension, tasks are done by fluid teams uniting diverse capabilities, and the teams are organized in formalized processes. A collaborative enterprise combines both dimensions: jobs and hierarchies are still important, but teams and processes emerge as central; much of the art consists in combining the two ways of organizing.

## PROCESS MANAGEMENT

Processes in a collaborative enterprise get very complicated, which is what gives rise to the need for *managing* them rather than leaving them to informal cooperation. Since bureaucracies also have a horizontal dimension, they have processes, too—but only of the most basic and simple sort. As production moves through the organization—as a car, for instance, moves from design to manufacturing to sales—there is a series of programmed handoffs that are a kind of basic process. When there are problems, there is a process of moving up through the hierarchy to the official who encompasses all the parts of the problem and waiting for a decision. These "processes" are, however, limited in two fundamental ways: they are hardwired, built into the structure of the organization; and they are one-way, with one and only one actor having responsibility at any given point.

This change can be tracked visually through the emergence of a large number of "process-mapping" diagrams in recent years. These break with the long tradition of representing organizations as hierarchical pyramids, and instead create pictures that try to catch the dynamism of relations through the sequence of production events. The most primitive of these simply add a horizontal arrow to the organization chart (Figure 2). This does not really add any new information to the traditional chart, because each phase in the flow is identified with a fixed part of the structure. It does, however, draw attention, in a way that the traditional chart does not, to the *interfaces* between divisions or units: it makes vivid the reason why these handoffs are so often described as "throwing things over the wall." On one side of the wall (in this case) sales is in charge, and on the other side distribution assumes the burden. Accountability and decision rights remain unitary and clear, which is a fundamental principle of bureaucracy.

The critical development that makes process mapping essential occurs when the roles and the process no longer map into each other one to one: when people contribute to multiple phases, and when phases draw from multiple organizational units. Immediately one has to chart a two-dimensional matrix (Figure 3).

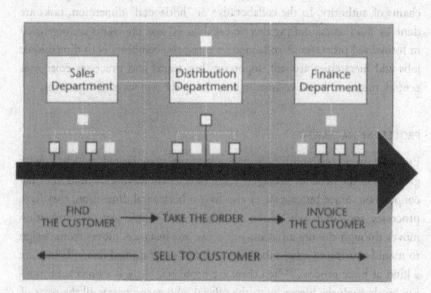

Figure 2: Bureaucratic "process." *Source*: http://www.pebbleage.ch/images/business-process.gif (accessed July 2, 2006). I have drawn illustrations from public domain sources. They reflect numerous similar examples from cases I have studied in depth, but companies are generally reluctant to publish them.

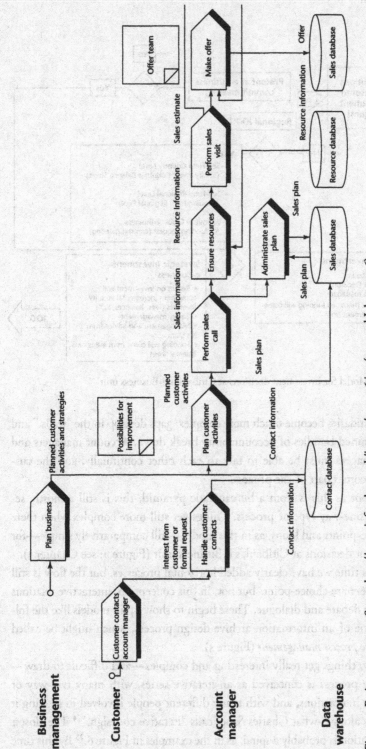

Figure 3: Basic process map. *Source*: http://www.infocube.co.uk/images/qpr_ss6.jpg (accessed July 2, 2006).

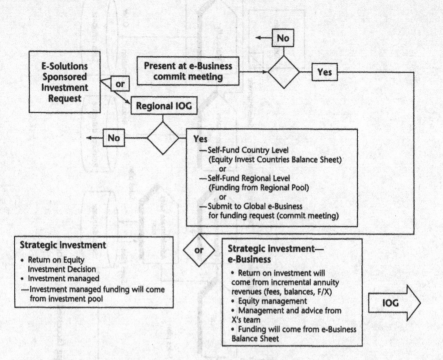

Figure 4: Model for investment decisions at Citibank's e-Business unit

Here boundaries become much more complex; gaps develop in the "walls," and self-contained bundles of accountability break down. Account managers and data managers must be able to talk to each other continually, and the customer becomes part of the process.

Different as this is from a bureaucratic pyramid, this is still a mostly sequential, one-way type of process. Things get still more complex when there are choice-points and loops, as in this model—still comparatively simple—for investment decisions at Citibank's e-Business unit (Figure 4; see Chapter 3).

By this time we have clearly added horizontal processes, but the flow is still linear; there are choice-points but not, in this conception, interactive relations involving debate and dialogue. These begin to show up in models like the following one of an information archive design process, which might be called *interactive process management* (Figure 5).

Finally, things get really interesting and complex—and difficult to draw—when the process is conceived as an iterative series, with many two-way or multiway interactions, and with many different people involved in shaping it as it goes along—what Charles Sabel calls "iterative codesign."[24] The closest representation is probably a spiral, as in the examples in Figure 6.[25] By this time

communication on and affirmation of clients' requests, quality and standard

**Client**

information

feedback, affirmation and fulfillment

**Marketing Department**

client's requirements

blueprint

price and delivery date

**Design & Engineering Department**

giving assignment

delivery feedback

shop drawing, standard and requests

manufacturing techniques feedback

**Comprehensive Management Department**

production program

production feedback

**Production Department**

quality feedback

quality inspection and improvement

**Quality Control Department**

Figure 5: Interactive process. *Source:* http://www.sz-wholesale.com/Products_Develop/images/ (accessed July 2, 2006).

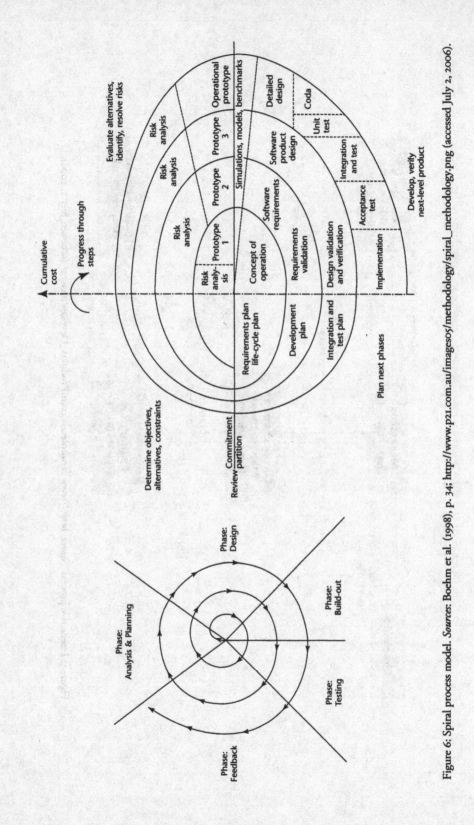

Figure 6: Spiral process model. *Sources:* Boehm et al. (1998), p. 34; http://www.p21.com.au/imageso5/methodology/spiral_methodology.png (accessed July 2, 2006).

the process has become almost entirely disconnected from the formal structure: individuals and jobs move in and out of processes on an as-needed basis.

Managers have similarly been struggling to reinvent the overall organization chart as something other than a pyramid of jobs. Probably the earliest attempt was the matrix, which showed jobs as nodes of two crossing hierarchies—for example, someone might report both to a marketing manager and to a production manager. But doubling the hierarchy just complicated life without reorganizing it, putting it on the individual at the nodes to somehow reconcile demands from competing structures that had not themselves changed. In the 1970s some companies began to try to capture a more radical notion—that those closest to the customer should be in charge—by simply turning the normal pyramid upside down (Figure 7). In this frame, managers began to speak of "supporting" their subordinates rather than directing them. But this simple inversion was both extremely crude and inaccurate as a real representation of relationships.

Customers/markets/competition

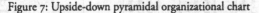

Shareholders

Figure 7: Upside-down pyramidal organizational chart

More lasting and fruitful have been attempts to conceive the organization horizontally. The "front-back" organization described by Jay Galbraith introduces this horizontal dimension as a relationship between two hierarchies— the production and the marketing—in a sequential process.[26] The most sophisticated models I am aware of view the organization not upside down but on its side, with business units aligned in terms of their flow, or contribution, toward customer needs and interactions, as in this example from a large consumer products company, developed to help move the organization toward a more customer-focused strategy (Figure 8).[27]

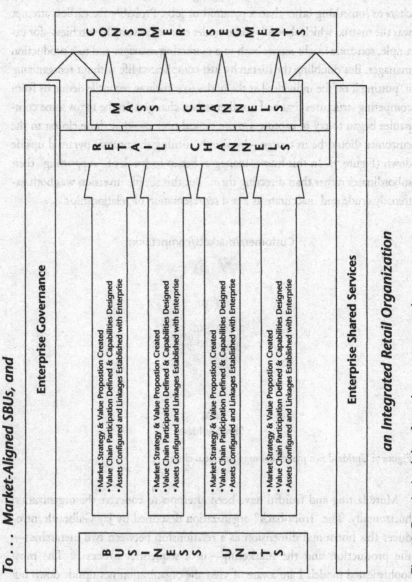

From Bureaucracy to Collaborative Enterprise     58

Figure 8: Organizational chart from a large consumer products company

**To . . . Market-Aligned SBUs, and an Integrated Retail Organization**

Enterprise Governance

Enterprise Shared Services

CONSUMER SEGMENTS

MASS CHANNELS

RETAIL CHANNELS

BUSINESS UNITS

- Market Strategy & Value Proposition Created
- Value Chain Participation Defined & Capabilities Designed
- Assets Configured and Linkages Established with Enterprise

In this representation the "pieces" of the enterprise are organized as flows toward customers, supported by shared services and integrated by governance systems. As the picture drills down and becomes more detailed, it highlights places in which the flows are disturbed by organizational bottlenecks, missed handoffs, and lack of communication. The visual and conceptual emphasis shifts from the identification of clear chains of command and accountability in the traditional organization chart, to the identification of value-adding processes moving toward the ultimate customer.

## PROCESS ROLES

The architecture of process management has led to a new vocabulary of roles that lie outside the familiar world of hierarchical responsibility: concepts like "process champion" (a high-level manager who supports a process without having formal authority over it), "process manager" (a kind of network orchestrator who must gather resources through influence around a project), and so on. In the early 1990s an AT&T manager told me, bemusedly, "So-and-so is my process manager, but this other guy is my hierarchical manager"— which was one of my first glimpses into the world of network roles.

The web of linking roles has gradually grown in sophistication and complexity. Many companies, for example, have developed customer relationships manager (CRM) roles intended to coordinate company activities around customer needs, rather than facing the customer with separate offerings and salespeople from each product and service unit. This has not been an easy innovation; CRMs by nature tread on the toes of powerful product managers:

> No, I have no authority over others here, over product groups. So—beg, deal, borrow, negotiate, flatter—yes, these are the behaviors I became an expert in! And probably above all that I am a good facilitator. (Citibank CRM)

At Citibank, as in other cases in our study, CRMs took quite a while to gain real effectiveness, and eventually did so only in the context of a larger shift in the organization's culture.

IBM developed "opportunity owners" in the 1990s to bring together resources across geographies and functions. This role was even more difficult than the CRM's: opportunity owners were temporary and sought to develop new and untested business lines rather than to satisfy existing customers. These roles have become increasingly important throughout the company.

## TASK FORCES AND OTHER TEAMS

Within these processes are sets of fluid teams with responsibilities for implementing or developing certain parts of the process. This is a primary topic of Chapter 2, where we will look at the role of different types of task teams in implementing strategies. From an overview perspective, we can sort task teams into types with increasing relational complexity:

1. *Semi-autonomous teams* are a kind of limiting case, since they exist entirely within the boundaries of bureaucratic organization—bringing together subordinates of a single supervisor. They change the rules of bureaucratic relationships by bringing these people into direct formalized interaction with each other rather than going through the boss. Semi-autonomous teams, usually at low levels of the corporation, must take on responsibility for issues that had previously been supervisory responsibilities, like scheduling and ordering supplies. Members typically have the same set of skills or work toward that goal; the benefit of the team comes less from diversity of capability than from the ability to share and cover for each other.

2. *Problem-solving groups* may cut across boundaries, bringing together people from different units and levels and using this diversity of knowledge to improve decisions. But such teams have no direct work role: they sit to the side of the main organization, making recommendations to someone who does have authority within the regular hierarchy. Total Quality teams are often, though not always, of this type.

3. *Linking teams* (my own term) bring together people from different units to argue or negotiate about priorities. These existed to some extent even in traditional bureaucracies, in the form of leadership councils, but they were generally rather ineffective and operated at best through log-rolling trade-offs. Increasingly, however, such teams are working in a collaborative manner to balance the priorities of each unit against the overall strategy of the firm. An example is the Amazon.com home page group, a cross-functional, cross-store group that decides each day how to structure the crucial home page to maximize cross-selling synergies. Degussa, a German auto parts supplier, draws its organization around the executive committee as such a linking team (Figure 9).

4. *Response teams* combine different kinds of expertise to deliver a solution or create an innovation. A typical case is in the consulting world, where projects are often taken on by groups with varied knowledge and levels of experience. These teams, unlike those mentioned earlier, are directly in the flow of work of the organization, responsible for creating and delivering value

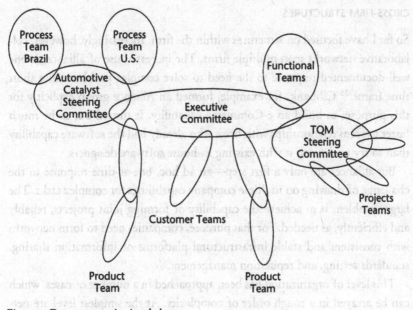

Figure 9: Degussa organizational chart

rather than merely making suggestions or linking organizational parts. Various kinds of customer teams have become widespread through the whole range of industries in our sample.

5. *Initiatives* are increasingly popular (though their names vary widely): they are broad strategic themes that do not define specific teams but are the focus around which teams may form. A famous case is the Microsoft Internet initiative launched by Bill Gates in 1995, which then became the backbone for a large number of shifting projects and task teams. At "NewTech," one of our research cases, the development labs are cross-cut by a set of strategic initiatives, defined as broad two- to five-year projects intended to transform the industry, such as "Internet media" or "broadband access." Citibank uses "initiatives" in a similar way; other companies in our sample call them "business plans" or other names but have the same concept of strategic foci providing structure for evolving task teams.

The first two of these task teams may exist at the margins of level 3 organizations without requiring wider changes, but the last three represent various types of collaborative level 4 organization that requires deep transformations in culture and infrastructure to overcome the divisions that are core to the workings of bureaucracy.

## CROSS-FIRM STRUCTURES

So far I have focused on structures within the firm. Increasingly, however, collaborative networks span multiple firms. The increased use of alliances is one well-documented response to the need to solve complex problems in a short time frame.[28] Citibank, for example, formed an Alliance group explicitly for this purpose: to build an e-Commerce capability. It turned out to be much faster to form relationships with firms who already had the software capability than to try to develop it with existing in-house software designers.

But alliances are only a first step—an ad hoc, one-at-time response to the challenge of drawing on multiple company capabilities for complex tasks. The larger problem is to achieve the capability of forming joint projects, reliably and efficiently, as needed. For that purpose, companies need to form networks with consistent and stable infrastructural platforms of information sharing, standards setting, and reputation management.

This level of organization has been approached in a number of cases, which can be arrayed in a rough order of complexity. At the simplest level are networks constituted by and dominated by one company; then there are those where a company drives but does not dominate the process of building a network; next are ones in which a few large companies join together on a peer basis; next are groups of many companies around simple processes, such as financial transactions; and finally, most difficult of all, are networks of many firms, governed by peer mechanisms, coordinating complex processes along entire production chains.

- The first level of difficulty in interfirm relations is found in supplier networks that are dominated by, but not owned by, a single firm with the power to set and maintain standards across the system. Among the best documented are automobile contracting networks, especially as structured in Japan, where there are stable relationships with common standards. As a result, when something breaks down—as in the case of a fire at one of Toyota's key suppliers in 1999—other members of the network can step in very quickly to fill in gaps and avoid breakdowns in the supply chain.[29] American auto companies have tended to avoid such stable relationships, preferring tighter control; thus they have stayed at the simpler ad hoc level of relating through particular contracts—with inferior results.[30]

- One step more difficult are cases where a powerful firm plays the "prime mover" role in constituting an interfirm dialogue, but without the kind of dominating role played by main automobile producers. The computing industry is marked by such efforts. Intel is particularly energetic in trying to build infrastructural platforms: one of the three pillars of its strategic definition, and a core measure in evaluating new initiatives, is the ability to expand the industry through technology licensing, the creation of new businesses, and the fostering of value-adding relationships to those businesses.[31]

- Up another level are networks that have independent governing mechanisms constituted by the member firms to define and enforce standard processes. Visa and NASDAQ consist of platforms that enable financial deals among many participants, and are governed by member boards with decision-making power based on contribution.[32] Another type is the standards-setting group: these have developed widely in the computer industry to enable companies to connect to each other's products, and have also gone beyond this in processes of quality certification like ISO, which has become almost mandatory for most companies engaged in international commerce.

- The most complex level so far in the competitive business arena consists of networks that span entire supply chains, and therefore coordinate interchanges that are more difficult and involve more parties than relatively simple financial transactions. One documented example is GHX, a set of health-care suppliers and distributors who set as their objective to eliminate more than $11 billion in annual cost from the industry supply chain. A member board establishes and enforces processes ranging from data ownership, to transaction processes such as purchasing, to the launching of new lines of business.[33]

These forms of collaboration are less common and still more unstable than intrafirm collaboration. The more advanced of them are particularly interesting at a theoretical level because they show the possibility of achieving collaboration without a hierarchical creator. GHX, Visa, NASDAQ, and their ilk have their own kinds of hierarchy in the form of governance systems with powers of defining processes and sanctioning violations. But they were created by companies coming together as peers without any one controlling entity. This is quite different from the usual in-firm dynamic and suggests alternate routes to collaborative systems.

## CONCLUSION

The structure of extended collaboration is far more complex than that of bureaucracy. Bureaucracy works in large part by sharply restricting the number of possible connections; collaboration multiplies them. In the former, each office in theory has only one upward connection and a few downward ones; in the latter, this restriction is lifted and anyone can reach out to wherever needed capabilities can be found. This is the essential reason why collaboration is potentially the more powerful system: it can organize diverse resources far more efficiently.

But this is true only if it works. If everyone is trying to talk to everyone all the time, the system will rapidly descend into chaos. Mathematical network theorists have suggested that this "edge of chaos" is in fact quite restrictive, and that only a small increase in the number of interdependencies can sharply reduce effectiveness.[34]

What this means is that the problem of structuring is much harder in a collaborative enterprise, not easier. It is not a matter of turning everyone loose, or of giving responsibility to small units. The first of these leads to chaos, and the second merely replaces bureaucratic narrowness with a different kind of narrowness. The difficulty is to develop ways by which people can find resources when they need them, over as broad an area as possible, without excessive confusion and time-wasting.

The problem has not been solved by any means, but the best efforts have taken the direction of the elaboration of process management and of task teams. Process management makes it possible to conduct systematic and organized searches over a wide area and to gather capabilities while keeping the overall mission in focus. Task teams focus a diversity of capabilities around manageable problems.

We can go somewhat beyond this general point. By now, with a decade or two of experience behind us, we can begin to specify which types of teams and processes work in which environments. That is the task for the next chapter.

## POSTSCRIPT: THE CONTRIBUTION
## OF NETWORK THEORY

The growth of collaborative systems in every aspect of social behavior has been reflected in both the management literature and the academic social sciences literature by the explosion of interest in "network theory." Where organizational theorists had spent most of the twentieth century exploring the variations and consequences of hierarchies, the focus of attention has clearly moved to peer-based relationships. This has produced an array of interesting insights. One major set of researchers, for instance, has turned a spotlight on people who play bridging or linking roles in organizations—"weak ties" that cross organizational "holes" (usually informally) so that needed information is transferred more rapidly than through the hierarchy. Others have looked at the value of marginal groups—people or units "out on the edges" of the main organization, who can be (if not too far separated) a key source of innovation.[35]

Nevertheless, the network approach is still in a very early stage and is far from coalescing in an overall picture of how real corporate organizations fit into these patterns or how they can make use of the knowledge. There are two basic weaknesses in network theories so far. First, many writers continue to treat networks as separate from hierarchy, or even as its opposite; they use the concept of "network" to refer to webs of mutual accommodation or "negotiated order,"[36] in which actors work things out among themselves. A few systems, such as the Internet or loose communal associations, may approximate such a voluntarist peer structure, but this version of the network image fails to capture much of reality in even the most advanced knowledge organizations. This equation of networks with mutual accommodation among peers often leads to a kind of extremism in which hierarchy and power are viewed as altogether irrelevant or harmful. Thus these approaches are blind to the vital interactions between hierarchical systems and webs of peer relationships.

For our purposes we need especially to distinguish between relationships that are structured hierarchically, where one person can command the other, and ones that are structured horizontally, where collective action comes from negotiation and dialogue. The first kind form vertical pyramids like the familiar organization chart; the second kind fall into the patterns of groups and holes described by Burt and other network analysts.[37] Network theory almost always assumes that relations are of one kind. But since complex organizations depend on both hierarchical and peer relationships, it is useful to think about not one but two kinds of interacting networks. Hierarchies and peer relations are both in fact forms of networks, coexisting and interacting.

The second blind spot in the network literature is the quality of the relationships. Essentially the dominant theories describe relationships in terms of only a few abstract structural variables: their number, strength (to use Granovetter's term[38]), or shape (degree of centrality, cohesion, or concentration). But there are other aspects that are crucial to understanding how corporate organizations have evolved in the past century.

- One critical quality is the degree of formalization: the same set of ties functions very differently if it is governed by deliberate rules and processes than if it is based on unreflective habits and affective ties.
- Second is the richness of the content that is carried across the ties. A simple market exchange, at one extreme, is a formal, peer-based form of network tie that carries very little information—essentially about supply and demand. At the other extreme, a scientific collaboration is also formal and peer-based, but it involves very thick exchanges of theoretical paradigms, hypotheses and proposals, plans and processes.
- Third is the degree to which the network is governed by shared norms or codes. At one end is a network of one-to-one relationships, which may connect many people without leading to any sense of unity. At the other is a set of relations among people engaged in a consuming shared mission, so that it is very clear who is "inside" and who is "outside." There are also networks that have a shared code but no shared mission: the Internet is a classic case, where in order to participate you have to use the HTML language, but you can say whatever you want.

Those are just the most important distinctions, but they already could produce many conceptual types. We are really concerned, however, with two main complexes.

1. *Traditional bureaucracy* is made up of a formal hierarchical network and an informal peer network, both of which can carry a good deal of information but that are not well linked to each other. There is a very strong sense of "inside" vs. "outside" based on shared history and cultural patterns. In addition, traditional bureaucracy operates within a market, which carries supply and demand information from the outside.
2. *Collaborative enterprise* is made up of a formal hierarchical network and a (relatively) formalized peer network. It operates both within a market and (typically) within a network of alliance relationships, both of which are extended peer networks, but the latter of which carries far more information. Thus inside and outside are less clear: there are extended relationships that cross the hierarchical boundaries.

The parentheses in this description—(relatively), (typically)—signal the fact that the collaborative type is less developed, and the terrain has been less fully explored, than that of bureaucracy. Personal relationships, for instance, continue to be important within collaborative systems, but they have declined relative to more formalized relations, and it is not entirely clear how they will evolve in the future.

Finally, it must also be emphasized that not all hierarchical relations are the same, nor are all associational relations. The former range from simple bureaucracy to the decentralized version developed by Sloan and du Pont to the "front-back" structure emerging in many customer-oriented companies today. The collaborative dimension ranges from informal cooperation based on common loyalties, through stable "linking mechanisms" like operating committees and cross-functional governing groups, to more fluid but still formalized systems of task forces and other temporary teams. The understanding of the evolution of relations therefore must take into account not only the two basic dimensions of networks but also the particular form and level of development of each.

# Chapter 2 Strategies and Structures: Varieties of Collaborative Enterprise

So far we have explored the fundamental divide between bureaucracy and collaborative enterprise. The main claim has been that business increasingly needs collaboration, mainly because of the growing importance of knowledge as a source of competitive value. We have also seen that the most important type of collaboration has moved beyond the level of small, decentralized teams to more complex, large-scale, and fluid sets of relationships that combine vertical and horizontal dimensions.

This distinction, however, is only a starting point. General claims such as "Business should adopt collaborative systems" or its opposite, "Collaboration doesn't work," are too broad and vague to be either true or false. Many kinds of collaboration don't work at all in a business context; other kinds work only in particular contexts.

There are, in fact, many varieties of collaboration with different qualities. One type looks like a swarming multitude of dynamic small teams with a great deal of autonomy: this is the "Silicon Valley" image, and also the image adopted by many firms that decentralize their structures to break the grip of bureaucracy. Another type is far more staid: it looks like a set of strongly linked hierarchies that share resources and build complex strategies. A third looks like a traditional bureaucracy much of the time, but periodically engages in widespread collaborative learning and reflection throughout the system to improve its processes. And there is a fourth, the most complex and interesting, that combines many of these elements: complex strategies, small flexible teams, and periodic reflection. Each of these is appropriate to particular situations, and each presents its own challenges.

A great deal of the existing literature looks at only part of this picture, and, as in the old story of the blind men and the elephant, gets a distorted view of the whole. Critics can find easy marks in the many failures characteristic of a period of transition. Some, looking at decentralized teamwork, note that it is bad at implementing coherent strategy; others, looking at early and unsophisticated efforts to reduce bureaucratic rules, argue that collaboration is too unstructured and loose; still others, looking at limited problem-solving groups, argue that they are only a new form of paternalism.[1] All these points are true—but only in part.

Those who advocate participation and collaboration have the mirror image problem: they often take temporary or particular successes and try to blow them up into solutions for all the ills of business. Some want to break apart hierarchy entirely and turn everything over to small groups, others want to invert the structure and treat managers as support for their subordinates, and still others want to encourage everyone to form learning communities. These efforts have their place, but that place is not everywhere or all the time.

To get beyond this very general level we need to understand in more detail the variety of challenges facing companies and the ways in which structural developments can help address them.

## TYPES OF STRATEGIES

The starting point is an old proposition in organizational theory, that structure is driven by strategy. If collaboration is growing in corporations, it is not because of a surge of niceness or democratic feeling among top managers, but because collaboration contributes to the achievement of strategic goals.[2]

The recent era has been marked by a major strategic discontinuity. During the twentieth century, value was derived primarily from the ability to master scale and scope—to produce and distribute for a mass consumer market.[3] This required strategies focused primarily on products—on developing and improving products, on making them with maximal efficiency, and then on finding a way to sell them. In the current period, this strategy is known by the pejorative term "commodity production," and most companies in advanced industrial countries try to stay away from it. The problem is that the capacity for effective mass production, which used to be difficult and unusual, has become common and easily replicated: companies in China and India can pick up most products and make them just as reliably and much more cheaply than anyone in the United States. It's hard to make a profit at this game except by wage cutting, which is a limited game.

The decline of commodity margins drives companies to seek profit from other kinds of value. Most of these are centered on knowledge, because the effective application of knowledge is still hard. Cost efficiency is necessary, but it just gets you on the playing field; pricing power comes increasingly from the ability to innovate, to customize, to integrate, and to provide solutions for customers.[4] This distinction is roughly the same one made a quarter-century ago by Michael Porter in his seminal work, *Competitive Strategy*, which turned on the distinction between cost-oriented strategies and ones that produce value through differentiation.[5] This shift involves (again, speaking very broadly) moving a mainly internal focus on improving operations to a mainly external focus on understanding and communicating with customers—from inside-out to outside-in.

This decline in the viability of commodity production is the general strategic pressure that has led to the decline of bureaucracy and the rise of collaboration.[6] Within that general trend, however, the kind of organization needed depends essentially on the type of strategy adopted.[7]

- The most familiar strategic focus, because the most important historically, is *operational effectiveness*—the dominant strategic dimension of the mass-production economy through most of the twentieth century. Companies adopting this strategy create value primarily by providing products for low cost over a wide distribution range. Traditionally the focus was primarily on cost control, and reliability was secondary. In the last few decades, however, product reliability has in many cases become as important as cost: most companies can no longer choose between positioning themselves for quality or cost, but must do both.
- Recently there has been a great deal of emphasis on uncertainty and change. A company can choose to position itself as a master of change: the value it offers is in helping its customers stay on the leading edge, producing the most advanced products, responding most rapidly to emerging needs, or absorbing risk for its customers. We can call this dimension *adaptiveness*.

• Somewhat less visible as a topic on bookstore shelves, but equally important in practice, is a strategic positioning that emphasizes the capacity to manage *complexity*—especially the ability to integrate very different capabilities around an offering. Citibank, for example, for many years had the largest international financial network in the world; but it is only in the last decade that they have chosen to turn this into a competitive advantage by creating the ability to do deals that involve multiple national regulatory systems and multiple types of offerings (credit cards, investment banking, and so on) into integrated wholes. The value offered is primarily one of integrating multiple services and products for the customer.[8]

Strategic choices are partially determined by the environment—but only partially. Certain environments with high uncertainty—telecommunications and computing in the last decade, for example—seem to require high levels of adaptiveness. In some industries, including banking and some heavy construction, the environment seems to demand high complexity. But even companies within these relatively strongly defined spaces have a great deal of choice. Some parts of ABB, for instance, chose during the 1990s to make complexity a competitive advantage, taking on large projects like the Oslo Airport on the grounds that it was better than the competition at integrating all the elements that go into such an effort; but GE, which competed with ABB in many areas, deliberately decided not to go after the Oslo Airport project because it did not want to stretch to that level of integration.[9] Similarly, within the "high-speed" industries there is a range of choice, with some emphasizing efficiency and reliability more than leading-edge adaptiveness.

These strategic dimensions require different capabilities, and they are therefore in tension with each other; it is hard to maximize on more than one. Companies that seek to become fast, agile, and responsive generally try to simplify their operations and to focus on a few core competencies; this reduces their ability to offer fully integrated products or bundles of services. Those that emphasize their ability to integrate usually lose speed. It is hard, in other words, to be both fast and big, and even harder to be fast, big, and efficient.

Bureaucracy can be somewhat effective on any of these dimensions, but not as effective on any of them as extended collaboration. The fundamental reason is the one sketched in the Introduction: every form of organization collaboration, if it is done right, adds the ability to make better use of intelligence. A bureaucracy can be highly efficient when it develops consistent routines and refines them over time, but it becomes more efficient when employees at all levels can participate actively in rethinking those routines and continuously applying new learnings. Bureaucracies can manage complexity through top-level strategic planning processes that are then driven down through the hierarchy, but they can manage far higher levels of complexity when employees at all levels understand the strategic priorities and tradeoffs and can make intelligent choices on their own. Bureaucracies can also respond to changing environments by gathering information at the center and decreeing new directions and structures, but they can respond much faster when employees can experiment and initiate changes quickly without going through the hierarchical process.

### HIGH-HIGH: THE TREND TOWARD SOLUTIONS STRATEGIES

The most difficult and interesting type of strategy, one to which many companies are drawn these days, involves both a greater focus on the customer, in order to take advantage of differentiated opportunities, and also greater complexity in terms of pulling together varied resources around customized needs—without losing operational effectiveness. The term "solutions" has emerged, more among practitioners than in the academic world, to emphasize close interaction between customers and producers, with at the limit shared problem-solving between them to bring together the right resources at the right time, and a sharing of risks.[10]

A solutions orientation requires more complexity than bureaucracies can handle, because it involves creating bundles of products and services that come from different organizations with differing histories and business models; it must also be high in adaptiveness because customer needs are differentiated and changeable.

The underlying reasons for the solutions shift can be traced to the continuing development of capitalist economies, which has led over more than two centuries to increased pressure on all three strategic dimensions. Within the local markets of the eighteenth century there was demand only for relatively simple products that could be made in small workshops. As transportation grew, markets expanded, and occupations differentiated through the nineteenth century, there was more demand for complex products that combined many skills—steamships, railroads, mechanical reapers; at the same time, these products had to deal with a wider range of consumers with differing needs spread over larger areas. Most important of all, however, was the dimension of operational effectiveness: the ability to radically reduce prices was the key to dramatic extensions of mass production. Throughout the twentieth century these trends continued, forcing continual organizational invention.

On the demand side, consumers—the ultimate drivers of the economy—are now far more sophisticated and demanding than they were a century ago, expecting continual variety and innovation. On the production side, there are more companies with more production capability, and with a high capacity to imitate and compete. In the earlier era, with fewer products and less variety within each category, the center of economic value was getting products into the hands of consumers through cost reductions and mass distribution networks. Today people are bombarded with so many choices that industries have sprung up to help make them, providing information and advice; and distribution has become trivial for some industries such as software, while even for larger products such as automobiles it has been eased to a degree that distribution is not a major barrier to worldwide markets. Thus the cycle from new technological capabilities to new products to consumer demand is greatly shortened, and the ability to keep abreast of these rapid cycles is a key competitive differentiator for many companies.

In many ways it would be more comfortable for companies to roll back these changes and restore some measure of oligopolistic control. It is even possible that the present period is a temporary one of unusually high competition driven by the expansion of markets to a global scale, and that the end-point will be a re-creation of the pattern of a few dominant companies that can dampen competitive pressures.[11] But this seems unlikely, because the sophistication of consumer markets is not easily reversible and will continue to encourage the capacity for higher rates of change driven by systematic invention and learning.

I have not mentioned technology among the drivers of post-industrial change, because it is not clear that this is new. While there have certainly been huge technological advances in recent decades, there were also enormous "breaks" in the late nineteenth and early twentieth centuries—centered first on transportation (the railroad and the automobile), then on the use of electricity, then on communications (the telegraph and the telephone). People complained about the "speed of change" as much then as they do now. The resulting economic and social upheavals were not in any measurable way less important than the current ones flowing from the microprocessor and the early phases of biotechnology.

The consequences, however, were worked out differently as a result of the level of sophistication of markets. In the earlier period, given the relatively undeveloped state of consumer markets, these inventions led to an explosion of new mass-produced products and of large-scale distribution systems, while in the current one, they led toward more customized and complex solutions.

Consider, for instance, the contrast between the histories of the automobile and the computer. Both are based on enormous technological transformations, and both have been central to periods of economic discontinuity. In the case of automobiles, companies that figured out early on how to build them cheaply and distribute them widely, by building effective bureaucratic organizational systems, were the ones that dominated the industry and, indeed, the economy for most of the century. The case of the computer went in another direction entirely. Most of the companies that figured out how to build it first—Digital Equipment, Wang—are no longer on the scene; their attempt to follow the auto model by locking in proprietary products could not succeed in an economy that can spawn competitors and imitators far more easily now than a century ago. Then there was a wave of companies that tried to win through low-cost mass production: Osborne Computer, with the first sub-$2,000 consumer box; Kaypro; and a number of others. These brands have vanished as well; their manufacturing efficiencies were too easy to duplicate.

IBM's trajectory is instructive. It entered the PC market in the 1980s with a mass-production strategy very much like that of Ford and GM in the 1920s and did very well for a short period. Soon, however, it came to be seen as slow and unresponsive. The challenge came first from a large number of small, agile competitors that could experiment with great flexibility; and then, more recently, a set of companies that have combined scale with customized responsiveness, like Dell or Cisco Systems. These pushed IBM to the brink of bankruptcy. When it recovered in the late 1990s, it was with a fundamentally new orientation, deliberately rejecting its mass-production history and adopting one of the more comprehensive and conscious solutions approaches within one company.

When he took over IBM in its hour of crisis in 1993, Lou Gerstner decided, against the advice of most of the financial community, to keep the company together rather than selling off pieces; the rationale was that in this way the company could deliver integrated packages of products and services to meet customer needs. The "one IBM" approach paid off handsomely in the ability to execute complex global business strategies. Gerstner and his successor, Sam Palmisano, then pushed the idea even further to the current core concept of "On Demand," which aims to bring together various kinds of knowledge around difficult problems. Palmisano's definition of his goal was "an enterprise whose business processes—integrated end-to-end across the company and with key partners, suppliers and customers—can respond with speed to any customer demand, market opportunity or external threat."[12]

In particular, Palmisano wanted to connect the company's technological expertise more directly to the needs of its business customers, and he understood that there was a gap between the two perspectives. This led him to the acquisition of the consulting firm PricewaterhouseCoopers (PWCC) in 2002. The perceived advantage was that it brought a deep understanding of business issues inside the company; the risk, a very substantial one, was that the business consultants and the technologists would be unable to work together effectively. The gamble is still in play as of this writing, four years later; IBM has taken highly creative steps to unify the differing cultures, but these are far from complete.[13]

The move toward solutions has become a very broad one. It began in the 1990s in a few industries, primarily those subject to rapid technological change, such as electronics and telecommunications; these domains were in a sense "forced" into an outward focus by technological discontinuities, and they were also open to it because they were relatively new organizations. Later in the decade, however, the trend began to spread beyond this category to more mature industries such as banking: Citibank, for example, implemented an approach of putting together complex financial products across national boundaries. This move was driven not by technological innovation but by an understanding that customer needs were evolving beyond traditional categories, and that there were opportunities that the company was unable to seize with its traditional product-based strategy (we examine this case in more detail later).[14]

Today the trend has reached even highly prosaic industries—for example, John Deere's approach to the manufacturing of farming equipment:

> [A]griculture is no longer driven by raw economic issues. We have farms of different sizes and types . . . and dual-career farmers, who might have full-time professions during the week and farm 1,000 acres on weekends. Technology allows us to farm differently, and a broad range of public policy issues also drive [the industry].
>
> These issues—such as management of resources like petroleum and water—and technologies—such as genetic modification and site-specific (GPS) monitoring— mean growers and retailers must deal with problems and how to solve them as much as with the products they are growing. At John Deere's Ag Management Solutions Group (AMS), the focus today is on providing these solutions.

The company believes there are advantages to this solutions-driven approach. "We can have integration of features and safety with our vehicles," says Than Hartsook of AMS, "and we can have a common source for information, namely our dealers."[15]

At Kodak, a solutions focus means (according to a senior operations manager) that

> we embrace all of the customer's needs, including everything from driving to stores and delivering chemicals to installing networks for mini-labs. . . . Kodak provides phone support whenever the store is open, enabling their counter personnel to call us whenever they need assistance. Beyond what I just described, which might be called "equipment support," we also help stores with their advertising. This helps them increase their business and, obviously, improves our relationships. We really don't leave any stones unturned in offering them a total solution that supports their efforts to make money. We are completely focused on improving their success.[16]

The move toward solutions, in this broad sense, demands the highest level of extended collaboration. A solution by definition brings together resources around customer problems or needs, without regard to where those resources come from. Thus it ignores existing organizational lines, histories, business models, and cultures. If I want to use a credit card while I travel, I don't care that my bank has separate divisions for each country or region and that each of them can offer me something excellent in one location. If I want an information infrastructure for my small business, I don't care that one company does engineering databases and a different company does customer management software. I want these dimensions to be integrated seamlessly for my purposes. As the integration issues grow more complicated and changeable, cost—while never unimportant—recedes from the primary to a subordinate priority.

There are of course still many industries in which operational effectiveness trumps solutions. Airlines remain an important example: most customers don't care much about the frills of on-board meals, putting their main emphasis on getting from point A to B cheaply and reliably. Yet even in these domains, collaboration has proved to be increasingly important. The low-cost providers, like Southwest Airlines, have generally achieved their operational effectiveness in large part through collaboration: employees are informed and work systems are highly participative, so there is little bureaucratic waste and low supervisory overhead. In the automobile domain, which is still essentially based on mass production, the GM–Toyota joint venture NUMMI has shown that employee participation can also lead to continuous operational improvements that have great competitive value.[17] Collaboration benefits operational effectiveness nearly as much as complexity and adaptiveness.

## ORGANIZATIONAL RESPONSES TO STRATEGIC CHALLENGES

Collaboration helps on all three strategic dimensions, but in different ways:

1. For strategies focused on efficiency and product quality, collaboration helps to smooth handoffs between units and to enable organizational learning. Such organizations continue to emphasize hierarchy and use extended collaboration mainly for episodic review and product development. I did not include examples of this type in my core research sample; I focus for the most part on the next three types.

2. For high-complexity strategies, collaboration helps in balancing multiple competing priorities. These systems are built around strong hierarchies linked through collaborative teams that argue out the management of resources for particular cases. They generally need to be large because they try to cover a large range of capabilities rather than focusing more narrowly.

    In our research the model high-complexity strategy is that of Citibank, which struggled for more than two decades to balance its traditional country focus with a broader customer and product focus; in the 1990s they, like many other companies, developed customer relationships managers as a mechanism to balance the various capabilities of the bank around the customer. IBM during the 1990s similarly tried to balance its traditional product focus with a stronger emphasis on responding to customer needs.

3. For strategies focused on adaptiveness, collaboration helps in gathering resources, especially knowledge, quickly around focused problems. These organizations reduce hierarchy considerably and emphasize project teams generated around opportunities. Size is not so important because this strategic approach narrows the focus to a small number of "core competencies."

    We take as our model of high adaptiveness the story of Nokia, which during the 1990s adopted a strategy of segmentation and "micro-marketing"— at the end of that decade it was introducing a new model every thirty-five days, in an attempt to maximize differentiation based on consumer segments.[18] Another good case is McKinsey itself, which has a strategy based on highly particularized responsiveness to individual customer needs.

4. Solutions strategies present especially difficult organizational problems. High levels of collaboration are needed to combine resources flexibly while

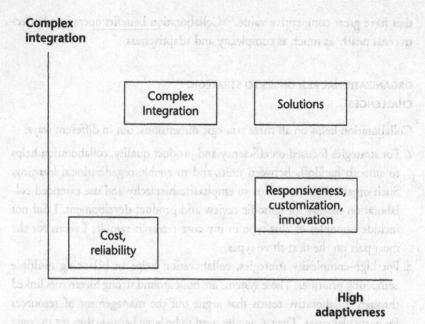

**Complex integration**

Complex Integration

Solutions

Responsiveness, customization, innovation

Cost, reliability

**High adaptiveness**

Figure 10: Strategic dimensions: Value to customers

maintaining strategic coherence. Such organizations have to manage both strong functional capabilities and an ability to work through problems collaboratively on the fly. They take the form of many fluid project teams operating in an environment of strongly standardized processes.

Our primary model of "high-high" strategy will be that of IBM in the 2000s era, as it has developed the concept of "on-demand": pulling together the business consulting capability of PricewaterhouseCoopers and the technical capability of the traditional IBM organization, to provide very complex bundles of products and services in rapid time frames for particular customers. Another central case is the recent move by Citibank to develop e-commerce capability, drawing all the bank's resources together in a common interface around Web platforms. We also draw lessons from Cisco and the "NewTech" development labs (Figure 10).

### High Operational Effectiveness:
### Collaboration Limited in Time and Space

Even in a post-industrial age, some companies—often but not exclusively manufacturing firms—are still driven primarily by operational effectiveness. A company positioning itself on this dimension offers products that above all are low in cost, and secondarily that are reliable. To accomplish this effectively, an organization must focus on consistency. Thus historically the companies best at this have been "tight" organizations with strong bureaucratic controls. The companies that took the lead in innovating bureaucratic systems and Taylorist control were also the companies that dominated the high industrial phase of economic development—General Motors, Ford, DuPont, and so on. They were able, through their developed control systems, to bring costs down dramatically, thus creating new mass markets. They did not ignore innovation, of course, but it was isolated in a separate part of the business—laboratories or product design centers—and the pace of innovation was controlled by the ability to absorb changes within the control system.

Since about 1980, however, when the Japanese threat became widely recognized, a new dimension has been added to the simple standard bureaucratic model: the notion of continuous improvement, embodied in the system of "Lean Production" and "Total Quality Management." Without modifying the basic bureaucratic control system, lean-production organizations add a capacity for learning: involving shopfloor workers in developing recommendations for improvement, bringing various parts of the organization together for periodic reviews. This has made possible the combination of quality and cost control cited earlier, and enabled companies to adapt more quickly to changing customer expectations.

The basic model was identified as early as the late 1970s and began to spread widely in manufacturing plants in the 1980s. By the early 1990s an influential analysis of the automobile industry identified lean production as a cornerstone of effective plants; another, meanwhile, found that the "new plant model" had spread in many other industries as well.[19]

The essential structure common to these descriptions involves:

1. A strong formal hierarchy with a relatively decentralized structure and large spans of control, sometimes as large as 50:1.
2. Local semi-autonomous work teams with significant responsibility for maintaining production and responding to normal fluctuations and problems.
3. Some form of "simultaneous engineering" that brings engineers and manufacturing managers together (sometimes with marketing representatives as well) to work together on the development of new products (see Chapter 1 for more on this mechanism).

The hierarchical structure is not essentially different from familiar forms of the last century, which have ranged from relatively centralized to decentralized forms and often oscillate back and forth, though by traditional standards the degree of decentralization in lean production is often extreme. The second element—use of autonomous teams—introduces a new element of formalized collaboration and has spawned a huge amount of learning about how to manage and sustain effective teamwork. This has converged over time on a model of systematic group problem-solving that differs in detail across many consultants and practitioners but is essentially consistent: teams consciously apply a process model starting with problem analysis, through generation of options, examination of alternatives, and prioritization of final solutions. There is convergence also on the basic culture of these teams, which stresses egalitarianism and openness (for example, all ideas are treated as equal in the generation of options, no matter whom they come from).

These semi-autonomous teams, as we saw in the last chapter, are a formalization of an old type of cooperation, based on small, stable, homogeneous groups. Homogeneity in this instance is formalized in the concept of "multi-skilling," which means that members of the team are encouraged to learn each other's skills. Thus they can all replace each other when necessary. The power of these groups comes far less from the exchange of differentiated skill and knowledge and far more from the much more developed mechanism of internal unity and exchangeability.

Where things get interesting and new is with the third mechanism, that of simultaneous engineering; this moves beyond local collaboration to the much more difficult level of extended collaboration, in which the assumptions of size, stability, and homogeneity no longer hold. I discussed this a bit in Chapter 1; the conclusions were that this approach leads to major improvements in product development, but that it is difficult to implement and in practice usually ends in a kind of compromise form of "overlapping design," which maintains some of the collaboration but reduces its intensity. The difficulties lie in getting people from different parts of the organization and with different knowledge bases to understand each other and overcome their natural tendency to fragment. These obstacles are common to all efforts at extended collaboration and are the focus of our discussions of infrastructure and change processes in subsequent chapters.

Sometimes these effectiveness-focused firms go still further and introduce another layer of collaborative mechanisms that are even more radical: periodic processes of review and learning that draw on wide swaths of the organization, crossing levels and unit boundaries. A particularly powerful and well-documented example is NUMMI, the GM–Toyota joint venture in California that has produced (among other models) the Pontiac Vibe and the Toyota Corolla. Unlike the more radical experiment at Saturn, NUMMI has maintained an essentially bureaucratic organization structure supplemented by shopfloor teams that have substantial responsibility for product quality. These teams have fewer job demarcations than traditional auto plants and engage in considerable job rotation and information-sharing. The culture emphasizes group harmony and stability, with a union contract that guarantees high levels of security but makes fewer formal distinctions than usual, and with a high level of dialogue between supervisors and workers.

What really distinguishes this plant, however, is its hansei (Reflection Review) process. During model launches, a task team drawn from many parts of the organization helps to certify that the workforce, machines, materials, and methods are capable of doing their intended jobs. After launches, all section managers work with their leadership to document what went right and what went wrong; then a series of meetings brings various parts of the organization together to review the reports and make recommendations for the next launch. A research team describes the process after the 1993 model passenger line reached full production:

> Before the lessons had time to fade, top management, Section managers, Assistant Managers, Group Leaders, and Pilot Team members began to document the launch. Topics included everything from the master schedule to training plans to workability and safety issues. NUMMI even sent out a questionnaire to its suppliers to capture the lessons they had learned.
>
> Each section's one- or two-inch-thick binder would be used by the next project team as a basis for its own work, thus ensuring cumulative learning in the organization. Using this documentation as a foundation, each section also prepared summaries of its performance against its targets, pointing out problems and proposing countermeasures for the next project.[20]

Other plants have developed similar processes under the label of Total Quality Management, or TQM. It should be pointed out immediately that the label by itself is often misleading, as it covers all kinds of initiatives from the most top-down bureaucratic interventions to highly interactive learning systems. It is the latter kind of TQM that resembles the NUMMI hansei process typically in building multifunction and multilevel teams that pursue a rigorous process of investigation of operational processes, identifying key variances, probing for root causes, and systematically testing various potential solutions against desired outcomes. These solutions then become in effect new sets of organizational rules implemented through a bureaucratic hierarchy, but open to future review through iterations of the TQM model.

## Knowledge Production

The teamwork involved in operational effectiveness, however, is not the leading edge of organizational change. It was the first focus for teamwork and collaborative systems, starting in the early 1970s, and the widely used and studied model of "Lean Production" includes it as a central element.[21] It generates new levels of learning and knowledge, but it remains within the frame of the manufacturing mode of production—focused on internal improvement and growth.

From the point of view of strategic analysis, an effectiveness-focused strategy is not solutions oriented, and it is not focused outward: the collaborative mechanisms are turned entirely inward on incremental, continuous improvement of existing operating systems. Thus even the most advanced of these enterprises remain in many respects close to traditional bureaucratic form; if one looked at them operating on a daily level one would be struck by the local teams, but the rest of the system of hierarchy and rule-based operations would look a lot like a factory from fifty years ago. The systems of extended collaboration—simultaneous engineering and learning reviews—are relatively episodic and limited.

By contrast, the other two dimensions of strategy change the competitive landscape in ways that are still hard to grasp. They put knowledge at the center of strategy—not as a means of achieving greater efficiency, but as the primary source of value in itself. The focus on complexity creates value by offering consumers integration among diverse and often competing products and services; the focus on adaptiveness offers them customization and rapid responsiveness. They require companies to turn outward toward customers and to recombine resources around customers' particular and changing needs. Collaboration adds to and improves operational effectiveness-focused organizations, but it transforms solutions-focused ones.

In what follows, therefore, I focus not on effectiveness—and therefore not on automobile companies—but on the dimensions of complexity and adaptiveness that are crucial to heavily knowledge-based solutions strategies. This also has the advantage of keeping us in two dimensions. The starting, point, in the lower left of Figure 11, is traditional bureaucracy with relatively low complexity and adaptiveness. Movement out to either complexity or adaptiveness can drive the system beyond the capabilities of bureaucracy and over the

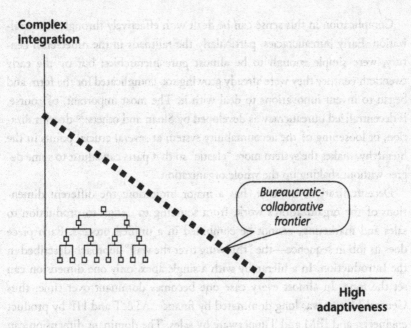

Figure 11: Dimensions of structure and strategy

line into collaborative enterprise. (In Figure 11 and the diagrams that follow, operational effectiveness is a hidden third dimension; I assume that all the structures I discuss are relatively high on it. This makes the problem harder, of course: if we were dealing with sectors where cost pressures were less urgent, the development of capacities for adaptiveness and complexity would be easier.)

A discussion of more systematic testing of the validity of this typology, and the conditions and mechanisms of these types, is provided in the Appendix at the end of this volume.

## High Complexity: Managed Collaboration

The strategic focus on complexity requires the ability to combine many different resources and types of value into final products. This is not necessarily the common-sense meaning of complexity, which usually refers to size or number of elements: a car in this sense would be complex because it has many parts, and General Motors would be more complex than Ford because it has more employees and more types of cars. This kind of multiplication of elements is not the problem we are concerned with; bureaucracies can handle it rather well by adding units and levels. It might better be called complication than complexity.[22]

Complication in this sense can be dealt with effectively through decentralization. Early bureaucracies, particularly the railroads in the nineteenth century, were simple enough to be almost pure hierarchies; but by the early twentieth century they were already growing too complicated for the form and began to invent innovations to deal with it. The most important, of course, is decentralized bureaucracy as developed by Sloan and others:[23] decentralization, or loosening of the accountability system at several crucial points in the hierarchy, makes the system more "elastic" so that parts can adjust to some degree without shaking up the whole organization.

Decentralization, however, has a major limitation: the different dimensions of the organization's work, from sourcing to design to production to sales and marketing, cannot be combined in a unified process. Each piece does its job in sequence—the "throwing over the wall" approach described in the Introduction. In a hierarchy with a single apex, only one dimension can set the tone. In almost every case one becomes dominant over time: thus General Motors was long dominated by finance, AT&T and HP by product engineers, and IBM and Tupperware by sales. The dominant dimension can be recognized most easily because it produces most of the chief executives; but it is also reflected in countless other cultural routines, large and small, that push it to the forefront. Employees are quite aware of which dimension rules the roost: in case of disagreement others defer to it. Daily routines of decision making are kept in order essentially through "hard-wiring" a hierarchy of priorities.

The problem today for many businesses is that they experience a need to focus simultaneously on multiple dimensions, without subordinating any one of them: one commonly hears things like, "we have to focus on geography *and* customers *and* products."[24] Many companies with a product or engineering focus have found that they cannot survive unless they also give major weight to customer demands; but those with a sales focus equally find that they cannot survive without stronger attention to product innovation. An AT&T manager told me:

> The old way things were done was that Bell Labs was king, and Bell Labs department heads and directors were the ones controlling what projects were being done and how they were done. Now you might think that's right, but we have a marketing organization and we have manufacturing, and typically that interaction between those three organizations had been top heavy leaning towards Bell Labs. So, now we're trying to integrate ourselves . . . and we're finding we're having rough times.

What I mean by complexity is this need to work simultaneously on multiple overlapping dimensions of organization, to balance competing values that cannot be simply lined up in a hierarchy of priority.

Here the case of Citibank is exemplary. The company's emphasis historically was on geography: country managers were kings. In the mid-1970s the top management decided that this country focus was blocking the ability to put together global solutions for large customers. For the next twenty years they tried various approaches to transcending the country boundaries; at each phase the resistance of the country managers, overt and covert, was fierce. In 1995 then-CEO John Reed declared that henceforth the hierarchy of priorities would be shuffled, with customers being at the top. Yet this did not solve the problem: the continuing importance of country differences meant that geography could not be simply subordinated to customers, but needed to be treated as an equal element in decision making. This balancing act remains hard for the bank to deal with.

Getting different dimensions to work together cannot be managed by decentralizing pieces and simplifying relationships: on the contrary, it has to be managed by getting units with different histories, languages, and priorities to talk to each other and work things out. It requires collaboration.

The pure "ideal-type" idea of managing this kind of complexity is through hierarchies linked at multiple levels through collaborative mechanisms. Thus disagreements or disparate points of view do not need to go to the top but can be worked out through discussions throughout the system. The simple ideal-type picture would look like the one shown in Figure 12.

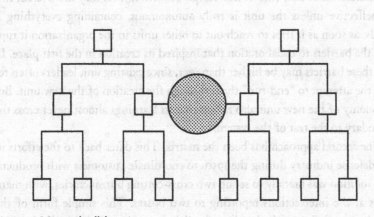

Figure 12: Managed collaboration

I use the term "managed collaboration" to describe organizations built around this principle because the hierarchy remains dominant and the collaborative elements are, in effect, interstitial—tying bureaucratic pieces together. Collaboration is therefore very dependent on direction and support from the hierarchy.

Managed collaboration does not mean collaboration driven by ad hoc interventions from the top leadership. We have some cases of the latter in our research sample, especially Microsoft and Sun, where the main operation of the company is on a decentralized project basis but is sometimes forced into integration by fierce high-level pushing, accompanied by lots of screaming. Managed collaboration has more consistent and pervasive linking mechanisms at various levels of the hierarchy.

Even within the bureaucratic framework it was common to use operating committees to connect divisions, with representatives from structural parts meeting regularly as peers to build unified plans. The problem was that these did not work well: in bureaucratic environments, such committees tend to be bogged down by defensive behavior and maneuvering for position rather than building toward a common vision. As Truman's Secretary of Defense Robert Lovett put it with unusual humor: "A committee is a group of individuals who, as individuals, can do nothing, but who, as a committee, can meet formally and decide that nothing can be done."[25]

As pressure for multidimensional balance has grown, it has become vital to have linkages that actually work. There have broadly been three types of approaches to resolving such complexity. Citibank's struggle began in the 1970s with the simplest one: putting representatives of multiple functions into a new and autonomous unit (the World Corporate Group). As they discovered, this is ineffective unless the unit is truly autonomous, containing everything it needs: as soon as it tries to reach out to other units in the organization it runs into the barriers to collaboration that inspired its creation in the first place. In fact these barriers may be higher than ever, since existing unit leaders often resent the attempt to "end-run" them through the creation of the new unit. But autonomy of the new unit also means that its learnings almost never cross the boundary to the rest of the system.

The second approach has been the matrix. This dates back to the efforts in the defense industry during the 1950s to coordinate customers with products. The solution was literally to set up two cross-cutting bureaucracies, with managers at the intersections reporting to two bosses. This simple form of the matrix essentially put the burden of collaboration onto individuals: they had somehow to reconcile conflicting pressures from the two dimensions. As one might expect, it didn't work very well in this pure form, and it has had a rocky history.[26]

In the last decade or so the matrix has evolved into a third solution. Many companies with historical strategies of improving on their core products have been shaken by increasingly complex customer demands. As Jay Galbraith has described it, the hierarchy in such cases has been decomposed into a "front end" focused on customer needs (sales and marketing) and a "back end" focused on production.[27] This is a new problem because the front and the back are clearly not independent and autonomous in the way that, for example, car divisions once were within General Motors; the front end needs to be able to work out plans and agreements with customers, and then get the back end to deliver them.

Thus the links between the front and the back become critical to success. The most common response among our sample companies has been some form of customer relationships managers (CRMs) whose responsibility is to work with the back-end production units to create solutions to the needs of major clients. These CRMs face directly the core problem of collaboration: with little power, they must persuade parts of the organization that are very distant in terms of formal bureaucratic links to cooperate to meet the customer needs.

In complex or multidimensional enterprises the hierarchy is generally elaborate, with considerable decentralization and many subdivisions. The collaborative system also has several aspects. These organizations may (and, in my experience, generally do) maintain a strong informal culture of loyalty and paternalism that helps with integration. This is not strong enough, however, to deal with the ongoing demands of complex strategies. Thus formal mechanisms are added—notably formal linkages between the front and the back through consensus-based committees.

A front–back representation of the IBM organizational structure in the late 1990s looks as shown in Figure 13. The boxes are essentially decentralized bureaucratic pieces, organized in the familiar pyramidal form. The arrows are collaborative linkages involving high levels of negotiation and influence.

The limitation of this kind of organization is that the hierarchical systems tend to dominate the collaborative ones; the former define the organization and the latter exist at the boundaries. Thus collaboration regularly runs into resistance from people who have no strong incentive to move outside their own turf. CRMs thus have a hard time: like the managers at the intersections

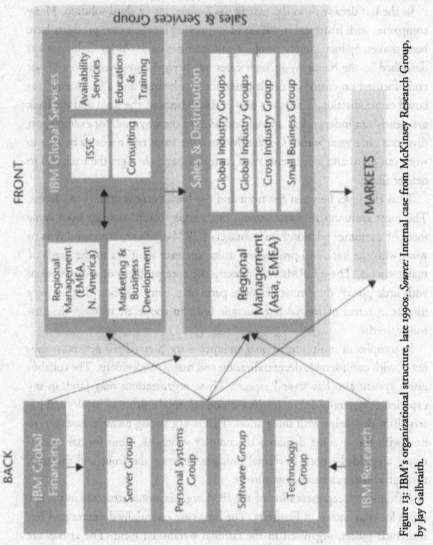

Figure 13: IBM's organizational structure, late 1990s. *Source:* Internal case from McKinsey Research Group, by Jay Galbraith.

of the old matrix systems, they have to take on themselves the managing of organizational tensions and conflicts, acting as ambassadors and mediators in their jobs. In the three companies where I have interviewed multiple CRMs (Citibank, ABB-Canada, and Lucent), I heard consistent stories of such obstacles.

In relatively stable settings, such as Citibank, the answer has been to choose CRMs who have long tenure and high prestige within the traditional networks, so that they can use informal means to negotiate reallocation of resources. But this proved to be insufficient; CRMs at Citibank continued to be frustrated by their inability to get the "back end" to focus effectively on customer needs. The collaboration did not begin to work until they gained some formal leverage for negotiating with their peers.[28] The outlines of this story are repeated in many other companies: to deliver complexity effectively to customers requires something more than the "interstitial" collaborative committees characteristic of linked hierarchies.

## High Adaptiveness: Project Collaboration

A second type of organization is that driven primarily by a strategy of adaptiveness—the ability to innovate and respond to change. Ford in the days of the Model T, and AT&T in the days of the basic black telephone, were almost at the zero point on this dimension: their competitive claim was almost entirely focused on reliability and cost. At the other extreme are consulting companies—McKinsey and its ilk—whose identity is largely based on the ability to stay on the leading edge of changes in the world of business, to anticipate better than others what will happen next, and to help their clients respond to these in tailored ways. Large production companies may also position themselves strongly on this innovative dimension: the battle between Intel and AMD is almost entirely in these terms.

This kind of strategy frequently leads companies to seek increased "focus": a large stream of strategic advice in the 1980s and 1990s was to focus more tightly on core competencies as a means of gaining speed and nimbleness.[29] In our sample, Nokia and Lucent adopted this notion with a vengeance; by contrast, Lou Gerstner deliberately rejected this pressure at IBM in order to maintain the benefits of complex integration.

The strategic claim to adaptiveness creates tremendous organizational pressure. Formalization, routinization, and mastery—the staples of traditional management—are hard to achieve in complex environments, but they come under direct attack when the emphasis is on adaptiveness. Relationships must be less hard-wired and more flexible; people (and the resources they control) must be able to combine in unexpected ways.

In non-business organizations focused on adaptiveness, there is a great deal of evidence that the best kind of organization is a network based on collaborative influence with very little hierarchy. One case for this is science as an institution, the best system we have yet discovered for innovation and discovery: it is based on quite independent scientists and relatively small laboratories, relating to each other primarily through peer evaluation and collaborations. Another is the Internet, an "organization" that has shown itself capable of extremely effective innovation, growth, adaptiveness, and resilience. But these organizations are different from businesses because they have little pressure for efficiency: both scientific investigation and communication on the Internet achieve their adaptability through a great deal of redundancy and tolerance of error. Business firms cannot afford the inefficiencies of such a pure network structure. Therefore even the closest approximations to free-wheeling networks within the business world—Silicon Valley startups or small professional-service firms—retain considerable hierarchical control.[30]

Business organizations with a focus on adaptiveness tend to emphasize heavily the customer dimension. The typical structure is of client-centered teams that collaborate strongly within teams, but have loose connections to the wider system. A simple picture would be that shown in Figure 14. Consulting firms, for example, typically build strong "client teams" managed by simple hierarchical links and common cultural orientations. They are accountable to practice managers or partners, but operate for the most part on their own. They are linked also to some degree by the core values or identity of the firm, which maintains a general consistency across client-facing engagements.

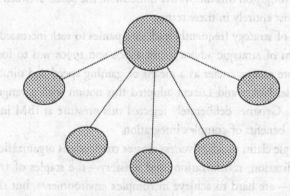

Figure 14: Project collaboration (adaptive)

What the diagram does not show well is the flexibility across teams. Unlike in "lean production" manufacturing, adaptive teams of this kind are not fixed for long periods; they must be able to reconfigure rapidly as clients and their needs shift. Typically this is managed to a considerable extent by the teams themselves rather than by assignments through the hierarchy. To do this, the organization needs to structure ways to help people to seek out and find those with the competence to help them on a problem—in particular, it needs good reputational mechanisms and systems of communication. This is not fundamentally different from a scientific field, except that here one adds a strong hierarchical element: unlike in science, where the highly inefficient institution of tenure is viewed as essential, in businesses those who do not perform well get evaluated and fired and teams that do not return sufficient revenues get disbanded.

This simple adaptive model has some key limitations. It is weak at integrative tasks, like pulling together different types of expertise for learning or coordination of complex solutions: the decentralized entrepreneurial teams tend to protect their own territories and to communicate poorly among themselves. It also works well only when teams can be matched neatly to clients. This may sometimes be the case for consulting firms, but in other situations this match is less clear. On one hand, companies may find that a single client must deal with multiple teams: when Lucent decentralized into eleven autonomous business units in the late 1990s, it found that customers were complaining of receiving sales calls from multiple agents for overlapping and even conflicting products. On the other hand, resources and capabilities held in a single organizational unit may be useful across many clients: McKinsey in the same period struggled with the inability to share general functional knowledge, such as organizational and marketing issues, across multiple product teams.

These limitations push many organizations "up" toward a greater ability to manage complex interdependent projects. Even consulting firms frequently try to strengthen the hand of overarching units based on industry, technology, or other integrative dimensions rather than on specific clients or projects. This turns out to be a major organizational change problem: the unidimensional culture of client focus leads to resistance to the attempts at multidimensionality.

## The Upper Right: Systemic Collaboration— Managing High Tension

The most difficult position is of course the maximization of both complexity and adaptiveness—an attempt to deliver integrated solutions in flexible and dynamic environments. Companies that have tried to inhabit this space, though often unsuccessfully, include large telecommunications firms such as AT&T or Lucent, faced with a rapidly changing technological landscape that requires integration of many emerging bases of knowledge with shifting customer demands; many major firms in the computer industry, such as IBM or Cisco; and global knowledge banks such as Citibank, during this period of international deregulation and technological change.

The organizational problem here is not merely to pull together projects "on the fly," but to pull together very large and multidimensional projects. These organizations need to keep a very diverse range of actors sharply focused while continually adapting to the unexpected. As a manager at Intel puts the problem: "Who should do a deal at Intel? The right anybody using the right process. Too restrictive a stance would seriously impede Intel's ability to keep up with the market."[31]

The organizational difficulties of this positioning are so great that companies may try to escape or avoid it. Some try to move to the "left," reducing the uncertainty of highly unpredictable markets by controlling the competitive environment. This is an age-old move: there is a strong tendency for most industries to consolidate toward a small number of players, so that they have an easier time watching each other and have less unpredictability to worry about. Adam Smith deplored it in *The Wealth of Nations*,[32] and Microsoft is widely accused of practicing it today by trying to eliminate rivals.[33]

Others try to escape the demands of the true solutions by moving "down" toward lower complexity. This is the main thrust of the frequent practice of "strategic focusing"—to drop some functions and activities so that the organization focuses on only a few that it can do well. Lucent is one example among many companies that have divested themselves of manufacturing because they felt they could not handle the integrative demands of combining a manufacturing environment, with its emphasis on continuity and cost control, with a knowledge-intensive organization dedicated to rapid innovation. Canadian-Pacific, which was trying to provide a complex offering including transportation, hostelry, car rental, and other elements of travel, decided in the end to break the company into separate pieces so each could better focus on its distinct businesses.

Nevertheless, the potential for the true solutions strategy remains extremely attractive: it is the only way to continuously match capabilities to opportunities. Many companies therefore find themselves drawn in this direction despite the difficulty of the task, and some find themselves more or less forced to

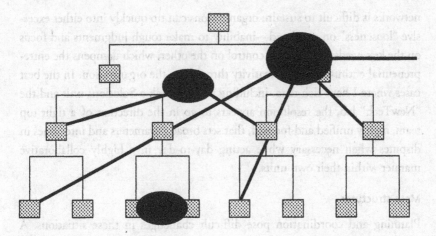

Figure 15: Systemic collaboration

take on very complex demands in environments that are also changing rapidly. The challenge is inescapable now in telecommunications and banking and aspects of the computer industry. In telecommunications equipment, for example, the problem is that there is a demand for enormously complex infrastructure, requiring huge investment and sustained processes of collaborative innovation, at a time when no one is really sure what technology will win out or what the shape of the industry will be.[34] This uncertainty was a major driver of the "bubble" mentality of the late 1980s, when every company seemed afraid that others would outdo it in gaining new technology—a fear that led to enormous overinvestment.

The basic organizational pattern of a high-high organization is one of strong functional units crossed by fluid teaming (Figure 15); it can be pictured with the diagram of complex teaming used in the last chapter. The hierarchical aspect is somewhat more pronounced than in the more purely adaptive systems, but it is strongly overlaid by shifting project teams; people may spend most of their working time in this formal collaborative activity rather than under the control of their bosses.

Like adaptive organizations, these systems require great internal flexibility to respond to unexpected demands; but they also need to maintain a high level of coordination and overall focus, rather than just a large number of quasi-independent initiatives. The bureaucratic aspect is needed for setting priorities, screening ideas and proposals, and allocating resources. The balance between these authority-based systems and the equally necessary peer-based networks is difficult to sustain; organizations can tip quickly into either excessive "looseness" on one hand—inability to make tough judgments and focus on the key needs; or excessive control on the other, which dampens the entrepreneurial enthusiasm and creativity throughout the organization. In the best cases where I have rich data, including the Citibank e-Solutions unit and the "NewTech" lab, the resolution appears to go in the direction of a tight top team, highly unified and focused, that sets broad parameters and intervenes in disputes when necessary while acting day-to-day in a highly collaborative manner within their own units.

### Meta-structures

Planning and coordination pose difficult challenges in these situations. A purely adaptive organization can allow a great deal of improvisation and local variation; a purely complexity-maximizing organization can organize through centralized mechanisms or a cyclical committees; but a solutions organization needs to maintain coherence around a plan while at the same time being very responsive to rapidly changing opportunities. They therefore need some form of what might be called "meta-structures"—processes that link the ongoing opportunity-spotting throughout the organization with the overarching strategic priorities, and that can change either side of the link as needed.

Meta-structures come in many forms. On one end are review committees that are fairly close to traditional management approval processes, but that operate with higher levels of dialogue and openness. In the Citibank e-Solutions group described in Chapter 3, a team of high-middle managers, crossing multiple units, reviewed project proposals, applied strategic criteria, assigned resources to those that pass, and modified the strategy as needed. But they strove to be something different from a management approval committee. First, employees at various levels had a great deal of room to experiment and develop early phases of projects before coming to the committee. Second, the meetings were structured as dialogues rather than as formal presentations; decisions generally emerged from the general discussion rather than from the "management" contingent.

In other companies meta-structuring is not the preserve of a single group but is a more open and fluid process, with a team acting as a hub for various processes of exploration and prioritization. The Monsanto Global Product Management Group (GPM), as of about 2000, was structured with co-leads from the seeds and chemicals sides of the business, and for product groups (corn, soy, Roundup, cotton) who come from both the front and back ends of the business. The product co-leads were responsible for integrating the roles of seeds, chemicals, and biotech for each of the products. There were extensive linkages between GPM and the geographies, and between GPM and the functions. In each geography there was a person responsible for product marketing and product development who are part of the product management network led by GPM. Similarly, there were people in the back-end functions who were part of the network. The GPM regularly talked and visited with the geographies and functions to understand new product ideas. In so doing, they became the "crossroads" of information streams, allowing them to set priorities and resolve conflicts.[35]

The examples can be multiplied: there has been an extraordinary amount of creativity applied to the development of processes to connect innovation to strategy and to make clear decisions on prioritization through open and transparent discussion. This is the place at which the tension between the hierarchy and the collaborative network is most visible. The Citibank e-Solutions unit started out with a highly open collaborative process and felt a need to tighten up the hierarchical decision making after a year or so; but there was a debate about whether this led to shutting down too many of the benefits of collaboration. It is too early to establish clear rules about which of the approaches just described works best, and in what situations. The answer depends in large part on the strength of the infrastructural elements of collaboration described in Chapter 5.

## CONCLUSION

There are three general points to underline from this overview. First, relational networks must combine the two dimensions of hierarchy and association, which are often in tension but cannot be separated. Second, the particular "shape" of the relational network is a function of the strategic positioning of the organization (which is itself partly a matter of choice). Third, there is a general pressure today to develop the associational dimension beyond the informal, loyalty-based version common in the dominant companies of the last century.

We have identified four "ideal types" of organization driven by differing strategic imperatives: operational effectiveness, complexity, adaptiveness, and the ultimate combination of complexity and adaptiveness that is the full flowering of a "solutions" organization. Taking the efficiency focus as a given

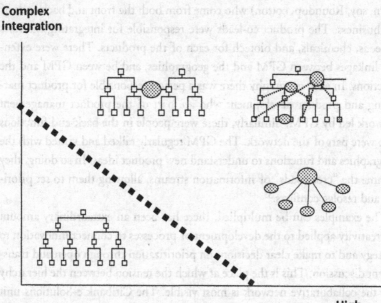

Figure 16: Strategies and structures: Varieties of collaborative enterprise

for business organizations, we map the remaining ones on two dimensions (Figure 16).

In each of the three collaborative configurations there is a break in which the traditional bureaucratic mechanisms of formal hierarchy and informal co-operation are surpassed; this break is marked by the addition of extended collaboration, bringing people together across organizational boundaries into wide-ranging, diverse teams. We have seen a number of types of such teams: the hansei (Reflection Review) teams of lean production, the linking committees of front–back organizations, the reconfigurable project groups of decentralized adaptive systems, and the multiscale emergent teams and meta-structures of the high-high solutions organizations.

All of these variants represent a step up in organizational capability in that they increase the number of possible working relations. Bureaucracy sharply restricts formal connections; in its paternalist variant, it adds informal links limited in number and extent. When organizations start drawing on the benefits of extended collaboration, looking for ways to bring together people with diverse skills and knowledge around evolving problems, they start to exponentially increase the potential links. In the Citibank case a credit card specialist in Lima may see an opportunity that requires the support of a finance specialist in Tokyo; a full solutions organization makes that connection possible, where a bureaucracy would at best require a long series of moves up and down the hierarchy.

But this increase in potential working relationships requires that groups break through the conditions that have previously limited collaborative relationships: it asks for cooperation between people who don't know each other well, who have no assurance that they will ever need each other again, and who have very different skills and viewpoints. Thus the problem is not just one of structure, but of transforming the background conditions—the infrastructure—that determine when and how people can trust each other, understand each other, and work productively together. That is the larger challenge, and the reason that the transition is so difficult.

**Table 4 Elements of Collaborative Enterprise**

| | Project Collaboration (High Adaptiveness) | Managed Collaboration (High Complexity) | Systemic Collaboration (High Complexity and Adaptiveness) |
|---|---|---|---|
| Overall character | Networks of relatively autonomous temporary groups, frequent recombinations; relatively weak strategic unity | Strong hierarchies focused on single dimensions (product, region, customer, function), linked by bridging processes | Rich networks with much overlap; strong planning and prioritization processes |
| Task teams | Decentralized temporary teams • delivery teams • innovation teams | Long-lasting linking roles and committees: customer relationships managers, prioritization councils | Initiatives (in addition to decentralized teams and linking committees) |
| Key processes | Reconfiguration: task definitions and self-organizing teams | Prioritization | Participatory planning, strategic dialogue, iterative codesign |
| Hierarchies | Thin hierarchies | Strong hierarchies | Hierarchies as resource allocators Meta-structures |
| Examples in research sample | Nokia McKinsey Spaarbeleg | Citibank overall IBM (1990s) | Citibank e-Solutions "Newtech" IBM (2000s) |

## Chapter 3 Citibank e-Solutions

At this point we break from the relatively abstract level and offer an extended example of how a collaborative unit actually operates. The following case is not meant as an ideal model: it had many difficulties and incomplete systems and faced continuing resistance from other parts of the organization. But it does illustrate in unusually rich detail the workings of extended collaboration.

Citibank e-Solutions was a part of an e-Business unit formed in April 2000. The mandate for e-Business, a global organization based on the old Cash Management group, was to move aggressively toward the development of Internet-based products. e-Solutions was essentially its innovation arm or product development group. The effort evolved rapidly through the two years of research, in 2001–2002. It was successful in that period in terms of meeting goals and surpassing its competitors, but faced continued resistance from other, more bureaucratic parts of the bank on which it depended.

In the 1990s the cash management and trade business was the core of Citibank, accounting for about 65 to 70 percent of total revenues, but its growth rate was only 3 to 4 percent a year. The organization was a stable and relatively bureaucratic one, with many separate units and "empires" that did not coordinate well. Geographic units were particularly strong and resistant to central strategies and directives. New product development in this unit and in the bank as a whole historically has been fair to poor.

In the mid-1990s a major process improvement effort was launched, involving training of more than 90,000 people in process management skills and the formation of thousands of teams. Many of these focused on improving processes that were ineffective because of differences across units of the bank. They succeeded in moving a substantial distance toward rationalizing everyday work processes on issues such as billing and management of statements. The effort also built a greater customer awareness throughout the bank.

In 1998 Jorge Bermudez took over the cash and trade business and began to consolidate the structure. He held meetings with all regions combined, developed combined goals across regions, and consolidated bureaucracies across regions: for example, he consolidated the financial management and regional sales groups into a global sales management organization with regional representation. It was "an ugly process for some of the regional managers."

During this period, CEO John Reed began to be concerned about meeting the nascent demand for Internet banking. He started the E-Citi initiative, an experimental "skunk works" for exploring Internet opportunities. It had a deliberate research culture, somewhat removed from business imperatives. As Sandy Weill took the reins, he pushed the Internet initiative toward more rapid revenue generation.

In the fall of 1999 Jorge Bermudez brought together about forty senior managers for a "team challenge" to explore opportunities in and develop a strategy for Internet-based products. The group spent four to five weeks of intensive, nearly full-time work, during which it came up with various initiatives to pursue, and with a strategy focused on breakthrough thinking. The key words, reiterated consistently after that time, were "expand, transform, connect."

In March of 2000 the corporate side of the E-Citi group was folded into the cash and trade business, and the whole, under Bermudez, was renamed "e-Business" to stress the Internet focus. e-Solutions was established as a separate unit within e-Business. Its goal was to accelerate the growth rate of cash and trade from 3 to 4 percent to a range closer to 20 percent.

## STRATEGY

As its name implies, e-Solutions was conceived as a solutions business, intended to create new and complex online banking products that could be tailored rapidly to customer needs. It sought to build stable Internet platforms for services such as clearing, trading, and collections, which would allow customers to get information much more rapidly and in more useful forms than through the traditional paper-based processes.[1]

A strategy manager expressed the challenge in this way:

Ultimately the goal is grow beyond financial services to providing commercial management services—in other words, to be a solutions provider. But our core competence is in financial management. So we need to work with other parties outside the bank, sometimes competitors, sometimes technology providers, in order to provide integrated end-to-end solutions. We can't do everything ourselves, we know that. The way to move forward is to form strategic partnerships with others.

Within the bank, the e-Solutions group was faced with trying to integrate many dimensions of the company in an environment of rapid change in technologies, regulations, and customer expectations. AOL and other providers had already enabled their customers to do online banking, trade stocks, buy mutual funds from a variety of sources, and view financial research and business and market news, all from a single screen. Citibank had been far behind, with relatively few customers and a much narrower range of services. To succeed in this arena the bank would need to integrate divisions that historically had been highly separate: credit cards, investment banking, private banking, and others. Further, the area was so new that no one was sure yet what would succeed; hence the problem could not be solved with a one-time restructuring but required open experimentation.

The strategic vision was not entirely clear from the start, but emerged through practice over time. The original E-Citi effort had been widely criticized in the bank for pushing technical leaps without connecting to business leaders. e-Solutions was launched after a careful review of these lessons and sought from the start to focus more heavily on business needs. The reorientation was gradual: the language in my interviews shifted subtly between the first and second rounds, a little more than a year apart. In the first round the watchwords, repeated and elaborated over and over in meetings and projects, were "expand, transform, connect": there was often a sense that innovation was an end in itself. Harder business objectives, such as 12 percent growth, were mentioned, but mostly in the background. In the second round of interviews, by contrast, the financial dimension was no longer in the background.

Thus pressures had grown for both complexity and adaptiveness.

- The complexity problem was to balance technical innovation with customer responsiveness, while raising the emphasis on financial results. One person complained that the cost focus had become dominant and had smothered innovation; but most felt that these dimensions must and could be pursued simultaneously. I more often heard financial numbers intertwined with broader or longer term issues of connection and transformation, and everyone was very aware of the need to make a case to business leaders for any project proposal.
- The adaptiveness pressure was a matter of shifting focus from the internal product-technology focus—how do we do cool things with the Internet—to more continuous interaction with customers and an attempt to respond to their needs. Strategic justifications paid more attention to the state of customer desire for online banking services.

Thus the collaborative problem became steadily more difficult over time, and the needed scope of collaboration widened to encompass more and more parts of the bank.

## STRUCTURE

e-Business included cash and trade management, which continued largely with its traditional tasks and organization and employed nearly 7,000 people; and the e-Solutions initiative, with about 300 people. Although e-Solutions was much smaller, there was a strong mandate for it to grow and become the core of the business. In the spring of 2001 Bermudez announced a target of 15 percent of revenues to come from new e-Solutions products and businesses by the end of the year.

e-Solutions was designed to enable rapid configuration of task teams not only across the immediate organization but across all of e-Business, the bank as a whole, and beyond the boundaries of Citibank through alliances. It went through a number of evolutions to build a framework that would enable teams to form quickly around opportunities, without heavy intervention from top management, while maintaining coherence around the major strategic dimensions.

In its first year it had a multidimensional structure of teams focused on initiatives, industries, and geographies; these dimensions overlapped and formed a kind of fluid matrix. In the spring of 2001 they reorganized into three segments to reduce these overlaps. One manager was responsible for facing "outward" against the industries and regions, another for focusing "inward" on the key e-Solutions initiatives, and a third for commercializing any new solutions brought to the marketplace. Geographies remained with the country leaders; there were e-Solutions teams within each major geographic area, as well as teams that cross-cut geographies (Figure 17).

The top four leaders of e-Solutions met regularly to review new initiatives. Though they controlled only some of the needed resources for any particular project, they enforced a consistent discipline of focusing on business value.

Within a very thin and fluid formal structure, much of the work was done in constantly reconfigured "virtual" teams. People at all levels went directly to the resources they needed without passing through the chain of command; when people felt they needed to work on a project they might check with their boss, but they rarely felt they needed formal approval.

Here, from an interview, is a typical example of how it worked. The interviewee was one of the members of the Alliance group who did not have a direct reporting relationship to the alliance leader, but who had other responsibilities in his region:

First I got an idea because I had a relationship with [a partner] in the past. I put that together with some opportunities I encounter in my daily work, and had a thought about something new we could offer.

A few years ago we did a small thing with [the partner], a local outsourcing effort. I kept the business card of the guy we worked with—keeping business cards is almost a religion with me. So when I had this idea I first put together a communication praising the local team with [the partner] on their good work and forwarded it to higher levels. Then I said to the senior manager, "We should look at how to advance these opportunities." I got response from him saying, "Great, here's my e-Business head from LA, talk to him."

Then I sat down in office and made a war map on the wall about who I needed to get involved within Citibank. I outlined under each of them what the alliance would bring to them: to a senior guy it will bring market share or revenue; for lower levels it should bring learning opportunities that could be added to their resume, and so on.

Then I hit the phone and talked to each of these main contacts, chitchatted a bit, then introduced this idea—sold it to them. I forwarded them documentation and presentations. Then I called back to talk to them again a week after.

That's how I start my "war."

People down to three or four levels below the top leadership engaged frequently in creating and developing such teams. The approach was needed not

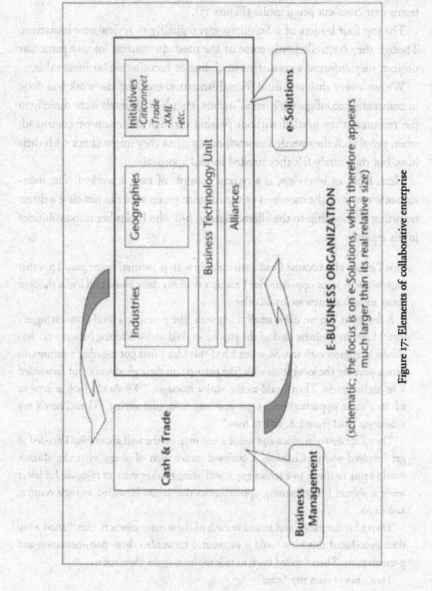

Figure 17: Elements of collaborative enterprise

just in cases of entrepreneurial invention; it was also needed on a daily basis because every project and sub-project required pulling together resources from different reporting areas of the bank. One person three levels from the top of e-Solutions listed his interfaces:

> [T]he e-Business management running legacy business other than e-Solutions; lawyers I spend more time than I like with; various investment and venture capital areas within the organization; the operations and functional areas: operations, technology, marketing. For part of the process you're working in the e-Solutions context; then you move on out into e-Business. And I've built a network of people outside of Citibank that I run things by on a regular basis—consultants, ex-bankers working on other businesses.

Another added: "If you drew me as a wheel, with all the spokes I have the wheel wouldn't roll."

When asked if there was any formal assignment process for his work with these different groups, he answered:

> Originally the alliance guy called me and asked me if I wanted to work on this, and when I said yes he said let me call [your boss], and she told him that it was fine for me to work on it. But we don't get knighted or anointed around here.
>
> As for the procurement side, I just started working with the team, and they accepted me.

Similarly, another person, asked whether he had been formally assigned a dotted-line relationship to alliances, said, "No, it's just a given, it's just natural."

## CULTURE AND VALUES

From the beginning, e-Solutions tried to symbolize a break with the "bureaucratic" Citi culture. The central offices in Connecticut were set up on an open plan, with Bermudez sitting in the center and easily accessible to most of the e-Solutions employees. A large number of managers were hired from outside Citibank—within a year an estimated 40 percent of e-Solutions managers had come from outside the bank, and some from outside the banking industry altogether. There was constant experimentation with communications vehicles, wider involvement, and so forth.

The core value that united members of e-Solutions was a "mindset of professionalism" or of "good business practices"; though these were not official terms in any sense, a number of people used them spontaneously in interviews. They seemed to have three main dimensions:

1. *Following through on commitments:* Those who tried to get by with free riding, or who made promises they didn't keep, produced a strong reaction. Unlike in other parts of the bank, there seemed to be little tolerance of "working around" such obstacles.
2. *Competence:* This was almost a given, but certainly those who did not have the skills to contribute to projects were quickly isolated.
3. *Contributing to the whole:* Several people noted in one way or another that they did things that had not been asked for and were not likely to be rewarded in any direct way. I asked one person working with the Alliance team, but not formally a member of it, if the Alliance leader had any input into his evaluation. He answered: "As far as I know, probably not." So, I pursued, why would he put time into this team? "Because I think it is an important function that we must fulfill in order to achieve our goal of being the leading e-business provider in the world."

Another put it:

> I don't look at it from my selfish perspective, because any good business person would try to look at things from as broad a perspective as possible. Anyone who's going to be successful in business is going to look at things from as many perspectives as possible.

The most valued "perspective," in other words, was a broad understanding of business success. Other dimensions of "culture" were generally downplayed or rejected.

> I don't buy into the cultural thing. The hard part is finding the people who do what you need done. At the end of the day it's a matter of what you contribute to them—articulate what the proposition is and what you need from them, a one-to-one relationship around the proposition rather than any culture hocus-pocus stuff. You can manage around the culture by having a tight buttoned-up approach to strategy.

### COLLABORATIVE INFRASTRUCTURE

The ability to form fluid teams required more than spontaneous good will and intelligence. Since work was not coordinated primarily by the chain of command, other kinds of support and coordination were essential. Thus e-Solutions developed an entire infrastructure of collaboration centered on building shared understanding and processes—a deliberately managed set of tools that enabled people to coordinate without direct intervention by their bosses.

## Shared Understandings and Knowledge

Collaborative interaction, according to many people, involved first of all a clear understanding of the value propositions for different actors in different parts of the bank. Daily work required a constant process of selling: "I have to show the value to them, I have to sell them the idea, as someone sells you a TV or a car; if I can show you value why you should do this you will do it."

To sell, one needs to have a good understanding of the needs and motivations of people in very different areas. A widespread understanding of diverse value propositions was underpinned with at least two organizational systems.

### Common Understanding of the Strategy and Priorities

The senior team spent a great deal of effort in articulating strategic priorities and reinforcing them consistently.

- The forty-plus managers involved in the initial intensive discussion and development of the e-Business strategy were scattered through the organization at several levels.
- The senior leadership conducted a series of seminars in the fall for everyone down to management associates. Bermudez himself held a meeting for all incoming managers, and other senior leaders then attended various meetings to reinforce the message.
- There were multiple continuing channels of communication and discussion of the evolving strategy.

Thus a person three levels from the top of e-Business said:

> The company does very well at having a clear sense of strategy and where we want to go. There are three basic strategies: expand, transform, connect—that's been clearly communicated in e-Business. The strategy has penetrated to all levels. . . . Part of why it has penetrated so well is because there is clear and consistent emphasis on three strategies and six tactics that we agree on. Often we have the very same slides up reinforcing what we are doing. Most people address these issues.
>
> The e-Business strategy research group is important in reaffirming that we are on the right track. They have a Web site and post some of their studies, such as compatibility analyses, so whoever is acting can pop in and look at it.

### Forums: Channels for Communicating Current Activities

It was essential for the functioning of this fluid system that people knew what was going on beyond their own horizons. A substantial communications industry had sprung up within the e-Solutions unit—some of it managed from the leadership, much of it created by people on an as-needed basis. "We got rid of monthly newsletters that everyone wrote and nobody read, and replaced them with Web pages, regular phone calls, and town hall meetings."

Meetings of different types evolved rapidly in the year's research on e-Solutions. One thing that seemed to be settling in was a series of conference calls focused on simple information exchange. There was a weekly "global-galactic" call for all of e-Solutions that anyone could join in on, during which people working on new initiatives had a chance to explain their goals and needs. Presenters came from multiple levels—though senior leadership were on the call they did not dominate it. Participants frequently picked up on the information shared in this call to identify available resources or new opportunities. Smaller, more focused versions of this information-sharing call began to emerge within initiative areas.

A second channel was a developing set of new communications channels driven opportunistically rather than organized from the top. While glossy newsletters declined, more people were creating their own broadcast channels. They appeared to be gradually moving toward a style that enables people to pick up the information they need with great speed and efficiency:

> I reach on a monthly basis between 5,000 and 7,000 folks. I have seven reports that go out every month. They are very focused around goals, strategies, milestones, what did we tell you we were going to do last month, what did we do, what will we do next month. They go deep in the organization, from senior managers to product managers.

This exchange enables people to find others who can contribute to their work in far-flung areas of the organization.

Web sites functioned as a second line of communication. Efforts to organize all information on the Web and to make it the first line faltered; it proved impossible to get people to input all the needed information. The "Compass" information system, which was touted by higher management of the bank as a way to coordinate initiatives and track commitments, languished almost totally unused. On the other hand, spontaneous use of the intranet grew as a way of supplementing the communications described earlier:

- Someone might give a brief description of her work on the "global-galactic" call and then refer those interested to a Web site for further details.
- One person kept records of all his conversations with potential allies in a Web folder so other team members could access it and so that if he became involved in other projects the information would still be available.

- The strategy group's analyses, as mentioned earlier, were frequently accessed by those planning new initiatives.

People expressed a need for an information system that would support new types of posting and communication as needed, rather than a highly standardized information format.

### Trust and the Reputational Marketplace

In addition to the need for understanding the functioning of the system, this kind of interaction required a high level of trust. People formed working relationships that were often brief and sporadic: many teams had "members" who interacted only a few times during the life of the project. They needed to be able to make rapid judgments about whether those making proposals were capable and trustworthy.

One basis for trust was personal relationships built over many years in the bank. Those who had been around a long time spoke of these relations as some of the most solid: "I've known X for fifteen years. We can laugh together and drink together, and that's an important part of our success." At the same time, it was realized that such a personal network was not enough for the task: the challenges varied too rapidly and required too wide a range of contributors. For the Alliance team the problem was especially severe, since they were constantly dealing with people who were outside the boundaries of the company and whom they had never met before.

"Rapid trust" worked effectively much of the time, and it depended most centrally on a strong reputational system. In the early phases of e-Solutions the formal performance appraisal system was rather weak—still in the process of development, not well understood. The reputational system, on the other hand, was very strong. People spoke frequently to each other about the performance of their peers, and most people participated in so many overlapping networks that the word got around in a hurry.

According to most people, the reputational network worked very effectively at maintaining accountability. In effect it worked in a natural way: those who did not contribute were not approached for further projects, and so were quickly marginalized; the formal appraisal mechanisms kicked in only when things got serious.

Communications are so open and expectations so high that you can't hide for long. Communication is so fluid and conference calls so frequent that sooner or later people begin to ask questions and make remarks. After a while someone says

"What is this person doing?" And then the boss and the country head and others talk about it.

Meanwhile, those who developed a good reputation thrived quite independent of their formal position:

> If you build relationships through credibility in executing, and people know that you are a person that brings value to the table then you can have access to them any day any time. If you're a roadblock, no matter how high your title or visibility you're going to get rejection.

This network based on reciprocal contribution had limits. It didn't extend very well to parts of the bank outside e-Solutions: other parts of the bank were often referred to as "bureaucratic" in contrast to the strong performance ethic of the e-Solutions unit. Other areas (in e-Solutions' view) valued sticking to the rules, or following established procedures, or not rocking the boat—all values that interfere with a focus on getting the job done and make it harder to work with them.

> In the regions there's a concentrated mindset of professionalism that gets diluted at the global level, in headquarters. New York is different; there are more levels, more bureaucracy. But the e-Solutions headquarters is similar in that you find a group of people dedicated to a single mission.

Thus when dealing with other sections of the bank it was generally necessary either to go through the formal hierarchy—go to one's boss to go to the boss of the person whose help you needed—or to utilize the "old boy's network" of personal ties. This may be why the top levels of e-Solutions are more heavily filled with people who had been around a long time: to break through resistances from product groups, from legal, and so on, one could not safely rely on the logic of mutual contribution; a personal call might be needed.

Dealing with groups outside the bank presented a different issue. For the most part the value dimensions lined up fairly well: because they were dealing with other people who were used to "rapid trust," everyone came to the table with a strong ethic of performance and contribution—and there were clear shared goals: "In some ways it's easier dealing with outside partners than with other parts of the bank, because in an alliance we have mutual targets in mind from the start."

Indeed, it seems that some of the key early alliances served to educate long-time Citibank employees about how this performance focus worked.

> [Our first partner] is very efficient about process: No meeting ends without the next meeting being identified, and a list of to-do items agreed on. They want to move

very fast, sometimes faster than we thought made sense. But we learned that we have to speed up. We have to learn the discipline of never leaving a meeting without an agreement on the next meeting, and the discipline of focus. I have trouble with focus, but if you don't focus in this business, you lose momentum. The compressed time frame keeps people focused.

There remained the problem of how to judge whether potential partners are trustworthy. Since they were not part of the reputational network, the judgment was heavily based on vague and intangible impressions.

You develop a feel for whether they can deliver what they promise—it's more an intuitive feel rather than an analysis. Obviously there's some tangible evidence like when you ask for delivery of things do they come on time; but in planning discussions you can feel instinctively whether they are being honest or not.

This appeared to work, though one wonders whether this was a strong enough basis for a system of long-term relationships.

### Negotiation and Process Management

As indicated earlier, the culture was based very heavily on negotiations of different types of value contributions. The language of "win–win" was current and widespread: everyone expressed a need to create solutions that met multiple needs inside and outside the organization. They were quite articulate about the kinds of moves needed when there was disagreement with a peer or a partner: setting operating rules at the beginning of negotiation, providing observable data, and so forth. Everyone I spoke to was quite comfortable with this kind of negotiation; I did not sense, as I often have in other organizations, a feeling that things were out of control and that more direction was needed.

This ability to negotiate was founded on a rich interdependency throughout the system: everyone knew that they could not get their jobs done without working with a wide set of other people. The Alliance group, for example, had virtually no formal power—it did not control access to partners or potential revenues, nor did it seek to do so. Nevertheless, as its leader said,

I can exert a lot of influence over my regional colleagues, which does not require reporting relationship: being smarter than they are on process; telling great war stories for them to learn from; helping them close deals.

More broadly, there was a strong understanding of and commitment to formalized process management. When they first met regularly, project teams held "roles and responsibility" sessions; they also frequently held "leveling" sessions when things got out of kilter, revisiting roles and responsibilities, doing root-cause analysis, and so on. The process discipline learned in Process Improvement Team training had been widely absorbed in the organization and was felt to have been a valuable foundation for the current organization. The difference was that the PIT processes were rather rigidly predetermined and drove teams in a patterned way from the start; in the current organization, processes were used and, indeed, invented as needed.

## THE ROLE OF HIERARCHY

So far I have stressed the "horizontal," associational dimension. The members of the organization themselves consistently emphasized this entrepreneurial, inventive, fluid side of things, and one generally had to dig rather hard to find an acknowledgment of the role of hierarchy and formal structure. Yet these clearly remained a vital background guiding the improvisational nature of the day-to-day work.

### Definition of Priorities

Probably the most important role of top leadership was to define the basic priorities of the organization. Everyone understood that there had been a shift in emphasis from "basic research" to relatively rapid revenue generation; one person in our sample did not support the shift, but everyone understood it. At the same time it was clear that rapid movement into an unknown space—Internet-enabled products—was also a priority. The constant refrain of "expand, transform, connect" reinforced the direction. These understandings helped a great deal in aligning people in the constant daily negotiations. "At the end of the day we all report to the same business head; and they have a clear directive that we're transforming the business; in the end it will be all Internet products."

Recently there has been an effort to be even clearer about the priorities by putting numbers on them. The people I talked to thought this had been positive:

> The best thing that's happened since e-Business formed was that Jorge articulated in December that by end of the year we had to have 15 percent of our revenue coming from e-Solutions. That was a galvanizing objective that motivated and tightened up a lot of processes just by articulating it. It gave people something crystal-clear to measure against.

Generally, though, superiors did not try to set priorities for individuals. The approach was more to discuss individual goals in the context of the overall priorities.

> I think embedded in what we have to do is it's not so much our boss coming to us and saying this is what I want you to do; his expectation is that you will have done your homework and had discussions with some of his peers about what the organization's requirements are and you come prepared to articulate to him what you're going to do.

The leadership group had also built a set of training programs, some of them mandatory, focused on "concepts, fundamental principles of e-space, the environment—to help people understand what was happening, what the new technology is and new ways of doing business—to enable people to start from common vocabulary."

There seemed to be some tension between people's desire for clarity and the desire for an open, interactive environment. Several of the interviewees veered abruptly from one pole to the other, on the one hand wanting strong leadership that absorbed some of the uncertainty, and on the other recognizing the value of an entrepreneurial environment that embraced uncertainty. Although on the whole the balance seemed to be working well, it was not easy for the participants.

## Resource Allocation

Although negotiation defined most of the day-to-day business, it worked against a background of resource allocation authority. The most common pattern was that people begin to put together an idea, as in the "war plan" described earlier, and when they found a certain amount of support they go looking for a "business leader"—someone who controlled needed resources—to back it.

After that they went to the senior team for formal project approval. This team asked two basic questions: Is there enough business leader support? and: Does it fit with the priorities of the organization?—especially: Does it help meet the goal of 15 percent of revenue from e-Solutions during 2001? Thus there was a kind of dual filter that strained out projects that didn't fit. Between April 2000 and April 2001 the Alliance group screened 171 companies; about 12 came to the "commit" group and received approval to proceed.

## Performance Management

The role of the hierarchy in performance management was different from, but not less important than, that in traditional organizations.

From middle management's perspective, most performance management came from peer commitments within teams and networks: "Accountability is mostly by our own initiative and what we psychologically or verbally contract to do."

Higher leadership did not appear to set strong fixed objectives for their subordinates. Most people agreed that their interactions with their superiors were more in the nature of conversations and discussions. Goals and action plans might be agreed on, but the expectation was that they would be frequently revised. "Goals change as you go along—[my boss] and I had a conversation over lunch today reshaping my goals—but some of them were left open, and they may change again."

People were generally very reluctant to use the hierarchy as a club to bring their peers into line. When someone did not perform well or blocked necessary resources, people generally said that going to that person's boss was an option, but they invariably added that they could not think of an occasion on which it had come to that. It was clear that such activities threatened the web of trust and influence on which the whole collaborative system depended. When hierarchical superiors were brought into the picture, the norm appeared to be that it was in the context of a data-based discussion of how to accomplish a given task.

Traditional MBO systems clearly did not play much of a role in shaping behavior. Repeatedly when I asked people how their bonuses were determined they were vague or uncertain. Superiors gained a great deal of "360-degree" information about individual performance by being plugged into the daily web of reputational discussions, and this appeared to be the most important basis for appraisals.

There was a bonus pool and a process for allocating it that was intended to encourage collaboration. The bonuses ranged from $5,000 to as much as 100 percent of salary. Members of the senior team made recommendations for bonuses for those they supervised, and those recommendations were then debated in a lengthy meeting of the entire top management team. The discussions brought out the cases either where people were failing to work effectively with other units, or where they were accomplishing things that might not be visible to their direct bosses. Yet although the process had been in place for four years (starting in Cash and Trade), none of the subordinate people I spoke to seemed to know much about it—certainly not enough to try to gear their behavior to it.

One person two levels down from the top of e-Business said:

> I don't have targets—but I have all of that network of people that I described earlier that will say—by perception and word of mouth—"he's got it under control, he's the one I want to work with," or "he's out in outer space." . . .
>
> There is a formal 360 process—at least I understand there is, I read it in an HR document at some point, but I don't know if it's actualized or not.

Nevertheless, the role of higher leadership was critical to the working of the system:

- The frequent conversations about goals and performance planning, even if they were more interactive than usual, clearly played a constant "steering" role in keeping people moving in a consistent direction. Without those conversations one would expect many more scattered and unproductive initiatives to go on far too long, and strategy to be much less coordinated.
- Although peers seemed to do a generally effective job of identifying poor performers, it remained for the formal superiors to take action when termination—or, more commonly, moving someone to another part of the bank—was necessary. The peer system alone, some people said, would probably not be decisive enough to deal with the exceptional problems; this could then poison the whole network of trust because people would no longer be able to rely on each other's commitment and competence. So the occasional hierarchical intervention to make clear who was meeting standards—and, most importantly, who wasn't—was essential to the health of the system.
- Though it seemed to be very rarely used, the fact that there was a backup authority that could settle disputes served to keep problems from escalating or going too far beyond the focus of the organization strategy; people knew that they would be held to account if they lost sight of the common purpose.

### Structuring

Although roles were fluid and often appeared to overlap, there was rarely much ambiguity about who was in charge. There might be a great deal of debate but little confusion about who got to "make the call" for any given type of issue.

The formal structuring process by top management was partly responsible for this clarity. They had clearly spent a lot of time and effort on structure, coming up with the three-dimensional model (geography, initiative, industry) described earlier, and several times shuffling responsibilities. After a year all of e-Solutions was put under one person's final responsibility, instead of being shared by two or three people as it had previously.

The top team of four also helped to clarify lines of authority in an ongoing way as they reviewed initiatives. They made it clear that the support of a business sponsor was an absolute requirement for approval. They did not appear to play a formal "arbitration" role, but in more informal conversations they constantly made sure that potential confusions were sorted out.

However, it was apparent that the general attitude of employees was also essential to the ability to reach decisions in this ambiguous environment. There was an explicit cultural expectation that people would seek not to gain control over resources, but rather to use influence and develop relationships. Throughout the organization there seemed to be relatively little battling for control of resources, or "empire-building." One person mentioned empire-building as a problem in the abstract: "The number one adversary of effective collaboration is personal need to want to amass responsibility and ownership of a turf "; but even he could not really cite instances within e-Solutions—he was thinking primarily of other parts of the bank.

One can only speculate about why empire-building, which was endemic in the larger organization, seemed relatively mild here. First, this was a relatively new organization; second, it was staffed with many people who were fairly new to the bank. Such "insulating" factors would decline with time. But the frequent shifting of projects and relationships was a more permanent feature of the organization and also worked against empire-building.

## THE ALLIANCE TEAM

One group represented in a particularly clear way the collaborative, networking nature of the e-Solutions effort: an Alliance team, consisting of only a few people and little power, was given the job of connecting outside resources to the internal bank resources. This was seen from the beginning as central to the Internet strategy; trying to do everything internally would be too slow and would result in missed opportunities. For example, electronic bill presentment over the Internet was a product they felt they needed immediately; to retrain internal programmers to build it would have taken far too long. Thus the Alliance team sought out companies that were already doing it and offered Citibank's distribution capability in exchange for the partner's software.

An early alliance was with AOL: Citibank bought high-profile marketing on AOL sites in an effort to expand its customer outreach, and it developed an online payment system for AOL users. Another was MyCiti.com, powered by a partner's technology, which consolidated all of a customer's financial information on one Web site. Other similar combinations of distribution channels and technologies were seen as essential to the ongoing development of the e-Business portfolio.

Roles were quite fluid and interdependent and often overlapped. The Alliance group generally had someone taking responsibility for the development of relationships with particular potential partners. As these persons defined opportunities, they would propose initiative groups involving people from many parts of the unit and the Bank as a whole, as well as from the potential outside partners. The process could also work the other way: someone in e-Solutions might come up with an initiative and go to the Alliance team for help. Then the initiative team would develop its own alliance manager, overlapping with another responsible alliance manager within the Alliance group.

The potential for confusion would seem substantial, yet people told us that the roles were relatively clear. The Alliance group manager was responsible for the overall relation to the partner cutting across multiple projects and relationships, and so was responsible for raising issues that might affect other aspects of the relationship. The manager within the initiative team, by contrast, was focused on maintaining the relationship for the specific project. This might sound difficult to an outsider, but I was consistently told that it worked out clearly enough in practice.

The head of the Alliance group was a member of the senior management team and participated in decision-making around priorities and rewards. The Alliance team included (depending on how and when one counted) about three people directly reporting to the Alliance head, and two or three more people who did not report to him but regularly participated in team phone calls. The latter were mostly strategy heads for e-Business in regions (South America, Europe, CEEMEA, and Asia).

The Alliance team itself, consisting of four formal members and three or four "virtual" members, operated in a very dispersed manner. Its members all spent most of their time elsewhere, on project teams with initiative groups or working with outside partners. For the first phase they apparently met very seldom as a group: their connections were largely through the team leader, and they were not very aware of what other members of the team were doing.

After a year there was a meeting at which they decided that they needed more interaction and set up a biweekly conference call for exchange of information. Still, at least one person saw it as "a group of high-performing individuals rather than a high-performing team."

The formal members of the team depended rather heavily on the team leader for organizational contacts: at least in the initial period, he was the source of most new opportunities, and in his role as a member of the top team of e-Solutions he was very plugged in to the strategic needs and directions of the organization as a whole. People saw his management style as very participative and effective: he was very good at the kind of ongoing interactive dialogues that served for performance management in e-Solutions.

## CONCERNS AND CHALLENGES

On the whole the picture was very positive, far more so than in most organizations in which I have interviewed: people felt work was getting done effectively with relatively little "political" distraction. There was some resistance and perhaps some empire-building, but no one saw these as major issues; most people seemed to be cooperating in pursuit of the key strategic objectives.

Nevertheless, there were some significant concerns. Internally, there were tense relationships with other parts of the bank with which interaction was vital; internally, there was running debate about how much formalization was needed.

### Dealing with the Rest of the Bank

One recurrent issue was dealing with parts of Citibank outside e-Solutions or e-Business. "We've figured out how to work with each other within solutions," said one manager; "now the problem is with other parts of the bank."

Because the products developed by e-Solutions needed to be developed and sold by other units of Citibank, the support and sponsorship of business heads was vital. Many of these leaders, however, pursued a traditional empire-building model very foreign to e-Solutions' partnership approach. The failure to overcome such resistance had doomed e-Citi, the previous effort at Internet development. The e-Solutions leadership knew that there was a serious danger of repeating that history, but there was no consensus on a way out.

The Consumer Bank was particularly hard to deal with, according to my sources, in part because they had a very "bureaucratic" culture—which meant that they operated by the book and protected their turf rather than focusing on the task—and in part because they were organized differently, with very decentralized geographic units, which made it difficult to do things on a global basis. The Corporate Bank was portrayed as having a very top-down culture. Salomon, Smith, Barney was so new that it was hard to know how to approach them; they relied heavily on one person who had contacts there to help them find the right people to help them.

In dealing with these parts of the bank it was much harder to establish a consensual problem-solving relationship. The leadership group itself took on much of the burden; their ability to politic in other parts of the bank was seen as vital. But some felt that this was too hit-or-miss a way to handle the heavy burden of interdependence among these groups.

Various control and audit functions of the bank could also present problems. One person described a case where they had agreed with an outside partner that at the end of the day they would share 50 percent of expenses; but the financial control system couldn't deal with that. They required line itemization, not a single check for 50 percent of expenses overall. This actually killed the deal in the end.

A strategy person raised a fundamental issue that involved reconciling different unit priorities. For some time the Global Relationships Bank (GRB) had had a strategy of maintaining only the largest customers and weeding out all but the most creditworthy:

> [B]ut e-Business has no boundaries or borders. Even if you're dealing with the big companies, very rapidly the supply chain would go down to smaller companies, and what do we do with that? We have won mandates from customers but haven't been allowed actually to sign them up.
>
> If we're actively engaged in e-Business then we need to find some way of fixing this. Without it there's no e-Business to speak of.

But the GRB had apparently been very resistant to changing its orientation. Thus this problem, which affected the way almost everyone in e-Solutions defined and pursued opportunities, had been bumped up to a committee at the highest levels and had languished there for some time without a resolution.

It was not at all obvious how to deal with these ongoing issues. One person suggested building systematic forums or linking mechanisms with these other parts of the bank; but someone else pointed out that such forums might well not work because these other units were not used to open discussion. Subordinates would not challenge their bosses, and each unit might well be more concerned with protecting its turf than with solving a common problem. Other proposals to build systematic processes for getting support from the business heads went nowhere, which was a perhaps ominous sign.

### Degree of Formalization

Over the two years of our study, e-Solutions shifted steadily from a very freewheeling, unstructured system toward more formalization. Most people saw this as a good thing: "Things are a little clearer than a few months ago. Now we have a strategy, an organization structure, an infrastructure, systems, a business direction, focused areas, revenue targets. We're innovative, but we're more disciplined."

Yet there were questions about how far this should go, and when it crossed over the line into needless bureaucracy. One person felt it had already gone too far, that the sense of empowerment had been lost and the hierarchy had become oppressive.

One debate centered on whether to mandate standardized process management. The Alliance group, like many others, relied heavily on voluntary maps and based their influence on being "smart about process" in their area. The group leader spent most of his Christmas vacation putting together a procedures manual for alliances, including tools, life cycle stages, tests for viability at each stage, and so forth. The members of his team seemed to use the procedures quite consistently: they could rattle off the five stages in the alliance process (targeting, screening, relationship with prospects, negotiation, and alliance relationship management) and situate their projects in relation to them.

Some people outside the Alliance group said they went to the Alliance team to make sure they did not miss important steps in working out agreements with partners. But the team also acknowledged that it was harder to get people across the organization to use structured approaches consistently. The Alliance leader's tactic was to tie the process to the audit procedures, which occurred regularly throughout the bank and were taken very seriously.

> The potential exists for it becoming a bureaucratic nightmare, but it also might make my life as person who runs alliances a lot easier. There were no operating rules for how to put together an alliance contract. The book I've developed includes a checklist—did you get all the legal authorities you need to get approval? and so on; that can prevent a lot of problems after the fact.

The advantages of a mandated process were clear: it would reduce the risk of errors, give people a common starting point and language for working together, and avoid many unnecessary debates. The Process Improvement Teams had used highly formalized process maps, "enforced" by facilitators, very effectively to get people from diverse parts of the bank to focus on a common problem. Mandated processes were also very helpful in planning. The tradeoff was that they might reduce the ability to be "opportunistic" and to work outside existing frameworks; some feared they might lead to an unstoppable momentum in which each process breakdown would lead to more process definitions, ending in a state of organizational clumsiness and rigidity.

Another area where more formalization might or might not be appropriate was in managing performance information. There had been some efforts at structured 360-degree feedback processes, as mentioned earlier, but they had not been taken very seriously. Most people seemed to feel that the more informal process of frequent hallway discussions did the job well enough. Yet this approach had some disadvantages:

• It put a heavier load on personal networks.
• It worked only within the e-Solutions group.
• Even within e-Solutions informal information exchange could well break down if the organization grew larger. It could become easier for poor performers to "hide" and for people to have trouble finding the right contacts.
• New people, who are very important in bringing ideas and contacts to the bank, were at a disadvantage until they built their personal web. One person noted, "Bringing in senior executives from the outside rarely works, but it will have to be overcome for the e-Solutions teams."

A more formal 360-degree feedback process could be a partial solution. Most of our interviewees thought this would be a good idea, though some worried about how it would be administered and how the information would be used. A key problem would be whether to make this information available to people trying to decide how to build a project team. Everyone seemed extremely nervous about opening peer feedback up too widely, and efforts to push it in other parts of Citibank's own Compass system had tended to bog down from resistance.

In summary, the Citibank e-Solutions group had developed a great many mechanisms of extended collaboration with considerable effectiveness and were able to identify and mobilize very rapidly around new opportunities. But there were also continuing major areas of fuzziness about how the systems would work in the long run, and resistance from the more bureaucratic culture of the wider organization.

# Chapter 4 The Culture of
##        Contribution

Structure, as described in Chapter 2, is relatively easy to change: top managers can establish new offices or even charter new teams and task forces by decree. But it is more difficult to make these structures work. Structures are animated by people, and the behavior of people is shaped by much more than formal directives, rules, and models. Managers can put in all the programs they want, but without understanding mindsets and expectations, they cannot improve the capability of the organization.

This brings us to *culture*—a familiar but notoriously hazy and ambiguous concept that keeps getting in the way of both management intentions and academic analyses. Virtually everyone agrees that culture is important, but few managers or academics know what to do about it—or even what categories are useful. The literature is fundamentally scattered: many analyses, drawing on anthropological traditions, don't pretend to generalizability beyond the immediate case; and those that try to be systematic, with very few exceptions, propose their own concepts and methods.

I approach culture through the lens of the shift from bureaucratic to collaborative systems—a change that requires certain fundamental and difficult transformations of collective mindsets: from autonomy to interdependence;

from deference to dialogue; and most central of all, from a primary focus on doing a job well to a focus on contribution to collective purposes. (See Table 5 at the end of this chapter for a formal contrast between these patterns.)

## UNDERSTANDING CULTURE

Culture sets a foundation of trust by establishing mutual expectations about how other members of a group will act. In any social interaction we have to have some idea about what others will do and how they will respond. When I start across the street in a crosswalk, I trust that oncoming cars know that they should stop for me and will be motivated to do so; when managers give orders, they trust that employees know and accept their role as subordinates. But if the driver of the car or the subordinate were from a different culture, he or she might neither know nor care about these expectations.

When people don't share a sense of what is right or appropriate, they cannot work together: they will continuously be surprised and disappointed in the way in which others respond, and they will misinterpret those actions. Very often such misunderstanding will lead to mutual contempt—a sense that the other is bad—and the relationship may spiral into conflict.

Most of the time culture is taken for granted because it is widely shared, an almost unconscious basis for action. It becomes most visible when groups with different cultures interact, or during periods of transition. At such moments most people feel intuitively that there are differences not just in particular policies or behaviors but in broader "ways of seeing"—and that these mismatches can result in mistrust, confusion, and resistance.

In the case of mergers and acquisitions, for example, observers of the actual process—as opposed to those who merely analyze the numbers—have often argued that one of the most pervasive causes of failure is cultural tensions.[1] The managers I have interviewed also regularly see culture as perhaps the most important obstacle to working together:

> Culture is critical for alliances—we learned that early on, we've talked about that a lot. That's the piece that will kill an alliance—the soft stuff people don't talk about. (Citibank e-Solutions)

The problem, however, is that there is little agreement beyond this general level. When I have pushed leaders for a definition of *what* aspects of culture are important, I have generally got only vague and impractical answers:

There are no analytic tools, it's sort of a touchy-feely. It's absolutely crucial, but not very clear.[2] (Citibank e-Solutions)

A few companies, such as Cisco, have developed metrics to assess the cultural "fit" of potential merger partners. But these measures are still based essentially on an intuitive sense of fit: "We walked away from one company that had fancy artwork on its walls, because we doubted it would fit into our culture of frugality."[3] Attempts to be objectively "scientific" about culture measures have produced little convergence on what is important (see the appendix, "Notes on Theory and Research Approaches to Culture," at the end of this chapter).

The haziness of culture is central to its function. Culture is important *because* it does not consist of unambiguous rules: it thereby enables people to act in new situations in ways that sustain trust and relationships with others. When a culture is strong, for instance, employees faced with a new customer demand or opportunity can make decisions that "fit" with the overall corporate approach, even though there is no rule or precedent for those particular decisions. This becomes increasingly important in high-adaptiveness strategic environments.

To achieve this paradox of consistent flexibility, culture must consist of a set of general principles, with room for interpretation, and where there is interpretation there is room for argument. Grasping cultural principles is as difficult as pinning down the core values of "democracy" or of "America." Particular actions are certainly shaped by the general ideas, but they can't simply be deduced from them, and people will have varying ideas of how to make the connection.

Culture has little to do with logical consistency. In this respect it is very different from ideology: ideologies are a simple and logically coherent sets of ideas, while culture is complex and grounded in practice. It emerges over time and through experience, governed only loosely by basic principles or a sense of style, and may incorporate contrasting elements. All that is important is that it enables people to predict, well enough to get along, how others will react and how the system will work.

With all those caveats, one broad cultural divide does run through the organizations I have studied, mirroring the basic distinction between bureaucratic and collaborative enterprise. There is one "way of seeing" that centers on autonomy, loyalty, and deference, and another that centers on interdependence, challenge, and contribution. Within each of the basic organizational types, these establish the broad frameworks that allow people to work together; they also cause divisions between two kinds of people who value different patterns of behavior.

## THE CULTURE OF PATERNALIST BUREAUCRACY

Bureaucratic culture is a combination of two rather different patterns with different historical roots. One layer is the highly rational, disciplined system described by Max Weber; the other is a paternalist mindset focused on informal community and loyalty. These two patterns are in many respects logically contradictory, and they create tensions in practice as well; yet they have managed to coexist for a long time and throughout the industrialized world.

### The Rational Layer

The familiar side of bureaucratic culture is the rational dimension; we can sketch it very briefly. Weber treats bureaucracy as built on the core concept of office, or "bureau." Bureaucracy more than anything else is the triumph of office over person—a priority of tasks, defined rationally in relation to an overall structure, over personal preferences and interests. Weber called this "the principle of fixed and official jurisdictional areas."[4]

Such a structure requires that participants share a basic cultural expectation that might be summarized as "do your job"—with the correlate, "don't try to do anyone else's job." This principle fits with the fundamental concept of autonomy sketched in the Introduction. Each person is expected—in the *official*, rational culture of bureaucracy—to be an expert in her own office, and it is not legitimate for others to challenge that domain; even those higher in the structure are supposed to avoid "micro-management" and to allow subordinates their zone of autonomy.

> What I like about this place, I've been treated pretty decently. I come in every day. I do my job. I go home. (Clark)

> What we are trying to get is where everybody has complete responsibility within his own role. (GM)

For peers, this implies the further expectation that people will not invade others' territory, publicly criticize, or even make suggestions that cross the line. Such behavior is considered extremely bad form and strongly prohibited in most organizations: it implicitly shows lack of respect for others' competence and expertise. If someone has an issue that may impact others at the same level, the expectation is that it will be bumped up to a higher level that has a view of all the pieces and can judge the relationships among them.

Robert Merton extended this analysis to define a bureaucratic personality that would support these cultural expectations:

If the bureaucracy is to operate successfully, it must attain a high degree of reliability of behavior, an unusual degree of conformity with prescribed patterns of action. Hence, the fundamental importance of discipline, which may be as highly developed in a religious or economic bureaucracy as in the army. Discipline can be effective only if the ideal patterns are buttressed by strong sentiments that entail devotion to one's duties, a keen sense of the limitation of one's authority and competence, and methodical performance of routine activities."[5]

A second central structural aspect of bureaucracy is the nested hierarchy of offices: as Weber put it, "The principles of office hierarchy and of levels of graded authority mean a firmly ordered system of super- and subordination in which there is a supervision of the lower offices by the higher ones."[6] This in turn requires a strongly shared cultural expectation that higher levels will set the boundaries of action for lower levels, and that the lower levels should not expect to know or understand the system as seen from higher up. There is no basis for challenge or argument from the bottom up, because—according to the system logic—lower levels can't possibly understand how their own piece relates to all the other offices. Thus the classic norm passed on in management texts since the early twentieth century: information should flow up, commands should flow down.

### The Traditional Layer

What has perplexed many observers, however, is that bureaucracy only partially follows this rational logic. In many respects it follows the entirely different and much older pattern of traditional community. Many observational studies of the high period of bureaucracy described relationships through the metaphor of "feudalism"[7]—complete with images or fiefdoms and baronies, and with a strong emphasis on deference and loyalty. This dimension, not described by Weber or other early scholars, continues to be less visible and less publicly accepted than the rational strand, but it is nevertheless universal and powerful.

Loyalty is an old concept, far more strongly rooted in traditional societies than the rational sense of duty sketched by Weber. It is telling that the duty of loyalty as applied to employment by the legal system is based on master–servant law, which is wholly at odds with the law of impersonal contractual obligations.[8]

In the corporation the most frequently used metaphor has been that of *families*: even today it is very common to hear employees speak of the company as a family, or to use parental language to describe their relationship to their subordinates. The traditional family, as analyzed by Freud and others, is held together by deference to the father and the desire to please him, but also involves solidarity among siblings that is partly opposed to and largely hidden from the parents. This pattern is mirrored in the paternalist firm, where the informal organization of peer relationships remains in an unsteady equilibrium with the desire to please the boss. Where the latter becomes too strong, the result can be destructive day-to-day animosities that undermine the informal organization; where it is too weak, the peer group may lose its commitment to the higher goals of the firm. But when the balance is maintained, the formal and informal organizations work in relative harmony and create powerful unifying bonds.

This master–servant or father–child pattern is a diffuse one: orders are assumed to be legitimate if they come from someone higher in status, and they do not have to be legitimated on rational grounds. It tends to be personal, focused on particular relationships rather than systems. It does not recognize the zone of autonomy based on expertise, which is central to bureaucratic culture. It does not make a sharp differentiation between the office and the person, but expects loyalty to extend into one's personal life.

Many aspects of this traditional ethic of loyalty made their way into corporate cultures from the 1930s on. Observers with a deep feel for culture have long noted, for example, that managers often imposed a kind of loyalty test on their subordinates by asking them to show that their jobs came ahead of their families; families were indeed made part of the larger corporate "family," in the sense that wives were not only expected to support their husbands but also to entertain the boss and to contribute to a good image for the company.[9] The authority figure was expected to be a protector, and deference was a way for the subordinate to ensure that protection. Here's an example (from an interview in 2006!) of how a subordinate viewed the ideal boss:

> I remember those days, my managers and employees always talking about [the Founder]. You would hear these legendary stories. These were true and they actually happened.
>
> There was a fellow whose wife was very, very sick. And the Founder had asked him, "Why do you come here?" And he said, "I have children. I need my paycheck." He said, "Look, your responsibility should be with your wife. Your paycheck will continue. I want you to go home and take care of your wife." And he found out if he had any big bills, and he wiped them clean. He was known for that.

In return, employees showed unqualified deference and conformity to the leader's wishes, down to the details of work style:

> The Founder wanted things done his way. His philosophy was that a cluttered desk is a cluttered mind. When you went to his office, on his desk was one piece of paper, a pencil, and his telephone. And that was it—nothing else. And if word got around that he was going to be walking around or come and visit some place, you were told to get everything off the top of your desk and make sure that it was not cluttered.

Observational studies regularly stress this pressure for conformity leading to a kind of moral abdication, particularly among middle managers, as they adapt their own principles to those that find favor in the organization and win them the trust of their superiors.[10]

In my own research in the early 1990s I found that the value of loyalty was deeply embedded in the world views of middle managers in a wide variety of companies. Attacks on the principle of loyalty, represented by unprecedented middle management layoffs, were widely seen not just as materially painful, but also as violations of a moral code.[11] I have also often been struck by how powerfully blue-collar workers, who in America have not been considered permanent members of the community as they are in Japan, nevertheless hold on to their pride in and loyalty to their companies. On hearing that his plant was slated for closure, one long-time union leader of a manufacturing plant put it with unusual poignancy: "This is like finding your wife in bed with another man. Our factory people are interwoven in the life of the company: most of the people feel it's their company, they're tremendously proud of it."

The cultural patterns of loyalty and rationalism coexist, producing a pattern with conflicting elements.[12] Within the rationalist frame, for instance (as Weber emphasized), the legitimacy of management authority is based on its rationality: if a boss gives an order inconsistent with existing rules and procedures, or that violates the zone of expert autonomy of a job, it should be legitimate to protest. Some bureaucracies do adhere to these principles. But more often the older pattern dominates: managers can act inconsistently and arbitrarily, playing favorites or engaging in political games, and (at least in the absence of union-enforced rules) no one protests. Here the governing principle is the more diffuse sense of deference, in which orders are legitimate *simply because of where they come from,* not because of their rationality.

In fact, it is not unusual for people to voice seemingly opposite values in a short period of time. The union leader I quoted earlier was on the one hand quite willing to absorb his sense of self into the higher identity of the company and to do whatever was necessary to help it, and on the other to lead frequent battles to protect the exact parameters of job jurisdictions and exact letters of the rules. In thinking of the middle management ranks, I recall one emblematic event at AT&T. I was having lunch with a group of managers who were strongly criticizing their new leader for trying to change things too quickly and ignoring their expertise. I had incidentally just spoken to that leader, who complained that no one would give him honest information on what was going on in the plant. So I suggested to my fellow diners that we walk to the leader's office and discuss the issues with him. The managers were full of moral bravado expressing their autonomy and integrity—"I'm the kind of guy who will always speak my mind, I don't care who I'm talking to"; but when they got to the office, they reverted to a deep paternalist deference mode, avoiding all suggestion of criticism of their superiors.

This complex pattern has defined the main cultural lines not only of American industrial companies, but of those in Europe and Asia as well. The famous Japanese corporate culture differs in degree but not in kind: blue-collar workers are more clearly included, and the rational-official aspects of the culture are perhaps somewhat less important relative to the duties of loyalty and deference. In much of Europe the emphasis falls on the other side, with loyalty being somewhat downplayed in favor of rule focus.[13] But all these elements show up in all these corporate cultures.

## "PERFORMANCE CULTURE"
## AS A TRANSITIONAL PATTERN

From quite early on analysts noted that bureaucracy did not always function as well as Weber suggested: that it indeed had systematic weaknesses, noted in a series of observational studies of bureaucratic corporations. The fundamental norms of stability, homogeneity, conformity, deference, and inwardness that characterize all traditional communities are in many ways ill suited to corporations that must compete for customers and seek continual growth. Even in good times paternalist cultures were subject to many pathologies such as rule fetishism and empire-building.[14] In oligopolistic industries these could be tolerated, but the rise of global competition in many core industries increased the pressure. Companies felt they could no longer afford these weaknesses, nor could they afford the obligation of employment security. Thus top managers began to seek a way out. The layoffs of the 1980s began a process of dismantling the traditional culture of loyalty.

The most common initial approach focused on the simple norm of "performance." Many people inside and outside the business world assume things have moved to a cultural pattern based on a very simple rule: if you don't perform you are out. This makes for good rhetoric—but, as it turns out, for bad practice, especially over time.

Among companies in which I have conducted research, the one that ran a true "performance" system was Figgie International. There the founder, CEO, and strongman, Harry Figgie, set absolute numeric targets for the presidents of his portfolio of companies, and if they failed to meet them he fired them publicly. Our interviews made clear that there was a complete absence of business understanding anywhere but at the very top, and that employees at all levels were concerned only with pleasing their boss; the best they hoped for was to be left alone. There was virtually no informal trust and cooperation. As for the CEO, "The general picture you get is people are afraid to talk to him. He gets yessed to death, even when the decisions he makes are impractical."[15] This worked while Mr. Figgie could personally keep an eye on everything, but as he aged and the business grew more complex it collapsed dramatically, and the company spun quickly into bankruptcy.

This version of "performance" essentially reverts to pure hierarchical control, either personalistic or rule-based. Everything centers on the boss, who sets targets and evaluates performance. This inevitably leads to fierce internal dynamics: extreme deference to the boss, accompanied by intense internal competition—not open competition, because people have to live together and work together over long periods, but rather covert forms of mutual undermining.[16]

Other than this case, I have seen simple performance orientations only in relatively brief periods of transition. It is not really a culture; it is an ideology— a simple, rational idea rather than a developed set of practical expectations. It serves primarily as a way of *breaking* existing culture—as a means of attack by leaders who want to undo the pattern of paternalist bureaucracy, an attempt to break a set of mutual expectations that are now felt to hold back progress.

In my own interviews I have found many cases of top management trying to drive change with strong performance reward systems. Inevitably it turns into a battle, open or covert. Middle managers in this transitional moment rail against pay for performance precisely because it destroys the bonds of trust that are central to effective performance in any system:

> The compensation curve doesn't motivate people. People want to know their wages are competitive. The amount of money isn't the key issue, but the fear of being put in the low category just causes discontent and undermines teamwork. (GM)

There's still a lot of feelings among people that in performance evaluation, you're rated only as one single individual, one single contribution, so why should you work with anybody else to make that work any better? (AT&T)[17]

I will return to this issue of the performance ideology in Chapter 6.

## COLLABORATIVE CULTURE: CONTRIBUTION
## AND THE COMMUNITY OF PURPOSE

But there is another meaning to the notion of performance—a more complex and nuanced one—that does not involve this kind of conflict. People in collaborative cultures are in one sense highly performance oriented: since they are interdependent with others, they are very intolerant of those who don't pull their weight. They put no stock in the local attachments and diffuse caring that are central to the paternalist notion of community. But their *measure* of performance is not the boss's judgment, and the *standard* of performance is not that of "doing a good job." Rather, what is expected in collaborative enterprises is performance that helps others and moves everyone toward achieving the collective mission and goal. It is, in short, a notion of *performance as contribution*.

This is a new basis for trust. In traditional communities trust is based fundamentally on the belief that others will stick to their assigned statuses and roles. Collaborative trust is based instead on the belief that everyone is working toward the collective goal, constituting a community of *purpose*.

We can construct an "ideal type" of collaborative culture by viewing it from two angles simultaneously: the values required by the logic of collaborative systems, and what I have actually observed among companies in my sample. My most extensive explorations of the collaborative expectations were in the Citibank e-Solutions case, but there is considerable converging evidence from interviews in other companies.[18]

Several things stood out in my interviews in collaborative settings that contrast strongly with the bureaucratic pattern. First, there was little or no expectation of long-term security or stable membership. About half of the members of the e-Solutions group, for instance, were recent arrivals at the bank, with less than five years' tenure, and the bulk of these were not young people at the bottom but mid-career people with substantial experience in other settings. They expected to be around for at least a few years—they were not just specialized technicians with a free-agent or subcontractor orientation—but when asked whether they would be around in ten years, most said that it was too far ahead to predict, and that it depended on whether the job still presented challenges.[19]

> I am excited by the challenge. . . . Some people are worried about another reorganization or a cut. My own perspective on that is you either worry about it or you work—so you'd better start working. I'm mobile, I'm not tied to one location, I can move.

A second significant contrast with bureaucratic culture was that people within e-Solutions did not expect to control their own areas or to have all the resources they needed to meet their goals. Consensus was vital, and dotted lines were everywhere; those who insisted on controlling particular areas are hindrances; and most people were comfortable with the ambiguity and negotiation processes required to manage:

> I have five or six bosses, with one direct boss and dotted lines to all the global heads. The feedback given by some of my dotted-line bosses sometimes doesn't mix. I get them on the phone and they resolve it. They say, "Don't allow yourself to be pulled in different directions."

> This place is all about relationships and personal credibility at the end of the day. Clearly there are infrastructural pieces, but in an organization of this type, where it's highly matrixed . . . the way to get things done is though influence.

In my interviews in more traditional organizations, by contrast, people have consistently advocated a norm of clear responsibilities and jurisdictions, entirely consistent with the Weberian conception. They are uncomfortable with shared jurisdictions and cross-boundary collaborative processes:

> In my previous job . . . there was a clearer feeling that there was nobody else that I had to get consensus with to get a decision. In my current job I am confused about which decisions are mine. Does the marketing division have the right to define suspension tunings? No one is ultimately accountable. I would like more autonomy, not more consensus.

> Dotted lines are useless because you can't keep control of anything.[20]

Thus the collaborative culture appears to reject two of the core cultural principles of paternalist bureaucracy: the assumption of security and the preservation of autonomy. Clearly the familiar mechanisms of sharply defined jurisdictions, rules, and reporting responsibilities are not the answer here. How, then, are these complex, fluid, large-scale interactions regulated? What are the core principles of a culture that enables people to work together collaboratively?

## Contribution to the Mission

The central organizing principle in e-Solutions was not the office but the mission, or collective purpose—or, as most people at Citibank called it, the "strategy." All of these terms have multiple meanings, so it is worth a little definition. People certainly did not mean by this any kind of broad, hortatory "vision statements"; the e-Solutions strategy was highly practical and quite detailed. They also meant a great deal more than immediate goals and numerical targets, though these were part of the picture: the mission stretches at least four or five years into the future, encompassing an array of initiatives that might not bear immediate fruit. Though it has a core logic, it is more than a slogan: it is a complex set of interpretations of the marketplace, of the competition, of the company's own best competencies—and most important, a plan about how to develop itself so as to achieve success in this landscape.

The core of the value system was contribution to this mission. No matter who you are, what your skills, your job title or level, what your personal life is like, how you wear your hair, the important question is: Can you help advance the mission? And the basis for trust is: Are you the kind of person—do you have the skills and motives—to contribute to it? Thus, from three different people in e-Solutions:

> My approach is to be transparent with the peers about the value you are bringing. It comes down to recognition. . . . If you've generated enough value recognition will come; people understand where the value is being generated.

> If you build relationships, through credibility in executing, and people know that you are a person that brings value to the table then you can have access to them any day any time. If you're a roadblock, no matter how high your title or visibility, you're going to get rejection.

> It all comes down to what you can contribute, what is your business proposition.

In Chapter 5 I discuss the infrastructure that creates this sense of mission; here the point is that it is the core element of the culture that organizes everyone's expectations of each other. This measure of value and standard of trust says nothing about office, and indeed, as we have seen, it is scornful of those who are bound by the restrictions of their job. When I ask about the indicators that people use to know whether another is someone you can work with, one response is whether the person is willing to take responsibility for the task regardless of office:

> If you're a nine-to-five specialist with limited skills, tunnel vision, encased in your little world, a yes/but person, then you're history. No one will work with you, especially when life becomes really challenging and complex. (Citibank e-Solutions)

It is hard to imagine a sharper contrast to Merton's definition of the bureaucratic personality centered around "a keen sense of the limitations of one's authority and competence."

## Peer Relationships: Dialogue and Acceptance of Criticism

In this context the willingness to challenge peers, to question their expertise, and to talk to others about their performance—all viewed as illegitimate in the bureaucratic frame—become necessary to the regulation of expectations: rather than threatening trust, they are the way in which trust is achieved in a fluid and unbounded situation. That is, rather than looking at a person's title and reading the expected relationship from it, one enters into a relationship asking whether the person can contribute to the shared task. One learns this in part by challenging people about what they can bring to this particular problem, and in part by sounding out networks of reputation. This works only to the degree that these reputations are accurate—which means to the degree in which people are willing to talk honestly about their peers.

Employees in the e-Solutions group not only were willing to criticize and engage in debates with their peers, but considered this a duty: within this collaborative culture, the norm was to argue things out before resorting to rules or bosses. For the "collaborators," bureaucratic avoidance of conflict was a source of annoyance and mistrust:

> [How do you decide whom to trust?] I look for someone who would be open to criticism or suggestions as opposed to someone who would get defensive, be scared by people meddling around. Some people are content with just managing their piece of turf and don't want anyone mucking around in it. In this business a lot of the role is to find out how pieces of the business are run if you don't already know. So it's important that the people you're talking to are open, and you not be overbearing and say, "Here's how you have to do things."

There is in these systems effectively no norm against "ratting out" a fellow employee, so common in most solidarity-conscious communities. The norm is that feedback should be honest, open, and based on direct evidence. Those who do not give that sort of grounded opinion are censured for making it harder for others to get their work done. At McKinsey, which holds frequent discussions about performance, a partner notes that those who are consistently too easy are prodded by reminders of those who have failed to live up to their billing. Here and elsewhere, people whose opinions are distorted are gradually asked for it less often, and are thereby pushed to the margins of the web of collaborative interactions.

### Sharing and Helping Others

Challenge, in a collaborative system, is not valued simply for its own sake or in order to achieve competitive victories: it is part of the general norm of openness that is essential to the workings of collaboration. These cultures also put far more emphasis on the other side of the equation: giving credit to others.

> The surest way to get cooperation from other people is not to hide who has contributed.

And openness applies also to knowledge sharing:

> There was a time when knowledge was power over here. What people knew made them experts and very valuable—so why would they share any of their expertise with others? But this model does not hold any more. So one of the behaviors we [emphasize] is knowledge sharing. If I am an expert I should be able to share this with others, with the network, with other teams. We can no longer afford one person to know everything about one thing—the business does not allow that.

### Hierarchical Relations: Interaction Rather than Deference

At e-Solutions, while there were clear levels of authority, there was very little deference in the traditional sense: people argued with their bosses, and they also did not think it wrong to talk openly to them about their peers. They frequently took independent action and then engaged in dialogues to try to convince superiors to provide resources and to change performance expectations on the fly.

> The relationship I have with my boss is a discussion—it's brainstorming, he gives his views which I respect a lot, and I will implement his views in my overall work. That energizes people and gives credibility.

People commonly told stories of buttonholing their bosses in the cafeteria and arguing with them about priorities and resources.

A nice published example of this collaborative norm is the story of IBM's Internet strategy, which was initiated from the middle levels of the organization and pushed through discussion and persuasion, gathering resources on an improvised basis, and gradually gathered higher-level support. The initiators framed their behavior in terms of "organizing an insurrection" and explicitly used orientation to the mission as their guide rather than deference to superiors: when people asked one of the renegades who he reported to, he said, "the Internet."[21]

### Openness to the Outside

A commonly noted pathology of bureaucracy is the "not invented here" syndrome, in which any idea that comes from outside is automatically rejected on the grounds that it cannot meet the particular needs of the group.[22] In collaboration, learning from the outside is crucial and built into mechanisms such as benchmarking, which ask managers to look to competitors for new ideas. It is visible in the e-Solutions case and others in the new emphasis on alliances, which require trusting relationships and complex interconnections with people entirely outside their corporate boundaries. Most of all it is visible in widespread attempts to become "customer-centric," trying to get the organization to respond quickly to customer requirements rather than refining existing products.

This shift requires far more than structure and behavioral commands: it involves a deep mindset. Ravi Venkatesan of Cummins India says that "it is virtually impossible to get a product person to think back from the customer."[23] An ABB interviewee captured nicely the distinction between traditional loyalty and the external focus: "I think we should target loyalty toward the client. If you are loyal to ABB, and then rip off the client, then it's worth nothing."

Collaborative enterprises must succeed in establishing an expectation of bringing the customers close to the decision process. Saturn represents one of the sharper instances: in an industry almost totally dominated by a closed product mentality, Saturn invited customers to celebrate at the site and to comment on the cars directly to the workers on the line, and it sent workers out to dealers to see how people were reacting. In e-Solutions there was a more elaborated pattern of looking for alliances that would work, in part by trying to judge whether the orientations of their counterparts in the other company are bureaucratic or collaborative.

### Diversity of Capabilities

Collaborative cultures also are more open to diversity than their bureaucratic counterparts, because they have less need for conformity as a basis of trust.

e-Solutions was one of the more diverse corporate environments I have seen, with many people from both genders and from all over the world at all levels. Collaboration does not value diversity of race and gender for its own sake, but can effectively treat it as irrelevant to the issue of trust because trust depends not on homogeneity—people being "like me"—but on organized processes of contribution to a shared task. What *is* valued for its own sake is diversity of skills and competencies: rather than separating people into homogeneous units so that they can work well together in an informal organization, a collaborative system like e-Solutions deliberately combines people from very different perspectives because the combinations will produce the richest outcomes.

> Before, culturally, we valued the longevity of a relationship; it was hard for non-bankers to make it. Then with whole dot-com movement we said, "We have to transform ourselves." There was a huge infusion of talent. We consciously looked for people with different thinking.

A by-product of the general orientation is that there is more openness to balancing private with public demands. The traditional concept of loyalty is an exclusive one: earlier studies of corporate managers showed how the family unit is made subordinate to corporate demands.[24] Within e-Solutions and other similar environments, by contrast, it is legitimate to ask for time off or to cite family obligations in assessing priorities. There is still a constant struggle between the obligations of work and family, and certainly many people in these high-paced organizations spend enormous amounts of time at work; but it is not considered disloyal to treat family demands on a par with those of work.

> I try to make every effort to be at any family function, birthdays, parent–teacher conferences, etc. I let the company know that I plan around those, too. In that respect I guess I am not considered the most loyal, because I will not override my family for business. (Shell-SEPIV)

> [The leaders of the unit] all have families and fully support that. But they come from the U.S. change process. I can't say that was so for past leaders. It is really good that those values are valued by the current leadership. (Shell-SEPIV)

## THE CLASH BETWEEN BUREAUCRATIC AND COLLABORATIVE CULTURES

Cultures are hard to validate empirically: they are, as I discussed earlier, necessarily somewhat fuzzy. A good way to test one's understanding of a culture is to ask the people involved whether it makes sense. Most people I have asked, on both sides of the divide, embrace the broad distinction I have sketched between the two types of orientation:

> If you want people to be loyal to you, there are two different ways. One is socially: my dad was in his job years back—you were loyal, you had a good job, you were going to get 7 percent cost of living increase every year. Now companies have more of an obligation to earn that loyalty, but we all know it's a business. When you go through these peaks and valleys that every business is going to go through, you have to use some of these key tools, be visible, listen, set clear goals: "We can only afford x amount, there are 10 general managers, we are going to six"—it's a business.

Some elements of the language are remarkably consistent across many companies: on one side, "family," "loyalty," "caring"; on the other "business," "professionalism," "bottom-line oriented." But the value charge changes dramatically depending on which side the speaker starts from.

An even sharper way of drawing the difference is to observe what happens when they interact. During periods of transition, in the early phases of layoffs and performance focus, the two perspectives often confront each other with particular clarity—and also mutual mistrust and suspicion. For those who embrace the loyalist orientation, the business side is cold and heartless, both toward employees and toward customers: it cares neither about true quality nor about long-term relationships:

> [T]here was a time when the attitude was you do your job, and the company will take care of you; it was a situation of trust in the company. Then the word "professionalism" came in, you come in and do your job, you do it in a highly professional manner. Never mind the word trust—you're here for this job, you're here for this purpose. And with professionalism came mobility, so loyalty and dedication went with it. The highly skilled professionals didn't care about trust, they didn't care about where the company's been, what kind of a family relationship we've had here. They say, "Hey, I'm a professional, I do my job, and if it works out, fine; if it doesn't work out, hey, I'll go to another company." That's the raw edge of professionalism, as opposed to the soft edge of trust which has gone. (Pitney-Bowes)

> I work for an organization that was able to get people to be so loyal because . . . they worked their way up this organization, and the Sam Walton philosophy of we're going to take you with us as we grow and prosper was very great there. But what happened I think is that we had to go through painful decisions that we had to implement, that we were not a part of making—with 20 percent of your workforce being laid off, having to sit across the table from somebody and saying, "You don't have a job." So then you begin to realize this isn't a family; this is a business.

It's like a husband who has an affair on you. What I mean is, you may forgive, but you never forget. (Wal-Mart)

But for those who start from a collaborative perspective emphasizing contribution, being trapped in a loyalist culture is deadly—repressive, conformist, conservative, missing the excitement and dynamism of present opportunities:

The problem we have here is nobody wants to do anything, say revolutionary, as opposed to evolutionary. Everybody wants everybody to be nice-nice to one another: "We're not going to embarrass manager so and so, or supervisor so and so, by telling them, Look, you've outlived your function, I want you on special assignment as a technical person only, we're going to retire you early." None of that has happened. And you can't do that. . . . You know, I want to make the business go. (Clark)

I have a very high level of frustration, I'm ready to quit, the system just isn't working. People walk in here at 8:00 and walk out at 4:30. They don't understand the risk that we're running in the market. (AT&T)

There are so many people that I have met in my career who get wrapped more around defining themselves by their job, and by their title and by their level. I have never defined myself by my job but I also look at the scope and scale of responsibility—whether in a new role I will be learning something and whether in a new role I will be contributing something. (Johnson & Johnson)

And there is a consistent sense of scorn, of lack of respect for those who try to play the old bureaucratic games of personalized relationships, political infighting, and self-protection:

If someone comes into the first meeting and starts throwing around names my hackles go up—because that means rather than focusing on capabilities and market proposition they're trying to establish credibility in terms of who they know and who they've talked to—and that at the end of the day doesn't move you an inch down the line. Or people who hedge, who don't share information: "I can't tell you this, or I've got to go talk to somebody." (Citibank)

On a few occasions I have actually heard both sides of this pattern of expectations both by observing public interactions and by holding private conversations. For example, in a period of severe competitive pressure on a division of a large company, two managers debated their response. On one side, a manager oriented to contribution argued strongly in public for a revision of work systems and rewards; on the other, a traditionalist manager, who was directly in charge, said little except to raise a few practical problems. In private, however, the latter manager hotly accused the other of being overly aggressive and pushing in where she had no right to be—saying that while she was very good at her own job she shouldn't be butting into his. Meanwhile, the contribution-focused manager's view was that it was vital to get the issues on the table, that the other was trying to avoid real debate and to protect himself. The level of trust and ability to collaborate, not surprisingly, were very low.

These are views across a chasm, two ways of patterning the world. I have rarely found people who appear to combine aspects of the two orientations. There are many who are confused, who—once one gets past rhetoric and groupthink—express uncertainty about where they fit and how to interpret the events around them. But those who embrace a culture almost always see the world from the point of view of loyalty and doing a good job, or from that of contribution and collaboration. These form the main coherent patterns of meaning in the corporate realm.

## CONCLUSION

The divide between cultures of loyalty and contribution, or between communities of tradition and purpose, is intuitively sharp to most managers and workers I have spoken with, but it has not yet been conceptualized publicly and consistently. In particular, there is a continuing blurriness around the notion of performance. What I have called a "simple performance culture" has a good deal of attraction to many—first, as a clear alternative to paternalism, and second as a way of recognizing individuality. This orientation has often become a basis for changing reward systems. But by itself it divides individuals rather than uniting them in a shared enterprise.

The notions of "contribution" and "purpose" define a complex performance orientation that enables people to trust each other in fluid situations—ones in which they do not know each other long and deeply, and in which they cannot rely on fixed routines. This value pattern makes it possible for people to work together in enterprises that, unlike traditional communities, are open, changing, and diverse (see Table 5).

## APPENDIX: NOTES ON THEORY AND
## RESEARCH APPROACHES TO CULTURE

The literature on culture is vast and particularly scattered: a review of anthropological studies fifty years ago famously identified 164 definitions of the term,[25] and agreement has not increased since then.

**Table 5  Two Cultures: Core Expectations**

| | Paternalist Bureaucracy | | Collaboration |
|---|---|---|---|
| | Recognized Norms | Common Pathologies | Recognized Norms |
| Organizing principle—core of commitment | Firm and offices | Rigidity | Collective purpose (missions) |
| Standard of performance | Technical competence, conscientiousness, consistency ("Doing a good job") | Job performance disconnected from organization purpose | Contribution to the success of the mission |
| Regulation of behavior | Respect for rules | Rule fetishism | Engagement in experimentation and co-design |
| Peer relationships | Autonomy | Conflict avoidance | Dialogue: challenge, debate, openness |
| Superior-subordinate-relationships | Deference | Subservience | Push for understanding |
| Relationship of individual to the firm | Loyalty | Conformity (dependence) | Balance of individual and group (interdependence) Valuing diversity of contribution |
| Relating to outside | Closed ranks: the outside as enemy or as recipient of products | Arrogance, failure to learn | Open: the outside as source of learning and potential alliances |

My own view falls into the broad Weberian tradition, which sees culture as providing a framework for social interaction. From this perspective, more purely hermeneutic approaches, analyzing culture as symbolic patterns of meaning, are deeply complementary: they tell us *how* culture works—but not *why* it works.

To sustain interactive trust culture must be *reflexive, consistent* over time, *flexible* in application, and supported by appropriate *sanctions.*[26]

1. Culture is *reflexive* in that it is a matter not just of what people think, but also of what they think *others* think; it is based on the notion that if I act in

a certain way I can expect that others will respond in ways that help us all. It thus demands that everyone give up some degree of freedom and follow some restrictive norms in order to benefit from the wider social group. It is quickly disrupted without that mutuality: those who violate the norms, trying to "cheat" by acting in ways forbidden to everyone else, gain personal advantage but threaten the functioning of the whole. Thus such violations usually generate extremely punitive responses. To take one of the norms discussed above: if there is a strong expectation of openness and sharing of information, one person might be able to get an "edge" by hoarding information and using that of others; if this violation goes unpunished, there would be a tendency for everyone to give up on openness and to scramble for position. This is the essential "prisoner's dilemma" dynamic in which the pursuit of individual gain hurts everyone. As a result, information hoarders in a healthy collaborative culture excite strong feelings of disdain and are excluded from the group before they can undermine it.

2. Culture must be *stable* to establish predictability: if I give up my "right" to act selfishly today, I need to believe that it will pay off tomorrow.

3. Yet it must also be *flexible*. Although we have to predict the future, we cannot predict it in detail; we often have to count on something happening without knowing exactly what it will be. Thus culture must also allow room for dealing with the unforeseen, for inventing new actions, while still maintaining continuity and collective confidence that everyone knows how others will respond.

To play this paradoxical role, balancing adaptability and predictability, and maintaining a capacity for change, culture must be not rules but *pattern*, which is to say that many elements are linked not in a mechanical or rational way but in a way that "makes sense." When we share a culture with others we believe that they will act in ways that seem *sensible* to us even when we cannot predict exactly what that will be. My interviewees frequently used the word "mindset" to express this sense of diffusely patterned expectations.

A useful analogy for this pattern-setting role is the relationship of a constitution to common law. The constitution lays out general principles and patterns, but it is often not at all obvious whether a particular action fits in or not. Thus there are courts that interpret those cases in terms of the constitution. The interpretation can be contested, and it can change over time, yet the constitution remains as a stabilizing orientation behind all the particular cases. In the same way organization culture is constantly interpreted— sometimes formally, as in process maps; more often informally—and can be fought over and debated.[27] Thus, especially in complex environments, no behaviors or rules can serve unambiguous indicators of a culture; people who share a culture may have different ideas about what it means in particular situations, and people may fake actions in order to appear to belong to the culture.[28]

4. Finally, like constitutional requirements, culture is not effective just as an idea; it must be *enforced* to ensure consistency in the culture and to identify those who don't fit in.

In general, culture is not enforced through formalized courts, but rather through the workings of opinion and reputation: indeed, we sometimes speak of "the court of public opinion." When people violate culture, their fellows make them feel shame. Another crucial basis of enforcement is through socialization: cultural norms become embedded in the personalities and identities of individuals so that they punish *themselves* for violations with feelings of guilt. This is the deepest basis for trust: when we build our expectations on a judgment of character, we believe that the other will come through even if the social environment changes.

This embeddedness has good and bad aspects. People can become stubbornly unable to change even as the society develops; on the other hand, they may be courageously unwilling to bend to collective fear or faddishness, maintaining their integrity despite attacks on their reputations. Often the same behavior can be interpreted both ways. In corporate change, there are always people who believe so deeply in the value of loyalty that they simply reject the move to collaborative norms even when their bosses begin talking a different language.[29]

Analysis of culture focuses both on the shared patterns and on the systems that maintain and interpret them. We don't learn much about culture if we just ask people what they think; we need also to know whether what they think is enforced in some way, through shame and reputation or through more formal mechanisms, and what happens when there are disagreements. Culture has to exist both in a set of expectations and in the social interactions that give them life.

## Research Approaches

It is difficult for scholars of culture to come up with convincing tools to research it. One well-known strand of research tries to build cultural dimensions by induction from factor analyses of individual survey questions. Hofstede's model of universal dimensions, based on surveys of IBM employees in many countries, has produced one of the relatively rare streams of empirical research in this field. But it has also been subject to severe criticism for oversimplifying and flattening out the nature of culture. Some have found, for example, that individualism and collectivism, rather than being opposite ends of a pole, can both be high, and that Americans are just as "collectivist" as Japanese; others have noted that small differences in scales and samples produced sharply different results.[30]

These problems flow from trying to treat culture as a fixed object of positivistic study. First, surveys, which have to rely simply on people's responses to standard questions, are almost inevitably distorted by the subtleties of language and beliefs. The same words may mean different things when embedded in different cultural patterns; people may have motivations to hide or distort their answers; it may just not be clear how a culture would respond to certain situations.

But the biggest problem with the survey approach is that it reduces everything to expressed norms—it assumes that what people *say* is the only important factor in behavior. In fact, as a little self-reflection will show, we all frequently act in ways that we don't really believe in in order to maintain our place in the culture. We tell "white lies" so as not to destroy a relationship with another—substituting a culturally legitimate excuse for one that might arouse a feeling of being wronged; we decide not to "rock the boat" in order not to be thought weird or crazy. People joining a new firm feel the pressure of group expectations and must spend a great deal of energy in trying to understand the cultural patterns so that they can "fit in" as well as possible.

In the framework just sketched, surveys are likely to capture the way in which (most) people *believe that they should be* formulating the broad principles of their social system—their "common language." This is unlikely to capture differences in the way in which these words are interpreted or adapted to new situations, or to distinguish thin types of conformity from deep beliefs.

This reflexive nature of culture becomes particularly important—and the survey approach is particularly weak—in capturing the dynamism of cultural *change*. At such moments people are particularly sensitive to what others believe and must often play a difficult balancing act between their own beliefs and those of the group. Thus their private answers to survey questions are likely to have less relation to their public presentation, and their public presentation is likely to be less consistent. As corporate cultures are faced with increasing pressure, people tend to speak the "official" language that everyone else speaks, but to actually behave quite differently. In early phases of change some people speak the familiar language of the past culture but begin adapting their behaviors to the new requirements. Later one can observe the opposite phenomenon, of people speaking the accepted language of entrepreneurship and performance while holding on to the older modes of behavior. In those conditions surveys necessarily give a very distorted picture of reality.

The major alternative approach to culture is often called "anthropological," though it is also used by many sociologists: it consists of trying to understand patterns of meaning from the *inside* through empathy and interpretation.[31] This method is better at capturing dynamic patterns and the balance between shared norms and individual viewpoints and responses, and therefore in practice is more useful in managing cultural change or conflict. That is why managers, who generally like clear metrics and algorithms, tend to reject them in this domain and to rely instead on their "touchy-feely" senses.

The major validity test of this approach is whether the interpretations make sense to the subjects of the research. Ideally theorists would "read back" their interpretations to members of the culture to see if they connect meaningfully to it. In most cases researchers have not gone this far but have used their own sense of meaning as the validity test. This has obvious drawbacks but has been justified by many on the basis of a human capacity for empathy that connects researchers to their subjects.

My own analysis is essentially anthropological in this sense, based largely on interviews and participant observation, seeking to identify through empathic reconstruction the patterns behind people's words and actions.[32] My interviews, with some 400 people in about twenty-five organizations over the past fifteen years, have not been systematically focused on culture, but they have aimed at understanding how people understand the changes going on around them; thus many of the issues of changing expectations can be found and analyzed. Many of these companies, especially those I studied in the early 1990s, still had fairly pure traditional bureaucratic cultures, though they were shaken by the layoffs and dislocations going on around them; others were already, even at that time, developing non-bureaucratic patterns. In some more recent studies, especially at Citibank, IBM, and Johnson & Johnson, I asked more precise questions about the norms of bureaucracy and collaboration. I also draw on published studies and on extended discussions with groups of managers at the Center for Workplace Transformation at Rutgers University.

In some of my most informative discussions I have in fact been able to try out my ideas of cultural patterns with practicing managers to see whether they make sense to them, and to ask them for stories of how these patterns play out in practice in contested or ambiguous situations. In interviews with middle managers in the early 1990s I asked for their reaction to my distinction between paternalist and "professional" orientations; they generally confirmed the distinction, but the idea of "contribution" began to emerge as key to the "professional" culture. In my interviews at Citibank I asked people how they decided whom to trust when they were forming working relationships, such as forming an alliance or creating an extended project group. The answers revealed a consistent divide between those who look for competence and contribution and those who look for connections and status. I have picked up this theme in more recent interviews at IBM and other companies.

## Types of Corporate Culture

The survey-based, factor-analytic approach to culture, when applied to the corporate world, has led to extremely diverse and inconsistent sets of distinctions. To take two examples from important players in the field: Hofstede's dimensions are "individual-collective," "power distance," "uncertainty avoidance," and "masculinity-femininity"; the Organizational Culture Inventory has twelve dimensions including "humanistic-helpful," "conventional," "dependent," and "avoidance."[33] I am unable to discern any commonality among these or the many other versions of cultural dimensions,[34] nor do they come close to connecting to the language of people I have spoken to or interviewed in corporations.

Anthropological approaches present a different problem: since they focus on understanding single cases, they are generally unable or unwilling to draw broad typologies. Those that have, however, do show an interesting degree of convergence with each other and with the broad lines I have drawn, which suggests that there might be an actual direction of progress in this field.

Earlier attempts, from before the mid-1980s, focus on varieties of what I call bureaucratic and paternalist cultures. Among the first such in the corporate field, for instance, were Douglas McGregor's "Theory X" and "Theory Y," later supplemented by William Ouchi's "Theory Z" or "clan" culture.[35] "Theory X" is essentially the Taylorist version of simple bureaucratic control. "Theory Y" is the later evolution of bureaucracy that I have called "paternalist": exercising control through a sense of participation and caring. "Theory Z" is also paternalist, but with a more collectivist tilt: rather than treating individuals better (as in "Y"), a "Theory Z" manager tries to motivate subordinates through feelings of collective loyalty and teamwork. But in my experience the distinction between "Y" and "Z" is not sharp; they are shades of the fundamental traditional culture. In my interviews during the 1980s and 1990s, I found that managers in American bureaucratic firms behaved in largely collectivist ways: encouraging group cohesion, defending expectations of lifetime employment, protecting "their" people in political battles, and refusing to make significant performance/reward distinctions among their subordinates. The "Z" approach described by Ouchi, based largely on the Japanese examples, goes a bit further in terms of involving subordinates in consensus decision making. Ouchi also fills out the paternalist model with a fuller description than McGregor's of the institutions and infrastructure of paternalism—especially lifetime employment and common values.

These cultural patterns share the core element that distinguishes them from the collaborative type: a key norm of hierarchical deference. Whatever caring, sharing, participation, and teamwork occur remains within the domain of a manager and subordinates, and is strongly shaped by the "family" dynamics of peers relating to an authority figure; they are subject to the restrictions (discussed in the Introduction) of strong boundedness, homogeneity, and stability. The theories of culture just mentioned share an inability to see beyond this restricted form of cultural unity: they assume that all "participative" management is of this bounded, familial type.

Some more recent studies, however, begin to sketch a type that approximates what I call "collaborative," enabling extended forms of trust. Cameron and Quinn begin with a theoretical view of cultural dimensions but also ground it in discussions within companies, including verification by explicit discussion among their subjects.[36] They distinguish four cultural dimensions. The first two, both internally focused, are familiar: "hierarchy" resembles what I call pure bureaucracy; "clan"—a term also used by Ouchi—is similar to what I call paternalism. The third, "adhocracy," has a good deal of similarity with what I have called "project collaboration": high on innovation, low on integration. The fourth, "market," is somewhat more problematic. It is similar to what I call "systemic collaboration" in emphasizing both external focus and internal control—that is, it orients to outside market demands while maintaining considerable strategic coherence.[37] It is also similar in seeing the central "glue" (as they call it) as a common orientation to strategic success. But it is different from my description in being considerably more hierarchically driven and competitive. These authors have, in my view, a too-simple notion of market orientation that focuses on "winning" against the competition rather than on meeting customer needs.

Denison's (1990) four dimensions also match at least roughly: "adaptability" aligns with project collaboration, "mission" with systemic collaboration,

Table 6 Correspondences with Other Studies

| | Bureaucracy | | Contribution | |
|---|---|---|---|---|
| | Pure Bureaucracy | Paternalist Bureaucracy | Project Collaboration | Systemic Collaboration |
| McGregor | Theory X | Theory Y | | |
| Ouchi | | Clan (Theory Z) | | |
| Cameron and Quinn | Hierarchy | Clan | Adhocracy | Market? |
| Denison | | | Adaptability | Mission? |

"clan" with paternalist bureaucracy, and "hierarchy" with pure bureaucracy. Again, the match is not perfect: Denison tends to talk about values from an ethical point of view rather than as a basis for interaction and trust; but the focus on shared mission does emerge once more as central.

Despite the differences, these correspondences suggest that those who actually observe what is going on in companies share at least a general intuition about the main cultural types. It is also interesting to me that they apparently share my view that the pure individualist-performance or "free agent" pattern, though much talked about, is not a significant cultural orientation in practice. The most complex and "leading edge" culture—the one required for systemic collaboration—shows the greatest divergence among the studies, though even in that case there are important similarities. It would be valuable for future research to see whether the evolutionary path continues as I predict, based on the analysis of collaboration, or whether it takes one of these variant forms (Table 6).

# Chapter 5 Collaborative
## Infrastructure

    While structure and culture are the most frequently discussed aspects
of organization, both depend in turn on a set of background systems that help
to create and sustain the organization's capabilities. I call these the "social
infrastructure."

On one side, infrastructure builds and supports culture. At the societal level
culture is defined and enforced through mechanisms such as churches, educational systems, and membership tests. Organizations similarly try, consciously
or unconsciously, to maintain the coherence of expectations through recruitment processes, training, and mentoring. The shift in expectations described
in Chapter 4, from loyalty to contribution, is embedded in a wide array of
mechanisms that constantly reinforce the importance of contributing to the
mission and helping others to do so, and that give people the information and
forums they need in this pursuit.

Conversely, fluid collaborative structures such as task teams and processes
also depend on a supportive infrastructure. This is less true in bureaucracy,
where structures are hard-wired directly by management; but in collaborative
enterprise processes and task teams must be able to emerge "on-demand"
rather than depending on higher level chartering and approval. To enable

this flexibility managers have to give up, at least partially, their directive use of structuring. They therefore need to establish infrastructural mechanisms such as process guidelines and reviews—systems that are one step removed from actually doing the work, but that help to shape it so that the organization can keep some control over ongoing and decentralized structuring.

For a collaborative enterprise, then, social infrastructure becomes more central than ever to effective management. In the bureaucratic world, and often still today, there was continual debate around whether to centralize or decentralize structure; but to succeed at collaboration, what is needed is *not centralization of structure but standardization of infrastructure*. The question is not whether to draw decision-making power up or leave it lower down, but rather how to create a common platform that enables everyone to communicate, understand, and share knowledge. Structures, such as teams and processes, can be created on a decentralized basis on these platforms.

Since the concept of social infrastructure is unfamiliar I have room to define it. I want to treat "infrastructure" as a practical concept. Thus social infrastructure, as I use the term, involves *deliberately manageable* systems that are not involved in the core work of the system but that shape work organization and culture.[1] There is a tremendous range of infrastructural systems, and many are in a state of flux and experimentation. Two of the most important, career patterns and accountability, are particularly unstable at this point. Other common ones include training, communication, mechanisms of voice, planning, learning, job design—the list is long, open-ended, and constantly subject to innovation.

This practical focus leaves out a number of aspects that are sometimes treated as broadly infrastructural. I put the more intangible aspects of action, including values and expectations and informal relationships, into the separate concept of "culture." Similarly, I don't use the popular notion of "social capital," which includes many elements that are diffuse or based on historical connections and so—as a legion of writers has discovered—is hard to connect to practical discussions.[2] Information technology is often thought of as "infrastructure": computer platforms increasingly enable people to communicate across boundaries of distance and position. But they are in themselves only empty vessels, abstract channels for communication. It is how they are formed and what they are used for that counts. Thus I focus on the social dimension; in what follows information systems appear as *facilitating* elements in almost all aspects of social infrastructure, from defining processes to building strategic alignment to dispute resolution.

## THE SOCIAL INFRASTRUCTURE
## OF PATERNALIST BUREAUCRACY

Much of the infrastructure built up during the bureaucratic era persists into the present, and much of it now undermines collaboration.

The main infrastructural task for bureaucracy is to provide clear and consistent job definitions, and to motivate employees to perform consistently and obediently within those jobs. After 1900, Scientific Management began to elaborate techniques of job analysis that eventually turned into the elaborate rule-based systems of classic corporations. At AT&T in the early 1980s there was a large room packed on four sides from floor to ceiling with books detailing every procedure for every job, and a good personnel manager could read directly from them to tell supervisors what their people should be doing in any given situation. This was bureaucratic infrastructure made visible with a vengeance.

On the motivational side, however, the formal controls of Scientific Management were never sufficient. Over time virtually all large companies adopted a set of policies designed to manage and encourage the informal organization and to build the culture of company loyalty. The infrastructural bases for this community were similar almost everywhere, including Europe and Japan, and across industries:

- Mechanisms to tie employee interests to long-term company loyalty—the most important being guarantees, implicit or explicit, of lifetime employment for those who demonstrated loyalty to the company.[3] Also vital and virtually universal are employer-based pension funds and internal promotion ladders, both structured so as to reward length of service,
- Development of staff roles, especially the personnel department function, which became a kind of specialist in bureaucratic infrastructure. Personnel managers provided training, managed pensions, managed promotion pipelines, guaranteed security by limiting supervisor authority, rationalized job definitions, and resolved employee disputes.
- Development of strong symbols of identity specific to the company to increase commitment to the organization. These included styles of dress and rituals of inclusion and recognition. In some instances, though not all, it included explicit values intended to be embodied by that corporation.
- Emphasis on promotions rather than short-term incentives as a reward mechanism.[4] Although there was always a formal system of periodic individual appraisals, in practice bureaucracies made few differentiations among

employees at the same level.[5] Instead they used promotions, which were diffuse, long-term, and infrequently implemented. This helped to maintain the
"family" culture that was central to the paternalist culture—limiting competition and perceptions of unfairness in the informal peer group, while cementing the pattern of loyalty and deference by forcing people to meet
subjective, diffuse expectations from their superiors.

In general the organizational system was gradually elaborated over time with
noneconomic incentives that tied individual interests and identities increasingly to those of the firm.[6]

This set of infrastructural policies encouraged the growth of loyalty and
informal cooperation. One-to-one peer ties were sustained in part by the fact
that people could expect that if they did favors for someone else, they would
be repaid in time. The needed deference to the organization was sustained by
caring leadership and the whole system of long-time career development.

In time these orientations were also embedded in wider social institutions
that extended far beyond the firm. These are also manageable, but not by the
enterprise; they become issues for the political arena:

- The role of government evolved from the antitrust focus of the early twentieth century to a focus on regulating large oligopolies. In the United States,
  incentives were created for businesses to provide benefits such as health insurance, which corresponded nicely to the "Human Relations" emphasis on
  firm loyalty. Courts recognized a duty of loyalty to employers.
- The educational system also supported the pattern of paternalist bureaucracy.
  In the context of closed, vertically integrated firms and strategies, companies
  primarily needed skills that were highly local, tailored to their particular needs,
  rather than broader technical abilities. Schools evolved to bring virtually everyone up to a level somewhat beyond the elementary level of education, and then
  turned them over to corporations for the rest of their learning needs.
- Unions, unexpectedly enough, also played a part by shifting from the craft-
  based focus on skills and certification to an industrial focus on stable employment and clear contracts. This fit nicely with the interests of mass-production
  firms seeking stability and interested in a stable and dependable workforce that
  would follow rules. Industrial unions negotiated for job security, emphasizing
  seniority, and insisted on codification of rules. By organizing entire industries,
  unions also succeeded in preventing competitors from undercutting each other
  on wages, which further stabilized the employment relationship and encouraged loyalty.

The fact that management always hated the "interference" of unions does not negate this profound underlying harmony: unions in effect forced management to live up to their own bureaucratic principles, to follow rules consistently and fairly, to avoid favoritism, and to reward loyalty. These principles were extended equally to layers of the organization that were not unionized—to technical workers and middle management—thus further cementing the general pattern.

## Weakening of the Supporting Pillars of Bureaucracy

It is obvious from the start that the core infrastructural element of paternalist bureaucracy, the lifetime career, is under pressure virtually everywhere. Though the numbers are far less dramatic than sometimes portrayed, there is little doubt that job mobility has increased, particularly among those who in the past had been the most stable: educated and skilled men, and those with long tenure.[7] In the heyday of bureaucracy there was a sharp line between the "primary labor market"—privileged workers who were part of the secure and stable career tracks of large corporations—and the "secondary market" of casual and generally unskilled workers; in general this line is being blurred by the increase in mobility among higher level managerial and white-collar employees.[8] Most important, there is strong evidence that companies have moved away from explicit and implicit promises of long-term security for their employees.[9]

Given the uncertain state of the data, it is important to emphasize that this argument does not depend on the more extreme claims that we are moving to a "free-agent nation" or that permanent jobs will disappear.[10] It is necessary simply that most people have lost the expectation that they will be able to move steadily through a process of growing compensation and responsibility through increasing seniority in a stable hierarchy. That seems difficult to question, and there are much data to support it.[11]

In many job sectors, particularly lower skilled ones, increased job movement is driven in part by corporate cost reduction efforts. But it is clear from both anecdotal and quantitative evidence that at least some of the increase is due to people and companies making choices about using skills and matching up to challenges. We have seen this in the Citibank case, where unlike the traditional pattern in the bank, a large number of people were new to the organization, and most had no firm commitment to a lifetime career there; they were attracted by and chosen for the challenge of developing an e-business.

On the quantitative end, recent research has found a particularly strong growth in movement not from work to unemployment, but from job to job.[12]

The bureaucratic infrastructure has been further weakened by the pronounced move among large companies to reduce the number of layers of management, thereby shortening career paths and tipping the balance for many people who can no longer sustain hope for continued promotions. This puts the motivational system in question: there is less incentive to defer to superiors, more incentive to look outside the company, and in general the danger of loss of loyalty.[13]

Other elements of the traditional infrastructure have also eroded under a combination of social and economic pressures. The main mechanism of voice in every industrialized country—industrial unionism—has declined everywhere and particularly so in the United States, where unions now represent fewer than 8 percent of private sector workers.[14] There is much disagreement about the significance of this decline, but it seems likely to be one cause of the rather dramatic decrease in job satisfaction found in polling results over the past thirty years, especially among non-supervisory workers.[15] The public education system, which supplied a steady stream of entry-level workers to the bottom rungs of the corporate ladders, has lost support and declined in quality. And it appears that the general attitude of deference toward authority has given way to a more individualist attitude in the Baby Boom generation, Generation X, and their successors.[16]

It is hard to trace cause and effect—whether the decline in career security and other elements of the bureaucratic culture have caused the shift in values or the reverse—nor is it necessary for this argument to do so. What is clear is that many fundamental systems and policies that underpinned the bureaucratic firm have weakened or crumbled.

## COLLABORATIVE INFRASTRUCTURE

The infrastructure of collaborative enterprises must support new cultural and structural premises: a culture that primarily values contribution to the collective task, and a structure that brings "horizontal," networked relationships to the foreground, or at least on an equal plane with the hierarchy. The development of these systems is still in a state of tremendous mutation and innovation. New efforts are springing up all the time: in the last decade the spotlight has swung from "performance management" and other forms of appraisal and compensation to "knowledge management," "communities of practice," and other ways of creating links among knowledge workers; to the "war for talent," with dozens of proposals for bringing on and retaining the best employees; to strategic outsourcing; and to many other proposals and fads. None of these is widespread or established enough to have clearly demonstrated its worth.

The profusion of infrastructural efforts can be organized roughly under four headings:

1. Practices that help to build and maintain a unifying sense of purpose;
2. Practices that organize and formalize peer or associational relationships;
3. Practices that connect the system to the outside world through planning and sensing; and
4. Practices that enable the system to learn.

As in the rest of this book, defining infrastructure involves more than describing existing reality. There is no perfect example yet of a completed collaborative infrastructure that I can point to as a model, and many of these practices are currently unproven and experimental. I have focused on those that meet two criteria that make them likely candidates for long life: ones that both fit with the general conceptual logic of collaborative enterprise and have been shown to work rather well in a number of our cases.

## 1. Shared Purpose: Strategic Understanding

A central element in the logic of collaboration is orientation toward a common purpose—not just timeless values, but realizable goals to be accomplished in the foreseeable future. Purpose for companies is essentially embodied in *strategy*, which defines the central medium-term directions of the collective enterprise—what strengths the company seeks to maximize, how it will position itself relative to the competition and what results it expects. In bureaucracy, strategy was the preserve of the top management: Alfred Sloan was indeed very explicit in drawing a line between the strategic functions of the top and the operational capacities of the rest of the organization.

This is one arena where the change over the past few decades has been unmistakable. As late as the 1980s the conventional wisdom in most corporations was that strategic plans needed to be kept confidential in order to avoid leaks to the competition; even the broad outlines of strategy were kept sealed within the top levels. The early 1990s, when I interviewed in a group of companies, were a transitional moment: some of my sample had opened up, others had not. Within General Motors I observed the contrast very directly. In the core CPC (Chevrolet-Pontiac Canada) division, middle managers had no idea what their competitors were doing or how the company was planning to address its severe market erosion; when I asked them about strategy, they replied that their quality and productivity numbers were up. Meanwhile, at Saturn, managed as a separate company within GM, I wandered on the floor and came across a group of assembly-line workers holding a quality meeting. When I asked *them* how they were doing, they answered that their initial focus on taking small-car share from the Japanese was nearing its end as a viable strategy; that they needed to find new ways to leverage the technological and productivity improvements that they had achieved; and that they therefore needed to find investors beyond GM, perhaps in Japan, perhaps outside the automobile industry. Unlike their CPC counterparts, these shopfloor workers were thinking outwardly and strategically, well beyond the confines of incremental operating improvements.

They were able to do this for two reasons: first, they had a tremendous amount of information about strategic intent, costs, competitive positioning, and other issues that were still closely held in most of GM; second, there were frequent lively and intense internal debates about these issues (often, in this case, organized by the union, which was an active partner in the enterprise). This focus on the shared purpose was critical to the high level of collaboration that enabled Saturn to operate successfully at the time with very low levels of management supervision and extremely good quality results.[17]

Saturn is an unusual company in many ways, but in this particular respect it was far more in the mainstream than its parent. Companies have been sharing increasing amounts of competitive information down through middle management to the shopfloor, and encouraging teams to discuss and debate how they contribute to the strategy. Citibank e-Commerce represents a highly developed case: people talked constantly about strategy and were strongly motivated by it.

> Our Internet strategy is well documented and communicated throughout the company. Twenty years ago a strategy document would have been only in certain hands within the company and kept very close. Now it's everywhere, on all the intranets.

A detailed "e-business road map" was available to everyone in the organization and continuously discussed and refined. Training sessions for new managers as well as regular meetings of subunits included detailed strategy briefings from senior management. The intranet was organized around the road map: projects were organized around its categories, and presentations regularly began with a review of the relationship to strategic purposes. Groups could communicate easily with each other because they used these categories in common.

Many companies hold regular meetings of strategic leaders with operational leaders to "mix" the two perspectives. Degussa, an automotive supply company, is one that I pick only because I have good notes on this aspect: they hold regular multiday cross-departmental process workshops that involve some training and some problem definition and solving; but they move beyond this level because members of the top team usually attend, deliberately aiming to teach the business to the employees and reciprocally to listen to emerging issues.[18] There are many other mechanisms as well. At GE, Jack Welch frequently conducted intense four-hour education sessions with managers from multiple levels, full of passionate arguments around issues of strategic definition and implementation; and the "Work-Out" process had brought this kind of debate deep into the organization.[19]

In our research coding of infrastructural elements, our main collaborative "level 4" enterprises all came out high on "understanding of strategic purpose throughout the organization," as we would expect. Some other companies that have struggled more with the move came out lower—in particular ABB and Hewlett-Packard. This confirms our suggestion that widespread strategic understanding is one of the central conditions for collaboration.[20]

### One-Way and Two-Way Strategic Dialogue

The discussions of strategy in these instances, it should be emphasized, were participative but not democratic. Top management's view of strategy was informed by the views of subordinates which they heard continuously in almost every meeting, but it clearly remained top management's prerogative to ignore the input if it wanted. It has been very rare for strategic ideas that originate in middle or lower levels of the organization to have any recognized impact upward. This sometimes leads to frustration, a feeling that the top is ignoring crucial aspects of the business that other parts of the organizations can see more clearly—such as evolving technological or customer needs.

There are a few partial exceptions. IBM's move to focus on the Internet came at least in part from middle managers who saw the potential of the medium earlier than their bosses did (and earlier than most other companies). They were able, in the climate fostered by Lou Gerstner, to push their perception upward and outward, gradually increase their support, and finally to have a significant impact on strategic direction.[21] At Veridian, a defense contractor, a middle management team challenged its superiors to overcome their positional rivalries and go after truly integrative projects and large contracts.[22] In these two cases the encouragement of strategic "pushing" from lower levels seems to have had significantly positive effects for the organization as a whole.

These examples suggest that there is value in creating opportunities for genuinely open dialogue about strategy, with room not only for upward disagreement but also for upward influence. At the same time, the logic of collaboration as well as observable practice suggest that it is vital that strategic vision be unified: it is because everyone shares a clear view of the overall imperatives that it is possible for them to work flexibly together and to coordinate very different types of knowledge. A free-for-all with many competing visions would do far more harm than good. Central management needs to ensure this coherence while also encouraging exploration and dissent. In the case of the IBM Internet initiative, top management was involved early on, knew about the initiative, and gave its blessing for continued experimentation and networking. In the Veridian case there was a formalized process for generating a strategic assessment from the middle layers of the organization and bringing it as a challenge to top management, followed by several rounds of continued dialogue before a final decision. These are two methods that seem to work, making it absolutely clear what aspects of strategy are binding on everyone while allowing room for debate.

In general, the evidence we have is that most companies have not gone that far; they communicate strategy from the top and encourage real discussion for the purpose of understanding, but they do not encourage pushback. It seems that this attitude, which carries the flavor of bureaucratic habits, restricts some of the possible benefits of wider collaboration.

### Vision and Values Statements

What about vision and value statements, which are often seen as central to change?[23] Though values as such are part of culture, formal value statements and discussions are infrastructural mechanisms that can be used to try to shape organizations.

Our sample is ambiguous on this issue. One case, IBM, did initiate a major effort in values redefinition (which is described in more detail in Chapter 9). Even allowing for the fact that our interviews were focused on this process, it did appear that values were a constant reference point in daily work. Employees at all levels were knowledgeable about successive value statements and how they had changed; they could give immediate and clear examples of the relevance of these statements to their work; they had strong opinions about them.

But this is not true of most of our other cases. Among our central ones, Citibank e-Solutions certainly had strong shared norms about collaboration (described in Chapter 4). but no formal statement of them, and people in general struggled to formulate them explicitly. The converse is even more common: many organizations in our sample had values statements that were on the wall in HR or leadership offices but were never referred to in interviews or other observations.

The difficulty seems to be that formulating visions is a delicate exercise that can easily lead to cynicism. If the value statement is not connected to daily behavior and interactions, it will simply make leadership seem "out of touch" with the operating core of the organization. Defining values ahead of practices, therefore, is dangerous. This is clearly the case in a number of places where I have conducted interviews: the wave of scorn, for example, when top management at GM's CPC division came back from a retreat in the early 1990s with a new vision of customer focus was overwhelming.

Thus the creation of value statements seems to work best as an interactive process over time, with a great deal of debate, rather than being established as an initial part of the infrastructure. Instead of common values, the early phases of change in our sample focus on common *purpose*, or strategy. The difference is that values are statements that define good and bad behaviors and are meant to be permanent; purpose simply defines what we are trying to do together, usually over a period of a few years. The latter is clearer and easier to use as a common point of orientation.

This does not, however, mean that a statement of values is not important as an element of social infrastructure. When we examine change processes in Chapter 6, I will argue that the process of making values explicit is essential to the later phases of the transformation. We see few formalized value statements because our cases are at relatively early stages in the move to collaboration.

## 2. The Formalization of Social Relationships

Another set of infrastructural elements aims at supporting webs of associational relationships. In both bureaucracies and collaborative enterprises people classically talk about "developing my network." But as described in Chapter 1, in bureaucracy this web is rarely managed in any deliberate way by the business; it is composed through haphazard personal contacts. In a collaborative system these "horizontal" linkages become more central, so that it becomes important to make sure that people can contact the right people at the right time and can form the needed relationships to solve tasks.

An academic literature on networks has emerged mainly to explore this formerly hidden world of peer relationships (see the "Postscript" at the end of

Chapter 1). Much of this literature extends from Granovetter's 1973 demonstration that for poorly structured tasks—including both high adaptivity and complexity in my sense—it is better to have a network that has many weak ties rather than one that is tightly linked around hubs. Weak ties, or "acquaintanceships," are connections that are infrequent and partial; they are crucial in crossing the boundaries of traditional communities and thus reducing the power of isolated cliques, opening them up to innovation and new combinations of resources.[24]

Many researchers have followed up this initial insight by exploring how weak-tie networks are structured and sustained—especially through the development of linking roles, such as gatekeepers, ambassadors, and others.[25] Recently the concept of a "network orchestrator" has become popular to designate a person or organization that has influence across a wide range of roles and can pull them together around a task.[26] But what is more important for our purposes is that many companies have begun to develop the idea in practice by deliberately assigning and managing these linking roles.

### Linking Roles

The most purely infrastructural roles are those that are not involved in delivering products and services at all, but are entirely focused on creating connections across the network. An archetypal example is John Gage, the Chief Scientist at Sun Microsystems in the mid-1990s. One of Gage's roles was to be a pure linker, "keeping the smartest people at Sun thinking, talking, and working together." He traveled the world looking to build connections among people in seemingly disconnected places. One of his major tools was e-mail distribution ("alias") lists: he watched the development of new lists as a signal of how the organization was forming around emerging initiatives, and he used his own list to create links across the formal system:

> [My alias list] lists the people I believe are the real players in Java, my personal view on the power structure. They're the people I send messages to. A fellow named Geoff Baehr is on my . . . list even though he works in a completely different part of Sun. But he's one of the drivers. You'd never know it from the org chart.[27]

Monsanto, as of the early 1990s, had a manager in the product that was effectively a global solutions developer. His responsibilities were to integrate geographies and functions to set strategy and prioritize solutions for business areas across seed, chemical, and biotechnical product lines. He worked closely with local marketing and technical people and convened representatives from geographies and functions to review strategy, performance and goals, and to share ideas and best practices. But for all this had no formal authority over the members of the network; he drew his ability to function entirely from the perception that the links he was creating added value to all those involved.[28]

Perhaps more significant than individual roles is the development of regular systems to encourage interaction and information flow—a kind of structured background chatter that enables people to keep track of what is going on in other areas and to spot possible new connections. Citibank e-Solutions developed a set of periodic, disciplined conference calls across areas in which a few people each time would talk about their initiatives. And for many, this keeping in touch across the system—the development of weak ties, in effect— became an essential part of everyday jobs. Two managers discussed their approaches:

> Credibility starts with communication—regardless of how good you are if you don't communicate constantly and routinely (I call it "air conditioning noise," a constant background), you can't succeed. You need constant communication on goals, milestones, accomplishments, constant reporting back; then there's an audience that listens and gives you the credibility; and there's another audience that uses your services, so it's good news for them.

> I reach on a monthly basis between 5,000 and 7,000 folks. . . . You don't know the 5,000–7,000 by name or face. If you need someone you work your networks. And when you talk to those people they've heard of you because of the communications you have put out.

Moving even further into formalization and extension of the network-shaping infrastructure is Shell's "core competencies" group, a boundary-spanning collection of people with expertise who were needed on many teams and task forces. It was designed to connect asset teams to each other and to the research labs, and in general to serve as a clearinghouse for technical service projects (Figure 18).

The infrastructure of network-shaping can also be done in part through technology. Most companies in our sample have begun to develop some form of computerized internal "yellow pages" (or, at IBM, "blue pages") that keep track of initiatives and skills, so that one can find people in other parts of the organization who could help or connect to what one is doing. It is worth noting, however, that these technological fixes are useful only when the collaborative culture has developed to a significant degree; when they are tried in bureaucratic systems, people are reluctant to enter their information. This is

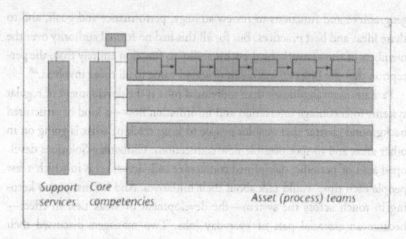

Support Core
services competencies

Asset (process) teams

Figure 18: Shell team organization, 1994

because in the bureaucratic culture, or set of expectations, information is seen as a scarce resource, to be protected as the basis of personal power rather than given away. Further, one is not expected to reach out directly to others in this way; connections are supposed to be made "through channels" to formally defined roles and positions. For these reasons the capacity for broad network linkages cannot depend primarily on technology, but must have a solid base of shared collaborative expectations.

The ability to draw accurately and quickly on resources across a wide span is almost entirely new. It goes far beyond the ad hoc personal connections of traditional organizations, or the restricted connections of the formal hierarchy. The use of individuals like John Gage as systematic linkers expands these connections by one significant degree. The development of disciplined organizational chatter, as in the Citibank example, begins to embed network-shaping in the fundamental infrastructure of the system.

### Information Transparency

It is not only strategy that has become much more widely shared than in the past; the same principle also applies more generally to the sharing of information that helps to overcome bureaucratic walls, build understanding, sustain relationships, and create accurate networks of reputation. The sociologist Talcott Parsons noted that freedom of information plays the same role in influence systems that freedom of contract plays in markets[29]: it makes it possible for the right resources to get to the right place by creating a platform of trust and shared knowledge.

There is a continuing tension between the need for confidentiality and the benefits of openness, but the latter seems to be gradually advancing its position. As early as the 1980s the Shell plant in Sarnia opened its information system entirely to shopfloor employees, which gave the union unusual leverage but also helped them to function as enormously effective problem-solving teams in crises. In our sample Saturn followed the Shell-Sarnia example in opening its computer system fully to unionized employees, with similarly beneficial operating results.[30]

Within the management ranks many companies have moved to develop transparent accounting systems that make clear where resources are being allocated. ABB's ABACUS system was one of the first, and most of our other collaborative cases have taken up the effort. ABB also measured the performance of units like factories and made the information and rankings available to everyone involved. The process is to encourage the lower ranking units to establish communications with the higher ranking units to exchange best practices.

In recent years the tendency to opening information has gone to a new level: many companies have asked outsiders, including customers and allies, to join in internal forums; and networks of companies have begun to share information at a deep level to form integrated value chains or platforms for transactions. Cisco uses the Internet as the glue not only for the internal workings of the company, creating great transparency among employees, but also for swiftly connecting with its web of partners. So high is the transparency beyond the formal borders of Cisco Connection Online that the entire constellation of suppliers, contract manufacturers, and assemblers looks like one seamless company.

A particularly interesting example is GHX, a network of health care production and distribution companies that has taken billions of dollars out of the process of getting health care products to market. This group, after substantial trust-building, has built a platform that enables the companies, many of whom are competitors as well, to share information needed to coordinate efficiently and to reduce transfer costs along the supply chain.[31] There are many other examples: Intel, for instance, has made it a major strategic priority to build the health of its industry, and therefore engages in open discussions with its competitors to find synergies. Cisco sends employees to talk with peers at companies that it is seeking to acquire, with instructions to be transparent, open, friendly, and aboveboard.[32]

### Formal Codes and Platforms

A common thread across collaborative innovations is that they are based increasingly on explicit rather than tacit processes. In bureaucracy, only a few top managers or specialists need to worry about structure; in collaborative settings, people at all levels need to be able to put together and take apart teams and processes to meet new challenges. They therefore need a shared platform of common tools and language to discuss and create these structures.

The clearest illustration is at the small group level. It is now quite routine in many systems for teams, when they come together for a task, to run through a structured set of questions around "roles and responsibilities." They discuss what needs to be done for their main tasks and, in a kind of negotiation, develop commitments from the members about who will do what. These discussions are repeated from time to time as the project advances to make sure that there is clarity and consensus, and they are usually recorded to be referred to in cases of disagreement. All of this is quite new in the last twenty years of organizations—often much newer than that—and has spread with great speed.[33]

The framework of roles and responsibilities is in effect a common process platform that can be used to produce an infinite number of collaborative projects through discussion, in the same way that in language a constant grammar enables us to create and understand an infinite number of sentences. If people understand the framework in the same way, they can use it to create something new together.

When a team's membership is already defined, this simple "roles-and-responsibilities" framework is enough; but there is another and more complicated level, involving the creation of new teams or new processes through peer negotiation. In an environment like Citibank e-Solutions such self-constitution does occur fairly often. Faced with new problems, people always sought to formalize processes that others could use and plug into:

> Over Christmas I had to put together a procedures manual for alliances. We want the whole management team to be able to put together alliances, not just the Alliance group. So we needed operating rules, tools, life cycle stages of alliance. We built a formal operating process.

The common language at this level is the language of "value-added": that is, people talk to each other about what value is needed for the project, how it connects to the strategic imperatives, and what will be given back to those involved. The alliance process was "sold" to others in terms of the value it would bring for the overall e-commerce strategy, as a way of quickly gathering resources for new offerings; and it also made others' lives easier by giving them a proven road map.

The code may be embodied in an infrastructure of software templates. Within e-Solutions strategic templates embedded in the information systems pushed everyone to use a common language to describe their initiatives, to justify their value for the strategic priorities, and to record their basic goals and commitments for public view.

In general, a key to generating processes quickly and flexibly is general acceptance of a few core rules that remain constant. The theory of complexity in physics and other scientific disciplines has shown how a few well-chosen rules can govern very complex systems. Dee Hock, the founder of Visa, used this idea explicitly; Kathy Eisenhardt has documented the effectiveness of "simple rules" at other companies like Yahoo![34] At Citibank e-Solutions one interviewee noted:

> Part of why the strategy has penetrated so well is because there is clear and consistent emphasis on three strategies and six tactics that we agree on. Often we have the very same slides up reinforcing what we are doing. Most people address these issues.

Without these basic rules, processes would tend quickly to harden and become rigid and unresponsive. But because of the core "code," teams and process maps can be constantly put together and taken apart without destroying needed unity and common understanding.

The formalization of codes and basic rules could be seen as a reemergence of bureaucracy, and indeed it is sometimes perceived that way by those concerned. But this kind of standardization is fundamentally different from the bureaucratic version in that it is created and maintained with the heavy involvement of the people themselves, rather than being handed down after rational analysis at a higher level. The primary value standard is whether it helps people get their work done, not (as in the Weberian analysis) whether it meets needs for rationality and control. Thus the Alliance head at Citibank e-Solutions went off to develop an alliance procedure in order to avoid continual reinvention of the wheel, but his initial draft was immediately modified in discussions with other task teams, and then continually updated thereafter as needs changed.[35]

### Negotiation: Skills and Systems

Collaborative networks depend much more heavily than bureaucracies on negotiation—agreements to exchange value. Bureaucratic systems, to be sure, negotiated informally a great deal: bosses, though they had formal power, negotiated with their subordinates so as to make everyone as happy as possible, and people negotiated resources with each other in the informal organization. But these were rather basic types of negotiation: almost entirely one-to-one, and based mostly on "log-rolling" exchanges of favors: "I'll do this for you if you do that for me."[36] In collaboration, negotiation moves to the center of interaction and becomes much more complex.

This is another area in which many of our sample companies have made a great deal of progress, though again there is still further to go.[37] It is notable that almost everywhere I have interviewed the language of "win–win" negotiation had become current. This language dates only from the 1980s with the line of research following the seminal book *Getting to Yes*.[38] What it signifies (which is not entirely the same as what the actual book said) is a set of principles that are essential to collaborative negotiation. First, in a win–win approach the parties are quite explicit and analytic about the value proposition of the exchange of value, as opposed to thinking of negotiation as a power game in which one side loses and the other side wins. Second, it is problem-centered, rather than seeking an exchange of favors; it tries to frame every negotiation in terms of a common problem that the parties are trying to resolve. Finally, it is impersonal, discounting personal feelings and qualities: it tries to "separate the person from the problem."

Thus a win–win approach is the foundation for a type of negotiation that can be repeated, in which the parties don't end up feeling bad about each other and the process, and that is focused on creating value together. It is therefore significant that so many managers not only use the language but have actually had training of some kind in this approach.

There has not yet been sufficient theoretical exploration of what it takes to make win–win negotiation work beyond personal orientation and skills. There is some evidence that it works better in conditions like the ones we are calling "collaborative," in which people already relate not through bureaucratic autonomy but are also trying to work together.[39] It clearly works better when people understand the shared goal in the same way, so that they can easily agree on the nature of the problem that they are both trying to solve.

In the cases I have looked at, I have been struck by a further condition: a good win–win system depends on a balance of resources. That is, everyone needs some value to exchange. This can be specialized knowledge that others need, but it usually needs to be backed up by more tangible resources. To illustrate what I mean, let me use another area of Citibank, the Customer

Relationships Management system of the Global Bank. In the early 1990s, trying to increase the bank's ability to focus on customers, John Reed set up a "front end" of highly regarded managers who were given responsibility for satisfying the needs of valued customers. To do this they had to pull resources from the various divisions—cash management, various countries, and so on—into integrated packages, in a kind of early solutions approach. But the power hierarchies remained in the divisions; the Customer Relationships Managers (CRMs) had to negotiate with the division heads to contribute to the customer solutions.

This didn't work very well. The CRMs had nothing much to offer except the chance to help in satisfying a customer and advancing the strategy; while this convinced some people some of the time, it was not enough. The system did not really begin to work until more than a decade later, when the country managers began to be rewarded in part on the responses of key customers. Suddenly they *needed* the CRMs, who had a unique capabilities in bringing things together for customers; and so they responded much more favorably to their overtures for "win–win" negotiations. By contrast, the e-Solutions group more often needed the support of the hierarchy to work with other parts of the bank:

> Unless top management is involved we can't get the product group to work with us. We do not have tools of CRMs—it's a result of our developmental state, we don't have revenue streams to promise, we don't have chips to negotiate with. When a decision is made to pull a product we have very little say about that.

A lesson in this is that a collaborative system works on two dimensions, not one. The motivation to contribute to a greater cause or shared purpose is essential to coordinating the diverse players, but they also have to need each other. One of the Citibank team managers reflected this double understanding in his description of trying to pull together a group around a new opportunity:

> I quickly brought a team together and said, "Here's our chance to make a difference in the institution." Then one-on-one I figured out what was in it for each of them. So in every meeting I made sure there was something important for every person—and they all came.[40]

### Mutual Understanding

A core principle of extended collaboration is that it works by drawing on diverse capabilities rather than by adding similar ones. An embedded difficulty is that these diverse perspectives have to understand each other.

This is not necessary in bureaucratic systems; people only need to understand their own jobs, not those of others. If you put them together in a task team, they tend to just state their own needs rather than building new understanding. In a cross-functional auto design team, for instance, it does not work for the marketer simply to lay out what works for marketing and the engineer to lay out what is good for engineering; that would lead to poor decisions at best and would not make use of the variety of knowledge available. What makes collaboration valuable is for the marketer to challenge the engineer on what exactly the problems are, and how they might be confronted in creative ways that come closer to dealing with marketing concerns. Thus the disciplines need to overlap enough to make such challenges effective.

To some extent this understanding may develop as a task team works. But teams can get up to speed more quickly and reliably when there is an existing store of understanding to draw on. Hence many organizations have begun to develop ongoing exchanges among different parts of organizations outside the context of immediate tasks. I use the term "forums"[41] for this kind of mechanism—a term that is actually used by some organizations, though others have many different terms for this general type of meeting.

Shell has used experience-sharing forums in a particularly deliberate way: they have an effort to create a "global community" that links knowledge groups across organization lines and also with each other in "communities of practice." This is basically a chance for exchanging experiences and knowledge in a general way without the pressure of task accountability.[42] They have systematic processes: coordinators, a software infrastructure for storing learnings, and a set of structured meetings. This has spread widely through the company and is seen as largely successful in improving cross-disciplinary problem-solving: As a well engineer said, "I understand better where my advice is coming from and understand the background thinking of why it should work."[43]

At Citibank e-Solutions the forum function was filled by a slightly less formal, but nevertheless regularized, set of mechanisms in which people could present the projects they were working on and the challenges they faced, and get feedback and support from other parts of the business. Several broad initiatives, involving multiple work teams, scheduled monthly phone calls for this purpose. "Town hall" meetings were businesswide and led by the head of the e-Solutions group.

### Personal Relationships in Collaborative Enterprise

Traditional bureaucracies, as I have stressed, rely heavily on networks of informal and personal relationships to overcome the extreme rigidity of pure rule-based systems. These relations are diffuse and social—based on "going out for beers" and other such shared non-work activities. As many authors have noted, this kind of personalized trust leads to discrimination and exclusion of new groups. From the aspect of collaboration, it also restricts the scope of enterprise to local and bounded communities.

For those reasons, collaborative systems put a great deal of effort into replacing personal relationships with more systematic process management skills. Citibank, for example, used to rely on informal networks to do deals for its multinational clients, but they became aware in the late 1990s that this resulted in much lost business. They therefore established formal global relationship managers and structures with the power to quickly assemble teams for their clients to make sure the deals got done. Every company in our sample that has pushed toward higher collaboration has gone through similar transitions.

Personal networks stand in a tense relationship to the formal processes. The first problem is that the informal networks are exclusionary, making it hard to incorporate new capabilities. One manager, for example, talked about the importance of drinking partners, but then acknowledged that it was difficult in such a culture to bring in executives from the outside: "It rarely works, but it will have to be overcome." Second, informal relationships can sometimes undercut the functioning of the formal system—as a McKinsey consultant explains about its internal systems,

> Everyone would like everyone else to be bound by the formal systems of team staffing, but to be able himself to use both the formal systems and his own personal contacts. So when you put together an engagement team you want to have full information about the capabilities and availability of others throughout the organization, but you want to be able to hoard the people you have had success with so that they don't get taken by someone else.

This creates a "prisoner's dilemma" problem that can quickly lead to a collapse of the more complex, formalized system of extended relationships and a regression toward more limited "empires."

Thus from the perspective of the system as a whole, it is important to control the use of informal connections and to keep them from being used in particularized ways that do not serve the larger collective purpose. In several cases, especially McKinsey and Veridian, this was done effectively by doing staffing through public discussions in which those who tried illegitimate manipulations could be "outed" by peers.

Still, personal networks have not by any means disappeared: the formal systems of process management and reputation are never enough by themselves to make the connections needed for fluid collaboration. People continue to work hard and continuously to develop their contacts, people whom they know and can trust. John Gage's alias list described earlier in this chapter is a classic illustration of their value in a collaborative setting. People over time build ties to others that cross-cut organizational lines, and go to those "nodes" first when they need to find new contacts or new paths through the formal systems.

There is, however, a crucial difference between this kind of personal network and the kind that underlie paternalist bureaucracies: the relationships are less diffuse, more focused on work performance and capability; they become in effect personal records of the things that matter at work rather than of a general "feeling" about someone else. Thus people are more able to differentiate between liking someone and trusting him or her as a work partner. This shift in tone was expressed with remarkable clarity by a purchasing agent in Lyon, reflecting on a recent shift toward a more formalized subcontracting partnership system:

> It is important to have a good climate in the working relationship and then the subcontractor becomes almost a friend. . . . Before [two years ago], it was different. The relations with subcontractors were mainly personal relations. That is to say, you were friends first because you knew each other socially and then you gave out the work to your friends. Now it's the opposite. According to the work given out and the quality of the work done, you establish a good relationship, but it's more of a professional relationship.[44]

This same pattern is also observable in the more directly corporate arena. A person who had gone through the transition from Hewlett-Packard to Agilent used somewhat different language for a similar perception:

> At HP we were more of a "family." If you got in, you didn't need to be held accountable; you just needed to be there. . . . So, if you have a crazy aunt you just hide her in the closet, you don't kick her out of the family. As we've become Agilent we've become more of a "team." You are part of a working unit. And I know some teams that are more functional than families, so it's a good thing. But, if you're not performing, you're out of there.[45]

As can be seen in this second quote, there is often a kind of nostalgia for the older, "warmer" familial relationships, but also a recognition of the essential need to ground relations on work performance.

*Activating* the network similarly becomes a far more differentiated and task-focused matter. When the Citibank manager quoted in Chapter 3 wanted to put together a task team, he "chitchatted a bit" but focused his conversations quickly on the value that could be exchanged through collaboration. The task-focused tone is accentuated when, as is increasingly the case, communication occurs through virtual means rather than face-to-face:

> You have some close buddies where you are going to shoot the breeze. But most people do not use the [messaging] system for shooting the breeze. It is mostly used very quick: "I need something—can you answer this question?" There is a little bit of the back and forth: "What you doing today?" There is very little of that casual flow of interaction.

Thus in collaborative enterprise the development and maintenance of personal networks remains a crucial aspect of successful performance. But these networks are not the diffuse social relationships characteristic of paternalist bureaucracies; they are records of direct experience with work performance. "Old-style" diffuse friendships must be differentiated and managed so that they do not interfere with the ability to get the best people together to get things done effectively.[46]

### 3. External Relationships: Planning and Responding

The move to collaboration in our sample is driven largely by increased pressure from the environment: consumer sophistication, international competition, technological transformations.[47] A major element of collaborative enterprise therefore must be mechnisms that keep the system in touch with what is going on outside and use experiences for effective learning and planning. In bureaucratic systems relatively few people have contact with the environment, and those who do tend to be at low levels—sales agents or clerks—with very little influence over planning processes occurring in distant headquarters. The problem in a dynamic environment is to add a lot of eyes and ears: to develop rich sensors for information from outside the company on customers, competitors, and industry trends.

The three major types of "level 4" companies we have distinguished—adaptive, complex, and solutions enterprises—have developed somewhat different systems. For the adaptive type, the main emphasis is on mechanisms of sensing and scanning; for the complex type, it is on mechanisms of planning and integration. The solutions type has to develop ways to pull these together into a single flexible loop of learning from the environment and responsive planning.

### Sensing and Scanning

For "adaptive" companies—those that are high on the dynamic dimension but not on complexity—there is a relatively easy solution: give customer-facing teams a great deal of autonomy to respond and innovate as they see fit. Thus the connection between sensing and action is very short. This is generally character- istic of consulting and other professional service firms, which can put a team in the field and let them deal on their own with the customer. In the simplest in- stances there is very little strategic coordination or prioritization; the relationship between the teams and the company is very loose and largely financial.

In our sample the clearest case of this positioning may be Spaarbeleg, the sales and marketing arm of the Dutch insurance company Aegon. The highly decentralized sales teams were governed by a simple model with two axes: risk and time frame; by locating their projects within this two-dimensional "house," teams were able to coordinate and integrate with other parts of the unit. We have already discussed other versions of this "simple rules" approach to coor- dinating networks.[48]

But the simple rules approach is sufficient only in simple situations. As the strategic world grows highly complex it becomes necessary not only to sense but also to integrate many sensings into a coherent strategy. The easiest way to do this is to increase the intensity and frequency of the top team scans. An early ex- ample is the famed Shell "Scenario Planning" process, which explores the princi- pal challenges to the business created by environmental change. Scenario scans are conducted every three years primarily through staff research but aimed at se- nior leaders, who use them in strategic decision making.[49] In the early 1970s the first scenario process pointed out the danger of severe oil price shocks driven by OPEC, and Shell was therefore in a far better position than any of its competi- tors to respond when this very pattern unfolded in 1974. Since then many others have picked up the idea. A substantial literature on "scanning" through the 1970s and 1980s focused almost exclusively on this type of process at the top levels.[50]

In our sample, Hewlett-Packard illustrates a somewhat broader approach. As of the early 1990s the company instituted two relevant kinds of teams:

- Scanning teams with marketers and engineers spending much time outside their offices scanning the environments of use of their current, former, and potential customers; gathering "premonitions" of future scientific and industry trends; and acquainting themselves fully with competitor products and direction.

• "Phase Zero" teams were partnerships of marketing and special representatives who visited customer sites. Interviews in the customer's environment allowed the team to observe and collect contextual, implicit, and qualitative information that would be overlooked in other methods of data gathering.

But even this approach still constricts the information flows to a few teams and cuts off involvement from most employees who have access to relevant information. By contrast, HP's Santa Rosa Systems Division, as part of its effort to develop a solutions capability, pushed further to a far more interactive, three-month market scanning process involving a more representative team and a strategic dialogue across the organization.[51] This created a wider capability to connect dispersed observations.

### Planning and Prioritizing

Systems of "managed collaboration"—managing complexity but with less pressure for rapid adaptation—need to focus primarily on a different dimension: bringing together multiple values and perspectives into integrated plans, and setting priorities among them. Complexity increases as strategies seek to reconcile multiple dimensions, of customer, geography, products, and internal functions. Once again, the simplest way to deal with this problem is to build top management into teams that can represent multiple parts of the organization in genuine debate about priorities. This is a significant theme of most companies, at least those in our sample: the top leadership has become less imperial and more of a forum for debate and argumentation.[52]

A great deal of power is added, however, when these discussions can include multiple levels, bringing in the knowledge of specialists lower in the system. A step in opening things up in this way is to establish settings where priorities can be argued out in a kind of "free-for-all." At Shell SEPIV, there were yearly meetings of this type involving a wide variety of positions, with a great deal of shouting and conflict. At ABB, projects were vigorously debated at several levels, and most people felt that the achievement of consensus in that process was a key to eventual success. For example, gas plants were debated among the Business Area and Segment leaders and chosen to be a priority, with successful results. On the other hand, waste treatment was similarly debated but without agreement; these projects failed.

Perhaps the most sophisticated approach, going beyond such free-for-all discussions, has been to build intermeshed resource structures—so that no single priority could dominate the others, but all needed to negotiate for the resources they needed. We have quite a few examples from our companies. At "NewTech," for instance, managers in charge of strategic initiatives determined requirements, including headcount, and petition the "owners" of resources—directors of research units and, if relevant, the marketing and finance department managers. Most issues were negotiated directly, though in difficult cases senior management was asked to weigh in. Since most unit directors were also responsible for initiatives, interests did not tend to "harden" along stable fault lines. This approach allows more continuous and complex resource allocation than simple open discussions do, but it also depends on a remarkably strong shared orientation to the strategic mission and a high level of trust.[53]

### Combining Sensing and Planning

In "high-high" strategies that combine dynamism with complexity, the problem becomes even more difficult. They have to simultaneously develop many channels for sensing environmental change, *and* link this information back to coordinating and planning mechanisms that steer the organization as a whole. Even frequent top team reviews or occasional middle-level scanning groups are too constricted, and specialized prioritizing mechanisms too slow.

The most complex cases are the "opportunity-driven" organizations like Citibank e-Solutions.[54] In addition to all the infrastructural elements already discussed—widespread strategic understanding, a culture of openness to criticism, and so on—such organizations may have regular opportunities for people at all levels to bring to bear their experiences on larger arguments about strategy.

Shell New Business Ventures had a structured process that has shown considerable promise in squaring this circle of uniting wide scanning with clear strategy: a system of "funneling" ideas through a series of reviews to assess their strategic impact and value, allowing for as many opportunities to enter the funnel while still screening for technical and economic feasibility as well as strategic fit. During the length of the process, projects were continually checked to ensure that they remained attractive to the organization both economically and strategically. The "checking" involved some self-management—the initiators of the opportunity were expected to evaluate it themselves against the strategic priorities of the organization. It also involved reviews by an Opportunity Evaluation Group, which involved people from multiple levels, and Business Development Coordinators drawn from higher leadership (Figure 19).

According to my interviews with employees at multiple levels, the various reviews have a very different "feel" from those in the more traditional parts of Shell: managers did not open or shut opportunities with a single word, but worked to engage all those parts of the organization that might be involved in or benefit from the opportunity under consideration, and to apply strategic principles that were visible to everyone and open to discussion. In this way the connection between strategy and environmental sensing was effectively broad, quick, and consistent.

The system described at Citibank e-Solutions in Chapter 3 shared most of these characteristics, though less formally and deliberately. Here, too, anyone could spot an opportunity and begin a process of trying to win support. Because

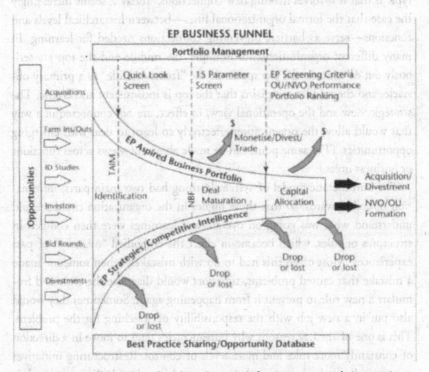

Figure 19: System of funneling ideas through a series of reviews to assess their strategic impact and value

of the strong strategic framework embedded in all the unit's processes, initiators needed to make the strategic case as well as showing benefits for the individuals to whom they appealed; and gradually, as the need for resources grew, they would need to appeal for them to higher levels. This produced the same "funneling" effect made explicit in the Shell model.[55]

## 4. Learning

Learning is a step beyond strategic planning. It involves not only the ability to pull together dispersed experiences into new patterns of action, but also the ability to reflect on basic values and principles. The pressure for responsiveness and innovation implies an increased need for systematic learning. As a result, a considerable industry has grown up around the idea of a "learning organization"; many companies have invested in everything from complex databases to building "communities of practice."

Probably the most important single thing we know about learning, of any type, is that it involves making new connections. Today it seems increasingly the case that the formal organizational lines—between hierarchical levels and functions—serve as barriers preventing connections needed for learning. In many different organizations, for example, the middle and the top are seriously out of contact: the top speaks of the "frozen middle" as a primary obstacle, and the middle complains that the top is inconsistent and erratic. The strategic view and the operational view, in effect, are not connected in a way that would allow the organization effectively to learn to deal with emerging opportunities. (The same point can be made about the views across functions or business units.)

The bureaucratic model of system learning had two main parts: information flowed upwards, so that those higher in the organization could see and understand what was going on overall; and learnings were then codified in structures or rules, which became in effect the embodied "memory" of past experiences. Most often this had to do with mistakes: when someone made a mistake that caused problems, superiors would diagnose the error and formulate a new rule to prevent it from happening again. Sometimes they would also put in a new job with the responsibility of watching for the problem. This is one of the key reasons why bureaucracies tend to move in a direction of constantly more rules and more levels of control. Restructuring initiatives may periodically hack away at the accretions, but unless the basic approach is changed they will inevitably grow back again.

This linear process exemplifies what Chris Argyris famously termed "single-loop" learning, going directly from problem to solution. Argyris proposed as an improvement a "double-loop" approach, which loops back to consider the significance of the experience for more general principles and values. He tried to apply this concept by getting individuals and small leadership groups to engage in reflective practice: analyzing the "theories in use" behind their decisions, testing them against data and experience, and modifying them as needed.[56]

Argyris always found it difficult to develop this reflective attitude among managers, even in small settings. The problem for a collaborative model of learning is immeasurably more difficult: to develop it on a large scale as an "organizational attitude"—to make it common to the way people operate across the system. Abstractly, this reflects the general problem of collaboration: to *distribute* learning capability, so more people in specialized positions can put things together in new ways, and at the same time to *coordinate* it so that it affects other parts of the organization as appropriate and enters into practical behaviors.

Cross-boundary task teams can be good at single-loop learning—as we have seen throughout this study, they do a good job at identifying new solutions by gathering diverse resources—but they are much less effective at the double-loop level. When they solve a problem, there is generally no good mechanism for reflecting on lessons that might be drawn for the future or for other parts of the system. In addition, the learning problem in collaborative systems is generally complicated by the fact that they are often in the midst of a major transition. The systems that did exist for learning are frequently dismantled before new ones can be instituted; institutional memory contained in the heads of long-term managers is often lost through downsizings.

> The problem is that people day-to-day just don't take the time to codify and communicate their learnings, except in personal networks. And you can't rely on personal networks any more. We've dismantled the functional departments which were the old structure for learning and put them into process flows. (Shell-SEPIV)

The companies in our sample showed enormous ingenuity and put great effort into attempts to solve this problem by formalizing the learning process. A number of these have succeeded in gathering data and connecting people more efficiently and thus generally improving the single-loop problem-solving process. They have been less successful, however, in double-loop reflection on principles:

1. Many initiatives have focused on building information systems that create connections across dispersed data. A number of cases suggest, however, that technology by itself rarely leads to sustained learning. If the traditional culture remains in place, units will resist giving up data—which was a key source of power in the bureaucratic model—and it will be poorly used. The different parts of the organization need to be *willing* to share and use data before the data are transformed into learning.

   The COMPASS system in Citibank is one example. This software system was designed to bring together many types of knowledge around new solutions and to create a database of knowledge that people could access when they needed it. The problem is that most people did not see its value and did not want to turn their information over to unknown forces. Thus it rather dramatically failed to take off despite considerable push from the top—as one manager put it, it was a case of "boom-splat."

2. A second widespread effort has been the formation of learning communities. Among our sample companies we looked particularly at efforts at Shell and the World Bank to develop "communities of practice" based on the theories of Etienne Wenger:[57] they built *deliberate* networks of people with shared interests, cutting across the formal organization boundaries and divorced from particular projects or tasks. In a sense, this approach differentiates learning from control: it says that learning can best happen in peer-based, knowledge-focused relationships that operate independent of the organization's control systems. This potentially "frees" learning from the defensiveness and limitations of the formal structure and, still more important, allows people to communicate across the normal organizational boundaries.

   Shell and the World Bank suggest a wide variance in success with this approach. The World Bank effort to establish "knowledge networks" was absorbed by the culture and became a manipulative tool for strengthening existing empires. By contrast, the Shell effort, occurring in an organization that had already gone a good deal further down the road of collaboration, was highly successful. The networks have compiled evidence of significant cost savings and new revenue generation. The networks also generated considerable enthusiasm and built ongoing discussions across widely different locations, business units, and even languages.[58]

   Yet there are limits even at this level, following directly from the separation between network and formal control structures. First, networks may have trouble "pulling things together" into a global perspective: they have no organized way of getting together all the people whose input is needed to validate their ideas. Second, if they do manage to pull together the people they need, they have few mechanisms for getting the learnings back out to the "line"; since these groups do not include those who have the resources they will need for implementation, they do not build up the support they need to break through to the operational leaders. They have to jump a considerable gap all at once at the end of the process.

The separation of structure from learning becomes problematic at the double-loop level, which is in its essence a connection between reflection and action. Though the learning community typically has links in to the "line" organization, they are relatively thin and late. Thus the looping process—the continual testing of connections to broader organizational policies and principles—is constrained for most of the process, and is likely to be dropped at the end. Our observation of even the generally successful case at Shell suggests a failure to systematically engage the policy-making level of the enterprise.[59]

A few impressive examples of reflective organizational learning do break through the "double-loop" barrier. I invent the term "review processes" to cover them, since this has not yet coalesced into a clear domain with a distinct name. By *review process* I mean bringing together mixed groups of stakeholders to look back over an initiative and draw lessons from it. An effective process then connects back to action—through effective involvement of decision makers, or through mechanisms that integrate the conclusions into the initiation process of future task teams.

ABB developed a number of review mechanisms as of the late 1990s and early 2000s, though we were unable to really document how well the learnings were put into practice:

1. A "Corporate Projects" group audited successful projects to see what was learned. These learnings were put into a three-day course on Corporate Projects. This course taught the corporate policies, provided a forum for project managers to share experiences and tell stories, and created a platform from which the leaders could communicate their priorities and values for projects. The course was also a way that cross-Business Area teams could reflect together on past lessons prior to launching a new project.

2. Every year starting in 1997, CEO Goren Lindahl met with the top 375 and included 25 people with less than five years of experience at ABB. These people were to observe what went on at the meeting and then report back to the Board about what was wrong and what needed to be changed.[60]

A still more thorough and sustained example of review processes are the Toyota "reflection reviews," which have been a major source of continuous improvement in the production process. Soon after a line reaches full production with a new model, Toyota documents the lessons learned through meetings and data-gathering among several levels from the front-line upward, and even extending to suppliers. The lessons are codified according to the usual *kaizen* process, identifying problems and proposing counter-measures. Finally, they include a formalized process for passing the knowledge gained onto the next launch team as a starting point for future work. This process, documented by careful observers,[61] is one of the closest I have encountered to a true double-loop organizational system, and it seems to have served the company very well.

In our own sample Veridian went through a "strategic fitness process" described more closely in Chapter 9. There a team of respected mid-level managers went throughout the organization conducting interviews to identify the obstacles to implementation of the strategy; they brought their learnings back to top management for an intense and often confrontational discussion that at times led to major organizational breakthroughs. As at Toyota, a major part of the process was a deliberate connection between the learnings and new action plans, which were reviewed by the study team and debated with strategic managers. In some companies, including parts of Hewlett-Packard, this internal study process has been regularly repeated for a number of years.[62]

At the far end lies IBM's plans—by its own admission, far from achieved—for "on demand learning." It has sketched out a highly elaborate "learning system architecture" as a central element of its move to a full solutions capability. This involves, among other things, replacing the separate databases in the different "stovepipes" with an integrating "middleware" of widely accessible information, and creating a "Learning Management Council" to coordinate and manage the processes of development and gathering of new knowledge.

These cases of systematic review, by broadening learning processes beyond the formal hierarchy, greatly increase the capacity of people to engage with each other flexibly and openly. The Toyota and Hewlett-Packard studies have been able to document the growth of collaboration and the overcoming of organizational barriers and stovepipes.

## CROSS-FIRM INFRASTRUCTURE

An important condition for the spread of extended collaboration has been the development of infrastructure that crosses firm boundaries. In the early phases of industrialism, as I have mentioned, crucial social institutions evolved to provide support for the changing demands of work. Schools, for example, increasingly emphasized virtues valuable in bureaucratic systems, such as dutifulness, exactness, and promptness. Cities developed in ways that provided labor markets near at hand. Later, roads built by the government became an essential base for distribution. A whole network of institutions grew up around the dominant pattern of long, stable careers within firms.

The move to collaboration creates new demands on trans-firm infrastructure. One rather striking one is the need for general business literacy. I have stressed that collaboration requires an orientation on the part of everyone to common strategy, rather than just to the performance of job duties. This requires as a foundation a *general* commitment to business values and a broad understanding of basic strategic issues—of competition, the role of innovation and knowledge, and basic financial concepts of profit and growth.

Until the 1980s these basic elements were largely missing except for a small group of elites coming out of business schools and destined for top management positions; the vast bulk of employees had no idea of how businesses worked overall and expected only to do the jobs assigned to them. But in the last quarter-century in the United States there has been a rapid spread of both commitment and understanding of business concepts to a much wider population. It is only in that time frame that business sections have become common in daily newspapers, that evening news shows have dedicated segments to international trade, that everyone down to the poorest classes have become aware of how credit works and have begun to think about money markets and other investment vehicles formerly reserved for the wealthy few. A key result is that employees at all levels are far more open than before to learning about the strategic issues of their companies and trying to contribute to them.

Comparisons with social infrastructure in emerging markets like India help to highlight a number of other ways in which institutions in advanced economies have evolved to support extended collaboration. There are, for example, far more developed certification systems that provide a broad basis of reputation for specialized skills, so that companies can reach with confidence beyond their own boundaries rather than relying on those they know from internal development. Labor markets—despite the confusions and struggles that we will look at in the next chapter—are relatively far more mobile, with better adult education and information systems for job-switchers. Consumer groups make product information much more widely available, which creates pressure for continual recombination and innovation.[63] Educational systems stress interactive learning and teamwork rather than rote memorization.

At another level, companies have been paying increasing attention to cross-firm business systems linking them to allies and competitors. In the computer industry, coalitions for standard-setting are now routine; they enable companies to pursue specialized products with confidence that these will "fit" with other elements sought by consumers, but made by other companies. This is an essential element in the success of solutions strategies like IBM's, which bring together whatever products are needed to fill particular needs. The International Standards Organization (ISO) establishes process standards and conducts certification inspections; though these are voluntary, they have become in practice mandatory in all complex industries because all companies want to have confidence that those who interface with them will be able to make reliable handoffs along the networks of interdependence.[64]

In general, businesses are thinking actively about their interdependencies with others and seeking actively to manage those relationships: Citibank's e-Solutions unit cultivates relationships with software vendors, auto producers build—in the most successful cases—webs of relationships to suppliers,[65] and so on. These have created a broader infrastructure that now makes it much easier than before for businesses to work together around complex tasks rather than trying to master all aspects internally.

## CONCLUSION

The extraordinary pace of innovation in infrastructural mechanisms—new ways of organizing processes, of building networks, of coordinating learnings, of building shared understanding—is an indicator of the rapid development of collaborative enterprise in the past twenty years. These mechanisms establish essential mutual understanding, standardization of codes and languages, and orientation to a common purpose. The ability to response to changing demands without strong top-down structuring depends on this consistency of the underlying systems.

These most important infrastructural systems for collaboration—though this is far from a complete list—include broad diffusion of strategic knowledge, information transparency, shared process codes, negotiation skills, new network roles, sensing mechanisms, and interactive planning. Other important areas are still very much in flux, and the resolution is hard to predict. I take up the two most important of these—accountability and career systems—in Chapter 6.

Chapter 8.

# Chapter 6 Two Unresolved
# Problems

Despite very considerable advances in recent decades, few of the infrastructural innovations described so far are stable or routinized; the general
condition of most companies is one of very active experimentation. But there
are two areas in which, for different reasons, the difficulties are particularly
significant and unresolved: accountability and careers.

## ACCOUNTABILITY

Of all the difficulties of collaboration, accountability may be the one that
presents the most day-to-day vexations; everyone wants to know: What is expected of me? How will I be rewarded? How can I get those who I am responsible for to do what they're supposed to? It is also an area that has seen
enormous change in recent years, an explosion of programs of "pay for performance" and "performance management"—and that remains highly contested
and confused.

Historically, accountability has been caught between the two contrary tendencies that we have seen throughout this study. On the one hand, pure bureaucracy is highly individualist and performance oriented and requires high

job performance. On the other, the need for cooperation and reliability has led bureaucracies to establish cultures of loyalty and "familial" caring that are softer and more diffuse, rewarding conformity and personal fidelity.

The result was traditionally an uneasy compromise. The formal appraisal system has always been highly performance based. The overwhelmingly dominant form was "Management by Objectives" or MBO, a system developed during the 1920s and 1930s in General Motors and other leaders of the bureaucratic revolution:[1] this required supervisors to establish yearly goals for their subordinates and then to reward them based on their achievement of those targets. Yet the reality always differed sharply from this formal system. Numerous studies have documented the startling fact that the actual spread in compensation between the best and worst performers rarely exceeded 2 percent.[2] Managers went through the motions of establishing objectives and doing appraisals but did not make sharp distinctions among their subordinates. They consistently felt that to make strong differentiations among their personal reports would sow discord and destroy the valued sense of diffuse loyalty.

The growing sense during the 1980s that bureaucracy was too slow and unresponsive, together with the rise in layoffs and restructurings, led to a major shift in attitude. Managers felt that they needed tighter, faster promotion systems that did not depend on the availability of promotion opportunities. So they began to emphasize short-term individual objectives, and to offer monetary rewards for good performance. The field of "performance management" was born and became one of the most widespread, highly touted reforms of the period; HR departments went through wave after wave of programs aiming to link pay to achievement of goals.[3]

The irony is that in this enormous, controversial, painful set of changes companies succeeded only in reinventing Management by Objectives. The operation of modern pay-for-performance systems are not in any significant respect different from that of Sloan's systems of the 1920s, or for that matter from Frederick Taylor's methods two decades before that: set targets for your subordinates, measure their performance against the targets, reward those who do well, and punish those who do not.

Not too surprisingly, this move has encountered fierce, though usually covert, resistance of very much of the same kind that it encountered in its first incarnation a century ago. Supervisors have balked at making distinctions among their subordinates, arguing (at least in private, and in my interviews) that setting people against each other does more harm than good. Thus over and over top-driven efforts to increase individual rewards have been thwarted at the middle levels. The response has frequently been to up the ante, forcing differentiation by requiring middle managers to grade their subordinates on a "forced curve," with a certain percentage in the lowest category. These are, in effect, a declaration of internal war, an attempt from above to force behavioral changes on unwilling middle managers. Eight of the fourteen organizations I studied in the early 1990s had recently instituted such programs.[4] I have seen several instances in which the middle managers continue the battle by devising evasive stratagems, such as rotating the bad rankings among their subordinates (and telling them all that they are doing so); top management then tries to invent new mechanisms to prevent this. The war has sometimes erupted into the open: in one particularly dramatic series of events at General Motors in the mid-1990s, the revolt from the middle became so loud that top management actually backed off and withdrew the requirement. And the pattern continues: IBM began the use of forced curves in the late 1990s for the same reasons, then backed off them in 2005.[5]

## The Transitional Role of Pay for Performance

I described in Chapter 4 how the performance ethic has played the role of "breaking" the culture of loyalty and bridging toward a culture of contribution. Pay for performance has been in effect the primary infrastructural tool in this transition. What it does do, quite clearly, is to shatter the whole pattern of expectations built around dependence on the supervisor and the informal teamwork of subordinates. In doing so, it frees up the system for more rapid action: goals can be readjusted more quickly and jobs can be more easily reassigned to those who are best for them; poor performers can be moved out, with resultant cost savings. Thus the battle over pay for performance does have a strong "ventilating" effect on slow-moving traditionalist organizations, forcing everyone to focus on new things. My own observation supports the notion that immediate improvements in performance do often flow from the "shaking up" effect of new systems, their ability to force people out of traditional patterns of behaviors, and the one-time impact of removing some of the low performers often hidden in the cracks of paternalist organizations.

Pay for performance in its usual form, however, is insufficient: it takes organizations one step forward but not two. It is effective in breaking the bureaucratic culture and taking apart the motivations and webs of informal relationships that have become obstacles to innovation—the empires and fiefdoms, the expectation of lifetime security; but it has been less successful in building a positive collaborative culture, leading instead to internal tension and poor cooperation.

The "good" side of pay for performance is reflected in a few broad surveys on pay systems and corporate performance. Though the research is remarkably sparse given the importance of the topic, there are some findings that competitive rewards broadly correlate with improved performance.[6] The "bad" side, meanwhile, is revealed in almost all detailed observational studies. Nearly every experimental observation of group behavior—the kind of research conducted by experimental social psychologists—finds that competitive reward systems are bad for group performance, and that more equal rewards work better; this is an enormous and long-running literature, with great sophistication, running back a half-century, and with rather consistent results.[7] Actual observational research in corporate settings similarly finds that individualist, competitive rewards lead to counterproductive dynamics.[8]

The generally positive survey results reflect the fact that firms that have instituted strong pay for performance plans have generally been aggressive in attacking the culture of paternalist bureaucracy, and that they have gained a considerable initial boost in performance by freeing up the system. But the underlying and longer-term cultural problems show up more clearly in the detailed observational or experimental studies. In terms of diagnosing the future, the latter kind of research is likely to be more accurate in bringing out the difficulties caused over time by competitive reward systems.

### Pay for Performance and Collaboration

Pay for performance systems, with few exceptions, are built on the same assumptions as traditional bureaucratic models.[9] In particular, they remain oriented to the immediate superior: both goals and evaluation come entirely from this one spot. When applied to collaborative systems, this creates several critical problems.

1. It assumes that the boss knows what needs to be done. This assumption was reasonably accurate in a world in which the supervisor had moved up through the same jobs and understood them well; it is entirely inaccurate in more dynamic systems with high levels of specialized knowledge. Lower level employees now often know things that the boss does not, and they often can spot and understand new opportunities faster, since they may be closer to the customers or at least have a different set of relationships.

2. It assumes that the boss can accurately evaluate subordinates' performance. Again, this is relatively true in a bureaucratic setting where the

span of control is five or six subordinates and the supervisor can follow performance closely; it becomes false when organizations are flatter and the span of control increases, as it has widely in industry, and even more false in complex collaborative settings when subordinates work on multiple projects, some of which may be entirely outside their superior's purview.

The response to this increasing complexity of evaluation has generally been to increase formal measurement. Consultants propose, and companies increasingly use, a bewildering array of measurement instruments from "hard" productivity to "soft" attitude measures; some business gurus say one should "measure everything."[10] This would clearly solve the problem of dispersed activity by allowing the supervisor to get accurate snapshots of subordinate performance.

But of course it isn't possible to measure everything: one can measure some things well, but not necessarily the things that are important. Increased measurement therefore has the perverse effect of focusing people sharply on particular aspects of their jobs rather than on the whole picture. If you try to measure all things, most of them will be measured badly—and a bad measurement may be worse than none at all.

To use the clearest example: creative activity is necessarily inconsistent and unpredictable; a person who has a brilliant idea generating millions of dollars one year may go fallow for another. Further, creativity generally results from "divergent" approaches—not following a specified track, but trying out unexpected avenues; thus it may come up with something different than the original intent, but still valuable. Attempts to measure these kinds of activity cannot capture the real value added, and so will only lead people to do the wrong things or to manipulate their reports.[11]

Assessing the value of ongoing complex work, in other words, requires *informed judgment*. Supervisors can apply that kind of judgment when they are close to the work, but not—as is increasingly the case—when they are distant and distracted. To apply rigorous objective measures that can be applied from a distance can only result in missing the point.

3. Performance measurement assumes that goals can be determined in advance. There are of course some general and long-term goals that remain constant in all systems; but the point of a responsive strategy is that it must be able to reorient its purposes as the environment changes. In successful collaborative systems, people must be able to spot new opportunities and

mobilize resources to develop them. If they are measured on objectives that are set at the start of the year, either those objectives must be very vague or they should be obsolete by the end of it.

4. Pay for performance is based on the assumption that people control the resources they need to perform the tasks that they are assessed on. This is of course a central tenet of bureaucracy, but it breaks down in collaborative systems where people are highly interdependent with others and must negotiate for resources.

> The big problem of course is the split of accountability and responsibility. In a capture team, everybody is accountable for his bit, so nobody is accountable for the total. The one who is accountable for the total is the AM or capture team leader, and that one has no power. (ABB)

> Supervisor-focused performance measurement as usually practiced almost inevitably leads people to try to gain greater control over resources so that they can manage their own destiny.

> No one wants to give up the business. The parties that didn't agree have many lapover initiatives and responsibilities. No one could resolve the conflicts, no one would cooperate. There is frequent tension from crossing boundaries—how does the ownership get fixed? (Citibank e-Solutions)

> The number one adversary of effective collaboration is the personal need to want to amass responsibility and ownership of a turf. I think that's the number one obstacle. (Citibank e-Solutions)

5. Finally, supervisor-driven performance measurement inevitably fails to capture one of the key dimensions in a collaborative system, which is people's willingness to help each other.

> A colleague called me, I gave him four or five people to bail him out of a problem. But that meant that they were not there to do the work I needed. Was it the right thing to do for the shareholder? You bet. Was it the right thing to do for my own performance appraisals? I don't think so. I doubt it.[12]

Thus accountability in collaborative settings is caught in an essential contradiction: the assessment of performance and the maintenance of accountability require higher levels of sophisticated judgment, but the supervisors, who are entrusted with the task, are less able to make those judgments because they know less about what their subordinates are doing.[13]

The companies in our sample had a great deal of trouble with accountability and reward systems. Virtually all of them had shifted tack multiple times, with most moving through the unhappy sequence I have described: energetic attempts to push pay for performance, followed by resistance, the institution of forced-curve ranking systems, and multiplication of measurements.

In interviews with middle managers and professionals in the more successful "level 4" organizations, I found a very interesting and paradoxical result: there is a curious disconnect between people's behaviors and the compensation system. Most people, especially the most energetic and successful ones, largely ignore the compensation system in their daily work. This is true of the interviews I did during the early 1990s[14] as well as more recent ones: I heard over and over that entrepreneurial middle managers do *not* try to orient themselves to the increasingly detailed and complicated measurements that they are subjected to; they don't even understand them very well.

> I can share my understanding of my compensation system [laughs]—I don't know
> if it will jibe with anyone else's. . . . There's a lot of confusion about the context in
> which reward decision-making occurs. (Citibank e-Solutions)

But this does not stop them from working hard and productively. They believe that they understand very clearly what needs to be done, and they go out and do it—with the expectation that somehow, in time, more or less, the compensation system will catch up and give them a fair reward. Thus, when I discussed accountability with one Citibank person who was involved in alliance projects, but not on the Alliance team, we had this exchange:

> [Does the alliance manager have any input into your evaluation?] As far as I know
> probably not.
>   [So why do you put time into this?] Because I think it is an important function
> that we must fulfill in order to achieve our goal of being the leading e-Business
> provider in the world.

"As far as I know": this person was not even sure whether this work was or was not going to be reflected on his evaluation. "Because it is an important function . . . to achieve our goal": he was committed to the mission of the organization and oriented himself to achieving it rather than to meeting artificial targets. Or, as another put it at Shell-SEPIV: "There is no way of measuring how the job is done. The question should be whether everything that you have done has added value to SEPIV." If there's anyone who really pays attention to the details of the measurements and compensation system in this environment, it is the lesser performers, those who are uncertain, those who seek an artificial "edge" by playing the system.[15] The best performers go straight to the mission.

This implicit appeal to people's better instincts, as it were, seems to work in these settings, but it is not an adequate system for the long term. People may plow ahead for awhile on the basis of collaborative values in the expectation that things will sort out, but sooner or later the compensation system actually has to support those values. And that is where we have very little solid experience and data: what kind of reward system would really work to manage collaborative activity? In my research, I have not yet found a level 4 organization where the professionals and middle managers say, "Our accountability system really helps."

### Collaborative Accountability: Reward for Contribution

Here we need to loop back to theory, to see what the logic of a collaborative system suggests about accountability within it; then we can see what actual practice suggests about working out, in place of "pay for performance," a system of "reward for contribution."

The question is *not* whether individual performance should be rewarded; that is a red herring that often confuses the issue. Collaboration is not a warm, fuzzy system that tolerates poor work. In fact, the only system that downplays performance—that can hide incompetent or uncooperative people for long periods of time—is traditional paternalist bureaucracy, with its strong emphasis on familial stability. Collaboration in its extended form, when people are helping with multiple projects extending beyond any local team or structure, puts a tremendous premium on individual performance: everyone needs to have confidence, in reaching out to people whom they don't know personally, that they will find in those people both competence and motivation to help. They are very intolerant of violations of this trust.

The problem is not the emphasis on performance as such, but the way performance is assigned and judged. In the bureaucratic form of performance management, supervisors assign jobs and judge their people on how well they do them. The logic of collaborative enterprise points to different solutions for two main elements of accountability:

• The first derives from the value of contribution, as described in Chapter 4. As the managers just cited indicate, *people should be judged on their contribution to the mission or purposes of the organization*—not on doing "a good job"

Table 7  Types of Accountability

|  | Bureaucratic | Collaborative |
|---|---|---|
| *What*:<br>   Assessment criteria | Fulfillment of specified objectives<br>with competence and reliability | Contribution to the<br>collective purpose |
| *How*:<br>   Assessment method | Supervisor judgment | Multisource appraisal |

in the sense of reliability and competence, not on merely meeting targets, but on whether they actually added value to the collective effort.

- The second follows from the fluid, interactive nature of the system, with a great deal of cross-boundary teamwork: people should be judged not primarily by their supervisors, but *by the whole range of people that they work with and contribute to.*

Thus collaborative accountability should differ from the bureaucratic logic on *what* is assessed and *how* it is assessed (Table 7). What does actual practical experience tell us about these elements?

### Assessment on the Basis of Contribution

If it is hard to judge how well people do their jobs in a complex environment, it is even harder to judge whether they have made a contribution to the larger enterprise. That would require something that is very far from the traditional mindset: driving strategic awareness through the entire system, and connecting rewards and sanctions to these broader themes.

At least one influential innovation in accountability in the last decade, however, has moved a long way in this direction: the "Balanced Scorecard" (BSC) of Kaplan and Norton, used by many of the companies I studied. Originally this was an effort to broaden the conception of accountability: it added qualitative measures such as employee satisfaction and customer loyalty to traditional financial and operational measures. In effect this initial emphasis of the BSC added a capacity for complexity to the system, pushing people to take into account multiple dimensions of strategy and to work through competing priorities where there was no algorithm for resolving conflicts.

As the approach has evolved it has moved even closer to the concept of contribution. Over the past decade, the emphasis has shifted from "balance" to "strategy"—that is, in the direction of tying accountability throughout the organization directly to strategic priorities. Kaplan and Norton's 2001 book focuses heavily on this theme:

*Make strategy everyone's everyday job.* Use the Balanced Scorecard to educate the organization about strategy, help employees develop personal objectives, then compensate them based on their adherence to and implementation of the business' strategies.[16]

This is the essence of the notion of assessment by contribution: rather than orienting people to narrow and particular pieces of the system, to orient them and assess them based on their contribution to the whole. The respondents at Citibank cited earlier were orienting themselves to the strategy—"our goal of being the leading e-business provider in the world"—in an intuitive and unsystematic way. The large industry of assessment systems that have grown up around the BSC in effect try to make this orientation the systematic core of accountability.

Like almost everything we have looked at, the BSC concept can be "reduced" to a bureaucratic version. This happens when it is implemented by first defining "balanced" strategic objectives, then defining particular jobs in relation to those objectives, then giving specific jobs to specific people and measuring them on those pieces. There is commonly a pull in this direction, because it fits so well the long-established logic: define the big picture from above and break it down into little chunks as you move down. But by advocating "Make strategy everyone's everyday job," Kaplan and Norton are running straight into the teeth of this "chunking" approach and of a century's worth of habits that sharply separate strategy from operations. Though they do not directly deal with the issue of collaboration, they are establishing in this way an essential piece of the infrastructure for flexible, boundary-crossing collaborative systems.

### Assessment through Multisource Appraisal

The next problem is how to make accurate judgments about individuals' contributions to the strategic goals of the firm. I have argued that the supervisor is not in a good position for this assessment, nor is there any simple *objective* way to do it. The resolution in collaborative systems must be to gather the judgments of those who are in a position to assess performance—which is the whole range of collaborators, people who have worked with and interacted with the person in question.

An innovation that leads in this direction is the strand often called "360-degree feedback": appraisals that seek input not just from the supervisor but also from subordinates and peers. Some version of the "360" or multisource method is used by most of the companies in my sample, and by all of those who have crossed the collaborative frontier. Estimates of its use from surveys vary considerably but perhaps cluster around 25 to 30 percent of companies.[17]

The actual experience of multisource or 360-degree efforts among our sample companies, like that reported in the wider literature,[18] is mixed. It is difficult to make these systems work: they are subject to resistance and manipulation. The fundamental reason, interpreting my interviews, is that these efforts directly confront some of the most powerful norms of the bureaucratic order: autonomy, deference, and peer solidarity. The first says that one should leave others alone to do their jobs (while they leave you alone to do yours); the second says that one should not challenge the boss; the third involves the powerful norm against "ratting out" one's peers to superiors, and also can legitimize peer cooperation to support each other against interventions from above.

But 360-degree feedback asks people to forget all of that. They are asked to evaluate their own bosses—infringing on a taboo as old as human history: the taboo against attacks on the father. Quite naturally, that generates fear and discomfort that come out in awkward jokes about honesty as a death sentence. At the same time, they may be asked to give honest evaluations of their peers, which breaks another, equally ancient taboo—that against turning against your brothers and sisters. It is not surprising that these efforts are widely disliked when they are first instituted, especially so when they are formalized in the hands of the HR department, which is widely seen in middle management as a secret agent of the top.

Thus a common reaction, according to some of my respondents, is for people to game the system by making deals with peers: I'll say good things about you if you say good things about me. It is also quite common for comments about supervisors to be muted and vague. Both of these responses greatly reduce the value of multisource feedback. In the end, the discomfort caused by the system is so high, that it, like other variants of pay for performance, sometimes fails outright: IBM had a strong initiative of this type in the late 1990s, and there was near-universal relief when it was shelved a few years later.

Can 360-degree feedback work in spite of all the obstacles? I have seen a number of successful cases in our research, but only in the environment of level 4 organizations with extended collaboration. Successful 360-degree feedback requires, first, open rather than closed communities; and second, strong connections to shared strategic purposes.

- In local communities and bounded groups, people do not want to evaluate others because they know they will have to deal with them in the future. Efforts to introduce peer appraisal into semi-autonomous teams have therefore had very limited success: in the best cases they are useful for developmental feedback, but are almost always resisted when used for discipline or rewards.
- Most multisource approaches also suffer by failing to make the link to the common purpose. The instruments commonly used involve elaborate and detailed lists of behaviors developed by outside experts; they are disconnected from the key issues of strategy that really matter to people and around which they feel a sense of interdependence.[19] Thus where I have encountered formalized systems, middle and lower managers regularly complain that the exercise seems abstract and academic: "It's another tick box exercise. It's that time of year again, let's get it out of the way and get on with some real work."[20]

Under conditions of extended collaboration and strategic focus, however, multisource feedback produces a strong sense of fairness and supports interdependence. Our research contains quite a few cases of success in level 4 organizations that have made the mental shift to a culture of contribution. Some are relatively informal: at Citibank e-Solutions, as described in Chapter 3, people spoke very freely about each other's performance—the taboo against criticizing peers had largely disappeared—and this communication was central to the whole process of creating teams around opportunities. I heard in great detail how those who did not contribute fully to team efforts were gradually marginalized in the group until they had few opportunities to succeed; only at that point might the hierarchical superiors step in to make a "performance" judgment.

> Communications are so open and expectations so high that you can't hide for long. After a while someone says, "What is this person doing?" And then the boss and the country head and others talk about it.

Other instances are more formalized. Another part of Citibank, the Customer Relationships Management system, assessed people in part based on twice-yearly internal surveys in which everyone ranked their peers on how they interacted with others, how much help they provided, and whether they had good ideas. Each person might rate more than 70 others—not only members of their own local groups, but everyone with whom they had regular contact, including people in Headquarters and in other countries. At "NewTech," which had a very strong purpose-driven culture, peer review showed up in almost every aspect. Projects received rigorous cross-department peer reviews at each of four major stages in their development; for individuals, managers served in effect as coordinators rather than as judges for the annual rank-and-review process, gathering data on their subordinates from various teams. And at a large consulting firm documented by Carlos Martin, those who are not honest and rigorous in their judgments of others, in the frequent peer review processes, are themselves sanctioned for undermining the system of information on which everyone depends.[21]

In these cases multisource evaluations are clearly built around the issues that everyone cares about—not elaborate behavioral "tick boxes," but small numbers of clearly relevant categories of the type defined in BSC processes. The combination of relevance to the purpose and involvement of a network of collaborators creates a powerful organizational advantage visible to everyone.

*Reputation.* To the extent that peer assessments become frequent, open, and accurate, they ground a reliable system of *reputation* that becomes the core of accountability. Reputation is in effect the history of past performance. In a bureaucratic order, the supervisor becomes the keeper of reputation, but no one else has much information. One result is that it becomes relatively easy to play games with reputations, through backdoor whispering campaigns or Iago-like suggestions to superiors; these insinuations are hard to shake because contrary data are few.[22] In the systems just described, by contrast, reputation is constantly being constructed from many sources, and it is therefore more robust and complete—and more useful in building effective task teams.

> If you give people tools, knowledge, intelligence, tips, hints, you get a positive reputation. It's saying to people, "I'm here to help you." (Citibank e-Solutions)

> I think when I get suspicious is when I hear things through Chinese whispers. (Citibank e-Solutions)

The systems have the advantage of being robust on a wider scale, rather than depending on personal conversations, and should therefore be better in the long run for larger networks.

Yet although reputational information has become more open, it has rarely become highly formalized: companies may use multisource feedback for rewards and accountability, but the results are never publicized widely. There are still severe resistances to openness. It would be hard to imagine companies, for instance, publishing "peer reviews" of people's performance as is done in science or in some open-source software efforts; this would be too deep a challenge to the traditions of hierarchy, and to the norms of peer banding for protection against superiors.

From a theoretical point of view, these limitations on the explicitness of reputation are harmful to collaboration, making it easier to distort the system and to maintain power based on hoarding information. This is an area where practice has not advanced far enough to make a good judgment about whether there is a better alternative, and it is an indication of the difficulty of the path to greater collaboration.

## Obstacles to Progress on Accountability

The arena of accountability and rewards has been particularly difficult, contentious, and slow in embracing collaborative principles. The problems lie in two deep conceptual and ideological obstacles common to corporate leadership.

First, accountability mechanisms are one of the easiest levers for leaders to pull when they are trying to transform organizations. They do produce rapid behavioral change: people will seek to meet new performance standards, especially when they are linked to significant rewards. In a turbulent environment which values leaders as heroic transformers, changing these systems is a dramatic and immediate way for leaders to make their mark.

The long-term problems show up only later. I have already discussed how often these efforts spark battles between levels and groups, and our cases indicate clearly that using compensation to drive change undermines collaboration.[23] When the culture as a whole remains bureaucratic, when people are still concerned mainly with what their boss thinks and believe that is what "really" counts, when people still believe it is wrong to talk about others' performance—then 360-degree feedback and the Balanced Scorecard will decline into cynical manipulation. People may fill out the required feedback forms or objectives, but they will not participate in a spirit of building a collaborative environment.

Worse, in the absence of other aspects of culture and infrastructure, performance-based compensation systems merely reinforce bureaucracy—making people focus on their own jobs and their own turfs, weakening even existing informal cooperative links:

There's still a lot of feeling among people that for performance evaluation, you're rated only as one single individual, one single contribution—why should you work with anybody else to make that work any better? (AT&T)

People are getting their salary grades all in line and checked and secured. And I think that's really created an environment where people compete in a very unhealthy way with each other. And instead of sharing information, they close information. (AT&T)

In general, the story from these cases and the interviews behind them suggests that compensation and the formal accountability system needs to follow other moves toward more collaborative expectations, and support those who go outside their defined job duties to make wider contributions—but not to try to impel people to take such actions. People are motivated to collaboration by enthusiasm about the mission of the organization and an attitude of wanting to help others, not by trying to hit numbers in an appraisal system.

I am kind of dedicated to every customer's success. It is not directly on my [appraisal form]. But I am going to do it, because I get great solace and trust in the fact that there is a value kind of steering me. (IBM)

The real task of effective leadership is to nurture such commitment rather than trying to force compliance through accountability systems.

### The Value Problem

A second and even more essential reason for the difficulty of accountability for contribution is that it comes up against a central aspect of the modern ethic: the notion of the morally autonomous individual. Locke and Rousseau in the seventeenth and eighteenth centuries formulated the revolutionary notion that the individual existed prior to and apart from society and that social order was merely an agreement among these morally independent creatures. The writers of the American Declaration of Independence took this up in their justification for rebellion: "All men . . . are endowed by their Creator with certain inalienable rights"—rights that need to be protected against the encroachments of social oppression.

In this performance mindset the use of accountability and rewards as tools of change are morally right because they respect the autonomy of the individual. If a superior offers pay for performance, the subordinate has (in theory) a choice about whether to accept or not, and so can maintain his moral independence. The pattern of paternalism, by contrast, makes everyone a bit uneasy by demanding moral deference to the social order. A legion of critics have elaborated on William H. Whyte's distaste for the "Organization Man's subordination and conformity to the collective."[24]

Thus Management by Objectives achieves a curious paradox: it actually increases managerial power, and yet is justified as liberating. This is just a special case of the larger paradox of modernity, in which the autonomy of the individual has gone hand in hand with the growing power of the state and corporate hierarchies.

The belief in the moral rightness of pay for performance, much more than any practical evidence, justifies senior managers in forcing performance-based compensation systems on unwilling subordinates. What is strange is that when I have asked them, they have been unable to come up with persuasive evidence that these systems actually work. Thus they frequently fall back on ideological justifications:

> The company is pay for performance, so everything comes down to the individual. Does that inhibit collaboration? I don't really . . . I don't know. Maybe—because in the end it is going to be me against my peers. However, I think it is the whole, you know—not just pay for performance good or bad versus pay everyone the same, which is socialism, you know.[25]

The academic literature has followed much the same path. To a remarkable degree it is concerned with working out the details of implementing the initial assumption rather than testing it. Major theoretical orientations have been built around the core assumption of the value of individual incentives—especially agency theory and psychological variants including the expectancy and reinforcement perspectives. Reward systems have then been tested on a wide range of dimensions: measurement accuracy, reactions and perceptions of usefulness, ratees' self-esteem, acceptance of evaluation results, the psychometric characteristics of the tools, gender or racial biases in evaluation, and internal validity. What is largely missing from most of this research is evidence on the core point: Do individual incentives actually improve organizational functioning? Studies focused on that question are astonishingly sparse for a policy that has been so widespread and controversial. There are many studies that look at the results on individual motivation; but for all the reasons suggested, this doesn't tell us much about whether the organization functions better. Individuals can be highly motivated and work very hard, yet not advance the performance of the system as a whole, or not in the right direction.[26]

The collaborative ethic stands on a different moral base: not performance, but *results* for the collective goal. It values not "doing a good job" but rather "making a difference." Clarity about this distinction is crucial to successful collaboration. It is quite possible to do a good job, and to have an organization full of people who do good jobs, yet fail to achieve the goal. This is in fact the quintessential bureaucratic pathology of Kafka's *The Trial*: individuals who perform perfectly rationally and competently yet produce an irrational result. Collaboration can have no tolerance for this type of failure.

But the standard of "making a difference" breaks with the modern notion of moral autonomy by centering on the individual's interrelation to a larger social group. Rather than contrasting dependence on the collective with individual independence, the notion of contribution is based on a conception of social order as a network of *inter*dependent individuals and groups. Thus it depends on things beyond the individual's control—one may work hard and "perform" well, yet fail to contribute. Middle managers in level 4 organizations, as I argued in Chapter 4, have generally adopted such an ethic; but even in the better enterprises we have studied, there is little connection between the formal compensation system and this sense of collective contribution.

I know of only one study, using methods of experimental social psychology, that tests the effectiveness of a reward system based on contribution. Fred Gordon and others used a laboratory setting to compare compensation approaches ranging from complete equality to pure individualistic performance; the most effective one was neither of these classic alternatives, but one that rewarded people to the degree that they contributed to the success of the group. The philosophical source of this model of reward was John Rawls's "difference principle," which justifies inequality to the degree that it benefits the least advantaged. This type of compensation indeed produced, in the limited experimental condition, the highest levels of collaboration and high overall performance.[27]

This is not sufficient evidence on which to base an empirical case for "reward for contribution," but it does at least bring into focus the paucity of research supporting other forms. This is itself an indicator that the pay-for-performance movement is driven more by values and ideology than by evidence of success[28]— leaving a continuing gap in practice between performance management systems and the increasingly collaborative nature of organizations.

## CAREERS

The economic turbulence since the 1974 recession has caused havoc with the stable, coherent career systems that had been built up in the previous half-century.

Starting in the 1980s the general rhetoric of career expectations shifted dramatically: as company after company was forced to engage in layoffs, leaders increasingly downplayed the value of loyalty and advocated instead tough performance standards and willingness to remove deadwood. It also appears that there has been considerable thinning of bureaucratic layers. This is harder to document: though many companies have claimed to have cut layers, I have certainly seen cases where they have grown back in short order, often in subtle forms using new titles that do not call attention to the renewed hierarchical positioning. Nevertheless, it is generally true that middle managers perceive much less upward opportunity than they did at the height of the bureaucratic regime.

Our sample reflects the wider trend: nearly all of them had been through the painful transition from a general, though tacit, expectation of high employment security to an acceptance of layoffs as a fact of life. Today there is hardly an executive-level leader in any company whom I talk to who does not embrace a language of "employability" and career flexibility, a value frame that says people should constantly learn new skills and be prepared to move in search of new challenges.

Though much of this change has been driven by simple cost-cutting motives, it is broadly consistent with the logic of collaboration. One of the core ideas is that it should be easy to gather resources around projects and tasks— to get people who know useful things to the right place at the right time; that capability is a huge strategic advantage in the solutions arena.[29] Long and narrow hierarchical career paths get in the way of this flexibility by locking people in to confined channels and creating barriers to collaboration. Thus one would expect these paths, and the promise of employment security that underlay them, to give way to more fluid networks of career movement.

In the ideal collaborative system, there would be a high degree of choice for both employees and employers. Rather than being "stuck" with their current situation, as in the paternalist model, both would feel free to seek opportunities and resources that fit their current needs. Employees would be able to define their basic interests, capabilities, and needs, and to find a company whose purposes and values matched them; employers would be able to adapt their strategic missions and to find people who could contribute quickly. Companies would not guarantee security but would promise challenges and experiences that would make people "employable," thus increasing their security not within the firm but over a labor market and career. This matching process would on the one hand maximize knowledge production, and also, from the point of view of the employee, increase diversity, choice, and involvement.

Though this vision fits with much current rhetoric, the reality is far less harmonious. There are great obstacles to achieving this kind of knowledge flexibility, and few models to draw on.

First, it seems clear that most of the costs of labor flexibility are currently borne by employees: they suffer on average significant permanent loss of income[30] as well as temporary loss of affordable health coverage and high uncertainty. Thus most employees quite accurately perceive mobility not as an opportunity but as something to be feared and avoided. More serious, the efforts that management has made to handle the growing demands for flexibility have unanticipated consequences that in the long run make the situation worse—favoring a few "winners" but displacing the costs of mobility onto a large number of "losers," who then are lost as potential contributors to complex systems, and who are increasingly driven by fear and confusion to resist change.

### The Danger of Dualism

A major motivational "carrot" for good performers has traditionally been the promise of promotion. As those opportunities have diminished, and the paths for mobility have increased, the best employees have begun to demand other kinds of rewards, and threatening to leave if they don't get them. Thus one of the biggest challenges for firms and HR managers has become retention. McKinsey propelled this into the public arena in the late 1990s with the catchy phrase "the war for talent," which advocated pulling out all stops to keep the best performers.[31] Simultaneously there has been a growing emphasis on making sure to (in the economist Michael Jensen's equally telling phrase) "release resources on the downside."[32]

This puts corporate managers in a difficult bind. The best performers have the most opportunities outside, so they are quite capable of starting "bidding wars" to increase their compensation. I know of no hard data on this phenomenon, but I do know that successful middle managers have told me since the early 1990s that they are frequently contacted by headhunter agencies and are always balancing the advantages of staying with the possibility of moving—a frame of mind that was unheard-of in the prior era. There is also considerable anecdotal evidence of how this affects compensation levels: Vinod Khosla, the cofounder of Sun Microsystems, recounts that he offered a software engineer a package worth a million dollars in the first year—and was turned down for a better offer.[33]

Meanwhile, on the other end of the spectrum, marginal performers are increasingly nervous and fearful about the danger of layoffs. Since they have few opportunities, they will do anything to hang onto their existing jobs, including tolerating slow pay growth; they also are motivated to engage even more intensely in internal political games to shore up their own positions at the expense of their peers, to duck responsibility for failure, and to claim credit for success.

None of these behaviors, needless to say, is very good for a collaborative environment. Both the self-interestedness of the good performers and the fear of the "normal" ones lead to internal rivalries rather than a concern for helping each other achieve the organization's mission. The bureaucratic culture at least encouraged informal and pragmatic cooperation; the current one often encourages people to throw spokes in each other's wheels. The perverse effects are greatly increased where management tries to force stronger performance rewards through forced-curve appraisal systems: there is a great deal of evidence that such systems are very bad for cooperation and teamwork, and generally reduce effectiveness in interdependent social groups.[34]

The damaging effects of internal competition are temporarily muted by the persistence of loyalty, even as the rational bases for that loyalty have been undercut. But this does not seem like a permanent solution, especially when the pressures for dualism appear to steadily increase. There is by now a great deal of macroeconomic evidence of increasing inequality in the United States,[35] and the effects frequently get right down to the working level of firms. As I write this, the Delphi Corporation has just filed for bankruptcy; among its first acts following the filing was to offer its executives bonuses averaging 100 percent of annual salary to keep them from jumping ship, while asking workers to give back up to two-thirds of their wages. This makes perfect sense in a market of unregulated mobility: the company has to protect itself from losing its core talent, and it has to squeeze wages for those who have no choices. In the long run, however, this equally clearly undermines the trust and incentives for cooperation between the core and the marginal employees, and even among the core employees themselves.

### Societal Support for Mobility

One of the reasons that careers are so difficult to manage at the firm level is that they depend increasingly on the development of societal institutions that are beyond the reach of the firm.

For labor markets to be truly flexible, as required by a collaborative system, a number of current obstacles to mobility would need to be removed. Employees would need to be able to sustain periods of unemployment as part of the normal career path, in inevitable moments of transition between companies and missions. They would need to be able to sustain their benefits and plan their finances effectively through a more uncertain lifelong flow of income. They would need to have very good information about job opportunities, both short- and long-term, and about the reputations of potential employers. They would also need excellent systems of lifelong education, so that they can continue to develop and shape their skills with the evolving demands of employers.

In the ideal image I have just described, all these capabilities would benefit employers as well as employees: they would make it easier to identify the right employees at the right time and to move them quickly into position, and they would reduce the resistance of those whom they wanted to remove.

The problem is, however, that none of these infrastructural conditions for mobile careers is yet in place, and in some respects we may be going backwards. In the past, when mobility was mainly a matter of moving upwards through hierarchies, companies supplied training and information to optimize the process. As mobility has shifted increasingly *across* firms, companies have tended to reduce their investments in these services. Many HR leaders ask: Why should we supply training to our employees when they can just take the knowledge to another company? They have also lost interest in sustaining expensive pension and health benefits as mechanisms for long-term retention.

But there has been only a little movement toward developing cross-firm institutions to pick up the slack. The United States is particularly weak, in the industrialized world, in terms of providing portable benefits that would make it less disastrous for people to lose their jobs. In the general population, not only does health care depend entirely on employment, but many people have also lost confidence in pension systems as the solvency of Social Security has been questioned and company plans have frequently been discontinued in times of crisis. On the information front, there has been some improvement with the rise of Internet sites and of headhunting firms, but this is still very far from an open and complete system that would enable employees and employers to make wide and informed choices about new commitments. Finally, adult education has also moved forward in small steps, especially with the rise of online programs targeted to those who cannot dedicate themselves to full-time programs; but again it is very far from being sufficient to meet the growing need for lifelong learning.

Though the labor market is far less flexible than economists and business leaders would theoretically want, there is no organized and systematic effort to build the infrastructure for mobile careers. In fact, the few experiments in this vein have for the most part failed. An emblematic story is that of the Talent Alliance: after a large 1996 layoff announcement, AT&T formed a consortium of fourteen large companies to share information to help laid-off employees find work and employers to identify skilled people quickly. One observer called the Alliance's approach "groundbreaking in that they're working for the greater good of all the companies and individuals rather being narrow in their thinking."[36] But in fact "narrow thinking" trumped the greater good. Within a short time it became clear that the companies were denying their best employees access to the Alliance's information; the only people given passwords were those who had already been designated for layoff, and the only ones listed were marginal performers. Thus the participating companies quickly saw that there was little value in the Alliance; in the first two years fewer than ten people were placed through its services.[37]

Though career expectations remain very unresolved, the problem is not yet acute. The U.S. labor market has fewer constraints on it than many others, and so we congratulate ourselves on our high mobility without noticing the growing strains on the system. On the broad scale of the society and economy as a whole, however, movement toward greater mobility is still just beginning to gather steam despite the dominant rhetoric. There seems to have been some decline in stability among those who used to hold the plum, high-security jobs, but only slight movement on a wider scale. There is no question that employees in the companies I have studied feel far less confidence than there once was in future security, but there is not widespread embrace of the vision of interfirm mobility.[38] The move to flexibility is new enough that it has not yet created significant pressure for support at the societal level.

As the value of collaboration spreads, however, based on its ability to mobilize intelligence and respond quickly to complex needs, it will increasingly run up against the limits of the current jury-rigged approach to careers. For an economy to function effectively on a collaborative basis, efficiently matching knowledge capacities with developing problems, there needs to be a much stronger and wider base of supportive institutions, including portable benefits, open information, and continuous education.

## CONCLUSION

The difficulties around accountability and careers suggest the depth of the changes required in the collaborative transition. These institutions are at the core of organizational effectiveness and of the relationships between economy and society. They are embedded in cultural expectations as old as human society, about the relationships of superiors to subordinates and obligations of loyalty and caring. It is not surprising that they remain the center of contention, but it is essential to the development of collaboration that the existing elements be put together in new patterns.

# Part II  The Transformation

# Chapter 7 Crossing the
## Collaborative Frontier

The move toward "level 4" collaboration involves every aspect of enterprises. For those leading or planning such a change, the problem is that everything is interconnected; it's hard to know where to start. As we have seen, structures do not work without the appropriate shared cultural expectations, or "mindsets," among participants; mindset depends on consistent infrastructures; infrastructures cannot be changed without regard for the power of culture. Further, this is not a linear chain in which you can change one aspect first and another later. If you try to create a task team without the right infrastructure, it will generally fail or run into frustrating blockages; if you try to institute process analysis with the wrong mindset it can turn into a parody of top-down control; and if you try to change the culture directly without significant changes in concrete work systems the outcome will be cynicism and resistance.

This is an old problem. Theorists have generally distinguished two types of change process: incremental and transformative.[1] The first, less difficult, brings dimensions of a system into alignment, gradually filling out and implementing an existing pattern; but the second changes the whole system, including its fundamental principles. The latter presents a seemingly insoluble contradiction: It seems essential to have a complete vision of the future in order to guide change, but if the vision is too divorced from existing practice it remains abstract and ineffective. In the change process, which comes first—the unified vision, or piecemeal behavioral change?

There is considerable evidence from our sample that the move from the decentralized bureaucratic form of level 3 to the collaborative form of level 4 is a transformative one. It is frequently experienced that way by the participants: managers at all levels have widely adopted the language of "paradigm shift"; a leader of Cummins Engine Company refers to the move to a cross-functional solutions orientation as "crossing the chasm" in recognition of the huge organizational leaps required and the real risks of falling into the abyss. Further, people on either side of the divide view each other with misunderstanding and mistrust. I have noted this before: from one side, "loyalists" who have grown up in the expectations of the bureaucratic world see the new performance-oriented types as selfish, aggressive, and shortsighted; but the latter see the former as rigid, self-protective, and underhanded.

## THE SYSTEM: STRUCTURE, CULTURE, AND INFRASTRUCTURE

I have so far divided the analysis of organizations into three segments—structure, culture, and infrastructure; but transformative change has to deal with them as an interconnected system. Managers may push primarily on one lever, most often by structural rejiggering or by creating new infrastructures of compensation. If the other dimensions are ignored for long, however, they begin to act as drags or to distort the direction of movement.

Culture is particularly important because it cannot be directly managed yet has significant effects, especially during change processes. When changes in infrastructure or structure do not "make sense" in the culture, culture in effect pushes back: people may try to ignore the initiatives, or more often they will assimilate them into their familiar overall patterns. In the worst cases attempts to "push" change through dramatic changes to structure and infrastructure can damage the culture so badly as to end in cynical manipulation: people try to follow the behaviors demanded by their superiors but maintain a disconnected set of values. At Sun, for instance, a reorganization in 2000 added a large number of infrastructural planning and integrating mechanisms, including "Relationships Mechanisms," "Readiness and Synergy Councils," "New Product Teams," and a "Pricing Committee." But a year later members reported

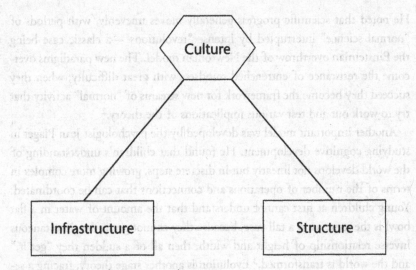

Figure 20: Culture, infrastructure, and structure

that although there was some behavioral conformity these councils were not functioning effectively:

> Our typical planning process is very stovepiped. Everybody stands up and makes their presentation, gets yelled at, and sits down. . . . We've managed to get people to follow the process; but if we don't solve some of these culture issues we're going to go back to ground zero every time.

Thus culture needs to be treated on another plane from infrastructure and structure because it integrates the whole. And while one element can change ahead of or behind the others, over time the three must form a coherent pattern for members of the system (Figure 20). In relatively calm and stable situations, when culture remains in the background as an unspoken set of expectations, one may be able to focus on one piece at a time; but in conditions of change, when expectations are in flux and emotions are charged, piecemeal approaches produce both descriptive and practical failure.

## STAGES

The best theoretical treatments of transformative change have used the concept of *stages*, based on the proposition that dynamic systems develop through a series of increasingly complex patterns. A famous version is Thomas Kuhn's analysis of the sequence of "paradigms" in the development of scientific theory.

He noted that scientific progress generally moves unevenly, with periods of "normal science" interrupted by intense "revolutions"—a classic case being the Einsteinian overthrow of the Newtonian model. The new paradigms overcome the resistance of entrenched mindsets with great difficulty; when they succeed they become the framework for new streams of "normal" activity that try to work out and test various implications of the theory.[2]

Another important model was developed by the psychologist Jean Piaget in studying cognitive development. He found that children's understanding of the world develops not linearly but in discrete steps, growing more complex in terms of the number of operations and connections that can be coordinated. Young children at first cannot understand that the amount of water in a flat bowl is the same as in a tall vase, because they cannot grasp the simultaneous inverse relationship of height and width; then all of a sudden they "get it," and the world is transformed.[3] Evolution is another stage theory, tracing a sequence of organisms of increasing complexity and adaptive capability.

These and other approaches to change share some key elements. They view development as a process in which dramatic leaps forward alternate with gradual working through of the implications. This view has been central to most literature on organization change. Business historians have generally divided its development into a series of stages very much like Kuhn's sequence of "paradigms." Alfred Chandler's great history of American business enterprise identifies three primary stages: the "unit firm" based on vertical integration, from the late nineteenth century; the "functional organization" composed of multiple product divisions, from the early twentieth century; and the "multidivisional firm" with substantial decentralization, initiated by General Motors and DuPont during the 1920s and 1930s. Many others have followed versions of this periodization.[4]

These models also suggest that "higher" stages are *better* in a particular sense—not morally, or even necessarily in terms of survival, but in the sense of having a wider range of adaptive capability. Newton's equations are just as good as Einstein's for everything we encounter in daily life; but Einstein's theory can solve all those problems *and* a whole range where Newton is lost; the functional organization similarly can do more that the unit firm. It is also important to recognize that the higher stage can operate at lower and simpler levels when appropriate. Humans operate most of the time using Newtonian, or even simpler theories, because it's much easier; only when confronted with difficult problems at the edge of physics do we "step up" to use the more powerful capability.

The concept of the collaborative enterprise here fits squarely in this approach to history. My proposition is that the collaborative enterprise is the next stage beyond the multidivisional firm: that it creates an ability to manage greater complexity and more connections. The stage is most clearly and objectively defined in terms of the density of connections: collaborative systems can manage more relationships than bureaucratic ones. In a bureaucracy, as the classic pyramid shows, only a few of the many possible connections are activated: people communicate to one boss and a few subordinates. A paternalist bureaucracy adds some interconnections among peers; but these are informal and poorly coordinated, and they generally remain within very restricted groups. A collaborative enterprise makes it possible for people to communicate systematically as needed with peers as well as subordinates and superiors in different units, crossing the boundaries of the bureaucratic model.

This is not just a matter of clarifying or tinkering with the multidivisional model, but of reconfiguring it—adding new processes and layers of relationships, new modes of coordination that operate on different principles from the bureaucratic model. Where the environment is stable and not too complex, people can fall back to the simpler mechanisms of bureaucracy—without losing the ability to break the bureaucratic mold when necessary, crossing levels and boundaries.

## MOVEMENT BETWEEN STAGES

But can these theorists help us to understand how the mysterious leap from stage to stage, such as the move to collaborative enterprise, occurs? Can they say anything beyond "Here a miracle happens"?

On the whole there is little systematic understanding of transformative *transition*. In the physical world changes seem to happen essentially randomly: a science of "chaos" has developed in recent years to explore the way in which events may have enormous and unexpected consequences—the flap of a butterfly's wings in Brazil setting off a tornado in Texas.[5] A variant, complexity theory, suggests that sometimes these transformations may "regroup" into patterns that resemble coherent stages; but this theory, too, has had difficulty in finding practical clues to shaping the transitional path.[6]

But the human realm may be different, because we—unlike butterflies and wind currents—have visions. A common theme through many of the historical and social science accounts of stage transition is the shaping effect of general images of the future that orient people's actions.

Writers on corporate change often have a simplistic view of visions, suggesting that what is needed is a visionary leader to create a new system of behaviors. Those who have looked closely at transitional phases in different realms, however, come up with something more complex than this one-directional view. Kuhn's description of scientific innovation is echoed by that of other theorists of nonlinear systems: "normal" phases are marked by a harmony of vision and action, in which it is fair to say that the former governs the latter; in transitions, however, they come apart, and practice becomes more loosely connected to the overarching system and more open to experimentation. At that point something novel happens: vision no longer *governs* practice, but it interacts with it. General patterns emerge from simple experiences, and in turn help guide the accumulation of further experiences while continuing to evolve.[7]

The Einsteinian revolution in physics, for instance, did not come from a new vision imposed by a new leader. Rather, it emerged after a long period in which the previous overarching Newtonian theory had come to seem inadequate, and many scientists had conducted experiments that didn't quite fit with the old model. In this increasingly fragmented scene, Einstein's intuition of a new pattern seemed suddenly to promise coherence. It was not embraced at the beginning on its provability; rather, activity began to crystallize around it—though not without resistance from many—because it made sense of many experiences and seemed "promising."

The new model would not have succeeded without the context in which many people had become frustrated with previous models. It was for this reason that Einstein, who was not a formal leader (or even, at the time, a professional scientist), was able to have such a powerful impact on the field. At the same time, the transformation developed much more efficiently than if scientists has merely tried several things randomly and eliminated the mistakes. The prefiguring vision guided experimental activity along a path that did indeed turn out to be fruitful.

The human capacity to see patterns behind the noise of particular actions and experiments in everyday life thus enables smoother transitions than mere blind casting about. The nature of an emerging stage can be recognized in a general way before it fully comes together; and this understanding can increase the speed and reliability of transformation by guiding ongoing experimentation.

The practical difficulty is to connect vision to practice. The business world contains innumerable cases in which vision is rejected or collapses (we will look at some of these shortly). One thing that does not work is to formulate a vision and then direct people below to carry it out. That approach, so congruent with the bureaucratic mindset, fails because transformative vision cannot be directly translated into behaviors. It is necessarily incomplete and partial, needing to be developed and filled through continuing experimentation. For that to work, however, the people doing the implementing also have to understand the vision.

## OBSTACLES TO CHANGE

Every transformation is faced by obstacles rooted in the "old" system. Existing mindsets or cultural patterns are deeply rooted in an array of habits and relationships that are hard to disentangle. And the process of change often creates distorted group reactions of defensiveness with a highly emotional charge.

### Mindset: The Stability of Culture

Culture, as we explored in Chapter 4, is the patterned set of expectations that allows people to orient to each other in a collective activity—to be able to act with the expectation that others' actions will complement theirs and lead to a good result for all. When cultural mindsets are out of alignment, people become narrow and suspicious because they cannot be confident of future harmonious working out processes.

This means that culture must necessarily be difficult to change; if it were easy, no one could have trust in the future. To achieve this trust, culture must be *embedded* in several ways that lock it in place—and that must be unlocked to make change possible:[8]

1. Culture is locked in place by the fact that everyone believes that others believe in it, and that anyone who deviates from it will be ostracized. As a result, if one person changes mindsets while those around do not, it creates mutual suspicion rather than new collective action. This is why it is so often difficult to publicly acknowledge issues that everyone is aware of in private—the "elephant in the room" phenomenon. Somehow everyone has to change at once.

2. Culture is locked by the fact that over time it integrates many specific routines and roles, so that all interactions become more or less predictable. If someone tries to act in an unusual way—going beyond the usual job descriptions, perhaps, or criticizing the boss in an open meeting—others will

be confused and perhaps disapproving, exerting subtle pressure to fall back to norms that are well understood. Thus there is constant collective "pull" back to the familiar in order to preserve the system of mutual confidence. A *new* vision, by contrast, is inevitably simple and abstract, leaving many problems unresolved. Acting on it is therefore a leap in the dark: no matter how exciting it may feel, there is no worked-through agreement on what it means in practical detail. This is why new visionary movements so often split into warring factions over time—and why people are generally reluctant to take the risk of abandoning familiar patterns.[9]

3. Culture is locked to place, finally, because it becomes embedded in individuals' personalities and motivational systems. One of the reason that people can trust each other to respond as expected in the future is that they know that the others to some extent *identify* with that way of behaving, that they will *not* change easily and casually. Thus the transformation process needs to overcome this necessary motivational "stickiness."

In these ways cultural expectations become almost unconscious, and people know without calculation what to do and what is expected. As one IBM employee put it:

> The reason the basic beliefs worked and people believed them was because they were demonstrated on a daily basis. You knew your manager, the way he was trained, and the management processes watching the manager so that he treated individuals with respect. So customer service, respect for the individual, and excellence was ingrained in me too, and in how we behaved.

In traditional bureaucracies it is the culture of loyalty and the informal web of relationships that are thus "ingrained." Individuals know how to act in this context, and they do not know how to act in a more formalized system. The personal networks that leaders have built over years are valuable properties, key to their success. They have built their own routines about how to judge people whom they can trust; they have retinues of subordinates whom they have helped and can go to for favors. They know how to run meetings, based on the conscious and unconscious rituals of deference that keep conflicts from getting out of hand. Many systems and rituals—the executive parking lots and dining rooms, the dress codes, the visible differences between departments and functions, and so on—reinforce the boundaries of the system that give people a sense of how and where to collaborate. The dominant relationships are within divisions and there are few live connections to customers; everyone may advocate cross-functional collaboration, but to get ahead one still needs to focus on pleasing one's boss. It is persistent and complex patterns like these that end up "freezing" things even without overtly intending to.

When faced with challenges that don't fit with the existing pattern, the first response of people and systems is to reinterpret them to make them look more familiar. This is the mechanism of "assimilation" identified by Piaget in his work on cognitive development. He noted that an infant learns, for instance, to grab his father's watch and put it into his mouth; then he does the same thing with a spoon and a finger, and he begins to "routinize" the pattern. Then he gets a ball, and he tries to do the same thing—and he is resistant to giving up what he has learned and accepting that he has to try something new.[10] This is fundamentally the same pattern that has caused a crisis in General Motors: for nearly a century they have formed business strategy primarily around finance, and they have built elaborate expectations and routines around it; it is therefore very difficult to move beyond it in a world that demands many more dimensions of performance.

The transition to collaboration is often derailed by assimilation—where new rhetoric and programs are turned unconsciously into old forms. Quality management efforts, for instance, are most effective when people from different parts of the organization, with different roles and expertise, are drawn into a genuine collaborative effort to analyze processes and to work continuously to improve them. But it is easily assimilated instead to the bureaucratic pattern: managers put together a team that gives them recommendations, and then they turn the recommendations into new rules and job descriptions. More generally, process management, which at its best creates linkages that focus everyone on the customer, can easily instead turn into a new tool of bureaucracy with large manuals that focus everyone on particular pieces.

This is a major source of one of the most common complaints of change leaders: the sense that there is a "frozen middle" in the organization that blocks new initiatives. Most of the time, when I talk to people at the middle levels, they are not deliberately trying to derail change—they may even embrace the new rhetoric; but they reinterpret it in familiar terms. They may advocate customer focus, but they frame it in terms of perfecting their service routines—a bureaucratic mentality—rather than genuinely listening to and interacting with the customer. They may advocate open dialogue with subordinates, but they frame it in terms of showing concern rather than encouraging the interplay of diverse ideas.

In the move to collaborative enterprise, the formation of task teams often becomes a key battleground between mindsets. Top management frequently sets up task forces to deal with complex cross-functional problems, but in organizations that are generally bureaucratic in orientation this usually fails. The members of the team are used to working within their own functions and denigrating others, and they expect the others to act the same way. They are used to competing with their peers vis-à-vis superiors, fighting for position and resources by exaggerating their needs—and they expect others to do the same. Further, they are generally not comfortable with the ambiguity and negotiation involved in task force management: they are used to having clear direction. Thus in General Motors or AT&T, when interviewed in the early 1990s, I found most middle managers disliked task teams:

> I don't like task forces and swat teams most of the time; it dismantles our ability to do the basics. The best thing is to just get out and talk with the folks. (General Motors)

All this leads to a self-fulfilling prophecy: task teams in these environments are largely ineffective.

But the new breed at places like Citibank e-Solutions naturally live and breathe in the flexible atmosphere of task teams: for them, as the case in Chapter 3 documents, this is the best way to get things done. To use a phrase that has become increasingly common in this period of clashing mindsets, they "get it": they are used to looking for diverse competencies that can help them in their tasks; they focus on the overall goals of the organization, and they expect others to do the same; they are comfortable with processes of mutual-gains negotiation, and they expect that of others. In this environment, the outcasts are those who protect their turf and look for clear direction from above.

### Sociodynamics: Collective Resistance and Defensiveness

I have referred to "mindsets" to suggest the patterned, interconnected nature of systems of action. But transformation is not merely about the mind; it is also about the gut. It is a process that affects deep feelings in individuals and deeply implanted social connections. The response of managers to layoffs, for example, is not merely intellectual: even those with continuing security often have reactions of confusion and depression. Nokia had a series of particularly painful experiences during its extraordinary transformation from a staid lumber company to one of rapid-response high technology: two of its senior executives committed suicide within a few years of each other, after having been pushed to the side by successive waves of change.[11]

Approaches to change that ignore such feelings generate collective emotions that can turn into pathologies similar to those that psychologists have found in individuals: regression to simplified past patterns, narcissistic inwardness, projection of fault to the outside, and disconnection between outward presentation and inward motivation. I use the term "sociodynamics" for these collective emotional defenses and distortions. The term draws a deliberate analogy to psychodynamics: just as in individuals childhood fears and anxieties can affect behaviors into adulthood, so in organizations norms often harden into resistant patterns.[12]

Occasionally these dynamics burst into open turmoil: cases from our sample include (among others) IBM, where Gerstner's efforts to redefine the direction of the company sparked several public revolts, notably around the changes in the pension plan, and in France a division flatly refused to carry out organizational changes decreed from above;[13] General Motors, where an attempt to force pay for performance led to similar widespread open rebellion; and Citibank, where, as mentioned earlier, the country managers responded to the CEO's efforts to weaken their autonomy with rather explicit declarations of war.

More often, however, the emotional strain turns into more hidden and complicated forms of resistance. The first reaction to moves that undermine the traditional community is often one of individualistic scattering, or a retreat to autonomy, where everyone loses faith in the social order and just tries to get by. This does not sustain people for long, however; soon they begin to group together for mutual protection and meaning, to create some kind of cultural unity that enables them to make sense of the world. They do this primarily by "regression": by grabbing and holding on to familiar past models of social relationships.

One major type of regression pulls back to a small homogeneous group set against the world; another holds on to and hopes to rebuild the image of a caring paternalistic hierarchy; and a third moves toward an ideal model of rational bureaucracy with strong autonomy. These are established ways of seeing the world and relating to others, with deep roots in historical societies. The pattern of group solidarity draws on the ancient notion of a "band of brothers," undifferentiated and united; the pattern of deference draws on the image of a paternal family, with a strong father figure protecting and demanding allegiance from the members; and the pure bureaucratic image, the most modern of the three, fits directly with the modern logic of moral autonomy and rationality. All three of these, with their strong emotional resonances and value commitments, coexist and interlock within the traditional firm. For the most part, the formal system is dominated by the rule of autonomy, with each person playing a rationally defined role; but the older patterns of deference and group solidarity govern the informal system, creating the dynamics of loyalty, of empire-building, and of inwardness that characterize all corporations that I know of.

These orientations provide, in effect, a set of common resources that people can fall back on to rebuild a sense of confidence in others and in the future. But they also are unrealistic in terms of dealing with the complex strategic pressures faced by most companies, and they retard and distort the necessary move toward collaboration.

### Retreat to Autonomy

Perhaps the most common emotion, at least in the early phases, is fear; and the reaction is generally to retreat from social commitments and adopt an attitude of individual defensiveness. People focus more intensely on doing their own jobs well, in the hopes that the larger storm will pass.[14]

> People keep their head down and try to do their jobs. The bunker philosophy has taken over. You know, don't get too visible, just do your job. (AT&T)

> The reaction to fear is to scatter and everybody's protecting their individual flanks. (Pitney-Bowes)

This clearly leads in the opposite direction from collaboration; on the contrary, it produces a perverse increase in bureaucracy. As trust is undermined and informal webs of exchange are taken apart, everyone retreats to the safety of rules, trying to avoid danger by doing everything "by the book."

> There was a decrease in the amount of trust, because people began covering their asses, which means they have to put everything in black and white. . . . Where formerly you could go and talk and say, "I've got this situation to solve," and he'd say, "I'll take care of it." (Pitney-Bowes)

And efforts to create a common focus on the strategy are emphatically rejected:

> (Q) Is there a clear understanding of the strategic direction of the organization?

> (A) Strategic direction! Who cares about strategic direction! I get enough if I keep my job for the next year. (Lucent)

### Small-Group Solidarity

A second common pattern is less individualistic but involves small groups pulling together in tight protective bands. An AT&T manager spoke of a small group of others at his level and division:

There's a togetherness, that life raft, or the log, whatever it is, to hold onto to survive. You're helping each other to survive in a hostile environment. And you talk to
people who have been in combat together, in situations where they didn't expect to
survive: there's a camaraderie that exists, there's a mutual dependency, an emotion,
that doesn't develop unless you've been in that situation.

This of course produces divisions at a different level:

I think there's really a sense that each little group bitches and moans about the other
little group and, you know, there is a feeling of fragmentation. (AT&T)

As organizations try to increase the scope of collaboration, the separate units
that have built up a sense of unity and "specialness" within the old
bureaucratic stovepipes resist efforts to meld them into a wider community.
The interdependence required by complex strategic challenges this type of simple, homogeneous security and creates feelings of tension and being "invaded."

Maybe part of what's going on is our realization that we are so dependent on other
parts of AT&T—which is somewhat depressing.

Commonly people respond defensively by asserting even more strongly
their distinctive independence. Bolstered by feelings of pride and identity,
they will fight fiercely to defend their groups. Veridian, for example, had
grown through acquisition of smaller companies that retained their own identities and resisted efforts to collaborate in larger cross-unit projects. One manager tried to get rid of all "heritage symbols" that reinforced the separate
company identities—taking the pictures of founders off the walls, forbidding
people to wear clothing with the heritage names; this was, as one person put it,
"a disaster: it reinforced people's defiance."

It gets worse: if they lose the battle they may continue the even more dysfunctional behavior of *denying* that they have lost, of continuing to insist that
their group will return to its former glory. They turn inward, at the extreme
developing a kind of "group narcissism" that denies the reality of the external
world, hanging on a sense of pride that can seem entirely disconnected from
the facts.[15] One place where I was particularly struck by this pattern of inwardness was in my interviews at General Motors' CPC division in the early
1990s. In a year when they had lost several billion dollars, I asked middle managers how they were doing; they replied with pride that they had achieved major improvements in quality and productivity. When I then asked what their
competitors were doing on these dimensions, however, they had no idea. One
engineer explicitly rejected the idea of looking outward to the marketplace

and the competition, launching instead a rhapsody about the beauty and line-age of their cars:

> A vehicle has a character, it has genes. There has to be a corps of people that retain the genes of the vehicle. I want to sense that my car is like a wife, it's your family, it's part of you. You can't have two wives, you can't have two cars.

## Dependence and Loyalty

Another avenue of regression is to maintain the image of paternalist commu-nity. The pattern of familial loyalty with deference to a father figure is ancient and powerful. I have emphasized throughout its strength in corporate cultures:

> It's a family-type thing, where you look at the people that look up to you for lead-ership and guidance, and that's probably all part of what turns us on as managers.[16]

In a set of several hundred interviews in the early 1990s I was surprised to find that most managers continued to be loyal in the face of unprecedented turbulence: they recognized that their companies were no longer holding up their side of the traditional bargain, but they were committed to the core of their identities to the value of dedication to the organization. This led to a great many confusing and inconsistent viewpoints, and above all to a deep conservatism. Most of those I spoke to were at one level cynical and disap-pointed in their company leadership, but they passionately rejected the option of retreating to me-first free agency. Many of them resolved the tension by hoping and believing that the current problems were a temporary crisis and that things would eventually go back to the way that they had always been.[17]

In the years since then I have been amazed at the continued persistence of this backward-looking view among middle managers despite overwhelming and continuing evidence that the traditional implied "deal" of loyalty for se-curity is no longer operative. Lacking a clear picture of an alternative, and es-pecially of a future that would provide some security and predictability for them, many hang on fiercely to the only image that makes sense to them—that of the stable hierarchical career. Thus I frequently find a huge gap be-tween the espoused values expressed by top management and the values in use by middle managers;[18] the former are full of dynamism and high performance and collaboration, while the latter are much more traditional and focused on doing a good job in a familiar bureaucratic sense. By 2005, to give one bit of poll data that reflects this theme, 59 percent of employees said they were loyal to their companies, while 26 percent of employees said that their companies are loyal to them.[19] The Conference Board found that promotion policies were the least satisfactory aspect of employment, with only 20 percent positive responses in 2003.[20]

Naturally, as this gap endures, cynicism increases. The gap in views leads to a deep alienation from higher management, which in extreme cases becomes open anger and resistance. Another survey nugget that captures the problem: a national survey in 2005 found only 40 percent of employees saying they trust their bosses to communicate honestly.[21] As one of my interviewees put it:

> I want to feel that the company is loyal to me and I do, to some degree; but I also know intellectually that they will only remain loyal for as long as they need me. When it comes time for them to make a choice if there is someone better, I'm out and they are in.

Subordinates who adopt this mode become more highly dependent than ever. They seek protectors, while those in higher positions, reciprocally, often try to protect "their" people from the surrounding turbulence.[22] Together, these strategies exaggerate the tendency for empire-building and personal cliques and sharpen the group infighting that prevents effective collaboration.

> There are people who are fighting tooth and nail to protect their people, and this encourages real loyalty.

And some middle managers with long records of success and highly developed skills become almost childlike in their pleas to be taken care of:

> I don't know what my motivation is anymore. Am I working just to retire? Why doesn't the company make use of all my knowledge and skill? Older people are still useful. We can teach the younger people. We are dedicated. Use me. I'm here. I'm willing and able.

### Longing for Bureaucratic Clarity

Finally, there are those who regress to an old model of bureaucracy. The formal bureaucratic system, as I have emphasized, respects spheres of autonomy defined by job duties. Collaboration, on the other hand, depends on building a sense of reciprocal *inter*dependence, with order emerging from combining different capabilities. The resulting ambiguity can lead to a simplifying reaction in which people just want to go "back" to focusing on a single piece and knowing exactly what they want to do. At General Motors, a supervisor caught up in a team effort said:

In my previous job . . . there was a clearer feeling that there was nobody else that I had to get consensus with to get a decision. In my current job I am confused about which decisions are mine. Does the marketing division have the right to define suspension tunings? No one is ultimately accountable. I would like more autonomy, not more consensus.

People who follow this line of retreat focus on doing what they are told, trying to please their bosses, not taking risks—coming closer to Merton's "bureaucratic personality," the "methodical performance of routine activities." Resistance expresses itself in the form of passive withdrawal:

The folks hear the strategies, they can't deal with them or keep them straight. And they're thinking, "Oh, we're losing money, but what can I do? I'll just cover my own little area here." They don't know their car line is losing money. And they're hoping that this astute set of leaders, if they work on a couple of strategies that they should and get the quality up, all will be well. . . . I've heard people say, "All I need to do is do Quality Now, and run my couple of strategies that are key to my platform, and all will be well." (GM)

All of this is indeed a change from paternalist bureaucracy, but it does not increase collaboration; indeed, it reduces it, by making everyone even more dependent on orders from above and more reluctant to take initiative, and by exaggerating the always-simmering competition for the boss's approval.

These various reactions are regressions to traditional cultural bases. Like all defenses, they make things worse: rather than leading to the kind of flexible, outward-looking entrepreneurialism that leaders seek, they produce more inwardness, more risk avoidance, more rigidity—and less capacity to deal with powerful environmental challenges.

# Chapter 8 Journeys: Winding

# Paths to Collaboration

Although transformative change requires simultaneous shifts throughout an entire system, and although it often feels to participants like a sudden "leap," the actual history is long and complicated. William James's classic study of religious conversion found that the apparent abrupt illumination experienced by many people was in fact preceded by long, painful, often subterranean processes of exploration.[1] The move toward collaboration has often been like that: long periods of experimentation and gradual shifts in thinking, coming together at last in a new shared vision.

The journey, moreover, has been full of failures—of efforts that have been greeted with fanfare at first but have disappeared, usually quietly, isolated and contained by the bureaucratic order. But as Winston Churchill once remarked, "Success is the ability to go from one failure to another with no loss of enthusiasm."[2] The failures have been necessary parts of the journey; each has led not to surrender but to other, more ambitious efforts. Crossing the line from level 3 to level 4 has been driven forward in this way despite all obstacles by an underlying enthusiasm—the belief that the bureaucracy creates barriers to effective business execution, and a gradually emerging vision of a collaborative system to replace it.

Failures are, of course, generally hidden: organization leaders like to portray themselves as succeeding in "forward-thinking" practices, and problems often do not become apparent for several years. For these reasons surveys tend to show higher levels of success than interviews, particularly interviews (like the bulk of those that ground this book) at the middle levels of organization, where the real implementation of complex collaboration takes place.

## THE EVOLUTION OF SHOPFLOOR
## WORK SYSTEMS

The pattern has most clearly played out in the evolution of work systems in factories and other mass-production units. On a macro level, the last forty years have seen a sustained erosion of Taylorist job control. But on closer inspection this trajectory is composed of a series of different efforts, each building from the problems of the last.

The first step was a rebellion against Taylorism and bureaucracy driven largely by ideological, "soft" beliefs. In the 1960s these led to the first significant reversal of the long prior tend toward the perfection of Taylorism: the move to job enrichment. Taylorism (and more generally, bureaucracy) operated by defining jobs as strictly as possible; job enrichment involved a loosening of those constraints, giving people more room to innovate and problem-solve. An assembly-line worker might be allowed to do two tasks instead of one. In the more adventurous forms, workers might assume a few supervisory responsibilities.[3]

There was a great deal of enthusiasm for these efforts at first. Ninety percent of employers reported increased productivity, and workers reported increased job satisfaction; there was a general win–win glow. Oddly enough, though, when studies stretched over time, there was a high level of mortality; somewhere between half and three-quarters of the efforts disappeared within a few years. The usual explanation for this seeming contradiction was that the efforts were too challenging to the existing cultures and succumbed over time to managerial resistance.[4]

But though the bureaucratic mindset had in a sense beaten back a challenge, the victory did not last long. Rather than seeing the "failure" of job enrichment as a sign of the inevitability of Taylorism, companies increasingly turned in the 1970s to an even more ambitious experiment: the development of problem-solving groups. In these groups, workers were not just given slightly greater freedom; they were asked to meet in teams to critique and come up with ideas for changing their own jobs. Some of these, called "Quality of Work Life" efforts, were sponsored jointly by unions and management; others, called generally "Quality Circles," were purely management driven.

This movement ran into the same peculiar contradiction: most studies showed significant improvement in business and work satisfaction measures; but larger surveys found that most of the studies disappeared within a few years. My own study at AT&T found that most of the groups started with great enthusiasm but could go only a short distance, dealing with minor issues, before they were stopped by a combination of their own lack of confidence and the subtle disapproval of their superiors. They soon reached a "plateau": energy ebbed, and generally they quietly stopped meeting.[5]

Once again, however, this high rate of failure only spurred a more ambitious effort. During the 1980s the major organizational fashion was the autonomous team. Here groups of workers were not only asked for advice and opinion, but also given substantial responsibility as a group for supervisory functions such as scheduling and ordering of supplies; sometimes their authority extended to hiring and even discipline. Some dramatic cases seemed to contradict every rule in the classic book: in a Volvo plant in Uddevalla, Sweden, teams of ten workers put together entire cars without any supervisors at all, doing away entirely with the assembly line. Again, the initial research results were positive on both business and human dimensions.

The story of successful failure was soon repeated, at least in part: the most dramatic cases, such as Uddevalla, were reined in or closed despite strong performance results.[6] By this time, however, the wider critique of bureaucracy had begun to take hold in many corporations and the cutting of middle management layers was proceeding rapidly. The resistance of bureaucratic officials was therefore not as powerful. Autonomous teams became *necessary* to the functioning of companies because there were simply fewer supervisors. The result is that they did not, as with the previous efforts, fade away over time, but they were encapsulated. As wider cross-functional efforts grew the autonomy of teams was reined in. The growth of "just-in-time" production systems meant that they could not be as independent as before; and rather than being integrated into cross-functional decision making, the authority of teams was simply narrowed.[7]

The final chapter so far in this continuing story is the growing integration of teams into wider networks of cross-functional decision making, often known as "high-performance work systems" (though the terminology remains very unsettled). Here again, the episode begins with a large number of failures

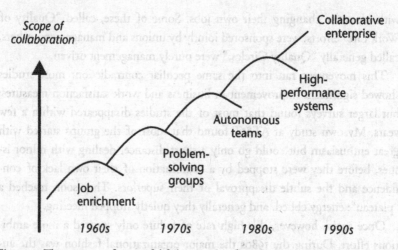

Figure 21: The sequence of successful failures in shopfloor work organization

and semi-failures, the most famous of which is GM's Saturn plant. There autonomous teams were just part of a web of governance, mediated in large part by the union, that drew workers into decision making at all levels. But despite the considerable success of the plant on every dimension, both GM management and the union's national leadership were highly uncomfortable with the radical challenges to normal ways of doing business; they starved the plant for investment capital and gradually hemmed in the more ambitious aspects of the system, moving it over time a long way toward a more traditional format.[8]

A widespread version of high-performance organization is Total Quality Management (TQM). As usual, this term is very loosely defined and covers many varieties of practice, but one essential idea is to involve all levels of the organization in diagnosing the sources of quality problems and finding solutions. Once again, after a huge burst of enthusiasm around 1990, there has been a growing wave of criticism; a 1993 survey found that two-thirds of HR managers thought it had failed in their companies.[9] But also once again the thrust of much criticism has been that the efforts have not done enough to involve a cross section of workers, and that they should reach further in developing cross-functional mechanisms and flexible collaboration.[10]

TQM has weathered this round of criticism and has continued to thrive throughout large companies. In many of our companies it has evolved toward a flexible system of linked teams focused on systematic quality analysis—a model of the collaborative enterprise. Thus, to close our loop, the particular case of the Citibank "Process Improvement Teams" and the later breakthrough in the e-Solutions team-based systems recapitulates and exemplifies the ongoing movement of TQM, and of team-based systems in general, toward full-fledged models of collaborative enterprise.

The general trend of this history is of an increasingly complex set of collaborative relations extending increasingly far and incorporating more diverse players. The details are erratic, because this has been an unplanned course; there has been much conflict, distress, anger, and confusion along the way. Equally, the future cannot be predicted in detail. But behind the particularities is an underlying driver that keeps things moving even in the face of repeated obstacles and plateaus (Figure 21).

## WHITE-COLLAR AND MANAGERIAL WORK

The organization of managerial and technical work has evolved along a similar path, from closely defined bureaucratic job structures with small spans of control, toward increasing use of teams and matrixes. The names of the programs are a little less coherent than at the blue-collar level, partly because white-collar work has been less studied by academics, and partly because this domain is more tightly bound than blue-collar work to idiosyncratic company cultures. But within our own sample we observed a number of examples of this pattern of stumbling forward through many failures toward a dimly perceived objective.

The Citibank case, one that my colleagues in the McKinsey group and I studied particularly carefully over a long span of time, provides a nice example of this pattern. The story as we know it began in the 1970s, with then-CEO Walter Wriston's insight that large companies increasingly needed the ability to manage funds on a global basis. He saw that while the company had an unequaled global reach, with operations in scores of countries, these countries operated entirely independently. In 1974 Wriston established the World Corporate Group (WCG) to integrate across geographic units for large customers.

The WCG achieved a few milestones in creating international transactions, but it also ran into strong opposition from powerful country managers who complained that it was taking away their clients. It was also isolated in the headquarters, with weak informal ties to the rest of the organization, and therefore highly vulnerable to the play of bureaucratic politics. In 1981, it was shut down. But the need for coordination remained pressing: in 1985 John Reed, who had succeeded Wriston the year before, revived it in a slightly different form—less headquarters-centered, more involving of the local operations.

Growth was slow but significant: by 1995 the WCG had 220 clients that numbered among the largest companies in the world.[11]

Yet Reed remained deeply dissatisfied with the amount of collaboration that was occurring across country units. He felt that the growth of multinational corporations represented a huge and growing opportunity that they had not yet tapped. His impatience increased when the bank went through a major crisis in the early 1990s. He called together the country managers and, in a dramatic moment that reverberated through the company, "shot" several of them on the spot for not cooperating with the global effort. He then initiated a major reorganization aimed at focusing on the customer, especially the 1,700 largest customers; he announced that henceforth the bank's priorities would shift from "geography, product, customer" to elevate customers to the first rank.

In an interview six years after these events, a senior manager on Reed's team said that this forceful intervention certainly moved things forward, but it was not a full success. "Reed *thought* he shot the geography managers. But I met with a group of them and said, 'Here is what's going to happen: customer first, geography third; and they said, 'No, it's not!'" The middle levels of the organization, he said, remained as a "concrete layer" blocking the goal.

In the late 1990s, a system of "customer relationships managers" (CRMs) was established to help coordinate the various facets of the bank around these global customers. The CRMs were chosen for their strong personal networks and reputations; they drew on these resources to try to jawbone and persuade their colleagues to contribute to the larger goal. Progress was very slow and difficult for a number of years. By the early 2000s, when I conducted interviews[12] among the CRMs, there was a sense that they were starting to get real traction: they had been given some negotiating leverage with other units by gaining some control over the credits that determined compensation, and they were able to use this leverage to put together some larger projects.

Looking back over a more than twenty-five-year history, the progress in achieving a global capacity was remarkable, and it gave Citibank a deep capability in the global marketplace that no competitor could match. As the effectiveness of the e-Solutions unit suggests (Chapter 3), the bank had rather clearly passed a boundary where a large range of people understood the need for collaboration and were able to relate to each other effectively in that framework. But from inside the process, it felt like a slow, hard slog with many blockages along the way.

It is important also to note that not all parts of the bank made this leap together. Indeed, in the early 2000s I also conducted interviews and surveys among nineteen "process improvement teams" (PITs), cross-functional groups aimed at improving operations. My general finding was that while many teams succeeded in generating enthusiasm, they could deal successfully only with incremental, focused, time-limited issues, but not more ambitious projects. Most of them hit a "plateau" after about six months, when the pull of the normal organization overcame the initial excitement of the team effort.

But in a few cases, the PITs broke out of this strait-jacket. The e-Solutions case described in Chapter 3, and especially the Alliance group within it, originated as a kind of "super-PIT" led by one of the former quality directors. He noted: "The difference from PIT is that here we play a really key role in the direction of the business; PIT was more tactical projects that couldn't be traced to the big strategy of business. So I'm able to get more cooperation than in my old job."

There are many other cases of this type in our sample. IBM stumbled forward in much the same way, starting with the "successful failure" of the original PC group, which was deliberately set up as a counter-cultural collaborative group outside the main hierarchy, which produced a wildly successful product, but was never able to mobilize the rest of the organization to support it.[13] Throughout the 1980s there was a battle in IBM between those who favored a more collaborative and entrepreneurial approach and those holding on to the older proprietary model; the former began to gain traction only after IBM's near-demise in the early 1990s.

These stories, and many others, suggest the importance of vision, which begins in a vague way—the need to coordinate across countries, the need to improve processes across functions, the need for customer focus—and gradually grow more precise as experiments are tried, plateau, and fall back to the familiar way of operating. The vision is what creates the disequilibrium that keeps things moving despite the inertial force of the shared bureaucracy mindset. Today we can characterize this vision as one of collaboration, but along the way it has taken many forms and names that expressed parts of this larger pattern.

## WRONG TURNS: TWO COMMON ERRORS IN CHANGE LEADERSHIP

In the many attempts to increase the scope of collaboration, two common mistakes stand out. The first is trying to drive change through behavioral mandates from the top; the other is to allow excessive autonomy and decentralization in the hopes of freeing people from bureaucratic habits.

## Leadership as Behavior Modification

The presuppositions of bureaucracy sneak into collaborative change when managers try to force new behaviors. The usual levers are structures and incentives: top executives can easily set up cross-functional task forces or units, and they can tweak the incentive system to collaborative behaviors. While these are often *parts* of successful transitions, they are unsuccessful as its primary drivers.[14]

There is certainly a role for strong leadership in this transformation, as we will explore shortly. At times leaders may even have to exercise power in dramatic ways, but they cannot force people to change their ways of acting. The notion that one can define a job and make someone do it reflects a bureaucratic mindset; to use that model to move away from defined jobs and controlled behaviors is too much of a contradiction to work. In fact, trying to force behaviors often leads to vicious circles of sociodynamic resistance that entrench the traditional model.

Our sample contains many such instances. For example, a large banking institution—*not* Citibank—tried to pull together coordinated services across their four main businesses for their high-net-worth customers. The president sent around a memo announcing that the organization's five-year plan was dependent on success in this segment and established a task force of the thirty most senior managers, led by one of three vice chairmen, to develop a plan. The two other vice chairmen, both of whom ran businesses that served the high-net-worth client, signaled to their organizations their dissatisfaction with the plan. The rest of the organization, recognizing the politics of the situation, sat on the sidelines and waited for the task force to render its conclusions. The result was that the task force was unable to agree on anything. The president's frustration was eventually taken out by firing the task force head; soon after the president himself left, and the wealth bank died as well.[15]

Another variant of structural driving consists in setting up special "innovation units" that are supposed to demonstrate the value of a new way of organizing. We have a number of these cases in our sample: Citibank's World Corporate Group in the 1970s, the IBM PC unit in the early 1980s, Shell's SEPIV exploration unit in the 1990s—all of which were intended as models of team-based, flexible organization.[16] The common thread is that the units became isolated; they had difficulty connecting to other parts of the firm because the gap in assumptions was too large. Managers in the traditional units had many reasons for not reaching across the boundary: they often resented the "special" status of the new unit; they didn't know whom to talk to because they couldn't identify titles and levels; lacking stable informal relationships across the unit boundary, they could not trust that cooperation would be repaid in the long run. These and other tensions meant that the work of the new unit was often sealed off—the IBM PC being a classic example—rather than serving as a model or impetus for change.

"Incenting" behaviors—instituting team- or unit-based reward systems—is another favorite approach. Once again, the experience is that by itself such initiatives are quickly reabsorbed by the bureaucratic culture rather than shifting mindsets. Compensation tends to focus people on how to please their bosses and beat the system, which produces a manipulative frame of mind rather than a focus on meeting the overall purpose of the organization. It also tends to reduce risk-taking and the seizing of new opportunities, since compensation schemes normally try to define expectations ahead of time and therefore almost by definition rule out risks.

A nice example in our research comes from the World Bank.[17] In an effort to build a learning organization, the Bank's leadership in the late 1990s created a structure of cross-unit thematic groups to discuss major issues of the organization. For a while there was very little activity; the expectations at the Bank were that each discipline worked in its own way on its own turf, and there was little interest in sharing. Then, in an effort to jump-start the process, a decision was made to give funding to all thematic groups. Suddenly the number exploded—by 2000 there were more than 140. But few of them functioned as intended to create collaborative learning. Instead, they tended to form around powerful figures trying to cement their positions, who used the resources to reward their followers. In effect, the collaborative effort was taken over by the classic bureaucratic dynamic of generating competing fiefdoms. Within a short time the attitude among the Bank's middle managers was one of high skepticism: "The formal groups are a waste of time," said one manager; "I just use the old-style informal networks."

An area where the difficulty of directed collaboration has emerged with particular clarity is around mergers and acquisitions, which in many cases are almost pure efforts to create collaboration by top-down fiat. The intent of joining companies is in most cases to draw on the potential synergies between capabilities—for example, between the distribution channels of AOL and the content creation of Time Warner; or between the computer capabilities of NEC and the telecommunications know-how of AT&T; or between the business understanding of PricewaterhouseCoopers and the technical capacities of IBM. These are in effect efforts to create strategic advantage through collaboration. But the problem is that the majority of these efforts, as illustrated spectacularly by the AOL–Time Warner case, do not work: various surveys indicate a failure rate of mergers and acquisitions of 50 to 80 percent. And the most common cause of the failure appears to be what are usually called "culture clashes"—what we would call a failure of collaboration.[18]

These efforts are typically marked by strong top management efforts to force people to talk to each other, by setting up cross-unit task forces or merging divisions from different companies or tinkering with incentive schemes.[19] Again and again these efforts are blocked by the walls that define bureaucratic domains and competencies. The AOL–Time Warner fiasco, for which I have seen some internal details, was a spectacular manifestation of this problem.

It is not, of course, a bad thing to exert strong leadership, to make structural changes or incentive changes, or to set up experimental units. The problem comes when leaders expect these to work by themselves, without addressing the wide range of cultural and infrastructural conflicts that result. This approach is simply one-sided, but it is very common because it fits with the familiar assumptions of bureaucratic leadership. Moving to collaboration requires two-sided, or interactive change.

Ravi Venkatesan, CEO of Cummins India, expressed this dual side in his analysis of guiding Cummins toward solutions, according to interviews with the McKinsey group. On one side, he was directive and forceful: he set firm priorities, and backed them with what he admitted was "brutal power" to drive back-end product support of solutions. In this mode he dismissed back-end managers who were not on board, hired strong market-facing executives to counter the product culture, and arbitrated disputes without debate. His second leadership mode, however, was one of patience, encouragement, and "letting go" to foster collaborative experimentation, in recognition that "no one has done this before." This most notably included tolerance of failure. When a Power Solutions team failed to adequately check customers' creditworthiness and ended up losing hundreds of thousands of dollars of equipment to a criminal syndicate, Venkatesen only focused on improving business practices to be more selective of future clientele.[20]

Thus it is quite possible, and perhaps necessary, for directed structural change to be a part of a change process; but this is successful only when it is driven by a collaborative vision and includes other elements of the interactive approach described below: connecting to the outside, challenging hierarchical relationships, building networks, and strengthening the shared purpose.[21]

## The Decentralization Trap

A second common move is the inverse of the first, and equally one-sided: it consists of trying to "free up" innovation and responsiveness by cutting back radically on centralized control. This is actually another structural move, but rather than trying to drive change from the top, it involves releasing energy at the bottom.

In our group of companies, ABB is a particularly dramatic case of radical decentralization: in the 1980s, in an effort to shake it from its highly bureaucratic and traditional culture, CEO Percy Barnevik divided it into more than 2,000 profit centers with high levels of independence. For a time this was touted by business writers and consultants as a model of how to break the power of bureaucracy. The bloom came off the rose as ABB struggled desperately to survive a series of reverses in the new millennium.

ABB's problems had many sources, but excessive decentralization was definitely one of them. One incident that caught management's attention was when a major customer complained that ABB had thirty-seven different sales people from thirty-seven different profit centers calling on them and were delivering thirty-seven different levels of service. Attempts to overcome this by putting all these salespeople into a single customer team did not work very well: the basic structural independence and competition among units hampered collaboration.

The same dynamic appears in less extreme cases as well. Lucent inherited a highly bureaucratic culture when it was spun off from AT&T; to spur innovation, CEO Rich McGinn divided it into eleven business units and insisted on high autonomy so they could experiment without constant clearing through the hierarchy. The results were the same as at ABB: customers complained about getting multiple uncoordinated sales calls. Even more serious, Lucent's products started drifting apart so that they no longer worked well together. Salespeople did not know what other parts of the firm were offering or what complementarities were possible. Within three years a new CEO admitted that the decentralization was a mistake and was making moves to reintegrate the company.

Other companies that have gone through the same experience, just drawing on my extended sample, include 3M, Ericsson, Cargill, Kodak, AIG, and the World Bank. These cases focused on achieving speed through decentralization, which did nothing to create a wider scope of collaboration: as one of our respondents put it, "We've lifted controls but left people in the cylinders."

In each case, there was eventually a partial or total reversal of the decentralizing moves.

It is also interesting that companies that have historically succeeded as highly decentralized bureaucracies are having a great deal of trouble in dealing with increasing demands for integration. Hewlett-Packard, for one, has tried repeatedly at least since the mid-1980s to coordinate aspects of business strategy and infrastructure across business units; all the major efforts have failed. They have been unable to agree on a single strategy for product architecture, unable to build strong project management, and unable to build a solutions capability for customers. Carly Fiorina's efforts to achieve unity around solutions were a particularly well-publicized chapter in this story, but there were several previous ones. For example, in the early 1990s an initiative was launched to focus around HP's core competence in technologies of measurement, computation, and communication (MC2). This "HP = MC2" effort began with an order from Ford to link test equipment in all its service and repair facilities worldwide with HP personal computers and printers. Despite the economic and strategic attractiveness of the Ford alliance, it was unable to gain the commitment of key managers in HP's decentralized product businesses or to integrate across diverse businesses with different business models and different processes. The initiative became a dead letter with spinoff of a Test and Measurement Group, which carried forward the traditional HP approach of creating a specialized autonomous unit but did not achieve the integration or flexibility that Ford had sought.[22]

The lesson from these problems is that the complexities of the modern market in many cases—increasing in number—require something more than focused responsiveness; they require a capacity to integrate a range of resources quickly and flexibly. The kind of company that can do this is neither centralized nor decentralized in the traditional sense. Units and individuals are neither highly dependent on the approval of their superiors, nor highly independent and able to operate autonomously. Instead, they recognize strong *interdependence* with other parts of the organization and operate on common platforms and standards so that they can quickly combine resources as needed.

### Pathways to Systemic Collaboration

As more and more companies have made the journey toward collaborative enterprise, the path—or rather paths in the plural—have become somewhat better cleared, with fewer false moves. As we tracked the histories of our sample companies, we found a set of sequences that may begin to show more direct routes to change. We did not find any that moved directly from strong bureaucracy to developed systemic collaboration; that may be too big a jump. Instead:

1. Some companies, such as Nokia, broke through the bureaucratic barrier by moving to the "right": that is by stressing decentralized experimentation, focused products or services, and high adaptiveness with relatively low complexity.[23]

2. Some, such as IBM and Citibank, broke through the barrier by moving "up," trying to build greater strategic unity out of what had been segmented organizations. Often these used the concept of "one company" to describe their new orientation.[24]

3. Several companies, such as Microsoft, did not need to break through because they started out as quite collaborative. They did, however, move from the relatively spontaneous form of a new startup to more organized, formalized systems.[25]

### IBM: "Up" to Complexity, Then "Right" to Solutions

IBM was known for its very strong paternalist culture and a strategic vision built around large products, especially its 360 line of mainframe computers. In the late 1980s it had a classic structure of decentralized bureaucracy: twenty business units, selling 5,000 hardware products and 20,000 software products. The operating model was around committee-based decisions. In 1992 this model collapsed in dramatic fashion, referred to by those who remember as a "near-death experience." IBM had to face the option of spinning off divisions into "Baby Blues" (similar to "Baby Bells" at AT&T) to avoid financial insolvency.

Lou Gerstner resisted Wall Street's pressure to break up the company, however, arguing it could provide more value as an integrated whole. He therefore reintegrated divisions into larger business groups and formed several strong linking groups, including the Corporate Executive Committee (CEC) of a dozen senior executives, and the Worldwide Management Council, composed of the top thirty-five people including geographic leaders and division presidents, which met monthly to define and execute global tactical strategy and operations. This pushed IBM higher up on the complexity dimension, enabling debates that balanced competing perspectives and strategic dimensions.

The move toward greater adaptiveness began in the late 1990s with the increased attention to the Internet. IBM moved decisively from an orientation to internal products to an embrace of open source and alliances, starting to build complex solutions. This gained more intense strategic focus with Sam Palmisano's concept of "On Demand" in 2002, which "would unite information, processes, and people to create an enterprise in which end-to-end processes were integrated across a company, an industry, and globally to enable it to respond with speed and flexibility to any customer demand, market opportunity, or external threat."[26] IBM acquired PricewaterhouseCoopers in 2002 to better combine business services with products into integrated solutions.

Delivering this model has required Palmisano to engage the organization in an intense interactive dialogue between the top and the bottom. By 2005, IBM had achieved considerable capacity for systemic collaboration.

### Nokia: "Right" to Adaptiveness, Then "Up" to Solutions

Nokia began as a highly traditional bureaucracy in the pulp and paper industry. In the late 1970s, when it began its move into high technology, it adopted a strategy of rapid innovation. The first move, under Kari Kairamo, was toward diversification, trying to develop new products rapidly and with an experimental mindset. At one point during the late 1990s it was introducing new models every thirty-five days. But in the 1990s the strategic focus began to shift toward globalization; to pursue this geographic broadening, there was a move to simplify and focus product offerings—suggesting that the company lacked the capability for simultaneous complexity and adaptiveness.

Around 1997 the strategy began to include simple bundling of products, which required some move toward integration; and in the early 2000s the company began to put together genuinely complex solutions (especially in the Nokia Networks division) and to seek to create standards across the industry— both efforts that required a more systemic level of collaboration and led to both turmoil and innovation in internal systems. These changes, including a stronger Customer Relationships Management structure and front–back organizational systems, had not yet been fully implemented by 2002.[27]

### CONCLUSION

The paradox of the last chapter—how do you change everything at once?—has been resolved not in a blinding flash but through many incomplete efforts from many different directions, each of which made somewhat clearer the vision and benefits of collaboration, even as they were temporarily driven back by the continued stability of the bureaucratic system. In the end, the accumulation of experiences with teams, participation, alliances, and other partial embodiments of collaboration has crystallized into a vision: the world of organization no longer looks the same as it did thirty years ago, and company leaders find it hard to believe that anyone could have embraced the bureaucratic past.

The role of leaders and change agents in this transformation has not been simple: it has not merely a matter of either forcing or releasing, centralizing or decentralizing; nor has it been a matter of ideological inculcation of new values. This brings us, for the next chapter, to the subtle process of interactive leadership.

# Chapter 9 Leadership: The Interactive Approach to Change

The next question is: Are there lessons in all this history that can help leaders and agents of change to smooth the path to greater collaborative capability? All transformative change is intensely difficult the first time through, but the difficulties diminish when others repeat the process. Today high school students can learn theories of relativity and quantum mechanics that took the greatest minds in the world decades to produce; can collaborative transformation be "taught" in a similar way?

Leadership of the change process—if it is going to do better than the uncertain lurches of the earliest explorers—must transform mindsets and deal with patterns of resistance based in culture, habit, and sociodynamic emotions—finding ways to use authority so as to encourage challenges to authority, to break down traditional teamwork in order to build collaborative teamwork, to take apart communities without forcing people into self-protective routines, and to create a sense of trust without clear rules for interaction.

There is considerable inconsistency and even disagreement in the existing change literature about how to do this. One major strand emphasizes the crucial role of top management. A second is critical of this and puts weight on wide involvement. A third recommends changing everything at once. There is also a wide range of ideas about sequence: whether to start with structural change or with cultural redefinition or a focus on strategy, and many other possibilities.[1]

My colleagues and I have documented the change sequence in most of our sample cases. All of them, like the Citibank move to global products described earlier, are long, cyclical, multifaceted, and uneven, full of false starts and changes in direction. We don't have examples—yet—of transitional processes that really know what they're doing. As a result we cannot point to any empirical case as a model; we need to try to abstract a smooth trajectory from this messy record.

I divide the analysis of change into "how" and "what." The "how" concerns the general interactive approach that runs through the entire transformation; the "what" is the sequence of substantive steps that mark successful change processes.

## HOW: INTERACTIVE CHANGE

As we saw in Chapter 8, transformative change does not work linearly through top-down implementation of programs. Rather, it works through pragmatic, opportunistic testing of new patterns of behavior combined with reflection and learning in an iterative cycle. This cycle frequently involves an inversion of the traditional, "normal" kinds of relationships: it involves the top learning from the bottom, and the inside learning from the outside. Each of these redefinitions is disruptive: there are deep existing patterns to overcome, requiring learning on both sides of the relationship. Thus the change process is essentially *interactive*, a matter of back-and-forth working out of new sets of expectations.

### The Challenge to Hierarchical Relationships

I have proposed that this shift from level 3 to level 4—from bureaucracy to collaborative enterprise—is a stage change, increasing the number and richness of possible interconnections. A number of abstract treatments of such changes in various sciences converge on a common point: the shift to higher levels of complexity requires a partial inversion of the usual pattern of hierarchical control, so that the higher levels listen to and reorganize themselves around the lower rather than the reverse. Thus Howard Pattee, a systems scientist and theoretical biologist, argues that evolutionary changes (increases in complexity) require that the structure become partially subordinate to "description"—that is, that the close-to-the-ground connection to "reality" becomes dominant over the usual representations and organizing symbols. This is very similar to Piaget's notion in cognitive psychology that practice leads representation in the transition to new stages of understanding, or Parsons's treatment of sociological movement as driven by "lower" cybernetic levels. It is equally echoed by an economist, Elias Khalil, in thinking about organization systems:

> Complexity is not basically the hierarchy of command, but rather a hierarchy of organizations where one organization is embedded within another like Russian dolls. . . . [Thus] a leader or a boss cannot crudely manipulate an organization. Since he is a member of the organization, the leader should listen and learn from the other members.[2]

Thus one central dimension of this kind of transformation is a reshaping of hierarchical expectations, a period in which the higher levels listen to the lower and to the outside in a very different way than usual—something that, as Pattee points out, nonliving systems cannot do.[3]

We have two very interesting examples in our sample.

### 1. IBM's Values Jam

A decade after the near-death of IBM and its powerful revival under Lou Gerstner, a new CEO, Sam Palmisano, felt that the company had lost the clear sense of internal values that had guided it for most of the twentieth century. Thomas Watson, the company's founder, had defined its initial set of core values: respect for the individual, the best customer service, and the pursuit of excellence. Gerstner had attempted to redefine this by (as company lore has it) sitting down at his kitchen table and writing out a new set of eight "principles." These, however, never had much impact; they were never widely understood, and when we asked managers at middle levels ten years later none could even remember more than one of them.[4]

Palmisano decided on a different approach. For three days in 2003 he opened the company's intranet to a wide-ranging, uncensored discussion of the company's core values, open to all of its 325,000 employees. Over that period a quarter of the employees tuned in, and many tens of thousands actively commented. For the first day or more, the discussion was dominated by people who were angry and bitter over layoffs and pension changes, accusing the company of "breaking the contract" with its employees. John Iwata, Senior Vice President, Communications, recalls:

I have to tell you, the first twelve hours, it was so overwhelmingly negative . . . that after the first twelve hours it was like, "We've gotta do something. This is ruining it."

So I was restrained by my colleagues here, they said give it a chance. Sam [Palmisano] didn't get upset, HR didn't get upset. Nic Donofrio [Senior Vice President, Technology and Manufacturing] deliberately went in and provoked people. He made a comment about the basic beliefs—and he's been here forever—that they've become dysfunctional; and this produced a huge reaction. And I said, "Nic, what are you doing?" and he said, "Hey, I'm just part of the dialogue here."

But after 24 hours, 36 hours, 48 hours, without management intervention, . . . what happened was what we really hoped would happen, and that was the rest of the employee population weighed in . . . and cumulatively it put it into more balance and perspective.[5]

The crucial significance of the Values Jam process is not whether it reached the "right" definition, but that it got everyone involved in a deep understanding of what the values meant. Earlier I noted the problem that general principles are too fuzzy to orient people in times of change. In this sense dialogues like the Values Jam serve the function of legal debate and common law, reinterpreting general values for evolving circumstances. The Jam dialogue gives to all its participants a similar kind of shared but flexible grounding. The first Jam was an intense debate about the meaning of fundamental principles such as respect and customer focus; in the second, a year later, the emphasis had a more practical tone of trying to apply the values to shaping everyday behaviors, identifying obstacles and problems—moving, in other words, from a transformative to an incremental type of change.

Thus the words that came out of the Jam at IBM are interesting in themselves, but not sufficient. The final statement of values was:

1. "Dedication to every client's success."
2. "Innovation that matters—for our company and for the world."
3. "Trust and personal responsibility in all relationships."

But only someone who had been through the Jam and the debates it engendered would understand the crucial subtleties in these words: why "client" is chosen instead of "customer"; why "dedication to client's success" replaces the old version, "the best customer service"; and so on. And only people who had been through that process could therefore interact collaboratively with confidence that the other person shared that understanding.

This approach runs counter to the logic and instincts of traditional bureaucracy, where values must be defined by a strong leader; values here serve more as a way of ensuring continuity of tradition than enabling flexibility. It is common in my interview in more traditional companies, or with senior employees remembering the old days, to hear stories of particular actions by a CEO or other admired leader: how one leader set a rule that no one could have coffee cups on his or her desk (UPS), and another wanted everyone to wear hats (this was a Watson-era feature at IBM), and so on; and these concrete behavioral indices became signs of loyalty and unity, a kind of template for the whole company.

The collaborative model illustrated by the Values Jam, by contrast, separates values from particular leaders and their idiosyncratic behaviors; it grounds values instead in a rich and repeated collective dialogue about their meaning. The former method encourages the kind of conformity which, as we saw in the last chapter, is a major feature of bureaucratic systems and central to the maintenance of trust; the latter enables very diverse and different people to interact by building a shared sense of basic principles that can be applied more flexibly and can be interpreted across a wider range of situations.[6]

### 2. The Strategic Fitness Process

Since the early 1990s Mike Beer, of the Harvard Business School, and his colleagues have conducted a remarkable set of interventions aimed at increasing organizational alignment around strategy. In nearly every case this has involved tremendous internal turmoil because it has required the kind of increase in complexity and collaboration that has been the theme of this volume. I have reviewed detailed material, public and private, on seventeen of these interventions; one of them, Veridian, is included in our core sample.[7]

The basic method is a perfect example of interactive inversion. A task team of middle managers is selected to take the top level's definition of strategy out into the organization, interviewing widely around the effectiveness of the strategy and the obstacles to its implementation. Most of the time this process brings out serious criticisms of top management. The task team then meets with their superiors—but in an unusual format. Rather than standing in front of them and making a formal presentation, the members of the task team sit in a circle and talk to *each other* about what they heard in their interviews, with the senior executives sitting outside the circle as observers. From this novel "listening" structure they move into a dialogue in which the leaders try to grapple with the views brought up from below.

Commonly the task team tells the top managers that their ideas of what are happening in the organization do not reflect reality. At Veridian, the top was in effect pushing for a solutions approach, trying to get beyond their legacy of fragmented products to a more coordinated approach to large projects. The task team told the top leadership that the rest of the organization was not seeing consistency around this initiative, that the actions of the executive committee did not match their rhetoric. As a result, continuing rivalries among divisions were hampering efforts at coordination. This discussion began a long and rather painful process of reassessment, including the development of more effective cross-boundary systems that encouraged wider collaboration.

One of the striking things in this process is the level of fear experienced by both the middle-level team and the senior leadership: "opening up" in this way is so novel that no one feels able to predict where it will go. The lower levels regularly engage in gallows humor about the dangers they are running in speaking honestly to their superiors; the latter regularly worry that they will lose control and fret that they could handle the change more efficiently by just telling people what to do. And, as at IBM, there is some reason for the fears: the emotions unleashed can be very powerful, and confrontations between the task team and its leaders can be sharp. At Veridian, the middle managers sharply criticized the executives for failing to match rhetoric to action in moving to a more unified strategy. Their overall assessment was remarkably blunt: "The [Executive Committee] as a whole is not seen as effective."[8]

Nor is this unusual. The senior leadership in these cases quite often leaves the initial feedback meeting shaken, and when it meets again on its own has to go through dealing with feelings of anger, hurt, and denial. And it's not yet over: when the leadership group then comes back with an action plan to address the task force's issues, they are often told that they missed the point, and another round of challenging follows. In several instances the criticism of senior leadership was so severe that the heads felt that they could not maintain their credibility and offered to resign. It's not surprising that in almost every case there are members of top leadership who retreat to various forms of resistance—who suggest (as one did at Veridian) that it would be much faster and more efficient just to tell everyone very clearly what to do; or who gather their own subordinates in defensive ranks.

Where senior executives have kept tight control, there has been much less increase in organizational capacity than in those where they put themselves at risk. One CEO, for instance, told the consultants that his experience in the military had taught him that leaders had to decide, and that the fishbowl feedback was useful merely as input to him; this is a company that has had continuing severe problems around innovation and coordination. At the other end of the spectrum, one unit of Hewlett-Packard in which the division manager offered her resignation was also one of the few parts of that company that have broken through to a cross-disciplinary solutions capability.[9]

### Bringing in the Outside

The sociodynamic tendency of groups under pressure to shut themselves down and turn inward is best overcome by increasing the scope of interaction with outsiders, particularly customers, and also other stakeholders. In paternalist bureaucracies the pattern is that the people closest to customers are those with the least power: salespeople out in the field, or even, as in the case of the automobile companies, franchisees with no formal organizational position themselves. Everyone else, right to the top, is essentially focused inward, working on how to improve what they are already doing and to generate new products, but without strong connections to the actual needs of customers. Competitors are seen as enemies, suppliers are treated instrumentally, and other stakeholders—political bodies, communities, environmentalists and other pressure groups—are regarded with wary hostility. All of these external relationships are highly colored by the strong in-group dynamics fostered by the paternalist culture.

A collaborative enterprise, oriented to a solutions strategy, has to open up to this whole gamut of "outsiders" and to engage them in mutual dialogue. This is most obvious and most widely recognized in the case of customers: most of our sample went through one process or another to "get to know the customers" more intensively and to connect more employees to them. But other outsiders have also been brought into the collaborative web. Stakeholder groups, which have grown steadily more assertive and effective, have forced many industries to take them seriously and to engage them in joint problem solving. Suppliers and subcontractors have in a growing number of cases been brought into a "partnership" relationship in which the dominant player tries to ensure the success of its suppliers rather than squeezing them as hard as possible.[10] Even competitors are increasingly engaged in this way. Lucent and IBM, among other companies, have sought to build the capability to sell and service competitors' products along with their own in order to provide true solutions for their customers; at an even more ambitious level is the GHX confederation, in which a set of producers and distributors of health care supplies have joined to build common standards and information systems across the entire supply chain.[11]

The breaking of the "inside–outside" barrier often starts with crisis and drama. At IBM, Lou Gerstner, taking over in the midst of the 1992 freefall, refused to take the usual turnaround-CEO steps of selling major parts of the company and radically restructuring around a new vision; he was widely criticized in the business press for not having a clear plan. Instead, he spent two years focusing on listening to the customers and understanding their requirements. One story widely told in the company is that when he first arrived he was told that he would need to make an appearance at a meeting of major customers. A senior manager recounts it:

We ran customer conferences for key CIOs, and in the spring of 1993 there was one in Virginia—Chantilly. I remember this like yesterday. We agonized about "Should we invite Lou," because nobody knew Lou then. "He's busy," we thought. Finally we said, "We should invite him." The invitation that went to his office was, "Lou, we want you to come and speak to our customers but it's only going to take an hour. You'll be back in your office by 10 o'clock in the morning." . . . "Well," he said, "shouldn't I stay and have lunch with them?" "No, execs don't stay," we said. He said, "I don't understand. These are your best customers." So he said, and I remember this: "I'm going to the whole conference. I'll be there the first night. I'll have dinner with them. I'll have breakfast with them. I'll have lunch with them. And any IBM executive who wants to attend must stay for the whole two days." We were all erasing our calendars, saying, "I was always going to be there two days."

He'd only been in the company for a short time and he gets up and speaks. And it was a speech like we'd never heard from an IBM executive. He opened into dialog with them and he started to single IBM executives out. "This executive will fix that and get back to you this afternoon." It was unheard of—the CEO's siding with the customers! . . . Lou turned the thing way upside down—the most important thing a CEO does, or any executive in this company does, is meet with customers. That was like a rocket through the company.[12]

This sort of CEO directive is echoed in other cases in our sample. For example, John Reed, after Citibank's own brush with death, ordaining that the priority order would change from "country, product, customer" to "customer, product, country"; or ABB getting the senior executive team to interview customer leaders to find out what they thought of the company.[13]

These strong interventions can be very powerful in getting attention, but they are clearly not sufficient. Engaging the outside is not like flicking a light switch from off to on; it is more like—in fact, it is—building relationships, with tentative tests and growing understanding, gradually coalescing into a pattern that all parties have confidence in. Drama can help, but it can also hurt if it distracts from the longer, less visible process of generating trust. In many instances the attempt to force in-group members to look outward only makes them more defensive. Often the resistance is subtle: people see criticism as a failure of others to understand them, and so react by going into an advertising or selling mode.

Indeed, it is very easy for these change efforts to go "off the rails" by adopting the rhetoric of change but falling back to the familiar behavioral patterns of the past. Most companies, when they engage the outside, begin not by listening but by trying to "get their message out," communicating with the outside through advertisements and statements rather than engaged dialogue. Wal-Mart has notoriously formed a "war room" to treat its stakeholder relationships like a political campaign, which so far has entirely failed to deal with the growing assertiveness and strength of a wide variety of claimants.[14] In another direction, U.S. auto companies have tried to follow the successful Japanese model of working with their subcontractors rather than treating them as outsiders to be manipulated and beaten down, but have not been able to do it.[15]

The more successful cases that I know of all involve a slow and steady increase in inside–outside interaction at all levels, with continued guidance from leaders or facilitators who understand the collaborative process. Only some, *not* all, involve a strong symbolic moment of inversion like the IBM example. One case we have studied that is short on drama but long on results is Avaya's effort to reach out to its larger customers in shaping its own strategy. It brought them into an "Executive Advisory Council" of high-level leaders to engage in an extended shared learning process, testing out various strategic ideas and building their approach to the market in a kind of partnership. One of the key ground rules was "No selling": everyone agreed from the start that the discussion would be about mutual exchange of value rather than about convincing others. In a series of meetings led by an outside facilitator, they tested strategic ideas and got strong feedback that identified major weaknesses from the customers' perspective. Avaya made important strategic and operational shifts as a result of these criticisms; equally important, the customers began to learn about the potential of emerging systems, and their own failure to maximize their use of it. As the process went on, both Avaya and its customers got closer to each other, more able to work on specific collaborative projects, and also more in touch with developments in the marketplace.[16]

In reaching out to political and social stakeholders, there is once again both drama and the "slow boring of hard boards."[17] Here an exemplar is Shell. A crisis in 1995 over the disposal of a North Sea oil platform made the company painfully aware of the power of public opinion and activist groups. Since that time the company has vowed to engage its stakeholders, including environmentalists and local community groups, in continuing and interactive dialogue—not just selling plans but trying to build them in partnership. This dimension has been built into management reward systems and into process definitions and measurements. A round of stakeholder forums has gradually built ongoing relationships quite different from the previous adversarial pattern.[18]

In short, though crisis can be a catalyst, it seems both possible and increasingly reliable to create change without crisis. The Avaya council and to some extent the GHX confederation of health care suppliers[19] involved a deliberate use of approaches that have been learned over decades of building simpler teams: consensual creation of agendas, agreement on rules of dialogue, use of neutral facilitators, public records, and so on.

The development of collaborative norms and values can happen fairly quickly within a defined group, sometimes as large as several hundred; but it is constantly running into trouble at the margins. Those *not* in the group continue to operate on traditional expectations: they may want more traditional hard-nosed negotiation, and they may be suspicious of their "representatives" for acting out of line.[20] Thus the dialogue process typically has to push continually outward through a series of phases, constantly bringing in new players. In the Avaya case the leaders gradually built a set of networks at different levels focused on various aspects of the customer relationship, each built around the same norms of collaborative interaction.[21]

These "process-based" approaches are not easy, and they do not eliminate emotion from the reconstruction of relationships; on the contrary, emotion is close to the surface. When Avaya's leaders were told bluntly by their customers in an early meeting that their strategy did not stack up, it was a shock on a personal level as well as an organizational one. But the process does help to smooth out the working-through, so that it is less likely to degenerate into defensiveness and more likely to keep open a path of steady growth of understanding.

## WHAT: A GENERAL MODEL OF CHANGE STEPS

Though the details of change processes are as varied as the organizations that engage in them, some general elements keep reappearing. One crucial step in the change process is building a shared understanding of strategy, which defines the common purpose of all members of the enterprise. A second is building denser and more formal process relations. They do not necessarily follow in sequence, but achieving a shared purpose is necessary before new relationships can "take" in daily work.

## 1. Building Shared Purpose

The thing that brings people together from different units, professional orientations, and levels in a collaborative enterprise is the sense that they are working on something together. In what I have called "adaptive" enterprises, focused on projects with relatively little strategic complexity, the focus on the outside customer is enough to provide this sense of shared purpose. But in systems that seek higher levels of integration, purpose must go beyond this customer focus to build a shared view of *strategy*. In a bureaucracy strategy is the preserve of top leadership, carefully kept secret from the rest of the organization, while for a collaborative system—especially of the "solutions" type—it is the common orientation for everyone.

In our collaborative cases this strategic understanding was a necessary early condition for progress. When it was lacking, network-building, task teams, and new initiatives were unable to gain traction. For example, the Global Corporate Bank at Citibank in the 1970s followed from a top management vision of global banking, but this strategic vision was not understood and shared widely through the system. It was not until after the crisis of the early 1990s, when it became more widely apparent that a new strategy was needed, that the international systems began to build momentum and overcome the existing internal habits and routines. This is a major root of the pattern of "successful failure" described in the last chapter: even when experiments accomplish everything they aim at, they generally become isolated unless they are widely understood as contributing to solving a shared problem.

The problem is to get everyone to take strategy seriously. It is easy to create training programs, but very difficult to make those programs seem relevant to the daily concerns of people who are used to more job-centered, bureaucratic forms of work. Shared purpose often begins to emerge around crises. IBM, like Citibank, went through near-death experiences around 1990, and in both cases this helped shift people's focus at all levels from the routine performing of jobs to the broader direction of the firm. At IBM, Lou Gerstner and Sam Palmisano did a particularly good job in directing this energy toward strategic images, beginning with the notion of "network computing," and moving some years later to the more complex strategy of "on-demand." These were difficult concepts that were far beyond what most employees had been expected to grasp in the past; it took intensive processes of discussion and education to begin to embed them in daily consciousness.

The development of shared purpose is not always, however, driven by crisis or by clear top management mandate. The Strategic Fitness interventions described earlier generate a ferment of inquiry around strategy. The interview process is often the first time that many people in the organization have heard about the strategic issues that their top leaders have been debating, and the openness of the format encourages them to explore them, understand them, and test their applicability. The messages that the task team carry back force the leaders to rethink them in terms of whether they can really be implemented with the resources of the organization. This then becomes the core orientation that brings together people who had formerly been isolated in bureaucratic "stovepipes."

In this process the very notion of strategy is revised—from a technical expertise to a mobilizing orientation, formulated in terms that everyone can relate to. In collaborative companies almost any randomly chosen person can discourse on the company's core competencies, the nature of the competition, the anticipated development of the market, and the ways in which they intend to position themselves for the future.

These stories follow the interactive pattern. Strategy *could* be defined by top leadership and "cascaded" down through the system; indeed, Wall Street generally encourages and applauds such "bold" and "visionary" leadership. But that is not how these successful cases work. At IBM, Lou Gerstner commented when he took over leadership that "the last thing IBM needs right now is a vision."[22] By this he meant that he did not want to come in with a full-blown strategic picture to impose on the organization. Instead, as we have seen, he pushed his employees to interact directly with customers, and he encouraged them to engage in strategic conversations. The key move toward the Internet was greatly affected by a group of middle managers who were able to bring the potential of the new phenomenon to the attention of their superiors.

In recent years the "Balanced Scorecard" approach has become another systematic tool for developing shared strategic understanding. This approach has in fact gone through an evolution from a unidimensional to an interactive approach. It started in the early 1990s as a rather technical tool for strategic planners, but it has developed into a change technique that, as its authors put it, aims to "make strategy everyone's everyday job" and to "make strategy a continual process." The emphasis has shifted from better measurement to better management—that is, the Balanced Scorecard has become the center of a process of continual dialogue at all levels around strategy. I did not see it used in this way in my own research, but accounts of its use in a wide range of firms—from Apple Computing to Shell to National Bank Online Financial Services (OFS)—suggest that it is taking to a larger audience the basic principle of putting the strategy at the center of the work process for everyone.[23]

## 2. Network-Building

The second major element in crossing to collaboration is the transformation of the routines and relations of everyday work. The traditional pattern is one of formal distance—mutual respect for others' "autonomy"—and informal deal-making. Building a collaborative system requires that people think in terms of organized networks of mutual interdependence. As we have noted, this is not easy: there is a strong tendency for people familiar with bureaucratic norms to protect their own zones of autonomy and to resent "intrusions" by others at their own level.

So far, from the evidence we have, the development of peer relationships has not been managed as well as it could be. Two things have been done fairly widely: the creation of interdependencies by putting people into formal cross-functional teams and creating other network ties and training in consensual problem-solving techniques. These initiatives often help people to find their own way to effective collaboration, but they fail at times to overcome entrenched differences. Difficult cases may also require deliberate definition of value contributions.

### Creating New Links

The most natural change lever, because most continuous with past habits, has been to direct people from above to form new relationships—and then hope that they will learn to function collaboratively. This comes in a large variety of flavors. Most obviously, managers form cross-functional task teams; as we've seen, this can be a hit-or-miss proposition, at best slow and uncertain, with many resistances.

Overcoming these divisions requires—in addition to the development of shared purpose and open dialogue—systematic attention to the network-building aspects of infrastructure. This is a slow process of creating new connections to encourage interaction across boundaries. Useful techniques discussed in Chapter 6 include deliberate linking roles; leadership policies that encourage the inclusion of diverse skills and nationalities on project teams; building "communities of practice" or "learning communities" that draw together people with common interests for discussion and experience-sharing; computer systems that spread information about capabilities and performance widely through the organization so that people looking for collaborators can locate candidates beyond their personal networks; and forums that enable people to learn about significant projects throughout the system.

### Consensual Problem-Solving Techniques

If simply creating teams and connections is not enough, it may help to provide structured experiences in team-building and consensual decision-making skills. This has been a significant part of the training function for a decade or more, and there has been tremendous innovation around it. When teams are formed nowadays among shopfloor workers or low-level managers, it is rare that they fail to get instruction in facilitative leadership, brainstorming, group prioritization, and win–win problem-solving—all of which were quite rare as recently as the late 1980s.

This kind of training clearly helps. It forces people who may otherwise be suspicious to go through a process, to take the steps of defining common problems and looking for common solutions; often this creates enough momentum to overcome the initial obstacles. So, for instance, when we surveyed Citibank's Process Improvement Teams, facilitation training turned up, as one would hope, as one of the top differentiators between the best and the worst teams.[24]

But a good deal of team-building training, especially the earlier forms, limits itself to the building of intra-team solidarity rather than building processes that link to the wider organization. This is, I believe, why these teams so often turn inward: they like each other, but they don't know how to articulate and leverage their value to the organization. Thus (as described earlier) they regularly hit a wall after a few months.[25]

### Deliberate Definition of Value Exchanges

Finally, there is some experience that suggests that it is helpful to deliberately discuss the value that the diverse parties bring to collaborative relationships. This is distinct from simply understanding the other party; it involves the further step of agreeing on the contribution expected from each actor. It is an idea that fits with the logic of contribution, but that has been implemented only in partial and scattered instances.

One of the experiences I would point to is the Citibank manager's description of his method of putting together collaborative groups (see Chapter 3). He began by systematically defining to himself what skills and resources were needed for the project, and identifying people who could supply them; then he defined the value that the project could give to each of them. This "contribution analysis" was the basis for negotiating for people's participation and defining their roles. This mode of action was in fact common in that unit, because it was the only way to create the fluid collaborative connections that were needed.

I find two other relevant cases. The customer learning group sponsored by Avaya begins with this same kind of analysis of potential contributions and makes them explicit as part of the process of recruiting and defining member roles. And the GHX health care alliance defines ownership stakes in part by the value contribution of the parties.[26]

It is interesting that the explicit discussion of mutual value happens most naturally where authority systems are weak—in intercompany systems or in unusually collaborative settings like Citibank e-Solutions. When one thinks about it, if a team is going to be put together by peers it has to begin by focusing on what the parties will contribute and what roles they will fill.

My speculation is that in most other cases authority gets in the way by taking over this function almost unconsciously: that is, bosses, when they put together task forces and project groups, consider what diverse skills are needed. The teams themselves, once constituted from above, then do not have a clear reason to build an understanding of each other's contribution; instead it is easy to just complain about each other to the boss, or to band together in an undifferentiated unit. This is one of the ways in which the use of authority is a double-edged sword, undercutting the principles of collaboration even as it tries to mandate the framework for it.

## THE ROLE OF COLLABORATIVE VISION

Vision, I suggested earlier, can help smooth the otherwise turbulent and uncertain transition from bureaucratic to collaborative enterprise. Here I am not talking about *strategic* "vision," which is a picture of where the enterprise is going in the next few years. The question now is what role may be played by the more fundamental, broad, and long-term vision of *collaboration* that is the subject of this volume. Does it help, in the transition from bureaucracy, to believe in collaboration?

It does appear from our cases that successful transitions have leaders who understand and believe in the value of collaboration, at least in an intuitive way. But they do not trumpet it loudly as a program to be followed or put it at the center of their value statements. They prefer to let it grow from small seeds.

On the smoothest path, collaborative vision seems to begin as private but gradually becomes public. That is, at first the general pattern of teamwork, contribution, and interactivity is grasped only by one or a few leaders. These values guide the key interventions just described—the building of strategic understanding, focusing on customers, network-building, and so on—and force a wider circle to collaborate as a practical matter.

Thus leaders in our sample have tended to follow their own consistent vision of collaborative systems, but to communicate it to the organization only incrementally, through specific initiatives. At Cummins India, Ravi Venkatesan's efforts to encourage customer focus met with "polite nods with no sign of comprehension"; to force new thinking he formed a customer council of "smart and influential" customers to get their voices in the room and scheduled a major customer exhibition in Delhi a few months out to force people to action.[27] At ABB, Percy Barnevik tried to build cross-boundary systems not by talking about values in general, but through specific "network-building" actions that forced people into interdependent relationships.

This "under the radar" approach, however, goes only so far: there comes a point at which organizations need more explicit discussion of the norms and values that guide them, and how the collaborative approach differs from the expectations of the past. It is essential that in time the general vision become public, shared and understood by everyone, in order to shape the countless daily relationships that make collaborative enterprise work.

The revival of IBM shows this sequence. From the first, Lou Gerstner had a clear and consistent sense of collaboration that differed markedly from the old pattern of personal exchanges of favors. Rather than articulating it openly, however, he quietly encouraged counter-cultural mid-level ventures. Those managers in immediate contact with him experienced a way of managing that was very different from the soft paternalism of the past, one much more like the culture of contribution described in Chapter 4; but this worked its way only gradually into the wider organization.

Later Gerstner ran into limits in how far he could push his vision through these "private" means. He sparked a major reaction, for instance, when he tried to change pensions to be consistent with a new vision of careers. By the time he left, the practical movement toward a more customer-focused, entrepreneurial system had advanced considerably, but the friction between the "old" and the "new" IBMers was like a chronic ache throughout the organization. People at all levels described a sense of malaise: though the company was doing very well, there was a sense of deep confusion about what could be expected for the future—whether the old "Basic Beliefs" of loyalty, stability, and excellence still governed, or whether a different orientation had taken over. Some saw the company as descending into a short-term world driven by Wall Street and callous toward employees; others saw it as opening up a new world of entrepreneurial excitement and promise; others still hoped for a return to the old pattern. Jon Iwata, senior vice president, Communications, commented:

> In late 2002, we did not have shared values across the company. There was a void there. We knew that if we did not fill that void, people would either continue to mourn or they would fill it themselves and there would be a proliferation of values, principles, and precepts.[28]

This was the source of Sam Palmisano's decision to hold the Value Jam process described earlier, which took the company another step along the iterative loop between articulating visions and working-through in practice. Palmisano described the way in which the Jam discussions then helped to overcome blockages based in old routines, such as the problems they had had in introducing unified solutions pricing:

> [W]e'd been debating the pricing issue at the executive level for a long time. But we hadn't done anything about it. The values initiative forced us to confront the issue, and it gave us the impetus to make the change. You know, there are always ingrained operations and habits of mind in any organization.[29]

The Values Jam is thus one example of a public conversation that clarifies vision. In many other cases there were less formalized but nonetheless crucial conversations of this type. At Citibank e-Solutions it was a "Team Challenge" that brought together a set of key employees to reflect on the lessons of a previous experiment in the development of electronic banking, and to formulate the principles that drove the e-Solutions organization. These conversations worked because they built on a base of common experience and articulated it into a broader shared pattern.[30]

For a contrast—a "wrong" way to do it—one might look at the short sad story of Jacques Nasser's tenure as CEO of Ford. Nasser tried to take on the Ford culture immediately and directly by *teaching* a different set of values—customer-focused, market-driven, team-based, anti-bureaucratic:

> [T]here is no question that we have to change our fundamental approach to work—we have to change our DNA. And teaching does that better than any other way I know. . . . Teaching allows you to replace the old mythology with a new and better one. . . . With teaching, we've been able to introduce new stories, to create a different folklore about what's possible at Ford. I tell a lot of stories that have the same moral—that working at Ford does not have to be about working in a single area. It can be about working and caring for the whole company. . . . That's how you build a new culture—through stories.[31]

Well, no, that's not how you do it: Nasser and his stories were emphatically rejected by the Ford culture. There were of course many reasons for his departure after less than three years on the job, but many of those voiced at the time had to do with the aggressive attack on embedded values.[32]

Nasser's experience shows the need to build a sense of collaboration on a base of real practical change, rather than through abstract exhortation. But many other experiences show that vision cannot be omitted altogether: at some point the key cultural elements of change must be brought to public consciousness. We can see, for example, the problems caused by the unwillingness of leaders to challenge the traditional expectations of paternalist caring. Corporate leaders increasingly want people to be entrepreneurial, innovative, and performance-centered; but often they want them at the same time to be loyal and reliable. As a result they may soften the message of change—playing down the difficulties of competition and shift in the rules of the game around layoffs. When they do this, they end with unstable cultures—the kind of unease that IBM experienced after a decade of Gerstner's leadership, the kind that I have found in many companies where the middle managers still hope for a return to past days of comfort and glory. This failure to address the changing vision of the future leaves employees at all levels adrift in very dangerous waters with no clear course of action.

It took vision for Palmisano to stick with the Values Jam process when many of his subordinates feared the undermining of authority. It took vision for Veridian CEO David Langstaff to stay the course when some of his senior executives wanted to clamp down on discussion, or for Venkatesan to force his reluctant managers to confront real customers. Each of these leaders had images that acted as compasses in the change process, keeping it steady along a path toward increased collaboration. As others in their organizations experienced new patterns of action, it became possible to reflect on them collectively and to articulate a changed culture through public conversations like the Values Jam or the Strategic Fitness Process, which in turn could guide further experimentation with less dependence on the leader. This is the best answer that I can see in our evidence for how to improve the otherwise random, error-ridden path of system transformation.

## CONCLUSION

It is hard to draw a process that is as multidimensional and iterative as what I have just sketched, but it may nevertheless be helpful to sketch a picture (Figure 22). The magic in the transformation process involves keeping two levels going simultaneously. An initial condition is an attraction to collaborative values among core leaders. The necessary foundation for expansion of practice is laid by the development of shared purpose or strategic alignment. Attention to network-building helps give the purpose meaning in everyday routines and work. Meanwhile, through periodic processes of reflection and dialogue, the vision is gradually made more public and sharpened as a framework of mutual expectations for all.

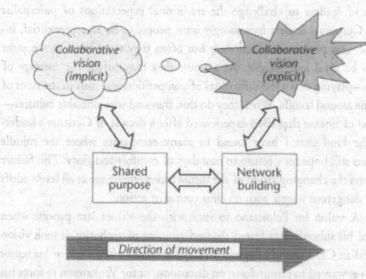

Figure 22: The change process

Organizations must manage a balancing act: being open to unplanned initiatives, but also bringing those initiatives into interaction with the vision to see whether it needs to be modified, or new experiments need to be tried. The closer this interconnection, the less discontinuous and "chaotic" the change process. There will still be moments of insight, of "tipping points," that will seem to open new vistas, but the groundwork will have been laid by ongoing development of capabilities at all levels, and so will not have the violence of revolutions that have less effective interconnection of vision and practice.

# Chapter 10 Recapitulation

This is a recapitulation, and not yet a conclusion, because the final chapter will go beyond the empirical study to consider the place of collaborative enterprise in the larger array of social values. But it seems useful, after this long excursion, to look back over the main points.

The central concept of extended collaboration is radically different from that of traditional communities and teams, which rely on closed, homogeneous, and stable relationships. Extended collaboration instead involves diversity of skills and perspectives, openness at the boundaries, and limited time frames. In general, it involves a strengthening of the "horizontal" or associational dimension of organizations, and therefore creates a set of new problems in linking this horizontal dimension to the continued "vertical" hierarchy.

I have tried to make claims about the development of extended collaboration in the business world that are empirically based. Although many of these claims are too complex to be proven or may need more time to work themselves out, there is relevant evidence for each of them in the sample of organizations that has grounded this study. The research methods and evidence are reviewed in the Appendix.

1. The main claim is that extended collaboration is the critical capability for long-term success in complex knowledge businesses. Despite the difficulty of this capability, firms are increasingly being driven to develop it, and some have now crossed a boundary where they are unlikely to fall back to bureaucratic patterns.

2. The need for extended collaboration is driven by major strategic imperatives or choices:

   a. For strategies based on efficiency, the need for continuous improvement and learning.

   b. For strategies based on integrating complexity, the need to balance competing priorities.

   c. For strategies based on rapid adaptiveness, the need to adjust quickly to changing environmental demands.

   d. In the most difficult case, these dimensions are combined in solutions strategies that seek to respond rapidly to customer needs with complex combinations of services and products, while maintaining cost efficiency and quality.

3. Each of these strategic needs has specific organizational consequences (see Table 8).

   a. A focus on efficiency (which has been in the background in this volume, as an assumed part of all strategies) requires a reflective capability. For organizations in which efficiency is the core of strategy, the daily work is organized in fairly traditional hierarchies, but periodic reviews bring together multiple segments of the organization to identify process blockages and to seek improvements.

   b. A focus on complexity requires *managed collaboration:* the hierarchy remains strong, with collaborative linking teams cutting across the hierarchy but under its control. Typically the hierarchical structure takes a "front–back" form: distinct units facing the customer, others responsible for product development, and strong linking mechanisms between the two.

   c. A focus on adaptiveness requires *project collaboration*, built around teams with considerable autonomy that are encouraged to innovate and respond quickly to opportunities; the hierarchy is relatively weak, and the teams initiate a good deal of their own activity.

   d. A solutions strategy requires *systemic collaboration,* with both strong hierarchies and strong teams. The hierarchy is strong in articulating strategic

Table 8 Organization Types

| High Complexity | | Managed collaboration (complex) | Systemic collaboration (complex and adaptive) |
|---|---|---|---|
| | Unitary bureaucracy | Integrated bureaucracy (modular) | *Project collaboration (adaptive)* |
| | Simple bureaucracy | Decentralized bureaucracy | |

*High Adaptiveness*

*Note*: Categories in bold italics are collaborative. The four bureaucratic types are described in more detail in the extended research chapter available from the author or online at www.heckscher.com/ CollaborativeEnterprise.

priorities, prioritizing, and developing cross-unit learning, but not in assigning tasks or governing daily operations. Most work is performed in teams that form easily across unit boundaries and gather needed resources around opportunities. The strategic offering is the ability to interact deeply with customers and to provide complex solutions.

4. Extended collaboration requires a deep shift in cultural pattern, from a paternalist bureaucracy to a culture of *contribution*. Central values in this cultural complex include:

   a. Focus on capability for contribution rather than on formal position.

   b. Dialogue and openness, including willingness to challenge peers and superiors.

   c. Helpfulness toward others, including free sharing of information.

   d. Openness to the outside.

   e. Embracing diversity of capabilities.

5. Extended collaboration rests on a set of stable systems of "social infrastructure":

   a. For creating and maintaining a shared understanding of the mission.

   b. For formalizing the building of relationships, especially with peers.

   c. For building continuous dialogue with external stakeholders, especially customers.

   d. For organizational learning.

6. The shift to extended collaboration requires overcoming sociodynamic resistances, expressed as tendencies to regress to simpler forms of organization and behavior:

a. A retreat to autonomy, just "doing my job" and trying to ignore the complexity of environmental demands.

b. Withdrawal into small-group solidarity based on homogeneity and defensive self-protection.

c. Dependence on and loyalty to powerful protectors.

d. One-dimensional rationality, especially the pure "performance orientation" that echoes bureaucratic Management by Objectives.

7. The transition to extended collaboration requires interactive leadership that partially inverts "normal" relationships:

a. From higher to lower: encouraging active dialogue and criticism of strategy and policy from lower-level positions.

b. From inside to outside: bringing customers and other stakeholders directly into the decision-making processes of the system.

8. The shift to extended collaboration occurs in two major steps:

a. Building a shared understanding of and commitment to strategy.

b. Building networks of collaborative relationships.[1]

9. Two major problems remain in developing extended collaboration:

a. Accountability: there is a need to move beyond the simple "performance" orientation in order to reward contribution to the strategic mission.

b. Careers: there is a need for far more support for mobility in order to realize the promise of matching specialized knowledge fluidly with emerging tasks and projects.

Table 9 Varieties of Collaborative Enterprise

| | Paternalist Bureaucracy | Collaborative Enterprise (Level 4): General Characteristics | Varieties of Collaborative Enterprise: Particular Characteristics | | |
|---|---|---|---|---|---|
| | | | *Strategic Orientation:* Integrative (complex)<br>*Organizational form:* managed collaboration | *Strategic Orientation:* Responsive (adaptive)<br>*Organizational form:* project collaboration | *Strategic Orientation:* Solutions (complex and adaptive)<br>*Organizational form:* systemic collaboration |
| Research examples | General Motors<br>IBM (pre-1990) | | Citi Global Bank<br>IBM (1990s) | Nokia<br>Spaarbeleg<br>McKinsey | Citi e-Solutions<br>IBM (2000s)<br>"NewTech" |
| Strategies | Product excellence<br>Efficiency, cost control<br>Mass markets | Customer focus/ integrated solutions | Product linkages, bundling | Customization, segmentation, and rapid innovation | Complex, dynamic solutions |
| Structure | Strong formal hierarchy<br>Informal peer organization | Thinner formal hierarchy<br>Task teams<br>Process maps | Hierarchies focused on single dimensions (product, region, customer, function) linked by bridging roles and committees (CRMs, task managers, etc.) | Loose network of relatively autonomous groups, weak strategic unity | Rich networks with high overlap; strong planning and prioritization processes |

| | | Contribution | Identification with system (organization, colleagues—long-term frame) | Identification with project/client | Identification with mission (three- to five-year frame) |
|---|---|---|---|---|---|
| Cultural core | Loyalty, obedience, caring, security | Collective strategy focus; Formalized peer relationships; Links to allies, customers, and stakeholders; Learning | Planning (negotiating priorities) | Sensing; Resource mobility | Adaptive learning (review and course correction); Strategic integration |
| Infrastructural | Offices and hierarchical control; Defining roles and responsibilities | | | | |
| Key intervention focus | Tension of centralization versus decentralization | Building shared strategic understanding; Creating networks | Establishing negotiating power of linking roles | Building reputational system ("360"); selection; strategic contest | Building shared strategic understanding and focus |
| Typical problems | | Tension of discipline versus flexibility | Overcoming established structural boundaries | System learning; Drawing on knowledge from other areas | Loss of focus and consistency (discipline) |

# Chapter 11  But Is It Good?

In the final chapter, I consider the impact of extended collaboration not just on economic performance, but on other values as well. The transformation I have described is after all a controversial one, in large part because it seems to threaten values that are deeply held by many in the workforce and the wider society—including security, loyalty, caring, quality, and community.

Social scientists still have a hard time in discussing values, more than a century after Weber tried to put the issue to rest by elaborating the distinction between values and social facts.[1] Most researchers would like to believe that their research is purely objective, modeled on classical physics, and built purely by finding regularities in data. But it turns out not to be so easy to escape the effects of values; they are powerful parts of human motivation and embedded in all action. Like unconscious drives, they push us in particular directions even without our awareness. This is, incidentally, not just a problem for the fuzzy social sciences: even natural scientists have become increasingly aware of the power of beliefs in shaping theories. Einstein, for example, was never able fully to accept quantum theory because it violated his deep belief that "God does not play dice with the Universe"; and Darwin noted that he had to work particularly hard to remember evidence that disconfirmed natural selection, because he tended unconsciously to push it out of his mind.

But the social realm is even more vulnerable to the effects of values, for there the data are almost always full of judgment and the emotional pull of their value consequences is strong. The results of studies on inequality in the United States, for example, can usually be predicted on the basis of the researchers' political beliefs. Even the most sober, careful investigators will find ways, in the myriad data sources and innumerable problems of interpretation, to bring the conclusions closer to their preconceptions. Liberal scientists trumpet data that seem to show sharp rises in inequality over the last few decades, while conservatives point out many flaws in the sources and draw lines between categories differently—in ways that end up minimizing this increase.

In the case of collaboration, the fundamental claim that I have put forward—that collaborative organization is necessary to economic success in major areas of the economy—is subject to several value-based distortions. Some people might accept it too easily because it seems to embrace values they like: diversity, involvement, and innovation; others might equally easily reject it because it threatens autonomy, security, and clarity of accountability.

There is also a second, more practical reason for addressing values: No social change can succeed if it does not win the "hearts and minds" of those who must make it work. Business organizations, to say nothing of society as a whole, are far too complex to be run as machines with detailed instructions from the center; they must have a strong cadre of people who both understand and believe in the basic direction of change and can help to make the daily decisions that determine how well it is implemented. This is increasingly true as systems become more interdependent and knowledge-dependent: they require not just a general willingness to accept authority but also a positive enthusiasm for its proposals.

Thus the excavation of the values within a theory helps both to test for bias and to clarify the practical conditions for use. But there is no generally accepted method for performing this excavation. It is quite a different process from testing hypotheses. Values are particularly slippery: their interpretation depends heavily on the point of view of the beholder. Generally, in fact, people define their own views as moral but those of others, if significantly different, as merely self-interested. Further, in practice, values are never unidimensional, all sunny or all dark. They have complex consequences and interconnections throughout the community they affect. Those who advocate corporate responsibility and caring toward employees emphasize the social good that can result, but they tend to ignore the side effects that are visible in most real corporations: conformity, subservience, hidden political infighting, and suppression of innovation. Those who advocate a collaborative perspective, in turn, put forward the relative openness and diversity of such systems. But there is a dark side here as well: tendencies to heightened inequality, to brutal treatment of those who cannot quickly contribute, to high stress and uncontrolled workloads. These consequences are not part of the espoused values, but they come along like uninvited guests and so cannot be ignored.

Thus the answer to the question, "Is it good?" is always likely to be, "It depends." It depends on how values are implemented, on choices made by leaders, on the depth of shared understanding among participants—in short, on action. And so the question morphs into another form: "Can it be *made* good? And if so, how?"

This will require retracing some of the issues discussed in earlier chapters, such as employment security, diversity, and inequality—but reframing them in terms of their consequences not for business effectiveness, but for other social stakeholders and values. I will begin by sketching the collaborative value position by comparing it to its main competitors, paternalism and the free market, and by sketching its own case, as it were, for why it is good. Then I will explore the dark side—the ways in which it may justify selfishness and self-interest, or in practice undermine its own ideals. Finally I will take up the question of whether there are actions that could help it realize its best ideals.

## COMPETING VALUE ORIENTATIONS

At the broadest level, collaboration is one of three competing patterns or complexes of values in industry. One side is a set anchored in the traditional firm, emphasizing loyalty, caring, security, stability, seniority, and dutiful or craftsmanlike excellence.[2] Slightly less conscious and deliberately held, but equally important to the overall complex, is the value of deference to authority.

On the other side, anchored in modern markets, is a set of values centered on freedom, individualism, risk-taking, innovation, and choice. Again, there is a slightly more ambivalently held but nonetheless central corollary: it involves the Calvinist notion that failure is a sign of lack of moral worth. As extended today by conservative philosophers and economists, it makes a moral argument that change is good, that those who can't keep up do not deserve to be supported, that we can't afford to carry the weak. Jack Welch of General Electric has often been seen as an exemplar, among the first to adopt a systematic policy of removing weak performers, appearing to revel in high stress and competition, deliberately pushing a culture of "edge."[3]

This market orientation is the more "modern" one that historically blew away the traditional loyalty and stability of traditional societies, but that has never fully supplanted them. Although freedom and choice are powerfully attractive to many, most people are not prepared to embrace them exclusively; stability and loyalty endure as moral as well as practical sentiments. Indeed, the whole period in the West since the Renaissance can be seen as a kind of oscillation between these poles.

Collaboration involves values that are distinct from both of these camps. In some respects it seems similar to the free-market ethic and is often assimilated to it by critics. Both stand as sharply critical of the paternalist-bureaucratic ethic of the past, with its burden of loyalty and subservience. Both value "freeing" individuals from the weight of traditional hierarchy and webs of rules; they both move in the direction of greater flexibility and innovation. Both are strongly opposed to institutions like seniority that reward longevity rather than performance.

But collaboration is also different in many ways from free-market morality. The latter essentially denies the moral weight of social relationships, emphasizes the rights of individuals, and promotes competition; the collaborative pattern values contribution to common purpose and promotes cooperation. From the perspective of collaboration, the pure free-agent ethic is just as bad as the traditional bureaucratic orientation. Free agency undermines trust, makes people less willing to share knowledge, and undermines relationships that make it possible to combine resources smoothly.

Collaboration is, in effect, the third leg of the triangle—in some ways intermediate between the other two, in some ways merely different. For example, the paternalist ethic values long-term relationships, the free-market one is very short-term—and the collaborative view is in between, seeing the value of stability in building and maintaining trust, but not to the extent of permanent locking-in. Collaborative types constantly assess the value generated by relationships; when things go bad, they try to repair them rather than quickly dropping them; but if repair does not work they are ready to cut ties and move on. This difference is nicely illustrated in MacDuffie and Helper's analyses of contractor relationships in the automobile industry. The Japanese, they note, have moved from the highly paternalist web of the past to a more collaborative stance, where they try to help their contractors succeed but make no permanent promises; American companies have stayed at the free-market pole, playing contractors off against each other and juggling contracts to get immediate cost savings.[4] Similarly, I have found a distinct set of time horizons among middle managers: traditional types expect to be at their jobs for their lifetimes; free-agent types make no predictions at all; and collaborators expect to be around for three to five years but are not comfortable in predicting beyond that.[5]

Similarly, while the loyalist ethic is highly collectivist and the market one highly individualist, collaborative values are neither, or both. There is certainly a strong emphasis in this orientation on assessing individual performance; but it is the performance of individuals in contributing to the multiple groups and projects of which they are a part. Collaboration assumes that success comes from the interaction of multiple people with differing skills and abilities, and sees individual stardom as denying that interconnection and undermining the conditions for its operation. At the same time, it assumes that success is not the result of any given, permanent group, but rather of a shifting constellations of resources—so that assessing individual contribution is essential.

Each of these orientations sees virtue in its own perspective and vices in the others. The basic patterns necessarily overlap significantly with the cultures described in Chapter 4, but connect to broader visions going beyond the economic and business worlds and crossing several centuries of social thought; the collaborative one, being the newest, has shown its vices less clearly than the others (see Table 10).

At this juncture, the collaborative and free-market perspectives are often unwilling allies, in that both are involved in the general revolt against bureaucracy. But they lead in fundamentally distinct directions.

### THE CASE FOR COLLABORATION

The case for collaboration is that it offers a combination of community and freedom. Against the backdrop of Weberian gloom about the "iron cage" of bureaucracy, and the fears of formal organization expressed from Michels to Whyte and Kanter, it appears immensely liberating. Employees (in this view) are no longer locked into tightly bounded "boxes," able to escape only by pleasing the boss and moving upwards through narrow channels, constrained to conformity in a hierarchical environment; their choices are vastly increased. At the same time, it avoids, at least in principle, the harsh "every-man-for-himself" individualism of the free-market ethic.

## Table 10  Three Value Complexes

| | Loyalty | | Collaboration | | Market | |
|---|---|---|---|---|---|---|
| | The good side, or how it looks to itself | The dark side, or how it looks to others | The good side, or how it looks to itself | The dark side, or how it looks to others | The good side, or how it looks to itself | The dark side, or how it looks to others |
| | Loyalty and status honor | Subservience | Human development Self-constructed individual identities | Lack of strong commitments | Individual moral autonomy Freedom/choice | Harshness Irresponsibility Selfishness |
| | Security | Risk-aversion Narrowness | Mutual support and help | Lack of moral clarity | Dynamism | Insecurity Inequality Inequity |
| | Diffuse communal caring | Conformity Inward focus | Respect for diversity of skills Wide participation | Lack of loyalty to primary group Insecurity | Individualism Tolerance | Mass culture Alienation |
| | Informal cooperation | Exclusionary **"old-boys' clubs"** | Broad cooperation, beyond narrow boundaries and clans | | Free choice (contract) | Adversarial competitiveness Lose-lose dynamics |

Collaboration takes its stand principally on three values, in addition to economic performance, that it holds more centrally than any competing orientation: participation, human development, and diversity.

### Participation

In many respects the move toward collaboration was initially driven, in the 1960s and 1970s, by values of employee participation. The early significant challenges to the principles of bureaucracy and Taylorism were heavily influenced by the concerns of those decades about alienation and participatory democracy. One of the key early players, for instance, was the Tavistock Institute, which had conducted some very early experiments in teamwork in the coal mines of Pennsylvania after World War II; its founders were explicit about their primary pursuit of democracy and human development. They and those influenced by them drew increasingly on models of "industrial democracy" developed in Scandinavia. Even the business leaders who first pushed the concept, such as Sidney Harman in his auto-mirror plant in Bolivar, Tennessee, were inclined to talk idealistically about the virtues of participation.

To be sure, all these pioneers also justified participation in terms of hard-headed business results. At that time, the argument generally was that involved workers would be more committed, and committed workers would work smarter and better: many studies at the time tried to demonstrate that employee involvement led to beneficial business results like lowered turnover and increased productivity. But these were not the driving motivations of those who led the charge; they were rather means of persuading mainstream managers.

This value orientation sometimes led off the historical track; people who took the notion of "democracy" seriously sometimes tried to create systems in which workers elected their managers. At some worker-owned companies, such as Rath Packing in Iowa, former workers were elected to the top management position; in other cases, especially in the steel and airline industries, worker and union representatives claimed seats on boards of directors and played a strong role in strategic decision making. Whatever one thinks of these efforts in value terms, they did not last as part of the mainstream in the United States; indeed, even in Europe, where worker rights are often ensconced in codetermination laws, there has been a decided shift in the last few decades away from this version of reform.

But the collaborative orientation has picked up the value of involvement and participation, though in a particular form that does not necessarily reflect the original ideals. Collaborative enterprises are highly involving compared to bureaucracies: people are expected to challenge their bosses, to go beyond their narrow job definitions, to seize initiative and responsibility. The basis for this involvement, however, is not general human rights, but rather individual knowledge and capabilities. One has a right to challenge bosses only if one knows something that they do not and can base the challenge on the grounds of contributing to the shared purpose.

Thus many of those who hold the value of democracy as primary will be dissatisfied with the collaborative model: it does not imply equal rights to power or processes of majority rule. Nevertheless, though it has little relationship to traditional debates about democracy, it does involve a radical challenge to hierarchy. Those who use power must in principle justify it on the basis of common purpose rather than on the basis of position. As a result, power may shift rapidly depending on issues and circumstances: an assembly-line worker can gain a decisive role in decision making, but only when and if strategic choice depends on manufacturing capability. Within a given team, the baton may pass from the marketing expert to the manufacturing expert to the strategist at different phases.

This development does not fit standard categories. Collaborative participation is not democracy; nor is it the most common alternative view, meritocracy. Meritocracy implies that those who have the highest level of general "merit" will ascend to positions of power. Collaboration minimizes the concept of "position" altogether, and it does not have much use for the concept of general "merit." The question that determines weight in decision processes is: What can a given social actor contribute to the problem under discussion? Some people may be useless a good deal of the time but have a critical value at certain moments. Some people will be highly influential on particular issues but not on others.

Collaborative organizations that I have observed, such as parts of IBM or Citibank, clearly engage their employees on a very active level; there is no sign there of "alienation" in the sense used by the early advocates of teamwork, who focused on the mind-numbing boredom of repetitive task performance. Some cases go further: they give employees of all levels a wide voice in overall direction. The Strategic Fitness Process described in Chapter 9 established a middle management team that collects views from every part of the organization on strategic direction and implementation, and then feeds back these views through an intense process that forces top management to respond and frequently to significantly modify their plans. IBM's Values Jam, also described in that chapter, gave all employees a chance to participate in an egalitarian, intense dialogue about the fundamental company values—a discussion that has had a real impact on leadership behaviors and policies.

Collaborative systems are in general lively, challenging, and make use of a wide range of capabilities: employees commonly echo one computer company manager in my interviews—"This is a great place to work. It's fun, it's a fantastic experience. It's addictive." This is part of their attraction.

### Human Development

The value of human development is related to democracy but can also be independent of it. John Locke, one of the first democratic philosophers of the modern era, did not use it: he grounded his argument on a notion of universal natural rights. Rousseau started on the same route, but then added the value concept of individual authenticity and development. The latter argument can be grafted on to the former by claiming that democracy is the best road to development, but it is not a necessary relationship. The ambiguity continues today: some writers believe that industrial democracy is simply a natural right, while others, such as Carole Pateman, justify it primarily as a road to the development of the self.[6]

Pateman's case was that participation at work forces people to develop their understanding of others and to take others' perspectives, which for her was an ultimate good. People who follow this line prize not just the abstract notion of democracy based on voting, but also a highly interactive notion with continual debate and negotiation and openness to multiple groups.

Collaboration, as it has evolved, has moved very much in this direction: that is, it has required people not only to work with others like them in small groups, but also to interact with people from very different groups with different views of the world. And middle managers in such situations are often aware of the ways they have grown and learned to deal with a broadened range of situations. So a Saturn manager said,

> It's a growth experience especially in terms of decision making and working with other functions. The 16 months I have been here have added four years of experience.

And one at IBM:

> I've had such varied experience—in the last few years I've probably worked on seven or eight different projects, which means I've had seven or eight different project managers and I've had had seven or eight different teams to work for. And it's

a fascinating experience, because each team is different, individuals are different, clients are different, requirements are different, geography is different, and what you bring to the table in terms of development and as a human resource is constantly being evaluated and tested, because you constantly have to keep adjusting yourself to what the requirements are. So I've been able to become very flexible in my approach, and I've been able to learn a tremendous amount, not just technically, but you know, dealing with different people, how you handle situations, how you communicate.

At times working with varied people in a team environment is even experienced as a kind of conversion—as by a manager at AT&T dealing in a problem-solving group with union officers:

I would say it was a significant emotional event in my life. It changed my way of thinking. I became a true convert to [collaborative] principles. I firmly believe that the only way AT&T is going to succeed is to work together, that the adversarial relationship is a relationship of the past. Now, there have been instances since that training where I personally have reverted back to old behavior—because I've been a manager a long time—but through the honesty of the team, they have called me on it. And it hurts at the time, but I've accepted it and I have tried and I continue to try to make the correct changes.

Development is also stimulated, according to most views, by increased personal choice and responsibility, and it is retarded by the converse: dependence and subservience. Here again collaborative systems fit the picture far better than the paternalist ones they replace. In the latter systems companies demand obedience and subservience, and even devise (as a number of observers have noted) loyalty tests to make sure that people are sufficiently willing to subordinate themselves to the organization—testing willingness to do the boss's bidding even in questionable circumstances, requiring managers to uproot themselves from their communities to follow the next job assignment. Managers who have grown up in such systems express attitudes of subordination often without any ambivalence, and they seem to be left totally helpless and dependent by the changes in their environment. One GM manager, contemplating the wave of restructurings in the early 1990s, expressed it this way:

Most of us are willing to be molded and bent in any direction that is a part of GM middle management. But we did not know in what direction they wanted us to be bent.

The contrast with those who have embraced the collaborative ethic is sharp:

I don't expect the company to come to me and say this is how we are going to help you get better. It's my obligation to say what I need in this position that I'm in. . . . I don't believe that the company has to come down to me.

Collaborative enterprise clearly encourages people to take this kind of responsibility for their own development and careers, and for many people it is a positive challenge. Senior leadership is naturally enthusiastic:

This whole issue of trust and responsibility for all of our actions is an enabling thought. I am not going to take care of you. I can't take care of you. I am going to give you an environment. I am going to commit to you to enable you. But in the end I will trust you, you trust me, you do your part, I will do my part, you are responsible and I am responsible but in the end you have to take the lead on these things. (IBM senior leader)[7]

But these values are also frequently echoed by people in middle and lower management levels:

The company tells us, "Build your skills so that you are marketable. We have good training; utilize it and make yourself useful so that you are marketable both outside and inside the company"—and everybody is expected to do that. This helps me and others to build a wider range of skills. I have found that I have grown in many ways both tangibly and intangibly, and that is what the company expects from us—to step up to the bat when needed. (Shell-SEPIV)

There are so many people that I have met in my career that get wrapped more around defining themselves by their job, and by their title and by their level. First of all I have never defined myself by my job, but I also look at the scope and scale of responsibility—whether in a new role I will be learning something, and whether in a new role I will be contributing something.[8]

And even at times on the shopfloor, as at Saturn:

We are like those pioneers who blazed westward. We've had lots of training in team development and team dynamics. . . . Job security, I really haven't thought about that; the biggest thing is that everyone is really excited about building the greatest car in the world.

(Let me remind those readers who view such statements skeptically that I will shortly turn to the "dark side" of the picture.)

### Diversity

Diversity often forms a pattern with participation and self-development, but also has an independent life. There are in fact two fundamentally different concepts of diversity that are often confused. Until the 1960s the dominant form was "tolerance," focused on personal freedom. Tolerance means that differences are treated as private and irrelevant to public life; the public and moral obligation is only to remain blind to such differences to the maximum degree compatible with social order.[9] The value of tolerance was revolutionary because most human societies have depended on a strong unity of values to maintain order and coherence. The notion that people could live together without sharing a common religion or other orientation was equally inconceivable to Catholics and to Communists. It is still controversial in much of the world.

It is important to recognize, however, that tolerance is possible only in what might be called a "thin" community, where there is relatively low interdependence and need for coordinated action. You can do your thing and leave me to do mine as long as we don't have to interact too strongly and can regulate our relationships through markets or simple rules. Corporations are not like this: they require much higher levels of cooperation, and therefore they have never been very tolerant. Traditional corporations, as I have noted before, insisted on rather strong codes of loyalty and conformity, extending to dress codes and other outward signs as well as to the more subtle cultural conformity of "old boys' clubs." There were fairly accurate public signs of whether people were competent in their jobs; but since cooperation was left entirely to the "informal organization" there were no good signs of whether you could trust them to help you out. Under those conditions one generally bases trust on how much the other is similar to you. These organizations were therefore very resistant to the intrusion of "different" people such as women and minorities.[10]

Collaborative enterprise is on the whole much more open to differences because trust is much less dependent on homogeneity. The cultural focus is on contribution, and there are strong mechanisms that generate accurate and widespread reputations about whether people do contribute. Thus other aspects of the person—dress, nationality, skin color, gender—can more easily be separated off as irrelevant. The more collaborative organizations I have observed are in fact remarkable in their openness about these issues. One person I interviewed at Citibank grew up in China, did graduate studies in England, and was living in the United States and working in teams with people from Germany and others of many races, with a female boss—and none of these relationships were problems to him as long as people were providing value for the projects that he was working on, and for the goal of building e-business.

In effect, the ethic of contribution and the shared purpose, which are very strongly supported in every aspect of the system, create sufficient unity that strong interdependence can be reconciled with tolerance on many dimensions.

But there is also another definition of diversity that has become more central in the last few decades, involving group claims to social respect and recognition. This creates entirely new dynamics and difficulties. Diversity in this recent sense means that the public and moral duty is not to ignore but rather to engage differences, to understand them, to find ways of accommodating them, to make sure that they are respected.[11] The claim and the burden on the wider community are much heavier than before. It is this image of diversity that has led to Affirmative Action and other highly controversial policy innovations.

From this perspective, the collaborative enterprise represents an interesting though incomplete advance. It is perhaps the first social system in which important kinds of diversity are not merely tolerated but actively embraced as a part of interactive dialogue: good project teams work not in spite of, but *because* of the fact that they involve people with differing points of view and knowledge. The central principle of collaboration is that people with viewpoints relevant to the shared should work together to pool their knowledge and experience. So it brings together, in an unprecedented way, people from different functions—the marketer has to actually talk to the manufacturer; from various levels; across boundaries of country, of customer segment.

Within this range, the principle of mutual recognition and respect is operative in the manner of the "new diversity." In most companies, marketers and manufacturers make fun of each other; in a collaborative environment they understand that they need each other and seek to understand the differences so that they can work effectively together. In most companies, the hierarchy defines some people as "better" than others, and underlings are expected to express general deference to their superiors; in a collaborative culture underlings legitimately challenge their superiors based on their particular knowledge, and negotiate for resources rather than begging for them. Of course, there are empirically many shades of gray, but I have been generally impressed by the dramatic shift in basic orientation observable in collaborative cases.

But this is not a full realization of the ideal of diversity because it engages only those dimensions relevant to the work. The *usual* definition of diversity around race, gender, and other social identities, is for the most part treated as irrelevant—tolerated but not engaged. The only exceptions might be—and I have only heard about such cases, not observed them—where a particular social group might have a perspective that would improve the business for a product: for example, deliberately putting women on SUV design teams so as to broaden the customer base; or ensuring that executive teams include multiple nationalities so as to represent the varying tastes and cultures of those countries in strategic decision making. On the whole, however, collaboration entails no *general* principle of respect and recognition for social identities; it furthers diversity in this sense only to the extent that it benefits the business.

Yet it should be emphasized that this step is in itself a big deal: many companies have worked hard, and it has required social learning, to make some progress in creating genuine interactive diversity. Percy Barnevik, former CEO of ABB and a strong proponent of having nationally diverse teams, said:

> Multinational teams do not happen naturally—on the contrary, the human inclination is to stick to its own kind. . . . At the end of the day, all people are "local," with their roots in some home country. It therefore takes a major, systematic and sustained effort to bridge borders, build the multinational teams and thereby create a truly international organization. It is sometimes necessary to intervene in the selection process to force people to overcome the "foreigner hurdle" and safeguard the idea of multinational teams. The value that is created is worth the risk.[12]

For those who value diversity, this is an important development.

## THE DARK SIDE: CRITICISMS
## OF COLLABORATION

There are also many reasons to object to these emerging systems from various value perspectives. Some of these objections are of the form, "The rhetoric is good but the reality is something else"; others don't even like the rhetoric.

Skeptics of the first kind generally focus on the ways in which recent changes have benefited corporate management while creating insecurity for employees. They are on the whole willing to accept the conceptual value of collaboration, but they view it as impractical and even harmful in the real world—in particular because of enduring power differences.

### Insecurity

The most widespread complaint is not specifically directed at collaboration, but it clearly touches it: this is the view that modern industry has led to heightened insecurity. I discussed this in Chapter 6 from the point of view of the dangers it poses for organizational success; but it is so central to current value debates that it is worth returning to it in this context.

We can leave aside for this purpose the debate among economists about the actual extent of job mobility and turnover; what is relevant here is that collaboration clearly calls for increased mobility and attacks the legitimacy of the old contract of loyalty. There is a pragmatic basis for this: if collaboration is basically about getting the right people to work together on a problem, then you need to be able to move some people out and move others in as the nature of the problem changes. The wider the scope of the collaborative project—if it spans nations and large markets and multiple steps—the more likely it is that people will be significantly displaced in the process.

The problem is that when people are displaced, given current institutions in the United States, the suffering is borne far more by individuals than by corporations. Most obviously, workers have a hard time maintaining health care protection when they are out of the umbrella of the corporate parent; despite weak government efforts to provide continuing protection, insurance remains out of range for most lower- and even middle-income people. This is not all: they lose many other benefits and protections as well—ranging from training, which is historically provided by companies and which is still poorly organized outside them; to information about new job opportunities, which remains very underdeveloped aside from the generic listings on Web sites; to financial advice about how to handle uncertain income flows, which remains far more available to the wealthy than to anyone else. For companies, however, displacing people carries little cost aside from the recruitment of replacements.

As a result, collaboration actually approaches its ideal only for elite employers. IBM can build a culture of real debate, openness, challenge, and mobility because most of its employees, if laid off, are easily able to find other jobs. Many Silicon Valley firms achieved high levels of collaboration, at least before the post-millennial crash, because their employees were highly sought after and had great market power. These people also are young enough and paid well enough that they can survive periods of uncertainty and unemployment.

For the much larger number of people who have no such prospects or safety nets, however, the promise of mobility, choice, and self-development is a sham. This includes most blue-collar workers and those with lesser education, but also the bulk of middle managers, especially those who have spent large portions of their careers working their way up through traditional hierarchies; and even many of the highly educated younger technical workers who are supposed to thrive in flexible environments. Many have found that the collaborative ethic is far too risky: rather than challenging the boss, one had better keep one's head down and try to survive.[13]

This problem cannot be blamed entirely, or even principally, on the spread of collaboration. Many of the worst effects are rather effects of the free market value orientation, which also attacks bureaucracy but has less concern for maintaining trust. Thus many companies are engaged in simple cost-cutting, taking advantage of a shift in the balance of power as unions have declined and the harsh free-market ethic has risen. Cases like "Chainsaw Al" Dunlap's wholesale chopping of heads at a series of companies he headed represent only the most extreme version of the swing to a harsh and short-term outlook. And the move has a self-perpetuating quality: as more companies cut heads and reduce benefits, it becomes harder for others to maintain them—and also less necessary, since their employees have fewer good options to move to.

The collaborative ethic is intertwined with this pure free-market ethic and shares some of the responsibility for its harsher consequences. Yet these consequences are also very harmful to the further spread of collaboration and to its potential business benefits. Collaboration depends on trust. When employees are fearful, they draw back from risk and are less willing to share, more apt to protect their position and hoard their knowledge. There is evidence that this is happening not only in many cases I have studied, but also on a societal scale: polls show increasing employee cynicism and mistrust toward their companies, and also an increasing reluctance to move—an unstable and potentially explosive combination.[14]

### False Participation

A second significant objection to collaboration is that the promise of participation is essentially false and dishonest—that in situations of grossly unequal power, such as that within corporations, the idea of open discussion and free exchange of resources is a delusion. This touches on an uncomfortable historical association: "collaboration" in World War II Europe meant cooperating with the dominant power, the Nazis. On a much less dramatic level, there is some aspect of this false cooperation in many "collaborative" efforts in companies.

Most team-based efforts in the past have faded out because they soon reached limits to their influence. Problem-solving groups, which took off during the 1970s, grew rapidly while they restrained their focus to minor hygiene issues like repainting the walls, but became highly unwelcome when they challenged supervisor decisions.[15] Later on, teams and individuals were asked to participate in Total Quality Management and other business improvement efforts, contributing their knowledge and their influence with their peers; but in such groups workers' issues such as pay, hours of work, or even the quality of supervision were generally off-limits. It is still broadly true that "weak" forms of involvement, such as suggestion boxes or teams with very limited scope, remain far more common than "strong" forms like the Citibank e-Commerce case described earlier, or ones in which workers' rights are backed with union power.[16]

Moreover, even the most successful cases, in which workers and managers of all levels have worked together over long periods of time and achieved excellent results, remain very vulnerable to market and strategic shifts. In a recent instance, General Motors' downsizing during its painful fall of 2005 included several plants that had been particularly praised for their cooperative relationships and had won major prizes such as the Deming Award for quality. Companies like AT&T, which had a huge employee participation effort in the 1980s and a second, more ambitious version a decade later, have ended up in highly adversarial fights with their unions and with broad disaffection at all levels.

It is therefore not surprising that some analysts want to write off the whole notion of collaboration or cooperation as merely a management trick to win commitment without giving up anything. What is more worrisome is that many workers feel the same way; in fact, union leaders who have led participation efforts have often lost subsequent elections.[17] And middle managers in my interviews often mingled enthusiasm about increased involvement with wariness and cynicism about its limits.

Some of this is, once again, not really the fault of collaboration in the sense I have used it: many employee participation efforts have simply been extensions of old-fashioned paternalistic "communication" in which there was never any intention of changing formal power arrangements. But quite a lot of cases do in fact involve falsity: there is a pretense at shifting power and responsibility to employees which is then pulled back at the first sign of trouble.

Even in the very best cases of collaboration, such as the Citibank e-Commerce unit, there is a continued uncertainty about the role of collaboration in key decisions around strategy. On one hand, the logic of the situation suggests that employees at many levels know things that should be part of the decision-making process and therefore need to be taken seriously; on the other, top managers are particularly reluctant to show any lack of certainty around strategic issues. With the partial exception of some Strategic Fitness Process cases, therefore, the central purposes of the system—the hub around which everything in collaborative systems revolves—remain separated off in another world, isolated from the lively interactions that give the system its effectiveness and ability to respond.

The typically limited and grudging nature of participation is a real and important flaw in collaborative systems, a violation of their own values and logic, and one that is not overcome by existing mechanisms.

### Dualism and Inequality

I discussed in Chapter 6 the tendency toward dualism created by managers' attempts to keep their best employees while making the rest contingent, and the ways in which this can undermine the business values of collaboration. But the problem of dualism has deeper roots: it appears to be a tendency within *all* collaborative systems, even those outside the mainstream of business competition.

The root difficulty is that collaboration sets up a kind of open market in reputations. Whereas reputations in traditional societies were heavily bound within local groups and communities, extended collaboration deliberately expands the scope of reputation so that people from outside this world can also get accurate information about performance and competence. But that can mean that a few people with wide reputations get a lot of requests, while those who may have been successful at a local level get left behind.

This is a good description of the culture of Hollywood, which has been touted by several authors as a model of post-bureaucratic systems. The project form of film organization replaced the more bureaucratic studio organization, with a relatively closed labor market, only in the 1970s. This change has resulted in increased flexibility, but also in a vicious form of elite dominance in which seven major studios are all going after just 3 percent of the total pool of guild members,[18] and salaries for this small group have increased at astronomical speeds. The same extreme dynamic has developed for top athletes with the elimination of the systems that kept them tied to particular teams, and with CEOs as their labor market has expanded to cross firms and even industries. Even software engineers, who would seem to fill a less glamorous role, have divided in this way: Vinod Khosla, a cofounder of Sun, noted in 1999 that the top 5 percent add disproportionate value, leading to intense bidding wars.[19]

These dualizing tendencies seem to create self-perpetuating cycles, in which the stars are more and more coveted and can command higher and higher compensation, while others are treated as expendable. Whatever the economic consequences, this clearly creates major strains for values that emphasize middle-class solidity and social solidarity.

## WHAT CAN BE DONE? OVERCOMING
## THE DARK SIDE

The three issues I have just raised—the insecurity caused by unsupported mobility, restrictions on participation, and the danger of dualism—are problems that are common in collaboration as it exists, but are clearly harmful to it over time. So the question arises: Could they be prevented? That requires going beyond existing cases and evidence and speculating a little.

It is in the interests of companies as well as employees, in situations of high complexity and uncertainty, to build strong collaborative systems. A major obstacle is the unwillingness of those who have held power in the bureaucratic order to give it up. This unwillingness may be justified in genuinely principled terms: giving away too much power could lead to chaos and even worse results. Resistance may, however, also have several admixtures of less noble motives, conscious or unconscious: fear of the unknown, unwillingness to give up the respect and perquisites of management for which they have worked, and lack of respect for the abilities of others. The combination of all these, in the hands of people who hold much power, is a daunting obstacle.

There are several kinds of things that could provide some counterweight. The first is the effort, to which this book is trying to contribute, to clarify the nature of collaborative enterprise, the details of its governance and organization, and the processes for getting there. To the extent that this is successful, it can mitigate the first problem, convincing those of good will that it is really possible to open up, to give up familiar forms of power, without putting the entire system in danger. It can also make it easier to identify distortions—bureaucracy or market in collaborative clothing. Obviously this is a task that goes well beyond one book or author, nor is it sufficient even then.

There are at least two other significant challenges that must be met to bring out the best aspects of collaboration: creating forms of representation, and reforming regulatory systems, so as to guarantee fairness within a collaborative order. Representation and regulation are the means by which the community expresses and enforces values other than purely economic ones. The pure "free-market" view has no use for them because it devalues the role of community. The "bureaucratic" view has created a set of institutions—industrial unions, rule-based regulations—that enforce stability, clarity of accountability, and other bureaucratic values. The problem is to develop a set of institutions that define and enforce collaborative value—that bring out the best aspects of this form of organization and limit its distortion by one-sided views or unacknowledged uses of power.

## REPRESENTATION

The founders of the U.S. government understood that relying on the good will of those in power is insufficient, and they therefore worked to actually spread the power around a bit—to create countervailing forces that force those in power to get outside their own point of view and take those of others seriously. Unions have historically provided one kind of countervailing force that has required managers to respect employee views, but unions in their current form are not well designed for the task of representation in collaborative systems. The essential structure of unions, or at least industrial unions, is one of counter-bureaucracy, matching up to the corporate bureaucracy, insisting that rules and procedures be followed consistently and fairly. With this mentality, the labor movement doesn't know what to do with teams and participation: these developments threaten the uniformity and clarity of contracts, yet they seem to further the broader goals of unionism and, moreover, members like them. It doesn't know how to confront increasingly mobile, flexible corporate structures, which can usually dodge with ease the cumbersome traditional weapon of mass strikes. Thus unions have remained hesitant in the face of current changes in corporate organization, which has contributed to their steady decline.[20]

Effective representation for collaborative systems must look different from that in bureaucratic systems, just as industrial unionism was different from the craft form that preceded it. The problem is both to redefine justice and to find ways of enforcing it. Justice will look different because the core values of the system are different: for example, seniority was a moral pillar on which industrial unionism was based, but it is far less valued in collaborative systems. Union "solidarity" in its familiar form of mass action and "hanging together" is devalued in collaboration—replaced not with pure individualism, but with more focused associational action.

Existing unions tend to oppose the basic principles of collaboration, which run against traditions and familiar forms of action, and to pull back toward stable bureaucratic relationships. But there is another way: not to turn back, but to "pressure" collaboration to live up to its own best values. This means pressuring for genuine mobility, in which employees gain at least as much as companies from the opportunity to make choices; and for genuine participation, in which employee views have weight and cannot be dismissed by the hierarchy.

It is possible that a successful model might come from outside the existing labor movement, just as industrial unionism once arose outside the dominant unions of that time. There are, for instance, many nascent efforts to build networks of mobile professionals to help themselves with their career development and to create genuinely open labor markets. One such model is Working Today in New York City—also known as "the Freelancers' Union"—which offers portable benefits, Web-based information exchanges, and research on companies' working conditions, and which compares companies based on standards for freelance work.[21] This is a promising idea, though still in an embryonic and local stage. It is even possible that employers might come to see its worth and support it, since it could provide a general benefit in terms of improved labor market efficiency that employers have trouble achieving on their own.

These are not impossible dreams, but they are very difficult. Mobility could be a good thing for employees as well as for companies *if* there were good systems in place for supporting mobile careers. These systems were unneeded in a bureaucratic order, but they are crucial now—and weak. Without such an infrastructure for mobility, employees will continue to get the short end of the stick, and in the end mobility as a whole will be reduced, harming the economy and businesses. Similarly, participation could be good if employee voice was organized so as to identify management problems and to create pressure around constructive solutions; without this there will only be a growth of cynicism that will undermine management.

Enforcement, or effective use of pressure, must also change: mass strikes are less effective than in the past, while collaborative systems are more vulnerable to other forms of action such as coordinated publicity campaigns and community pressure.

## REGULATION: CHANGING NOTIONS
## OF GOVERNMENT, PROPERTY,
## AND OWNERSHIP

A century ago, the growth of large bureaucratic firms put enormous pressure on existing government systems—banking, interstate commerce, and other aspects of economic regulation, as well as systems to prevent corruption and crime, and the protection of workers and communities. At the same time it challenged essential aspects of law, including the notion of property: the legal system, based on the notion of individuals as economic actors, didn't know how to treat unified organizations of thousands of people. All these issues were worked out over decades, through the Progressive era, the swing back to free markets in the 1920s, and finally the New Deal version of government and law.

It appears that the development of the forces of collaboration will require no less of a change. The New Deal regulatory institutions are having a very hard time holding accountable organizations that are highly flexible, international, and complex; rules passed through existing processes seem consistently to miss the point or to be easily evaded. We have been through several rounds of seeking a new model of flexible regulation—decentralization, negotiated rulemaking, and so on—none of which has yet come close to solving the difficulties; corruption and illegitimate behavior are far from under control.

Equally difficult, the definition of property—the core institution of capitalism—is also in question and shaping up for a major battle. The lines have been drawn around the notion of "intellectual property." Both the free-market approach and the bureaucratic one agree on the importance of attaching ownership to knowledge so that rewards are given clearly to the ones responsible for it. The collaborative view puts this principle in question, because it starts from the assumption that knowledge is created by interdependent groups in which many people play critical roles. Thus collaborative systems create problems for existing definitions of property built around individuals and corporations.

The battle is shaping up most dramatically around open-source software, which has become a very substantial enterprise. Run on highly collaborative lines, with strong principles of sharing and open discussion, open source has come to threaten the business even of some large corporations. The leaders of the latter have fired back: Bill Gates calls those who question intellectual property rights "new modern-day sort of communists"[22]; Shai Agassi, president of the product and technology group at SAP, says that "Intellectual property [IP] socialism is the worst that can happen to any IP-based society."[23] Proponents of open source in turn accuse the IP side of monopoly tactics that interfere with "the users' natural right to copy."

This problem is not confined to open source, however: it is characteristic of knowledge work in general, and has been raised for a long time by scholars of science. As early as the 1940s the sociologist Robert Merton characterized science as a form of "Communism": he noted that it is characterized by common ownership of goods; recognition and esteem are the sole property rights; and products of competition are treated as open to all. Merton argued that this scientific organization of knowledge was incompatible with the definition of technology as private property.[24]

The solution is not yet clear, but there is no reason to believe that it will be any more impossible than the development of corporate ownership in the early part of the twentieth century. Capitalism, it turns out, is highly flexible and inventive; it does not depend on the narrow individualist definitions of ownership, but has learned to encompass organizations and the separation of ownership from control—although it took many decades of struggle to do it. There is no a priori reason to believe that the concept of ownership cannot similarly adapt to the concept of creation in networks. IBM, Sun, and other fully capitalist companies have already embraced the concept of open source. Eric Raymond, one of the leaders of the open-source movement, has suggested ways of defining ownership of collaborative projects that he compares directly to definitions of land tenure as systematized by John Locke in the early phases of capitalism.[25] Whether or not this points to the eventual resolution, it certainly suggests that traditional definitions of ownership can be adapted to the challenge of reconciling the needs of capitalist markets with those of collaborative knowledge networks.

## CONCLUSION

Where does that leave us? Of course at a certain level value differences cannot be resolved through argument. Those who believe that, for example, loyalty or seniority or deference to authority are ultimate goods in themselves will never support collaboration, which denies their fundamental value; the same is true of those who believe in pure individualism without social entanglements.

What we can do, however, is to clarify what is essential to the orientation and what is not. It is true that collaboration has been part of a social trend that has been very cruel for many categories of workers and managers, and that has left large parts of the workforce with inadequate security for retirement and other life changes. Many criticisms are based on the assumption that collaboration inevitably produces these inequitable results, whether by intent or not— that it is incapable of overcoming inequalities of power, and that it can therefore never be anything more than a mirage, distracting attention from real social problems, creating illusions of promise that are doomed to be crushed.

My claim here is that this insecurity is not a part of collaborative values, but rather harmful to them. The conclusion is that action is needed to create the conditions for true collaboration. Economic forces have taken it a certain distance, but they have failed to address the social needs that are equally important to its long-term success. Without appropriate forms of representation, regulation, and legal framing, collaboration will inevitably be distorted—restricted perhaps to small, elite sections of the economy, but never realizing its potential for maximizing economic value for the society as a whole. For that, economic value must go hand in hand with the development of participation, diversity, and human development.

It is not at all clear how to go about building the social side of collaboration. We can argue empirically about whether or not it is possible to do it within the current society, but it is not entirely an empirical question; it is partly a matter of will. As I have suggested, it does not seem on the face of it to be a bigger task than the creation of the representative/regulatory framework that made possible the growth of the mass-production economy in the last century. On the other hand, it is not any smaller, and for those who find collaboration of value it is time to accelerate the effort.

# Appendix: The Research Base

*Charles Heckscher, Carlos Martin, and Boniface Michael*

*Note: for those who would like more detail on the research approach, an extended version of this chapter with additional data and analysis is available from the author or online at:*

- *http://Yalebooks.com/Heckscher*
- *http://www.heckscher.com/CollaborativeEnterprise*

This study makes a very broad argument for a long-term change in the nature of organizations. Such propositions are inherently hard to test. Nevertheless, in the last few decades there have been many claims of this type, trumpeting "paradigm shifts" or "transformations." Generally they tell their readers, "Forget how you've thought about the world before; everything is new." They are persuasive because they appeal to readers' widespread sense that things are disjointed and don't make sense within familiar ways of thinking. Indeed, it often seems that the more radical the claims, the more they succeed in convincing readers that here is something really new that might relieve the sense of confusion.

The foundations of these claims range widely. At one end of the spectrum are those that use simple homespun anecdotes meant to resonate with the personal experience of readers. The modal type, at least in the ones I have looked at, goes a bit further—using real business cases from the authors' experience to *illustrate* the arguments being made. A few claim greater rigor because they choose a sample of successful cases and draw lessons inductively about the roots of that success: this is the method used famously in one of the most successful of all modern business books, *In Search of Excellence*.[1]

But an essential problem with all these approaches is that they are free to pick and choose their evidence: there is little or no attempt at falsification. They develop ideas or propositions that seem to fit with experience and present examples, but they do not make a systematic search for cases that *don't* fit. If you don't look for disconfirming cases you can build up evidence for almost anything. Over the years a long string of fads and companies held up as exemplary (including many of the *In Search of Excellence* cases[2]) have declined or crashed soon after, but there are few attempts to draw lessons from this counter-evidence.

Researchers who try to be more rigorous are caught, however, in a serious dilemma. The justification of broad claims requires broad knowledge. If the claims are about the functioning of companies, you need to know a great deal about many companies. But it is very difficult for academic researchers to get this kind of knowledge, and essentially impossible to get it in a systematic way: it is impractical to try to pick a random sample of companies and get them to submit to in-depth investigation.

Thus research that seeks to be scientific has been pushed into two major approaches, both with serious weaknesses. One type is based on extensive access in a single company, or at best a few, using observation based on anthropological methods. This type gets good data and can achieve deep insight, if it is disciplined with a solid use of theory. A classic model is Rosabeth Moss Kanter's *Men and Women of the Corporation*,[3] based on a single case observation, but resulting in understanding that has proved broadly applicable and has withstood the test of time. The link between the single case and universal insight was provided by Kanter's deep knowledge of theories including those of classic sociologists, and her ability to connect her observations to these abstract concepts that had been generated in widely different social environments. The vast majority of these studies, however, are far less disciplined and therefore less reliable; and even in the best of them one would like to know more about how well they apply to other companies.

At the other end are studies that have tested specific hypotheses across a large enough number of companies to achieve statistical significance. This type can generalize directly, but only on narrow issues and from very bad data. The method is narrow in that it can test only questions that have been turned into specific measures; it excludes of necessity many crucial issues where useful data must be based on *judgment* by people with real knowledge of the situation. The data are bad not only because response rates are typically low, but more essentially because they must be based on standardized language and categories; on any difficult question, especially in periods of uncertainty and change, the meanings of these responses are subject to many uncontrolled contingencies.

As a result, a great deal of current research produces very misleading pictures. If you ask HR managers if they are conducting pay for performance efforts, for example, you will get a very high proportion saying "Yes," because that is the current sign of being up-to-date. But if you talk to the middle managers in their organizations you find that many of the programs are honored more in the breach than the observance. Further, even ones that are actually being used may mean very different things under the same language: pay for performance may focus on separating top individuals from the pack, or it may help identify those who build collaboration and contribute to the work of others. The results of such studies may therefore be statistically significant but meaningless.

## DATA-GATHERING AND INTERPRETATION

We have not been able entirely to escape these problems, but we have tried to improve the research method somewhat by a method that might be called one of disciplined judgment.

We began with a broad point of view based on a combination of existing theory, discussions with colleagues, and our own extensive knowledge of a few cases. We then put this point of view to the test as rigorously as we could. The research team of Carlos Martin and Boniface Michael created a database by coding twenty-one cases for which we had a considerable amount of "deep" knowledge based on observations or interviews at multiple levels of the system. (Table 11 is a summary of the cases and our data sources.) In almost all these cases we have primary interview and observational data either by ourselves or by close colleagues in the McKinsey study group or elsewhere.[4] In the vast majority we have direct interviews at high and middle levels of the organization, and in several we also have such data from frontline blue-collar employees.

This sample is in no sense random; it consists of enterprises to which for one reason or another we, or people whose research we trust, have had extensive access. Thus we cannot generalize directly from these examples; we have to *interpret* them. Part of this involves using theory, and part involves other data—including other studies and our own "secondary" sample which is less systematic than the core—to see whether the insights hold up on a less rigorous but wider basis.

These cases were coded at three levels, using all available sources of evidence, including our own interviews or surveys, private internal documents, published and unpublished case write-ups, and scholarly or news articles. First we organized relatively observable, objective data under consistent headings. Then we sorted these base data into more abstract categories drawn from the theory. Finally, we assessed the truth of key propositions from the theory. By doing these different levels of coding we were able to ensure that the more difficult judgments in the later codings were grounded as closely as possible in data that we could review in cases of disagreement.

The coding allows us to deal consistently, across many cases, with propositions that cannot be answered simply or "objectively," but that require an extensive knowledge of context. It has enabled us to look thoroughly and quickly over the available evidence on many issues over the whole core sample, and to quickly spot disconfirming evidence. The final result is, as much as we can make it, consistent *both* with sociological and business knowledge drawn from a wide range of contexts, *and* with the particular set of cases that constitute our core sample.

This method is essentially constructionist and interpretive. We made many judgments that went beyond directly observable and replicable data, but we worked hard to make them *consistently* across the range of cases. Judgments are essential in this kind of research because we are dealing with complex, changing, systems of human interaction. At times it was very difficult to assess, for example, whether an enterprise was in transition from a complex strategy to a solutions one, or whether its rhetoric was at one level and practice at another, or whether it was simply confused and trying to do two things at once. Such assessments require interpretation of meanings—of what is people in interviews are "really saying," and to what extent formal statements are in conflict with hidden resistances or distortions.

There were at times significant disagreements among the members of the research team, especially in coding high-level abstract propositions. Resolving these debates required that we have a shared understanding of the general theory and that we be able to refer to a wealth of direct evidence from interviews and other material. To build alignment and develop our understanding, we spent a great deal of time early in the process on a few cases. They were coded by two or more people, and we used discrepancies to explore our understanding of the theory and the categories and to build a shared view. Later cases were coded by only one person (it is a very labor-intensive process), but in most instances more than one person had some knowledge of the case and could challenge codings.

Thus the process was not a linear one of forming propositions and then testing data. It was rather a lengthy iterative sequence of using the data to build the theory, and then testing this new understanding against other cases, which led to further theoretical development.

## VALIDATION OF PROPOSITIONS

The problem for constructivist or interpretive method is discipline—avoiding closed circles of self-validation. In classical science the basis of discipline is clear: hypotheses are formulated independent of the tests that validate them; the tests are objective and can be replicated by others. These particular controls are either too limiting or entirely infeasible in dealing with complex human systems.

We did, however, use other controls to avoid solipsism. First, the involvement of several researchers ensured that many disagreements would surface and be debated. We resolved disagreements or ambiguity by going back to primary data whenever possible. The lower, more directly observable levels of organizing and coding were done first, and independent of the more abstract theoretical judgments. Thus when there were doubts or disagreements about the more abstract judgments we could return to more "basic" levels of evidence for justification.

Second, we tried to validate every essential proposition against the entire range of cases in our main sample. A major strength of the database is that it enabled us look relatively easily and systematically for counter-evidence. We could go beyond finding examples that *illustrated* the points we wanted to make; we could search to see whether any cases *disconfirmed* it. We did this most directly by entering codes about whether key propositions were true or false for each case (these codings can be accessed. In addition, as I have elaborated the theory in writing this study, I have gone back frequently to the database to test the validity of particular statements).

Our basic rule was that *any disconfirming case* needed to be investigated and resolved—either by finding evidence that changed our judgment, or by rethinking the theory. This is not, in other words, a study based on statistical probabilities. The propositions—about the conditions for moving to collaborative enterprise, about the necessary infrastructural elements, about the match between strategy and structure—may be hedged with conditions, but they are intended to be *true*, not merely "true more often than not." Thus even a single case where they are *not* true upsets the whole structure. The consistent application of this principle, and the development of data in a form that we can check for truth relatively well over a range of cases, moves this study a step beyond the modal type of research in this field.

We started by coding a set of propositions derived from a working paper at the start of the research (the full coding can be found in the Web site material). These propositions are not "operationalizable hypotheses": as mentioned before, they require a great deal of judgment. Nevertheless, they helped to focus us on the variety of ways in which all these cases were dealing with organizational change, and on areas where the data did not support our original hypotheses.

Because these propositions were generated at the start of the process, they are relatively crude. It turns out that some of them were disconfirmed to one degree or another. We were forced as a result to make significant modifications to the theory, which are reflected in the body of this study and summarized in Chapter 10. The most important of these are:

1. We thought initially that systemic collaboration was still highly experimental and unstable, but we found that there was more movement in this direction and more stability than we expected. We were particularly struck by examples like IBM or Cisco which seem to have established collaborative capability across entire companies rather than just within experimental units. This leads us to believe that the shift has gone past the earliest phase and is reaching at least a form of adolescence.
2. We thought that mobility of people would be quite high in these systems. Instead we find that it is more often moderate—intermediate between the high stability of the traditional bureaucratic form and the high mobility of the market.
3. We believed that highly decentralized organizations were a form of adaptive collaborative system, but we found that in many organizations decentralization preserved the essence of bureaucracy: subunits remained autonomous rather than developing interdependence, and thus engaged in the kind of turf battles and resistance to the outside more characteristic of bureaucracy. They turned out also not to be very adaptive at all.

In addition, many other propositions that were implicit or generated during later discussions or writing turned out to be false when we reviewed the cases. A single example: I believed at the start in the importance of public discussion of collaborative values as a driving force in the change process. It turns out, however, that such discussion rarely happens: the only place where it did to a considerable degree was IBM, and to a lesser degree at HP SRSD and Veridian. Thus I modified the proposition to the form found at the end of Chapter 9, suggesting that in successful cases vision begins as a private guide for leaders and only gradually becomes open to public discussion.

## DESCRIPTION OF THE SAMPLE

Two types of cases form the research base for this study. At the core are twenty-one units that have been fully coded on a long form, using all available data. These "units" are not necessarily companies: they simply relatively autonomous, culturally coherent groups. Some of them are divisions within companies; they might in theory extend beyond company boundaries to include industrial districts or alliance networks. In several instances we include two units from a single company.

For a secondary sample of forty-two units or companies we also have direct observational and interview data, but we have not fully coded them. Most of them have been coded at the first level of consistent categorization, but have not been fully assessed in terms of the theory. This is due mainly to simple time constraints: the gathering of information and coding requires weeks of work for each case. In some instances we felt we didn't have rich enough data for a full coding. But this extended sample did play a significant role in building the theory of collaborative enterprise and to illustrate various mechanisms. I also used it frequently as a double-check: scanning the list of enterprises and making sure that at least from a quick review this evidence supported my claims.

All these types of data have at least one serious weakness that should be addressed in future research: they are entirely company-centered and have no cases of federations, alliance groups, industrial communities, or other such cross-company networks. The theory of collaborative enterprise suggests that the boundaries of corporations are weakening and these cross-boundary relationships are becoming more important. As a practical matter, however, it is easier (though not easy!) to identify and get access to a corporation than a looser network, and most of my research has been on those lines.[5]

The final coding form can be reviewed in the Web sites listed at the start of this chapter.

**Table 11 Summary of the Cases and Data Sources**

| Company and Research Time Frame | Summary of Case | Personal Observation and Relationships | Personal Interviews | Other: Surveys, Working Group's Case Knowledge, etc. |
|---|---|---|---|---|
| **ABB** 1994–2003 | Traditional company trying to become more customer-focused and entrepreneurial. Strong top-driven initiation of radically decentralized structure and matrix resisted, much confusion. Eventual serious operational problems. | Ongoing consulting relation with colleague Michael Maccoby ABB-Canada member of collaborative organization network, 1999–2001 | Interviewed 10 ABB-Canada business unit heads, 2000 | McKinsey case, 2000 |
| **Aegon Netherlands** 2000 | Mature insurance markets, stable products, segmented marketing front end. | | McKinsey research interviews | McKinsey case, 2000 |
| **Aegon-Spaarbeleg** 2000 | Moderate uncertainty and complexity, but increasing; creation of innovation unit with high decentralization and innovation. | | McKinsey group interviews | Case based on interviews and experience, 2000 (Galbraith) |
| **Cisco** 1999–2001 | Highly collaborative enterprise with strong emphasis on alliances and customer solutions. | Two personal contacts at mid-levels | McKinsey study, 2000–2001 | McKinsey group case and extensive documents |

*(continued)*

Table 11 Summary of the Cases and Data Sources (continued)

| Company and Research Time Frame | Summary of Case | Personal Observation and Relationships | Personal Interviews | Other: Surveys, Working Group's Case Knowledge, etc. |
|---|---|---|---|---|
| **Citibank** 1974–2003 | Bank as a whole moving towards greater complexity and adaptiveness. Customer relationships managers aiming for upper right; long period of resistance, finally thawing. Process improvement teams pushing against bureaucratic resistance (level 3 boundary). | Member of collaborative organization network, 2001–2002 | ~40 in spring 2001 Follow-up Spring 2002: • e-Solutions unit • Customer relationships managers, Global Bank • Process improvement teams | Several cases from 1975 onward, based on personal experience and secondary sources 61 surveys in 19 process improvement teams |
| **Citibank Alliances unit and e-Solutions unit** 2000–2001 | Alliance was part of e-Solutions unit, total about 150 people, highly innovative and customer-focused; strong systemic collaboration. | Member of collaborative organization network, 2001–2002 | 20 interviews, 2001–2002 | |
| **Cummins-India** 2000–2001 | Stable equipment manufacturer seeking to move to solutions strategy and customer focus. | | McKinsey study, 2000 | Case based on interviews and experience, 2000 |
| **Hewlett-Packard** 1980–2005 | Great flexibility within business units; efforts to build new levels of customer responsiveness that pull together business units consistently resisted. | Close long-term relationship with colleagues Mike Beer and Jay Galbraith Several personal contacts at various levels Rich secondary data | | McKinsey case based on long-term interviews and experience, 2000 Further detailed case information from colleagues, 2000–2005 |

| | | | | |
|---|---|---|---|---|
| **Hewlett-Packard Santa Rosa Systems Division** 1994–1997 | A transition from traditional product focus to solutions capability, with major reorganization. | Consulting relationship with colleagues Mike Beer and Russ Eisenstat | | Harvard Business School case, 1997 |
| **IBM** 1998–2005 | Strong move in last decade toward responsiveness while maintaining complexity; very creative development of collaborative systems. | Ongoing discussions with a top manager; two site visits for Values Jam process in 2003–2004 Personal relationships with employees at various levels | 20 interviews, 2004–2005; multiple levels | McKinsey team case (Galbraith and Miller), 2001 (primarily from secondary sources) Harvard Business School case, 2006 |
| **Johnson & Johnson** 2004–2006 | Strong firm with highly successful decentralized, bureaucratic, paternalist culture; seeking increased cross-unit standardization and collaboration, finding it difficult. | Multiple personal contacts at various levels | 20 interviews 2004–2005; multiple levels | |
| **Lucent** 1997–2005 | Attempt to adapt research capability and bureaucratic structure to high-speed industry; decentralized, then severe problems and slow, halting recovery. | Ongoing consulting involvement, observation of management and union-management meetings, discussions with senior managers, 1998–2005 Member of collaborative organization network, 2001–2002 | 20 managers and union officials in 2 plants, 2000 | |

(continued)

Table 11 Summary of the Cases and Data Sources (continued)

| Company and Research Time Frame | Summary of Case | Personal Observation and Relationships | Personal Interviews | Other: Surveys, Working Group's Case Knowledge, etc. |
|---|---|---|---|---|
| **Lucent IP&T** 2004–2005 | Stable internal service provider with strong paternalist culture, driven by a new leader towards adaptive solutions orientation and expansion of focus beyond firm; much resistance. | Ongoing relationship with leader | 30 interviews at all levels, 2005 | |
| **McKinsey** 1999–2005 | Highly decentralized, project-oriented professional firm seeking to move toward greater integration and systematic learning, encountering significant resistance. | Participant observation, 1998–2001 | 5 structured interviews in 2005 | |
| **Microsoft** | Project collaboration. Windows-centric product development shows high adaptiveness but some problems of integration across products, with much integration coming directly from the top. More recently attempting to shift to a solutions-services model. | Data from secondary sources and limited amount of "inside" knowledge from colleagues that have consulted with it | | Secondary accounts of product development at Microsoft based on on-site observations and confidential records. |
| **"NewTech"** (A large Silicon Valley manufacturing company) development lab 2000–2001 | Specialized innovation unit, high-high (upper right), very creative formalized systems for prioritization, reputation, and communication. Somewhat isolated from rest of organization. | | McKinsey interviews and observation, 1999–2000 | Confidential case based on observation and interviews. |

| | | | | |
|---|---|---|---|---|
| **Nokia** 2000–2002 | Strong firm culture in highly unstable environment; rapid innovation. | | McKinsey group case interviews with top and middle managers<br>Ongoing long-term consulting relation (Galbraith) | Case based on interviews and experience, 2000 (Galbraith)<br>Later updates |
| **Saturn** 1988–2004 | An "experimental change unit": Higher adaptiveness through internal level 4 systems of collaboration, but poor collaboration beyond the company. | Repeated training interventions with union management teams, 1999–2001<br>Close ongoing relationship with colleague Saul Rubinstein | ~15 interviews, 1986–1990<br>Many interviews by Saul Rubinstein | Network analyses, book by Rubinstein and Kochan (2001) |
| **Shell SEPIV** (new ventures unit) 1998–2002 | "Experimental change unit": high internal collaboration through level 4 formal systems, much isolation from rest of organization; increasing focus on efficiency as well as adaptiveness. | Member of collaborative organization network, 1999–2002<br>Ongoing contacts with staff member of unit | 10 in new ventures unit, 2000 | |
| **Sun** 2000–2001 | Decentralized "cowboy" culture attempting to achieve solutions strategy, having difficulty with integration and discipline. | | Discussion with change team, 2001<br>Galbraith/McKinsey interviews with top and middle managers, 2000 | Case based on interviews and experience, 2000 |
| **Veridian** 2001–2003 | Defense contractor built by acquisition, trying to achieve strategic integration. | Ongoing relation with (former) CEO and change consultants | Interviews with (former) CEO and 5 employees, 2004 | Case writeup (Heckscher and Adler, 2006) |

# Notes

## INTRODUCTION

1. Chandler (1977).
2. Chandler (1977); Smith (1776). Markets and hierarchies are, strictly speaking, the essential organizational forms of modern society; I am leaving out here key "traditional" forms such as the bund and the status hierarchy.
3. See Pagels (2003). Schmalenbach used a similar concept, *bund*: see Hetherington (1994). Recent feminist writing has stressed the "sororal" nature of much historical collaboration, but that is not crucial to the point here; what is crucial is that there are few cases of genuine collaboration that crossed the gender divide.
4. Gerth and Mills (1946), p. 228.
5. The seminal works were those of Taylor (1911), who applied the principles of bureaucracy to shopfloor work; and Fayol (1916/1949), who did the same for managerial work.
6. Mitzman (1969); Whyte (1956); Riesman (1950).
7. Academic treatments of teams include Lawler, Ledford, and Mohrman (1989); Hackman (1990); and Guzzo and Dickson (1996). Managerial treatments include Katzenback and Smith (1994). On lean production, see Womack, Jones, and Roos (1991) and Oliver, Delbridge, and Barton (2005).
8. See Osterman (2000).
9. See notes 7 and 8.
10. The notion of "boundarylessness" achieved fad status during the 1990s; it was one of Jack Welch's top principles of management at GE. There have also been some academic

treatments of the concept, for example, Sabel (1991). There is also an extensive literature on the dynamics of industries and "clusters," which are geographically proximate groups of firms. The collaborative enterprise, however, need not be bound by either of these limits, either: see, for example, the notions of process networks and global network orchestrators in Brown, Durchslag, and Hagel (2002).

11. Bell (1973), pp. 378ff.; Holton (1996).

12. For an elaborated argument connecting network complexity to the demands of knowledge creation, see Hage and Alter (1997).

    The connection of collaboration to the expansion of knowledge work has been made by many authors in various ways. An early and broad theoretical treatment in this line is Parsons (1971), esp. pp. 103ff. More recently, for an argument and extensive references, see Adler (2001).

    I have used the concept of "interdependence" somewhat in passing. Not all interdependence requires collaboration—it is possible to structure stable interdependent processes through bureaucratic routines. Knowledge interdependence, however, has become a major driver of business value and requires a new level of interactivity: in terms used widely in the literature, it requires reciprocal interdependence as opposed to sequential or pooled interdependence (Thompson, 1967).

13. Bell (1973); Castells (1996).

14. Clark, Chew, and Fujimoto (1987).

15. Hamel (2000).

16. Taylor (1911).

17. Adler, Goldoftas, and Levine (1997).

18. For a good example of Total Quality Management (TQM), see Harkness, Kettinger, and Segars (1996). For a general discussion of effective TQM, see Mohrman, Lawler, and Ledford (1996).

19. Shakespeare, *Richard II,* act II, scene 3.

20. Barnard (1938), p. 220.

21. The phrase is Adam Smith's from the opening of *The Wealth of Nations.*

22. Simon (1969), pp. 90–92.

23. Merton (1940).

24. Holton (1996), chapter 3.

25. Hayek (1945) makes a famous argument about the power of decentralized bureaucratic activity.

26. I differ in this from Eisenhardt and Martin's (2000) treatment of "dynamic capabilities," which at first glance have a great deal to do with collaboration. They reduce these capabilities, however, to routines that are relatively concrete and easily attained. These "routines" are close to what I am calling "collaborative infrastructure." My argument, however, is that infrastructure is just one part of collaboration, and that the whole is not achievable without systemic coherence which is in fact very difficult to attain.

27. Lee (1992).

28. Michael Maccoby was one of the first to describe this shift in "social character" in *The Gamesman* (1976).

29. Important analyses of bureaucratic dysfunction include Crozier (1964) and Blau (1963).

30. Heckscher (1995).

31. These cases are detailed in Heckscher et al. (2003).

## CHAPTER 1. FROM BUREAUCRACY TO COLLABORATIVE ENTERPRISE

1. Weber (1921/1968), pp. 650–678.

2. The argument that these two structures constitute fundamental types is bolstered by the fact that they reflect basic categories of mathematics and logic: the hierarchical pyramid is a real-world form of the mathematical (semi-)"lattice," and the peer group reflects the mathematical use of "groups." Piaget (1952, 1953) has shown how the interaction of operations based in those two types is central to cognitive activity. I am proposing—loosely, so only in an endnote—that they are equivalently important in other systems of action.

   There is also intriguing supportive evidence, though highly preliminary, from neuroscience. Goel argues that ill-structured problems involve "lateral transformations" and that well-structured ones involve "vertical transformations" and that the prefrontal cortex is involved in the former. The real world of mixed well- and ill-structured problems seems to involve interaction of the prefrontal cortex with other "vertical" parts of the brain. See Goel (2005).

3. Roethlisberger and Dickson (1939); Mayo (1949); Barnard (1938). Interestingly, the effect of group norms on the work is not what has been most remembered from the Hawthorne studies, though it was vital to Mayo. The more usual presentation of the results is psychologistic, having to do with expectations (the "Hawthorne effect"). This finding has not held up so well over time—see Franke and Kaul (1978)—but the social effect has.

4. Mintzberg (1973); Dalton (1959); Blau (1963). For a historical treatment of how workers can informally work against management, see Mathewson (1931); and for the converse, the informal but essential ways they help with production, see Kusterer (1978).

5. Such a brief summary of the literature on professions and crafts necessarily simplifies a great deal. There were of course rather elaborate organizations of guilds and secret societies built around crafts and professions, and there was even a kind of hierarchy built on the apprenticeship system, which enabled masters to be in effect managers of shops rather than associational equals. But despite these caveats I would stand by the general statements that associational mechanisms until the mid-twentieth century were based on low levels of interdependence, and that their governance was primarily aimed at boundary-maintenance and self-protection. See Adler and Kwon (2005).

   Things are changing: many professions are under a great deal of pressure to increase the level of accountability and to create multidisciplinary collaboration. The difficulty they are having in responding to these demands is further support for the view I am adopting of traditional professions and crafts.

   I should also stress that this characterization of the professions does not apply to science, which has always been a more interdependent activity in which each person's activity is always intended to make a contribution to the whole. See Hagstrom (1965).

6. Gerth and Mills (1946), p. 228.

7. Guilds, of course, were characterized by more hierarchy, though not for the most part a hierarchy of power. They were closer to traditional hierarchies of value commitments, of which the Catholic Church has been the long-term exemplar: the hierarchy is not generally one of offices that can give and enforce orders to each other, but rather one of "closeness to God" in which the lower have a moral duty to follow the "ex cathedra" pronouncements of those higher up. Thus their formal hierarchy can be, by modern standards, very thin and accountability can remain diffuse.

In the background of this analysis is Parsons's treatment of the media of social interactions. He defined two pairs of media that fit the distinction I have drawn, though he does not do it quite in terms of types of networks. One pair is essentially hierarchical, as the term is used here: it consists of power (familiar enough) and value-commitments (as just described). The other pair is essentially negotiated: it consists of markets mediated by money and communities mediated by influence. See Parsons (1969), chapter 14; Parsons (1963).

8. For a very detailed account of this interaction between occupational communities and emerging corporations, see Bensman (1985). For a wider view, see Montgomery (1979).

9. The Weberian concept of bureaucracy was developed and applied to corporate organizations by theorists such as Fayol (1916/1949).

10. Taylor (1911). Accounts of resistance to Taylorism include Braverman (1974); Mathewson (1931); Nelson (1980).

11. On restriction of output, see Mathewson (1931). "Soldiering" was Frederick Taylor's term for what he saw as the tendency of workers to collude in reducing the intensity of work.

12. These patterns of bureaucracy were well documented in some studies during the 1950s and 1960s—especially Crozier (1964) and Blau (1963). But managers had clearly become aware of the problem much earlier, as demonstrated by the growth of internal "community-building" efforts.

13. Barnard (1938), pp. 123, 220.

14. See, e.g., Vogel (1979); Clark (1979); Heller et al. (1988).

15. Mintzberg (1973), reviewing literature from the 1950s and 1960s, found that managers spent most of their time in lateral communications (pp. 45ff., 204). For my own research, see Heckscher (1995).

16. The best studies that I know of such "bad" bureaucracies are Crozier (1964) and Blau (1963).

17. Heckscher (1995), pp. 28–31.

18. The Harris poll has been tracking confidence in "institutions" for decades. In effect this essentially tracks confidence in bureaucracy—in large, strong organizations such as the military, the government, and major companies. Between the 1960s and 1970s this index dropped by nearly 50 percent, and it has hovered around the new level ever since. Confidence in major companies went from 55 percent in the 1960s to 27 percent in the 1970s; in 2005 it was at 17 percent (www.harrisinteractive.com). The shift from the 1960s to the 1970s is extraordinary in its size and decisiveness; I have not seen it sufficiently analyzed.

19. In theoretical terms, I am treating the paternalist system as using a primitive form of influence, similar to economic barter; the collaborative system develops a more fluid "market" in influence. See Parsons (1963).

20. Hard data on increases in spans of control or degree of decentralization are difficult to come by, but there is not much doubt of the overall trend. Urwick's classic 1947 textbook recommended that no one should supervise more than five, or at most six people; and people I have talked to with memories of the 1960s and 1970s remember those ratios as being the norm then. By the 1990s even mainstream companies like AT&T were regularly pushing to 12:1 or 15:1 ratios; ABB had a "span of management" of 42:1 (interviews); Volvo-Uddevalla and Saturn had ratios of 50:1 (Hancke, 1993).

21. Chandler (1977); Sloan (1964); Gouldner (1954).

22. Any attempt to schematize historical sequences necessarily generates many caveats. I do not mean to imply that each stage wipes out the one before it: there are still many "level 1"—personally managed small businesses, some with strong occupational communities—today, as well as levels 2 and 3. The meaning of the sequence is that the most elaborated and complex, and generally the most profitable, forms are the ones on the leading edge of the sequence at any historical period. It is also true that very few examples get ahead of their time: there are few "level 3" exemplars today, but thirty years ago they were far rarer, existing only in partial form in odd niches. Though I don't want to stake much on this argument in this context, my belief is that the "levels" do form in this sense a sequence that cannot be skipped.

 The table as set up implies that the hierarchical and collaborative dimensions develop simultaneously. In fact, in most cases (if not all) the collaborative aspect lags: change is initially driven through the application of power, and the building of networks of peer relationships comes afterward.

23. An extensive literature has examined the structure of teams. Many have converged in distinguishing two dimensions: stability of membership and complexity of task (e.g., Scott and Einstein [2001]). I am using the term *task team* to designate relatively complex and dynamic teams.

24. Sabel (2006).

25. Boehm et al. (1998), p. 34; http://www.p21.com.au/images05/methodology/spiral_methodology.png (accessed July 2, 2006); http://www.cs.uga.edu/~eileen/ 4800/Notes/spiral.gif (accessed June 29, 2006).

26. Galbraith (2005).

27. From a presentation at the Human Resources Planning Society, San Francisco, June 2005.

28. There is a large recent literature on alliances, e.g., Doz and Hamel (1998). I am not aware of good research documenting the number of alliances, but it is hard to doubt that they have become increasingly important in many large corporations.

29. Sabel (2006), pp. 129–130. His source is Nishiguchi and Beaudet (1998).

30. MacDuffie and Helper (2006).

31. Another such case in telecommunications is documented in Bonchek and Howard (2006).

32. On NASDAQ, and these interfirm networks more generally, see Applegate (2005).

33. See Applegate and Ladge (2003); Applegate (2006). I am continuing to omit even more ambitious forms of collaborative networks, like open source software development or scientific research, in order to maintain a focus on the realm of competitive business.

34. Carroll and Burton (2000).
35. Granovetter (1973; "weak ties"), Burt (1992; "structural holes"), Mandell (1984; "multilateral brokerage roles"), Krackhardt (1995); etc.
36. Munch (1986); Gray (1989).
37. See note 2, on Piaget.
38. Granovetter (1973).

## CHAPTER 2. STRATEGIES AND STRUCTURES

1. Criticisms of collaboration include Jaques (1990), who believes it is too loose and unstructured; Barker (1993), who argues that it is merely a more subtle form of management control; and Eccles and Nohria (1992), who conflate it with informal cooperation and thereby see it as nothing new.
2. Organization change can be spawned for any number of reasons; in fact the origins are frequently based in value-driven or "crackpot" ideas. The current move toward collaboration owed much of its early impetus in the 1950s and 1960s to soft values of participation derived from the broader political climate. But the continued growth and survival of any organizational change depends on strategic success.
3. Chandler (1990).
4. This concept of solutions strategy was developed in the McKinsey research group described earlier, with Jay Galbraith playing a central role; he has recently published his version of the solutions argument in Galbraith (2005).
5. Porter (1980).
6. This argument about the decline of mass or commodity production has been made by many economic historians; I have been most influenced by Michael Piore and Charles Sabel (1984). Their idea for what would replace it was also generally "collaborative" in my sense, though at that time the outlines were far less clear than now.
7. Most dimensions of strategy, though not all, depend heavily on the organizational capacity to execute them. The exceptions, where a company is successful without a good organization, are relatively short-term—for example, where the key is financial tactics implemented by one person or very few people, or a major technological breakthrough from a single inventor, or a brilliant (or lucky) choice in market positioning from the brain of a CEO. A major type of strategy of the 1970s, the building of conglomerates of unrelated firms, relied much less on organizational strength than on financial balances.
8. A general theory that similarly treats uncertainty and complexity as drivers of "network governance"—roughly what I am calling collaborative organization—is Jones, Hesterly, and Borgatti (1997). Hage and Alter (1997) focus on complexity.
9. More recently, however, GE has pushed more toward the "high-high" model of solutions and is trying more to integrate diverse offerings—for example, by reorganizing so as to offer "one-stop shopping" to developing countries. See Claudia H. Deutsch, "G.E. Becomes a General Store for Developing Countries," *New York Times*, July 16, 2005.
10. See Foote, Galbraith, Hope, and Miller (2001). This concept is a close kin to Ramirez and Wallin's (2000) notion of "co-production."

11. This is one scenario explored, for example, by Piore and Sabel (1984).

12. From multiple company documents, 2004.

13. For details of this strategic evolution at IBM, see Applegate, Austin, and Collins (2004).

14. A nonscientific but indicative 1999 McKinsey survey of 230 of its customer teams found that they expected rapid increases in solutions strategies in virtually every one of the twelve industries covered, including "prosaic" ones like Auto & Assembly and Petroleum; the only partial exceptions, where they expected that fewer than 50 percent of companies would have more than 25 percent of sales through solutions, were Chemicals and Power (electricity and natural gas). (Internal document from McKinsey & Co.)

15. http://apply-mag.com/news/Systems-provide-solutions-092004/ (accessed June 24, 2005).

16. Frank Diorio, General Manager and Vice President of Kodak Service and Support; in Dorio (2002).

17. Gittell (2003); Adler, Goldoftas, and Levine (1997).

18. I draw this information in part from an internal case by the McKinsey research team and in part from a draft case by Shazad Ansari of Rotterdam University (2005).

19. Womack, Jones, and Roos (1991); Lawler (1990).

20. Adler, Goldoftas, and Levine (1997); the preceding description is drawn largely from this article and discussions with Paul Adler.

21. Lawler (1990); Womack, Jones, and Roos (1991).

22. Atlan (1991) uses these terms in a somewhat similar, but not identical way. By "complexity" he means the capacity to self-organize, while "complication" is simply any kind of order.

23. See Chapter 1 at "Level 3: Decentralized Paternalist Bureaucracy."

24. This idea originated (for me) in the McKinsey group described elsewhere. Russ Eisenstat and Nathaniel Foote framed the task originally as a matter of "managing multiple dimensions"; Jay Galbraith was particularly helpful in detailing the way in which different companies were combining dimensions of geography, customer, product, industry, and function. More recently I became aware of a piece by Baron and Besanko (2001) that tells much the same story.

25. Isaacson and Thomas (1986), p. 669.

26. What is often called "matrix" today is a far more evolved form of team-based management, as described later in this chapter.

27. Galbraith (2005).

28. Based on interviews with nine Citibank customer relationships managers, 2001.

29. For example, Quinn and Hilmer (1995).

30. Jones, Hesterly, and Borgatti (1997) elaborate a general theory of networks that is consistent with mine here. They draw the connection of networks to uncertainty of demand and also argue that hierarchies facilitate complex, customized exchanges, but not when need for adaptiveness is high.

   They argue explicitly that increased uncertainty of demand pushes more toward "network forms—in the sense of strong peer linkages, weak hierarchy (pp. 3ff.).

31. From company training materials.

32. Adam Smith, *The Wealth of Nations*: Book 1, chapter 11, "Conclusion of the Chapter."

33. Some, but not all, of our sample companies tried this move: details are provided in the expanded research chapter available online (see Appendix), especially proposition 9b.

34. The data for the following remarks on "high-high" organizations are drawn especially from my study of the e-Solutions group at Citibank, which is one of the best examples I know of. I have checked these lessons against other examples such as the Shell new ventures unit, IBM, ABB of Canada, and the "NewTech" architecture lab.

35. This description comes from a case written for the McKinsey group by Nancy Taubenslag.

## CHAPTER 3. CITIBANK E-SOLUTIONS

1. For more details of the e-Business strategy see Yu et al. (2002).

## CHAPTER 4. THE CULTURE OF CONTRIBUTION

1. Nahavandi and Malekzadeh, (1993); Olie (1994).

2. This is from an interview at Citibank e-Solutions, where as mentioned earlier, "culture" is treated as central to the alliance process.

3. Deutsch (1999). I have also spoken directly with a member of Cisco's culture group, and been part of another study; these confirm the general impression.

4. Weber (1921/1968), p. 650.

5. Merton (1940).

6. Weber (1921/1968), p. 650.

7. See, for instance, Mayo's treatment as described in Whyte (1956), pp. 32ff.; Jackall (1988), p. 197 passim.

8. Atleson (1983); Hylton (1996), pp. 583–593.

9. Notably Margolis (1979).

10. On the abandonment of moral autonomy, see, for example, Jackall (1988); Margolis (1979). Other works emphasizing the conformity of managerial life, and the paternalistic nature of the culture, include Mills (1951), Whyte (1956), McGregor (1960), Kanter (1977), and Kunda (1992).

11. Heckscher (1995).

12. From this perspective, William H. Whyte's classic study, *The Organization Man* (1956), is very interesting: he sees the emphasis on corporate loyalty as new (p. 161), but also stresses the growing importance of expertise, the notion of management as an expert role. He dislikes both these trends because they suppress individual "genius" and lead to leveling downward.

13. A classic European study is by Crozier (1964): he finds that the elaboration of rules is a primary dynamic and mechanism for playing the political game, and that the values of autonomy and expertise are very high in the pantheon. Conflicts between expertise and positional hierarchy are very tense (p. 112)—whereas in the United States they are more likely to be resolved in favor of the hierarchy.
    On Japanese paternalism, see Ouchi (1981); Clark (1979). Khatri, Tsang, and Begley

(2006) consider Japan and the United States similar in producing cronyism, which is an outcome of what I would call paternalist culture.

14. Merton (1940) noted that the bureaucratic personality often led to a "sanctification" of rules: "devotion to the rules leads to their transformation into absolutes; they are no longer conceived as relative to a set of purposes" (p. 564). Gouldner (1954) suggested that rules may become in effect a group defense mechanism, a way of protecting themselves against outside pressures. There is also the simple issue of elaboration of rules over time: whenever something goes wrong in a bureaucracy the response is to add rules to prevent it from happening again; this one-directional process inevitably leads to an accretion of rules to a point where they make it hard to focus on the work.

Many observers have also noted the hardening of internal divisions and the development of dysfunctional "politics." Merton once again provides a useful analysis of how long-term attachment to the organization tends to produce groups with a strong sense of community that defend themselves against encroachments from the outside or from above. The built-in element of autonomy in the bureaucratic culture may serve as another self-protective weapon (Crozier, 1964).

15. From interviews with middle managers.

16. See also Mohrman, Mohrman, and Lawler (1992) for a similar analysis of how pay for performance strengthens hierarchy and the role of supervisors.

17. The battle very often escalates into "forced curve" programs: see Chapter 6.

18. My description of the "professional ethic" in Heckscher (1995), chapters 7–9, already had many of the elements of what I now call the culture of contribution, though some pieces—especially the notion of contribution itself—have come into sharper focus as a result of later research.

19. The exceptions to this generalization were some people older than age 50 who had been with the bank for a long time and did express a hope that they would finish their careers there. Not all older people by any means expressed this view, but all who expressed it were older than 50.

20. The first quote is by an engineer at this same automobile company; the second a high-level manager in a manufacturing plant.

21. Hamel (2000).

22. See Husted and Michailova (2002).

23. From interviews with the McKinsey research project on solutions organization.

24. Margolis (1979).

25. Kroeber and Kluckhohn (1952).

26. These dimensions are drawn from Parsons's functional framework (e.g., Parsons and Platt, 1973), though I don't believe he ever formulated them in exactly this way. For Parsons, values and culture perform the "pattern-maintenance" function; I use the concept of pattern in a similar way. This function is particularly concerned with maintaining consistency over time. It permits flexibility through its reflexive relations to the systems of integration, which govern concrete internal relationships, and goal attainment, which focuses on external relationships. Sanctions are essential to each of these institutional systems.

27. The radical or Marxist literature puts special emphasis on the contested nature of culture; see Wright (1998); Kunda (1992).

28. There are other ways of thinking about the "pattern-setting" role of culture. In some respects it is like a grammar: a set of rules that can produce an infinite number of meaningful actions that have never occurred before, but that can nevertheless be judged as "right" or "wrong." This image is not quite right however, because culture is less clear cut and rule based than grammar. A better image is of an artistic style: an expert can usually identify a Picasso or a Monet that has never been seen before, not on the basis of clear rules but on the basis of an empathic grasp of the style. The judgment is not perfect—forgers can sometimes fool the experts, just as con men can sometimes fool people into thinking that they share cultural beliefs. In general, culture is closer to this sense of "pattern" than to generative grammar.

29. Treatments of shame and guilt in this context include Riesman (1950); Scheff (2000).

30. See Oyserman, Coon, and Kemmelmeier (2002); Fiske (2002). To be fair, Hofstede himself has never relied purely on survey data, but has used wide-ranging qualitative reflections to validate the "sense" of his dimensions. His analyses are therefore generally far more nuanced than those of many of his followers.

31. Weber (1907/1948) used *verstehen*, usually translated as "empathy," as a major methodological foundation.

32. See the Appendix at the end of this book for details on these interviews and sites.

33. Hofstede (1983); Cooke and Rousseau (1988); Denison (1990).

34. A 1988 literature review found more than twenty dimensions (Cameron and Ettington, 1988).

35. McGregor (1960); Ouchi (1981).

36. Cameron (2006).

37. Cameron and Quinn (1999).

## CHAPTER 5. COLLABORATIVE INFRASTRUCTURE

1. This treatment is superficially similar to Schein's (1985) distinction between culture and "artifacts," the latter being visible manifestations of culture. But in fact I am turning it around: where for Schein culture is reality and artifacts are "merely" its expression, I am defining infrastructure in terms of visible systems that *shape* culture. I am also emphasizing not only visibility but also actionability.

   There is also some similarity between infrastructure and Eisenhardt and Martin's (2000) notion of dynamic routines. I treat these routines, however, much more as part of a systemic and patterned whole rather than as isolated mechanisms.

2. Adler and Kwon (2002).

3. Employment security is often seen as distinctively Japanese, but this is not so. American and European corporations until the 1970s were as strong in their implicit guarantees of job security for managerial workers as were Japanese firms (and, incidentally, the Japanese commitment to this policy is currently weakening as well). There was some difference at the blue-collar level, where in the United States it was more common to view these employees as a variable expense and therefore routinely subject to layoffs; but even here there was considerable security, in part enforced by unions, so that General Motors

assembly-line workers or AT&T operators typically did come to identify themselves with their companies rather than viewing themselves as free agents.

4. Baker, Jensen, and Murphy (1988).

5. For evidence, see Baker, Jensen, and Murphy (1988).

6. This use of noneconomic incentives was a central theme of Barnard (1938).

7. Some economists have doubted the significance of the supposed increase in job mobility, but the tide seems to have turned. Henry Farber, of Princeton University, was one of the most prominent skeptics until the mid-1990s, but in the latter part of that decade found that the percentage of workers with long-tenure jobs was dropping significantly (Farber, 1997). See also Ruhm (1995). For some reason there has been little further research on this question since 2000; the recession of 2001 would of course have affected the numbers.

8. See especially Stewart (2002). The theory of dual labor markets is most associated with Doeringer and Piore (1971).

9. Lawler, Mohrman, and Ledford (1995) found that by 1996, only 9 percent of firms offered employment security assurances to more than 80 percent of their employees—down from 26 percent in 1987.

10. See, for example, Bridges (1995); Pink (1997–1998).

11. Academics have not agreed that there is a major change going on in career patterns; few have examined this proposition that *expectations* have changed. The best review I know of is Cappelli (1999), chapter 3. There are many journalistic surveys indicating that workers are more willing to change jobs than in the past.

12. Stewart (2002).

13. The reduction in management layers has not been documented, to my knowledge, aside from some journalistic surveys; but it is widely perceived as significant by my middle management interviewees.

14. In the European Union, union membership declined from 44 percent to 32 percent in 2001 (Ebbinghaus, 1990).

15. Surveys from the 1970s regularly reported job satisfaction levels of more than 80 percent in the "fairly" or "very satisfied" categories in the 1970s; in the early 2000s the norm was closer to 50 percent; contrast, for example, Quinn and Staines (1979) with the Conference Board (2003). Without writing a treatise on polls in this footnote, I find that this decline is consistent with many other surveys from these two periods.

16. See, in general, the longitudinal work of Geert Hofstede, which despite my criticisms of its methodology in Chapter 4 does seem likely to capture some broad trends. One article that traces the longitudinal development of individualism is Hofstede (1987).

17. Saturn's story since then has not been an entirely happy one: they were unable to break free of the GM bureaucracy and to find outside financing, and GM—which never trusted this collaborative system—starved it for new models. The plant is still alive and doing reasonably well, but the models are behind the curve and it has lost its competitive edge. See Rubinstein and Kochan (2001).

18. This description is provided in an internal case by Jay Galbraith.

19. On Welch's education effort, see "How Jack Welch Runs GE," *Business Week* online, June 8, 1998 (cover story). After 17 years of tenure at that time, Welch had run such sessions

more that 250 times, covering more than 15,000 managers and executives. On "Work-Out," see Bartlett and Wozny (2001).

20. For an overview of this issue in our research sample, see the online treatment of research methods referred to in the Appendix, especially proposition 2b.

21. See Hamel (2000).

22. Heckscher and Foote (2006).

23. For example, Peter Senge: "You cannot have a learning organization without shared vision" (Senge, 1990, p. 209).

24. Granovetter (1973).

25. Stephenson (2001); Ancona and Caldwell (1992).

26. Applegate (2006); Brown, Durchslag, and Hagel (2002).

27. See an interview with Gage in Rapaport (1996).

28. Drawn from case studies by Kristina Wollschlaeger at McKinsey.

29. Parsons (1963), p. 49.

30. Rubinstein and Kochan (2001).

31. Applegate (2006).

32. See the online treatment of research methods referred to in the Appendix, especially proposition 8d.

33. See, for example, Weisbord (1987), Dyer (1987), and Schein (1987).

34. Eisenhardt and Sull (2001); Caulkin (1995).

35. See the online treatment of research methods referred to in the Appendix, especially proposition 8c.

36. Kaplan (1984).

37. See the online treatment of research methods referred to in the Appendix, especially proposition 2c.

38. Fisher and Ury (1981). This book did not actually use "win–win"—its term was "principled negotiation"; but the Harvard Program on Negotiation that arose from the book quite soon began using this catchier language. The other frequently used term is "mutual gains."

39. Heckscher and Hall (2004).

40. Though this quote sounds rather like the person quoted in Chapter 3—"That's how I fight my war"—it is actually a different person in an entirely different kind of position; this fact indicates how widespread this sort of attitude was in the organization.

41. I must note that I know the correct Latin plural is "fora"—but that's not what people in companies generally use.

42. See Wenger (1998), Wenger and Snyder (2000), and McDermott (2000).

43. McDermott and Jackson (2000). See also McDermott and O'Dell (2001).

44. Lorenz (1993b), p. 320.

45. From an internal case study by Barry Sugarman for the Center for Organization Fitness.

46. Much of the "social capital" literature is hobbled by the failure to distinguish between diffuse social relationships and performance-focused work relationships: they treat all "personal relationships" as equal in building system capability (for example, Nahapiet and Ghoshal, 1997). My argument suggests that diffuse social relationships are useful for paternalist firms and specific work relationships for collaborative enterprises.

47. See the online treatment of research methods referred to in the Appendix, especially propositions 6a and 7a.

48. See p. 151.

49. See De Geus (1999).

50. See, for example, Daft, Sormunen, and Parks (1988); Garg, Walters, and Priem (2003).

51. Beer and Rogers (1997).

52. See the online treatment of research methods referred to in the Appendix, especially proposition 6b.

53. Other examples in our sample include the ABB corporate projects debates, the front–back links in the Citibank product management process, and the "NewTech" "business linker" role.

54. I would include Saturn here, since employees at all levels were unusually tuned in to strategy and full of ideas; unfortunately the connection to actual strategic decisions at GM was almost entirely absent, so their ideas went nowhere (Rubinstein and Kochan, 2001).

55. Citibank, for instance, had "team challenge" processes that involved representatives of wide swaths of the organization in intensive, multiweek processes of study to assess major new challenges and initiatives. Other good cases from our sample include the IBM opportunity management system and the "NewTech" initiative review process.

56. Among many works by Argyris that elaborate the notion of double-loop learning and defensive routines, see, for example, Argyris (1990).

57. Wenger (1998).

58. This analysis of both Shell and the World Bank is based on interviews and meetings with middle managers and on presentations to the Center for Workplace Transformation in 2001; in the Shell case I also had access to unpublished internal studies. For a published treatment of the Shell learning communities, see McDermott (2000).

59. See the online treatment of research methods referred to in the Appendix, especially proposition 10a.

60. These descriptions of ABB learning mechanisms are from case studies by Jay Galbraith.

61. Adler, Goldoftas, and Levine (1997); Helper, MacDuffie, and Sabel (2000).

62. For published descriptions of this process, see Beer and Rogers (1997); Heckscher and Foote (2006).

63. This comparison is nicely made by Khanna and Palepu (1997).

64. Guler, Guillén, and Macpherson (2002).

65. See MacDuffie and Helper (2006); also Brandenburger and Nalebuff (1997).

## CHAPTER 6. TWO UNRESOLVED PROBLEMS

1. Though apparently not *named* until the 1950s, by Peter Drucker (1954).

2. This 2 percent figure is drawn from a 1986 Hay Group study (Greeley and Ochsner, 1986), and it is also consistent with much other evidence, such as Lee (1989). See also Baker, Jensen, and Murphy (1988), pp. 595ff.

3. Good summaries of the performance management literature include Jenkins et al. (1998); Beer and Cannon (2004). Carlos Martin (2006) finds that "there is a substantial lack of literature linking the organizational context with assessment tools, which is a major limitation in evaluating the effectiveness of the existing (mostly hierarchical) practices designed for and implemented in advanced collaborative work."

4. This is based on a review of the data at the base of Heckscher (1995). In five of these cases the forced curve was rigidly enforced, at least for a time, while in three others variations from the pattern were permissible but discouraged.

5. For a public case describing this dynamic of forcing and resistance in pay for performance, see Hall and Madigan (2000).

6. For example, Becker and Huselid (1998).

7. These findings are summarized in great detail in Johnson and Johnson (1989). A similar conclusion from economists is Fehr and Gachter (2000).

8. For example, Beer and Cannon (2004); Mohrman, Mohrman, and Lawler (1992).

9. For evidence of this relation see Mohrman, Mohrman, and Lawler (1992).

10. Among others, Sewell and Brown (2002), which was a business best-seller. See also Neely (1999).

11. See, for example, Lester and Piore (2006).

12. I do not have permission to identify sources of individual quotes from this company.

13. An extended theoretical argument in a similar vein critiquing the use of individual performance measures in knowledge settings is Offe (1976). For shorter and more business-oriented critiques, see Pfeffer (1998); Beer and Cannon (2004).

14. Reported in Heckscher (1995), pp. 153–154 passim.

15. For an economist's argument that traditional incentives can undermine collaboration, see Fehr and Gachter (2000).

16. Kaplan and Norton (2001), part III (emphasis in original).

17. The most recent estimate I have comes from a 2002 Mercer Compensation Planning Survey of 1,600 organizations covering more than 15.5 million workers, which finds 28 percent using "multi-rater performance management" and another 19 percent considering its adoption. ("2003 Compensation Planning Briefing," Human Resource Association of Central Indiana, September 19, 2002.)

18. The existing literature on 360-degree feedback is best summarized by Atwater, Waldman, and Brett (2002). There are estimates that 12 to 29 percent of large organizations are using some form of multisource, multirater feedback, and that the use of this method is increasing (Waldman, Atwater, and Antonioni, 1998; Antonioni, 1996). There also are diverse estimates of the success of the method. The *APA Monitor*'s July 1995 overview said that "anecdotal information indicates that these [multisource] feedback methods heighten managers' awareness of their strengths and weaknesses; create an atmosphere of constructive dialogue; remove personal blind spots; and are a powerful incentive for change." Other scholars have shown a positive relationship between implementation of multisource feedback and firm performance (Bracken et al., 2001; Walter and Smither, 1999). However, a number of studies have questioned the real impact and the positive outcomes of multisource feedback in terms of its overall effectiveness (Atwater et al., 2000; Timmreck and Bracken, 1997), true impact on behavioral

change (DeNisi and Kluger, 2000; Kluger and DeNisi, 1996), or the acceptance of the feedback (Lepsinger and Lucia, 1997).

19. This failing is noted by two recent reviews of the practice of multisource feedback: Atwater, Waldman, and Brett (2002); Morgan, Cannan, and Cullinane (2005).

20. Silverman, Kerrin, and Carter (2005). For empirical evidence of this association between organizational "politics" and negative responses to multisource feedback, see Ford (2002).

21. Martin (2006), section 3.2.4, "Servico."

22. For good examples of reputational infighting, see Shorris (1981); Dalton (1959).
    Uzzi (1966) notes the inadequacy of reputational mechanisms in the traditional firms he studied.

23. See the online treatment of research methods referred to in the Appendix, proposition 4a.

24. Whyte (1956).

25. Martin (2006), p. 254.

26. Becker and Huselid (1998) suggest that "performance-contingent incentive compensation" has a relatively powerful effect on corporate performance when it is integrated with total systems changes. This evidence is, however, inconsistent with many other studies that show that performance is not unidimensional or so easily correlated with specific policies (see Rousseau, 1997). In my own interviews I have found no one at any level who claims to have strong evidence of a positive link between performance-based pay and organizational effectiveness; I have, however, found many who believe the link is negative!

27. Gordon et al. (2000). For the "difference principle" see Rawls (1971), p. 303.

28. At least one study, moreover, has made a quantitative case that the theoretical framework is an important variable affecting research findings: Jenkins et al. (1998), p. 783. These authors themselves then seem to fall into the same trap: they conclude their meta-analysis by saying that incentives do help performance, but omit a fundamental qualification noted earlier in the text that this applies only to quantity of output and not to quality.

29. See Chapter 2.

30. Farber (2005) finds that full-time job losers who find new full-time jobs earn 17 percent less on average on their new jobs than they would have had they not been displaced.

31. Michaels, Handfield-Jones, and Axelrod (2001).

32. Michaels, Handfield-Jones, and Axelrod (2001) For critiques that extend the argument in this section, see Heckscher (2000); Pfeffer (2001). The line from Jensen is from an interview: "Kingston Employees Take Bonus in Stride," *Los Angeles Times*, December 16, 1996.

33. Speech at Wharton Conference on New Organization Forms, March 19, 1999.

34. For a summary of this evidence see Gordon et al. (2000).

35. See, for example, Blank (2000); Kennickell (2006).

36. John Epperheimer, director of corporate services for Cupertino-based Career Action Center, quoted in Silverstein (1997).

37. Based on interviews in 2000 with Talent Alliance leadership.

38. Dueling economists: Gottschalk and Moffitt (1999) find little change in tenure or mobility; Osterman (2001) finds "substantial evidence that there have been shifts in the

American labour market in the direction of weaker attachment between firms and their employees"; Farber's (1997) results are similar.

## CHAPTER 7. CROSSING THE COLLABORATIVE FRONTIER

1. Two of the more famous modern statements of this distinction are Burns's (1978) typology of transformational versus transactional leadership, which has generated a substantial research stream, and Kuhn's (1962) notion of "scientific revolutions" as distinct from "normal science." But the basic idea underlies innumerable older notions, such as Weberian charisma, Freudian transference, Hegelian synthesis, and so on.

2. Kuhn (1962). Scientific paradigms are very similar to what we have been calling cultural "mindsets," but with some differences: they are more rigorously integrated by logic, and they are more susceptible to proof. But they play essentially the same role, providing a broad vision that then shapes and integrates many details of daily behavior.

   Other important stage theories appear in widely diverse fields, such as evolutionary theory and neuroscience (see Dennett, 1996), etc.

3. Piaget and Inhelder (1958).

4. Chandler (1962); similar treatments include Child and Kieser (1981).

5. This is a famous example from a lecture by Edward Lorenz (1972); see also Lorenz (1993a).

6. There has been very important work describing the characteristics and constituent elements of "self-organizing systems" but much less success in developing a theory of key interventions. See, for example, Holland (1996); Comfort (1997), pp. 375–383.

7. See Khalil (1996); Atlan (1991). Atlan argues that complexity of meaning, which is central to human systems, is still more difficult to grasp than "natural complexity," and of necessity proceeds through "bricolage" rather than through formalizable paths.

8. This treatment somewhat resembles Lewin's (1951) notion of "unfreezing." My analysis of obstacles, though, is not in terms of restraining forces, but in terms of the interconnections of a system of action.

9. This difficulty of change resulting from the interlocking of expectations has been modeled by economists and game theorists: for instance, Sapienza (2003).

10. Piaget (1945/1962).

11. The two were former CEO Kari Kairamo and former head of the China office Topi Honkavaara.

12. The notion of sociodynamics is related to but not the same as the claim that emotions matter in social exchange theory (see an extensive review in Lawler and Thye, 1999). Sociodynamics are specifically distorted and defensive forms of group emotion. This is much closer to the concepts developed by Vasconcelos and Vasconcelos (2002).

    There is also apparent overlap with Argyris's theory of "defensive routines" (1990). Argyris tends, however, to treat these routines as individual failings, and to believe they can be overcome through evidence and reasoning: "People can be taught how to recognize the reasoning they use when they design and implement their actions" (Argyris, 1991, p. 12). Sociodynamics as I propose it is essentially social, a result of interactions and the conditions for maintaining trust in a group, and it is definitely not solvable by reasoned discussion.

13. See Vasconcelos and Vasconcelos (2002).
14. Heckscher (1995), p. 7 passim.
15. A powerful exploration of group narcissism at the level of nations is Brunner (1997). Thomas Scheff has deeply analyzed the dynamics of pride and shame in various kinds of social strain (e.g., Scheff, 1988).
16. A middle manager quoted in Heckscher (1995), p. 101.
17. Heckscher (1995), chapter 4.
18. This distinction of "espoused values" and "values in use" is drawn from Argyris and Schön (1974) and other works by Argyris.
19. As reported by the staffing firm Randstad in the *2005 Employee Review*, based on a survey of 3,000 employees done by Harris Interactive.
20. Conference Board (2003); this figure had declined from 23.4 percent in 1995.
21. This study by Mercer Consulting was based on a survey of 4,000 employees in 800 organizations; reported at www.ocregister.com/ocr/2005/07/22/sections/business/business_nation/article_606141.php (accessed September 15, 2005). Other polls in this period also find high cynicism about the integrity of top management.
22. Jackall (1988); Heckscher (1995), chapter 6.

## CHAPTER 8. JOURNEYS

1. James (1902).
2. This line is quoted in many places, but I have never been able to trace its origin—like many of Churchill's "mots," it seems to have originated in luncheon conversation and been passed on by word of mouth.
3. Herzberg (1966); Ford (1969).
4. The success level is documented by Srivastva et al. (1975). The problems of mortality are described in Hackman (1975).
5. U.S. Department of Labor (1985). See also Goodman (1980).
6. Hancke (1993).
7. For a case study of this dynamic, see Harvard Business School (1986); for a wider survey, see Mohrman, Mohrman, and Lawler (1992).
8. Rubinstein and Kochan (2001).
9. Jacob (1993).
10. Taylor (1993); Beer (2003). It's fair to say that like almost everything else in this study, there are two types of criticism: some say that the problem with TQM is that it's not being controlled tightly enough; others, like the authors cited earlier, say the trouble is it's too focused on control and not enough on collaboration.
11. So far the story is told by Yoshino and Malnight (1995), and supplemented by the personal experience of Jay Galbraith.
12. With my colleague Anat Lechner.
13. See the discussion of the limitations imposed on the IBM PC by "mainframe thinking" in Applegate, Austin, and Collins (2004), pp. 3–6.
14. For an extended critique of top-driven change, see also Beer, Eisenstat, and Spector (1990).

15. This case is not part of our coded sample, but was one of those looked at in the McKinsey process; Susan Dunn provided this information. For a publicly available case showing some of the same resistances, see Margolis and Donnellon (1990).

16. A famous example of a failed "innovation unit" is Xerox PARC, which produced many inventions that became crucial to the computer industry but were not adopted by Xerox.

17. The World Bank is not part of our coded sample but was represented in the series of meetings on organization change at the Center for Workplace Transformation from 1999 to 2002.

18. A McKinsey study published in 2005 found that 70 percent of mergers failed to achieve the revenue benefits that were predicted by melding two companies, and that managers consistently overestimated the benefits and underestimated the costs (Christofferson, McNish, and Sias, 2004). Another review of mergers in the 1990s found that that various studies estimated the failure rate between 50 and 80 percent, and that only 17 percent of cross-border mergers and acquisitions add shareholder value (Melewar and Harrold, 2000).

19. We have one detailed case of this merger dynamic from the McKinsey group but it is difficult to tell a story at this level without breaking confidentiality.

20. This description of Venkatesen's leadership is drawn from an internal memo for the McKinsey working group by Quentin Hope and Danny Miller, 2001.

21. On the value of structural change as a driver of transformation, see Galbraith (2000). I see this view as consistent with my argument about the role of structure within an overall interactive process.

22. Johnson & Johnson is very similar to HP in these respects. The tradition of decentralization has served them well but is now felt increasingly as an obstacle to efforts to achieve value-chain integration and create complex solutions.

23. The best case in our sample besides Nokia is Aegon-Spaarbeleg. Nokia then proceeded to move "upward" toward greater complexity, addressing multiple customer segments, products, and services in complex solutions.

24. Veridian was starting to move in the same direction. In all three cases, they then began to move toward more adaptiveness and a full solutions approach.

25. These include, besides Microsoft, McKinsey, Cisco, Sun, and "NewTech" development labs.

26. Applegate, Austin, and Collins (2004), p. 1.

27. This information comes primarily from internal cases and discussions of the McKinsey research group, and from an excellent case study by Ansari (2005).

## CHAPTER 9. LEADERSHIP

1. The top management focus is much the most common, especially in best-selling books like Peters and Waterman (1982), for example. For more involving approaches, see Beer, Eisenstat, and Spector (1990); Pascale, Millemann, and Gioja (1997); Heckscher et al. (2003). "Change everything at once" is actually the title of a book (Neumann, Holti, and Standing, 2000) and the theme of other cases such as Oticon (Kao, 1995). An

argument for starting (sometimes) with structure is Galbraith (2000). The strategic approach is exemplified by Kearns and Nadler (1992) For a culture-driven approach, see Charan (2001).

2. Khalil (1996), p. 316. Pattee's argument is in Pattee (1973); Piaget's in Piaget (1932/1965); Parsons's in Parsons and Shils (1953). It is worth pointing out that all these theoretical approaches stem from a notion of complexity involving reconciliation of fundamentally differing dimensions of value; it is quite different from mere complication, or from nonlinear systems explored by chaos theory. Khalil (1996) details the latter distinction, Atlan (1991) the former.

3. Pattee (1973), p. 144.

4. This case is consistent with other research on the limits of the top-down approach to value transformation: see Beer, Eisenstat, and Spector (1990). Robert Simons has also studied cascades and found the same problem (personal communication; the study is documented in Simons (1991), though the conclusions do not focus on this aspect.)

   A small clarification: the "Watson values" were not actually written down until the 1960s by Thomas Watson Jr.; but they were meant to capture unchanged the "Basic Beliefs" laid out by Watson Sr. in 1914.

5. Applegate et al. (2006), p. 7.

6. I am applying here Parsons's concept of "Value Generalization" (Parsons, 1966).

7. On Strategic Fitness Profiling and for more details on the Veridian case see Heckscher and Foote (2006), chapter 12. See also Beer and Rogers (1997); Beer and Eisenstat (2004).

8. This case is told in detail in Heckscher and Foote (2006), chapter 12, pp. 502ff. The quote from the Veridian task team is drawn from the company's written summaries of the meeting.

9. The latter case is detailed in Beer and Rogers (1997).

10. MacDuffie and Helper (2006).

11. Applegate et al. (2006).

12. Austin and Nolan (2000).

13. Reichheld (1996, chapter 7) describes this process in another set of companies.

14. Barbaro (2005).

15. MacDuffie and Helper (2006); Applegate (2006).

16. Bonchek and Howard (2006).

17. This is Max Weber's phrase to describe political action and social change (Weber, 1919/1946a).

18. Heckscher et al. (2003), pp. 208–209 and personal interviews.

19. Applegate and Ladge (2003).

20. This is the well-known sociological problem of "institutional isomorphism" (DiMaggio and Powell, 1983).

21. Bonchek and Howard (2006). For a discussion of the same problem in mutual-gains labor negotiations, see Heckscher and Hall (1994).

22. Palmisano, Hemp, and Stewart (2004).

23. Kaplan and Norton (2001).

24. This was an unpublished study of nineteen teams engaged in the Citibank Process Improvement Process in 2000–2001. We interviewed eighteen of the team leaders on their assessment of the teams' performance and the factors affecting their success; we then used these discussions as the basis for a survey of sixty-one team members, which we subjected to statistical analysis.

25. This describes not only the Process Improvement Teams at Citibank, but also the outcomes in most Quality of Work Life effort during the 1970s and 1980s (see Heckscher et al., 2003).

26. See Applegate (2006); Bonchek and Howard (2006).

27. Foote et al. (2001), p. 87.

28. Applegate et al. (2006), p. 3.

29. Palmisano, Hemp, and Stewart (2004), pp. 8–9.

30. This notion of public conversation as generating shared values is of course used by many change theorists. I would trace its modern use to Dewey (1927). It is heavily used by both the Habermasian and Communitarian "schools" (see Habermas, 1994); Habermas (1971) and has been introduced to the business world by authors like Beer and Eisenstat (2004). It is also consistent with Piaget's view of stage change, which begins with experience and moves to conceptualization; see Piaget (1932/1965). But Piaget never could figure out how leadership or teaching could work, and so had an extremely romantic view that development occurred through pure peer interaction.

   I am not aware, however, that any of these uses elaborates the threefold sequence that I have sketched here, drawn from the evidence of my sample, in which the leader's private vision is made public through iterations between specific practices and broader reflection.

31. Wetlaufer (1999). The order of sentences is slightly changed.

32. For example, Muller (2001).

## CHAPTER 10. RECAPITULATION

1. These two steps are, I suggest, in a "value-added" relationship: the second one may come first, but it will not be effective until the first one is in place.

## CHAPTER 11. BUT IS IT GOOD?

1. Weber (1919/1946a, 1919/1946b; 1907/1948).

2. Merton (1940), p. 562.

3. See Krames (2005). A somewhat more moderate form of this ethic is the claim that it is not business's responsibility to consider social values (see Friedman, 1970).

   I don't mean to take a position on Welch myself, since I don't know enough; there is some evidence that he was more collaborative than generally perceived. The point here is just about the perception.

4. MacDuffie and Helper (2006).

5. Heckscher (1995), chapter 8.

6. Pateman (1970).

7. Applegate et al. (2006).

8. I do not have permission to identify sources of individual quotes for this company.

9. This was the essential position of John Stuart Mill (1869), who had an enormous influence on modern Western political thought.

10. See the famous analysis by Kanter (1977), and also Chapter 4 in this volume.

11. See Taylor (1994).

12. Case for McKinsey & Co. research group on opportunity-based design.

13. The pain caused by current increases in flexibility, and the unfairness of its imlementation, are graphically documented in many books, including Gordon (1996), Newman (1989), and my own *White-Collar Blues* (1995).

14. See Chapter 7, p. 209. A survey by Walker Information in 2005 found that loyalty—those planning to stay with their companies for at least two years—had risen to 34 percent in 2005 from 24 percent in 2001; but that dissatisfaction with companies remained high, especially around training and career opportunities. *Workforce Management Week* 7, no. 1 (January 1–7, 2006); http://www.workforce.com (accessed January 3, 2006).

15. See Kaus (1973) for a particularly rich description of such a case.

16. See Rubinstein (2006).

17. Among many other cases, the articulate leader of the Saturn local, Michael Bennett, was defeated when the mood in the plant soured, and the plant shifted in the direction of more traditional relations; Don Ephlin, the founding spirit of the effort as head of the UAW's GM division, was relegated to a basement office at the union headquarters.

18. Jones, Hesterly, and Borgatti (1997).

19. From a presentation at a conference on New Organizational Forms at the Wharton School, March 19, 1999.

20. This argument is developed at much greater length in Heckscher (1988/1995).

21. See http://www.workingtoday.org.

22. Michael Kanellos, "Gates Taking a Seat in Your Den," *News.com*, January 5, 2006, http://news.com.com/Gates+taking+a+seat+in+your+den/2008–1041_3–5514121.html (accessed January 10, 2006).

23. "SAP Dismisses Open Source Innovation," *Vnunet.com*, November 10, 2005, http://www.vnunet.com/2145809 (accessed December 28, 2005).

24. Merton (1940, 1968). Similarly, see Strathern (1996).

25. Raymond (2006), especially section 4, "Ownership and Open Source."

## APPENDIX

1. Peters and Waterman (1982). This is also the method of the book that has overtaken *In Search of Excellence* as the best-selling management book of all time: James Collins's *Good to Great* (2001). Peters has in fact been quite cavalier about his research methods: though he probably didn't really "fake the data," as he once claimed, he does continue to believe that the most important knowledge comes from following your gut rather than being rigorous about evidence (see Peters, 2001).

2. Two-thirds of the publicly traded "excellent companies" in Peters and Waterman's book underperformed the S&P 500 in the 1985–1995 period. The authors themselves acknowledged that only one-fifth remained excellent in 1995 (Reichheld, 1996, p. 189).

3. Kanter (1977).

4. The two exceptions are Microsoft and BP, which members of the research team became intrigued by and worked to gather a wide range of data; in both instances there are rather good published observational studies.

5. There are some studies of cross-company networks. One of the most extensive is Lynda Applegate's review of twenty-nine such over nine years (Applegate, 2006).

# Bibliography

Adler, P. S. (2001). "Market, Hierarchy, and Trust: The Knowledge Economy and the Future of Capitalism." *Organization Science* 12, no. 2: 214–234.

Adler, Paul S., Goldoftas, Barbara, and Levine, David I. (1997). "Ergonomics, Employee Involvement, and the Toyota Production System: A Case Study of NUMMI's 1993 Model Introduction." *Industrial and Labor Relations Review* 50, no. 3: 416–437.

Adler, Paul S., and Kwon, Seok-Woo. (2002). "Social Capital: Prospects for a New Concept." *The Academy of Management Review* 27, no. 1: 17–40.

Adler, Paul S., and Kwon, Seok-Woo. (2005). "The Evolving Organization of Professional Work." Draft Version, November 27.

Ancona, D., and Caldwell, D. (1992). "Bridging the Boundary: External Activity and Performance in Organizational Teams." *Administrative Science Quarterly* 37: 634–665.

Ansari, Shazad. (2005). "Resource Value and New Markets: The Case of Mobile Telephony." Draft, Rotterdam School of Management, Erasmus University, presented at Academy of Management.

Antonioni, D. (1996). "Designing an Effective 360-Degree Appraisal Feedback Process." *Organizational Dynamics* 25: 24–38.

Applegate, Lynda M. (2006). "Building Inter-Firm Collaborative Community: Uniting Theory and Practice." In Charles Heckscher and Paul Adler (eds.), *The Firm as a Collaborative Community: Reconstructing Trust in the Knowledge Economy*. Oxford: Oxford University Press, chapter 9.

Applegate, Lynda M., Austin, Rob, and Collins, Elizabeth. (2004). "IBM's Decade of Transformation: A Vision for On Demand." Harvard Business School Case N9-805-018 (July 21).

Applegate, Lynda M., Heckscher, Charles, Michael, Boniface, and Collins, Elizabeth L. (2006). "IBM: Uniting Vision and Values." Harvard Business School Supplement 805130 (September).

Applegate, Lynda M., and Ladge, Jamie. (2003). "Global Healthcare Exchange." Harvard Business School Case 9-804-002 (July 21).

Argyris, C. (1990). *Overcoming Organizational Defenses*. Boston: Allyn and Bacon.

Argyris, C. (1991). "Teaching Smart People How to Learn." *Harvard Business Review* (May–June): 5–15.

Argyris, C., and Schön, D. (1974). *Theory in Practice: Increasing Professional Effectiveness*. San Francisco: Jossey-Bass.

Atlan, Henri. (1991). "*L'intuition du complexe et ses théorisations.*" In Françoise Fogelman Soulié (ed.), *Les Theories de la complexité: autour de l'oeuvre d'Henri Atlan*. Paris: Seuil, pp. 9–44.

Atleson, James B. (1983). *Values and Assumptions in American Labor Law*. Amherst: University of Massachusetts Press.

Atwater, L. E., Waldman, D., Atwater, D., and Cartier, P. (2000). "An Upward Feedback Field Experiment: Supervisors' Cynicism, Follow-Up and Commitment to Subordinates." *Personnel Psychology* 53: 275–297.

Atwater, Leanne E., Waldman, David A., and Brett, Joan F. (2002). "Understanding and Optimizing Multisource Feedback." *Human Resource Management* 41, no. 2: 193–208.

Austin, Robert D., and Nolan, Richard L. (2000). "IBM Corporation Turnaround." Boston: Harvard Business School Case 9-600-098 (March 14).

Baker, George P., Jensen, Michael C., and Murphy, Kevin J. (1988). "Compensation and Incentives: Practice vs. Theory." *Journal of Finance* 43, no. 3: 593-616.

Barbaro, Michael. (2005). "A New Weapon for Wal-Mart: A War Room." *New York Times*, November 1.

Barker, James R. (1993). "Tightening the Iron Cage: Concertive Control in Self-Managing Teams." *Administrative Science Quarterly* 38: 408–437.

Barnard, Chester I. (1938). *The Functions of the Executive*. Cambridge, MA: Harvard University Press.

Baron, David P., and Besanko, David. (2001). "Strategy, Organization, and Incentives: Global Corporate Banking at Citibank." *Industrial and Corporate Change* 10, no. 1: 1–36.

Bartlett, Christopher A., and Wozny, Meg. (2001). "GE's Two-Decade Transformation: Jack Welch's Leadership." Harvard Business School Case 9-399-150.

Becker, Brian, E., and Huselid, Mark A. (1998). "High Performance Work Systems and Firm Performance: A Synthesis of Research and Managerial Implications." *Research and Personality in Resources Management* 16: 53–101.

Beer, Michael. (2003). "Why Total Quality Management Programs Do Not Persist: The Role of Management Quality and Implications for Leading a TQM Transformation." *Decision Sciences* 34, no. 4: 623–642.

Beer, Michael, and Cannon, Mark D. (2004). "Promise and Peril in Implementing Pay-for-Performance." *Human Resource Management* 43, no. 1: 3–48.

Beer, Michael, and Eisenstat, Russell A. (2004). "How to Have an Honest Conversation About Your Business Strategy." *Harvard Business Review* (February): 82–89.

Beer, Michael, Eisenstat, Russell A., and Spector, Bert. (1990). *The Critical Path to Corporate Renewal.* Boston: Harvard Business School Press.

Beer, Michael, and Rogers, Gregory C. (1997). "Hewlett-Packard's Santa Rosa Systems Division (A): The Trials and Tribulations of a Legacy." Harvard Business School Case N9-498-011 (August 11).

Bell, Daniel. (1973). *The Coming of Post-Industrial Society: A Venture in Social Forecasting.* New York: Basic Books.

Bensman, David (1985). *The Practice of Solidarity: American Hat Finishers in the Nineteenth Century.* Urbana: University of Illinois Press.

Best, Michael H. (1990). *The New Competition: Institutions of Industrial Restructuring.* Cambridge, MA: Harvard University Press.

Blank, Rebecca, M. (2000). "Enhancing the Opportunities, Skills, and Security of American Workers." In David T. Ellwood, Rebecca M. Blank, Joseph Blasi, Douglas Kruse, William A. Niskanen, and Karen Lynn-Dyson (eds.), *A Working Nation: Government Work and the Economy.* New York: Russell Sage Foundation, chapter 4.

Blau, Peter M. (1963). *The Dynamics of Bureaucracy.* Chicago: University of Chicago Press.

Boehm, Barry, Egyed, Alexander, Kwan, Julie, Port, Dan, Shah, Archita, and Madachy, Ray. (1998). "Using the WinWin Spiral Model: A Case Study." *Computer* (July): 33–44.

Bonchek, Mark, and Howard, Robert. (2006). " 'The Power to Convene': Creating Collaborative Community with Strategic Customers." In Charles Heckscher and Paul Adler (eds.), *The Firm as a Collaborative Community: Reconstructing Trust in the Knowledge Economy.* Oxford: Oxford University Press, chapter 13.

Bracken, D. W., Timmreck, C. W., Fleenor, J. W., and Summers, L. (2001). "360 Feedback from Another Angle." *Human Resource Management* 40, no. 1: 3–20.

Brandenburger, Adam M., and Nalebuff, Barry J. (1997). *Co-opetition: 1. A Revolutionary Mindset That Combines Competition and Cooperation; 2. The Game Theory Strategy That's Changing the Game of Business.* New York: Currency/Doubleday.

Braverman, Harry. (1974). *Labor and Monopoly Capitalism: The Degradation of Work in the Twentieth Century.* New York: Monthly Review Press.

Bridges, W. (1995). *Jobshift: How to Prosper in a Workplace without Jobs.* St Leonards, NSW: Allen & Unwin.

Brown, John Seely, Durchslag, Scott, and Hagel, John III. (2002). "Loosening Up: How Process Networks Unlock the Power of Specialization." *The McKinsey Quarterly*, no. 2 (Special Edition: Risk and Resilience): 59–69.

Brunner, José. (1997). "Pride and Memory: Nationalism, Narcissism and the Historians' Debates in Germany and Israel." *History & Memory* 9, no. 1–2: 256–300.

Burns, James MacGregor. (1978). *Leadership.* New York: Harper and Row.

Burt, Ronald S. (1992). "The Social Structure of Competition." In Nitin Nohria and Robert G. Eccles (eds.), *Networks and Organizations: Structure, Form, and Action.* Boston: Harvard Business School Press, pp. 57–91.

Cameron, K. S., and Ettington, D. R. (1988). "The Conceptual Foundations of Organizational Culture." In John Smart (ed.), *Higher Education: Handbook of Theory and Research.* New York: Agathon, pp. 356–396.

Cameron, K. S., and Quinn, R. E. (1999). *Diagnosing and Changing Organizational Culture.* Reading, MA: Addison-Wesley.

Cameron, Kim S. (2006). "A Process for Changing Organizational Culture." In Thomas G. Cummings (ed.), *Handbook of Organizational Development.* Beverly Hills, CA: Sage (in press).

Cappelli, Peter. (1999). *The New Deal at Work.* Boston: Harvard Business School Press.

Carroll, Tim, and Burton, Richard. (2000). "Organizations and Complexity: Searching for the Edge of Chaos." *Computational and Mathematical Organization Theory* 6, no. 4: 319–337.

Castells, Manuel. (1996). *The Rise of the Network Society.* Cambridge, MA: Blackwell.

Caulkin, Simon (1995). "Chaos Inc." *Across the Board* 32, no. 7: 32–36.

Chandler, Alfred D., Jr. (1977). *The Visible Hand: The Managerial Revolution in American Business.* Cambridge, MA: Harvard University Press.

Chandler, Alfred D., Jr. (1990). *Scale and Scope: The Dynamics of Industrial Capitalism.* Cambridge, MA: Belknap Press.

Chandler, Alfred Dupont. (1962). *Strategy and Structure: Chapters in the History of the Industrial Enterprise.* Cambridge, MA: MIT Press.

Charan, Ram. (2001). "Conquering a Culture of Indecision." *Harvard Business Review* (April): 74–82, 168.

Child, J., and Kieser, A. (1981). "Development of Organizations over Time." In P. C. Nystrom and W. H. Starbuck (eds.), *Handbook of Organizational Design,* vol. 1: *Adapting Organizations to Their Environments.* Oxford: Oxford University Press, pp. 28–64.

Christofferson, Scott A., McNish, Robert S., and Sias, Diane L. (2004). "Where Mergers Go Wrong." *McKinsey on Finance* (Winter): 1–6.

Clark, Kim B., Chew, W. Bruce, and Fujimoto, Takahiro. (1987). "Product Development in the World Auto Industry." *Brookings Papers on Economic Activity* 3: 729–771.

Clark, R. (1979). *The Japanese Company.* New Haven, CT: Yale University Press.

Collins, James C. (2001). *Good to Great: Why Some Companies Make the Leap—and Others Don't.* New York: HarperBusiness.

Comfort, Louise K. (1997). "Toward a Theory of Transition in Complex Systems." *American Behavioral Scientist* 40, no. 3: 375–383.

Conference Board. (2003). *Special Consumer Survey Report: Job Satisfaction.* The Conference Board Executive Action Report No. 68, September, available at http://www.conference-board.org/economics/press.cfm?press_ID=2227 (accessed September 24, 2003).

Cooke, Robert A., and Rousseau, Denise M. (1988). "Behavioral Norms and Expectations: A Quantitative Approach to the Assessment of Organizational Culture." *Group & Organization Studies* 13, no. 3: 245–273.

Coriat, Benjamin. (1997). "Globalization, Variety, and Mass Production: The Metamorphosis of Mass Production in the New Competitive Age." In J. Rogers Hollingsworth and Robert Boyer (eds.), *Contemporary Capitalism: The Embeddedness of Institutions.* Cambridge: Cambridge University Press, pp. 240–264.

Crozier, Michel. (1964). *The Bureaucratic Phenomenon.* Chicago: University of Chicago Press. (Original French edition Paris: Editions du Seuil, 1963.)

Daft, R. L., Sormunen, J., and Parks, D. (1988). "Chief Executive Scanning, Environmental Characteristics, and Company Performance: An Empirical Study." *Strategic Management Journal* 9, no. 2: 123–139.

Dalton, Melville. (1959). *Men Who Manage: Fusions of Feeling and Theory in Administration.* New York: John Wiley & Sons.

De Geus, A. D. (1999). *The Living Company: Growth, Learning and Longevity in Business.* London: Nicholas Brealey.

DeNisi, A. S., and Kluger, A. N. (2000). "Feedback Effectiveness: Can 360-Degree Appraisals Be Improved?" *Academy of Management Executive* 14: 129–139.

Denison, Daniel R. (1990). *Corporate Culture and Organizational Effectiveness.* New York: John Wiley & Sons.

Dennett, Daniel C. (1996). *Kinds of Minds: Towards an Understanding of Consciousness.* New York: Basic Books.

Deutsch, Claudia H. (1999). "The Deal Is Done. Now the Work Begins." *New York Times,* April 11.

Dewey, John. (1927). *The Public and Its Problems.* New York: Henry Holt.

DiMaggio, Paul J., and Powell, Walter W. (1983). "The Iron Cage Revisited: Institutional Isomorphism and Collective Rationality in Organizational Fields." *American Sociological Review* 48, no. 2: 147–160.

Doeringer, Peter B., and Piore, Michael J. (1971). *Internal Labor Markets and Manpower Analysis.* Lexington, MA: Heath.

Dorio, F. (2002). "Developing a Total Service Solution: Moving from Products to Solutions." *Service Business Review* 9 (July), available at http://www.internetviz-newsletters .com/clicksoftware/e_article000071058.cfm (accessed June 24, 2005).

Doz, Y. L., and Hamel, G. (1998). *Alliance Advantage: The Art of Creating Value Through Partnering.* Cambridge, MA: Harvard University Press.

Drucker, P. F. (1954). *The Practice of Management.* New York: Harper.

Dyer, William G. (1987). *Team Building: Issues and Alternatives.* Reading, MA: Addison-Wesley.

Ebbinghaus, B. (1990). "Does a European Social Model Exist and Can It Survive?" In G. Huemer et al. (eds.), *The Role of Employer Associations and Labour Unions in the EMU.* Aldershot: Ashgate, pp. 1–26.

Eccles, Robert G., and Nohria, Nitin. (1992). *Beyond the Hype: Rediscovering the Essence of Management.* Boston: Harvard Business School Press.

Eisenhardt, Kathleen M., and Martin, Jeffrey A. (2000). "Dynamic Capabilities: What Are They?" *Strategic Management Journal* 21: 1105–1121.

Eisenhardt, Kathleen M., and Sull, Donal N. (2001). "Strategy as Simple Rules." *HBR Onpoint* (January): 107–116.

Farber, Henry S. (1997). "Trends in Long-Term Employment in the United States, 1979–1996." Princeton University, Industrial Relations Section, Working Paper No. 384, available at http://www.irs.princeton.edu/pubs/pdfs/384.pdf (accessed November 17, 2006).

Farber, Henry S. (2005). "What Do We Know about Job Loss in the United States? Evidence from the Displaced Workers Survey, 1984–2004." Princeton University, Industrial Relations Section, Working Paper No. 498, available at http://www.irs.princeton.edu/pubs/pdfs/498.pdf (accessed February 18, 2005).

Fayol, Henri. (1916/1949). *General and Industrial Management*. London: Pitman. (Original edition *Administration Industrielle et Générale*, 1916).

Fehr, Ernst, and Gachter, Simon. (2000). "Do Incentive Contracts Crowd Out Voluntary Cooperation?" University of Zurich, Institute for Empirical Economic Research, IEER Working Paper No. 34, February.

Fisher, Roger, and Ury, William. (1981). *Getting to Yes: Negotiating Agreement without Giving In*. New York: Houghton Mifflin.

Fiske, Alan Page. (2002). "Using Individualism and Collectivism to Compare Cultures—A Critique of the Validity and Measurement of the Constructs: Comment on Oyserman et al. (2002)." *Psychological Bulletin* 128, no. 1: 78–88.

Foote, Nathaniel W., Galbraith, Jay, Hope, Quentin, and Miller, Danny. (2001). "Making Solutions the Answer." *The McKinsey Quarterly*, no. 3: 85–93.

Ford, John M. (2002). *Organizational Politics and Multisource Feedback*. Ph.D. dissertation, Louisiana State University and Agricultural and Mechanical College, Department of Psychology.

Ford, R. N. (1969). *Motivation Through the Work Itself*. New York: American Management Association.

Franke, Richard Herbert, and Kaul, James D. (1978). "The Hawthorne Experiments: First Statistical Interpretation." *American Sociological Review* 43, no. 5: 623–643.

Friedman, Milton. (1970). "The Social Responsibility of Business Is to Increase Its Profits." *The New York Times Magazine*, September 13: 122–126.

Galbraith, Jay R. (2000). "The Role of Formal Structures and Process." In Michael Beer and Nitin Nohria (eds.), *Breaking the Code of Change*. Boston: Harvard Business School Press.

Galbraith, Jay R. (2005). *Designing the Customer-Centric Organization: A Guide to Strategy, Structure, and Process*. San Francisco: Jossey-Bass.

Garg, Vinay K., Walters, Bruce A., and Priem, Richard L. (2003). "Chief Executive Scanning Emphases, Environmental Dynamism, and Manufacturing Firm Performance." *Strategic Management Journal* 24, no. 8: 725–744.

Gerth, H. H., and Mills, C. Wright (trans. and eds.). (1946). *From Max Weber: Essays in Sociology*. New York: Oxford University Press.

Gittell, Jody Hoffer. (2003). *The Southwest Airlines Way: Using the Power of Relationships to Achieve High Performance*. New York: McGraw-Hill.

Goel, Vinod. (2005). "Project 3: The Differential Roles of the Prefrontal Cortex in Real-World Problem Solving." http://www.yorku.ca/vgoel/project3.frame.html (accessed March 18, 2005).

Goodman, Paul S. (1980). "Realities of Improving the Quality of Work Life: Quality of Work Life Projects in the 1980s." *Labor Law Journal* 31, no. 8: 487–494.

Gordon, David M. (1996). *Fat and Mean: The Corporate Squeeze of Working America and the Myth of Managerial "Downsizing."* New York: The Free Press.

Gordon, Frederick M., Welch, Kathryn R., Offringa, Gregory, and Katz, Nancy. (2000). "The Complexity of Social Outcomes from Cooperative, Competitive, and Individualistic Reward Systems." *Social Justice Research* 13, no. 3: 237–269.

Gottschalk, Peter, and Moffitt, Robert. (1999). "Changes in Job Instability and Insecurity Using Monthly Survey Data. Part 2: Changes in Job Stability and Job Security." *Journal of Labor Economics* 17, no. 4: S91–S126.

Gouldner, Alvin W. (1954). *Patterns of Industrial Bureaucracy: A Case Study of Modern Factory Administration*. New York: The Free Press.

Granovetter, Mark S. (1973). "The Strength of Weak Ties." *American Journal of Sociology* 78, no. 6: 1360–1380.

Gray, Barbara. (1989). *Collaborating: Finding Common Ground for Multiparty Problems*. San Francisco: Jossey-Bass.

Greeley, Thomas P., and Ochsner, Robert. (1986). "Putting Merit Pay Back into Salary Administration." In Robert C. Ochsner (ed.), *Topics in Total Compensation*. Greenwale, NY: Panel Publishers.

Grobstein, Clifford. (1973). "Hierarchical Order and Neogenesis." In Howard H. Pattee (ed.), *Hierarchy Theory: The Challenge of Complex Systems*. New York: George Braziller, chapter 2.

Guler, Isin, Guillén, Mauro F., and Macpherson, John Muir. (2002). "Global Competition, Institutions, and the Diffusion of Organizational Practices: The International Spread of ISO 9000 Quality Certificates." *Administrative Science Quarterly* 47: 207–232.

Guzzo, Richard A., and Dickson, Marcus W. (1996). "Teams in Organizations: Recent Research on Performance and Effectiveness." *Annual Review of Psychology* 47: 307–338.

Habermas, Jurgen. (1971). *Knowledge and Human Interests*. Jeremy J. Shapiro, trans. Boston: Beacon Press.

Habermas, Jürgen. (1994). "Three Normative Models of Democracy." *Constellations* 1, no. 1: 1–10.

Hackman, J. Richard. (1975). "Is Job Enrichment Just a Fad?" *Harvard Business Review* (September–October): 129–138.

Hackman, J. Richard (ed.). (1990). *Groups That Work (and Those That Don't): Creating Conditions for Effective Teamwork*. San Francisco: Jossey-Bass.

Hage, Jerald, and Alter, Catherine. (1997). "A Typology of Interorganizational Relationships and Networks." In J. Rogers Hollingsworth and Robert Boyer (eds.), *Contemporary Capitalism: The Embeddedness of Institutions*. Cambridge: Cambridge University Press, pp. 94–126.

Hagstrom, Warren O. (1965). *The Scientific Community*. Carbondale: Southern Illinois University Press.

Hall, Brian, and Madigan, Carleen. (2000). "Compensation and Performance Evaluation at Arrow Electronics." Harvard Business School Case 9-800-290 (December 11).

Hamel, Gary. (2000). "Waking Up IBM: How a Gang of Unlikely Rebels Transformed Big Blue." *Harvard Business Review* (July–August): 5–12.

Hancke, Robert. (1993). "Technological Change and Its Institutional Constraints: The Politics of Production at Volvo Uddevalla." Science, Technology, and Public Policy Program, Kennedy School of Government, Harvard University, Working Paper 93-05.

Harkness, Warren L., Kettinger, William J., and Segars, Albert H. (1996). "Sustaining Process Improvement and Innovation in the Information Services Function: Lessons Learned at the Bose Corporation." *MIS Quarterly* 20, no. 3: 349–368.

Harvard Business School. (1986). "Sedalia Revisited." Harvard Business School Case 9-687-004 (rev. 1988).

Hayek, Friedrich. (1945). "The Use of Knowledge in Society." *American Economic Review* 35, no. 4: 519–530.

Heckscher, Charles. (1995). *White-Collar Blues: Management Loyalties in an Age of Corporate Restructuring.* New York: Basic Books.

Heckscher, Charles. (2000). "HR Strategy and Contingent Work: Dualism vs. True Mobility." In Françoise Carré, Marianne Ferber, Lonnie Golden, and Stephen A. Herzenberg (eds.), *Nonstandard Work: The Nature and Challenge of Changing Employment Arrangements.* Champaign, IL: Industrial Relations Research Association (now Labor and Employment Relations Association), pp. 267–290.

Heckscher, Charles, and Foote, Nathaniel. (2006). "The Strategic Fitness Process and the Creation of Collaborative Community." In Charles Heckscher and Paul Adler (eds.), *The Firm as a Collaborative Community: Reconstructing Trust in the Knowledge Economy.* Oxford: Oxford University Press, chapter 12.

Heckscher, Charles, and Hall, Lavinia. (1994). "Mutual Gains and Beyond: Two Levels of Intervention." *Negotiation Journal* (July): 235–248.

Heckscher, Charles, and Hall, Lavinia. (2004). "La négociation quotidienne et le règlement officiel des disputes dans les entreprises" [Everyday negotiations and formal dispute-resolution in business enterprises]. *Négociations* (May): 63–78.

Heckscher, Charles, Maccoby, Michael, Ramirez, Rafael, and Tixier, Pierre-Eric. (2003). *Agents of Change: Crossing the Post-Industrial Divide.* Oxford: Oxford University Press.

Heckscher, Charles C. (1988/1995). *The New Unionism: Employee Involvement in the Changing Corporation.* New York: Basic Books, 1988; 2nd ed. Ithaca, NY: Cornell University Press, 1995.

Heller, Frank, Drenth, Pieter, Koopman, Paul, and Rus, Vefjko. (1988). *Decisions in Organizations: A Three-Country Comparative Study.* London: Sage.

Helper, Susan, MacDuffie, John Paul, and Sabel, Charles. (2000). "Pragmatic Collaborations: Advancing Knowledge While Controlling Opportunism." *Industrial and Corporate Change* 9, part 3: 443–488. Also available at http://www.law.columbia.edu/sabel/papers/ICCpragcoll.pdf.

Herzberg, Frederick. (1966). *Work and the Nature of Man.* New York: Thomas Y. Crowell.

Hetherington, Kevin. (1994). "The Contemporary Significance of Schmalenbach's Concept of the Bund." *Sociological Review* 42, no. 1: 1–25.

Hofstede, Geert. (1983). "The Cultural Relativity of Organizational Practices and Theories." *Journal of International Business Studies* (Fall): 75–89.

Hofstede, Geert. (1987). "Relativité culturelle des pratiques et théories de l'organisation." *Revue Française de Gestion* (September–October): 10–21.

Holland, John R. (1996). *Hidden Order: How Adaptation Builds Complexity.* Reading, MA: Addison-Wesley.

Holton, Gerald. (1996). *Einstein, History, and Other Passions.* Reading, MA: Addison-Wesley.

Husted, Kenneth, and Michailova, Snejina. (2002). "Diagnosing and Fighting Knowledge-Sharing Hostility." *Organizational Dynamics* 31, no. 1: 60–73.

Hylton, Maria O'Brien. (1996). "Legal and Policy Implications of the Flexible Employment Relationship." *Journal of Labor Research* 17, no. 4: 583–593.

Isaacson, Walter, and Thomas, Evan. (1986). *The Wise Men: Six Friends and the World They Made.* New York: Simon and Schuster.

Jackall, Robert. (1988). *Moral Mazes: The World of Corporate Managers.* New York: Oxford University Press.

Jacob, Rahul. (1993). "TQM: More than a Dying Fad?" *Fortune* 128, no. 9: 66–72.

James, William. (1902). *The Varieties of Religious Experience: A Study in Human Nature.* New York: Longmans, Green.

Jaques, Elliott. (1990). "In Praise of Hierarchy." *Harvard Business Review* (January–February): 127–133.

Jenkins, G. Douglas, Jr., Mitra, Atul, Gupta, Nina, and Shaw, Jason D. (1998). "Are Financial Incentives Related to Performance? A Meta-Analytic Review of Empirical Research." *Journal of Applied Psychology* 83, no. 5: 777–787.

Johnson, D. W., and Johnson, R. T. (1989). *Cooperation and Competition: Theory and Research.* Edina, MN: Interaction Book Co.

Jones, Candace, Hesterly, William S., and Borgatti, Stephen P. (1997). "A General Theory of Network Governance: Exchange Conditions and Social Mechanisms." *Academy of Management Review* 22, no. 4: 911–945.

Kanter, Rosabeth Moss. (1977). *Men and Women of the Corporation.* New York: Basic Books.

Kao, John J. (1995). "Oticon (A)." Boston: Harvard Business School Case 395144.

Kaplan, Robert E. (1984). "Trade Routes: The Manager's Network of Relationships." *Organizational Dynamics* (Spring): 37–52.

Kaplan, Robert S., and Norton, David P. (2001). *The Strategy-Focused Organization.* Boston: Harvard Business School Press.

Katzenback, Jon R., and Smith, Douglas K. (1994). *The Wisdom of Teams.* New York: HarperBusiness.

Kaus, R. M. (1973). *Job Enrichment & Capitalist Hierarchy.* B.A. thesis, Harvard College, Department of Social Studies, April.

Kearns, D. T., and Nadler, D. (1992). *Prophets in the Dark: How Xerox Reinvented Itself and Beat Back the Japanese.* New York: HarperBusiness.

Kennickell, Arthur B. (2006). "Currents and Undercurrents: Changes in the Distribution of Wealth, 1989–2004." *Federal Reserve Board,* January 30, available at http://www.federalreserve.gov/pubs/feds/2006/200613/200613pap.pdf.

Khalil, Elias L. (1996). "Non-linear Dynamics versus Development Processes: Two Kinds of Change." *The Manchester School of Economic & Social Studies* 64, no. 3: 309–322.

Khanna, Tarun, and Palepu, Krishna. (1997). "Why Focused Strategies May Be Wrong for Emerging Markets." *Harvard Business Review* (July–August): 41–51.

Khatri, Naresh, Tsang, Eric W. K., and Begley, Thomas M. (2006). "Cronyism: A Cross-Cultural Analysis." *Journal of International Business Management* 37, no. 1: 61–75.

Kluger, A. N., and DeNisi, A. (1996). "The Effects of Feedback Interventions on Performance: A Historical Review, a Meta-analysis, and Preliminary Feedback Theory." *Psychological Bulletin* 119: 254–284.

Krackhardt, David. (1995). "Entrepreneurial Opportunities in an Entrepreneurial Firm: A Structural Approach." *Entrepreneurship Theory & Practice* 19, no. 3: 53–69.

Krames, Jeffrey A. (2005). *Jack Welch and the 4 E's of Leadership: How to Put GE's Leadership Formula to Work in Your Organization.* New York: McGraw-Hill.

Kroeber, A. L., and Kluckhohn, Clyde. (1952). *Culture: A Critical Review of Concepts and Definitions.* Cambridge, MA: Papers of the Peabody Museum XLVII, 1, p. 149.

Kuhn, Thomas S. (1962). *The Structure of Scientific Revolutions.* Chicago: University of Chicago Press.

Kunda, Gideon. (1992). *Engineering Culture: Control and Commitment in a High-Tech Corporation.* Philadelphia: Temple University Press.

Kusterer, Ken C. (1978). *Know-How on the Job: The Important Working Knowledge of "Unskilled" Workers.* Boulder, CO: Westview Press.

Lawler, Edward E., III. (1990). "The New Plant Revolution Revisited." *Organizational Dynamics* (Autumn): 5–14.

Lawler, Edward E., III, Ledford, Gerald E., and Mohrman, Susan A. (1989). *Employee Involvement in America: A Study of Contemporary Practice.* Houston: American Productivity and Quality Center.

Lawler, Edward E., III, Mohrman, Susan A., and Ledford, Gerald E., Jr. (1995). *Creating High Performance Organizations.* San Francisco: Jossey-Bass.

Lawler, Edward J., and Thye, Shane R. (1999). "Bringing Emotions into Social Exchange Theory." *Annual Review of Sociology* 25: 217–244.

Lee, Dennis M. (1992). "Management of Concurrent Engineering: Organizational Concepts and a Framework of Analysis." *Engineering Management Journal* 4, no. 2: 15–25.

Lee, Tony. (1989). "Performance Pays Off When Salary Hikes Are Set." *National Business Employment Weekly*, October 19, 31.

Lepsinger, R., and Lucia, A. D. (1997). *The Art and Science of 360 Degree Feedback.* San Francisco: Pfeiffer/Jossey-Bass.

Lester, Richard, and Piore, Michael. (2006). *Innovation—The Missing Dimension.* Cambridge, MA: Harvard University Press.

Lewin, Kurt. (1951). *Field Theory in Social Science: Selected Theoretical Papers.* D. Cartwright, ed. New York: Harper & Row.

Lorenz, Edward. (1972). "Predictability: Does the Flap of a Butterfly's Wings in Brazil Set Off a Tornado in Texas?" Paper presented to the Global Atmosphere Research program at the 139th meeting of the American Association for the Advancement of Science, Washington, DC, December 12.

Lorenz, Edward. (1993a). *The Essence of Chaos.* Seattle: University of Washington Press.

Lorenz, Edward H. (1993b). "Flexible Production Systems and the Social Construction of Trust." *Politics & Society*, 21, no. 3: 307–324.

Maccoby, Michael. (1976). *The Gamesman: The New Corporate Leaders.* New York: Simon and Schuster.

MacDuffie, John Paul, and Helper, Susan. (2006). "Collaboration in Supply Chains: With and without Trust." In Charles Heckscher and Paul Adler (eds.), *The Firm as a Collaborative Community: Reconstructing Trust in the Knowledge Economy.* Oxford: Oxford University Press, chapter 10.

Mandell, Myrna. (1984). "Application of Network Analysis to the Implementation of a Complex Project." *Human Relations* 37, no. 8: 659–679.

Margolis, Diane Rothbard. (1979). *The Managers: Corporate Life in America.* New York: William Morrow.

Margolis, Joshua, and Donnellon, Anne. (1990). "Mod IV Product Development Team." Boston: Harvard Business School Case N9-491-030 (September 4).

Martin, Carlos. (2006). *Establishing Accountability Systems in Advanced Collaborative Work.* Ph.D. dissertation, Rutgers University.

Mathewson, Stanley B. (1931). *Restriction of Output among Unorganized Workers.* New York: Viking Press.

Mayo, Elton. (1949). *The Social Problems of an Industrial Civilization.* London: Routledge & Kegan Paul.

McDermott, R., and O'Dell, C. (2001). "Overcoming Cultural Barriers to Sharing Knowledge." *Journal of Knowledge Management* 5, no. 1: 76–85.

McDermott, Richard. (2000). "Knowing in Community: 10 Critical Success Factors in Building Communities of Practice." *IHRIM Journal* (March): 19–26.

McDermott, Richard, and Jackson, R. Jeff. (2000). "Developing Global Communities: Lessons Learned." Shell Global Communities.

McDermott, Richard, and Kendrick, John. (2000). *How Learning Communities Steward Knowledge: Shell Oil Company.* Boston: Linkage Press.

McGregor, Douglas. (1960). *The Human Side of Enterprise.* New York: McGraw-Hill.

Melewar, T. C., and Harrold, John. (2000). "The Role of Corporate Identity in Merger and Acquisition Activity." *Journal of General Management* 26, no. 2: 17–31.

Merton, Robert K. (1940). "Bureaucratic Structure and Personality." *Social Forces* 17: 560–568.

Merton, Robert K. (1968). "Science and the Democratic Social Structure." In Robert K. Merton, *Social Theory and Social Structure,* rev. ed. New York: The Free Press, chapter 18.

Michaels, Ed, Handfield-Jones, Helen, and Axelrod, Beth. (2001). *The War for Talent.* Boston: Harvard Business School Press.

Michels, Robert. (1911/1962). *Political Parties: A Sociological Study of the Oligarchical Tendencies of Modern Democracy.* New York: Free Press.

Mill, John Stuart. (1869). *On Liberty.* London: Longman, Roberts & Green.

Mills, C. Wright. (1951). *White Collar: The American Middle Classes.* London: Oxford University Press.

Mintzberg, Henry. (1973). *The Nature of Managerial Work.* New York: Harper & Row.

Mitzman, Arthur. (1969). *The Iron Cage: An Historical Interpretation of Max Weber.* New York: Grosset & Dunlap.

Mohrman, Allan M., Mohrman, Susan Albers, and Lawler, Edward E. (1992). "The Performance Management of Teams." In W. J. Bruns (ed.), *Performance Measurement, Evaluation and Incentives.* Boston: Harvard Business School Press, pp. 217–241.

Mohrman, Susan A., Lawler, Edward E., III, and Ledford, Gerald E., Jr. (1996). "Do Employee Involvement and TQM Programs Work?" *Journal for Quality & Participation* 19, no. 1: 6–10.

Montgomery, David. (1979). *Workers' Control in America: Studies in the History of Work, Technology, and Labor Struggles.* Cambridge: Cambridge University Press.

Morgan, Arthur, Cannan, Kath, and Cullinane, Joanne. (2005). "360° Feedback: A Critical Enquiry." *Personnel Review* 34, no. 6: 663–680.

Muller, Joann. (2001). "Ford: Why It's Worse Than You Think." *Business Week Online*, June 25.

Munch, Richard. (1986). "The American Creed in Sociological Theory: Exchange, Negotiated Order, Accommodated Individualism, and Contingency." *Sociological Theory* 4: 41–60.

Nahapiet, J., and Ghoshal, S. (1997). "Social Capital, Intellectual Capital, and the Creation of Value in Firms." *Academy of Management Best Paper Proceedings*: 35–39.

Nahavandi, Afsaneh, and Malekzadeh, Ali R. (1993). *Organizational Culture in the Management of Mergers*. Westport, CT: Quorum Books.

Neely, Andy. (1999). "The Performance Measurement Revolution: Why Now and What Next?" *International Journal of Operations & Production Management* 91, no. 2: 205–228.

Nelson, Daniel. (1980). *Frederick W. Taylor and the Rise of Scientific Management*. Madison: University of Wisconsin Press.

Neumann, Jean E., Holti, Richard, and Standing, Hilary. (2000). *Change Everything at Once! The Tavistock Institute's Guide to Developing Teamwork in Manufacturing*. Didcot, UK: Management Books.

Newman, Katherine S. (1989). *Falling from Grace: The Experience of Downward Mobility in the American Middle Class*. New York: Vintage Books.

Nishiguchi, T., and Beaudet, A. (1998). "The Toyota Group and the Aisin Fire." *Sloan Management Review* 40, no. 1: 49–59.

Offe, Claus. (1976). *Industry and Inequality: The Achievement Principle in Work and Social Status*. London: Edward Arnold. (Original German edition 1970.)

Olie, R. (1994). "Shades of Culture and Institutions in International Mergers." *Organization Studies* 15, no. 3: 381–405.

Oliver, Nick, Delbridge, Rick, and Barton, Harry. (2005). "Lean Production and Manufacturing Performance Improvement in Japan, the UK and US 1994–2001." Available at http://www.cbr.cam.ac.uk/pdf/WP232.pdf (accessed June 13, 2006).

Osterman, Paul. (2000). "Work Organization in an Era of Restructuring: Trends in Diffusion and Impacts on Employee Welfare." *Industrial and Labor Relations Review* 52, no. 2: 179–196.

Osterman, Paul. (2001). "Flexibility and Commitment in the United States Labour Market." Geneva: Employment Sector, International Labour Office, Employment Paper No. 18.

Ouchi, William G. (1980). "Markets, Bureaucracies, and Clans." *Administrative Science Quarterly* 25, no. 1: 129–141.

Ouchi, William G. (1981). *Theory Z: How American Business Can Meet the Japanese Challenge*. Reading, MA: Addison-Wesley.

Oyserman, Daphna, Coon, Heather M., and Kemmelmeier, Markus. (2002). "Rethinking Individualism and Collectivism: Evaluation of Theoretical Assumptions and Meta-analyses." *Psychological Bulletin* 128, no. 1: 3–72.

Pagels, Elaine. (2003). *Beyond Belief: The Secret Gospel of Thomas*. New York: Random House.

Palmisano, Samuel J., Hemp, Paul, and Stewart, Thomas A. (2004). "Leading Change When Business Is Good: The HBR Interview—Samuel J. Palmisano." *Harvard Business Review* (December): 60–70, 148.

Parsons, Talcott. (1963). "On the Concept of Influence." *Public Opinion Quarterly* 27: 37–62.

Parsons, Talcott. (1966). *Societies: Evolutionary and Comparative Perspectives.* Englewood Cliffs, NJ: Prentice-Hall.

Parsons, Talcott. (1969). "On the Concept of Political Power." In Talcott Parsons (ed.), *Politics and Social Structure.* New York: The Free Press, chapter 14.

Parsons, Talcott. (1971). *The System of Modern Societies.* Englewood Cliffs, NJ: Prentice-Hall.

Parsons, Talcott, and Platt, Gerald. (1973). *The American University.* Cambridge, MA: Harvard University Press.

Parsons, Talcott, and Shils, Edward. (1953). *Working Papers in the Theory of Action.* Glencoe, IL: The Free Press.

Pascale, Richard, Millemann, Mark, and Gioja, Linda. (1997). "Changing the Way We Change." *Harvard Business Review* (November–December): 126–140.

Pateman, Carole. (1970). *Participation and Democratic Theory.* Cambridge: Cambridge University Press.

Pattee, H. H. (1973). "Postscript: Unsolved Problems and Potential Applications of Hierarchy Theory." In Howard H. Pattee (ed.), *Hierarchy Theory: The Challenge of Complex Systems.* New York: George Braziller, pp. 129–156.

Peters, Thomas J., and Waterman, Robert H., Jr. (1982). *In Search of Excellence: Lessons from America's Best-Run Companies.* New York: Harper & Row.

Peters, Tom. (2001). "The Confessions of Tom Peters." *Fast Company* 53 (December): 78ff.

Pfeffer, Jeffrey. (1998). "Six Dangerous Myths about Pay." *Harvard Business Review* (May–June): 109–119.

Pfeffer, Jeffrey. (2001). "Fighting the War for Talent Is Hazardous to Your Organization's Health." *Organizational Dynamics* 29, no. 4: 248–259.

Piaget, Jean (1932/1965). *The Moral Judgment of the Child.* New York: The Free Press. (Original edition *Le Jugement Moral Chez l'Enfant.* Neuchâtel, Paris: Delachaux & Niestlé, 1932.)

Piaget, Jean. (1945/1962). *Play, Dreams and Imitation in Childhood.* C. Gattegno and F. M. Hodgson, trans. New York: Norton. (Original edition *La formation du symbole chez l'enfant.* Neuchâtel, Paris: Delachaux et Niestlé, 1945.)

Piaget, Jean. (1952). *Essai sur les transformations des opérations logiques; les 256 opérations ternaires de la logique bivalente des propositions* [Essay on the logical operations: The 256 ternary operations of the bivalent logic of propositions]. Paris: Presses Universitaires de France.

Piaget, Jean. (1953). *Logic and Psychology.* Manchester: Manchester University Press.

Piaget, Jean (ed.). (1967). *Logique et connaissance scientifique* [Logic and scientific knowledge]. Paris: Editions Gallimard.

Piaget, Jean, and Inhelder, Barbel. (1958). *The Growth of Logical Thinking from Childhood to Adolescence.* Ann Parsons and Stanley Milgram, trans. New York: Basic Books.

Pink, Daniel. (1997–1998). "Free Agent Nation." *Fast Company,* no. 12 (December–January): 131.

Piore, Michael J., and Sabel, Charles F. (1984). *The Second Industrial Divide: Possibilities for Prosperity.* New York: Basic Books.

Porter, Michael (1980). *Competitive Strategy*. New York: Basic Books.

Quinn, James Brian, and Hilmer, Frederick G. (1995). "Strategic Outsourcing." *The McKinsey Quarterly*, no. 1: 48–70.

Quinn, R. P., and Staines, G. L. (1979). *The 1977 Quality of Employment Survey: Descriptive Statistics, with Comparative Data from the 1969–70 and 1972–73 Surveys*. Ann Arbor: University of Michigan Institute for Social Research.

Ramirez, Rafael, and Wallin, Johan. (2000). *Prime Movers: Define Your Business or Have Someone Define It Against You*. Chichester: John Wiley & Sons.

Rapaport, R. (1996). "The Network Is the Company." *Fast Company*, no. 2 (April–May): 116–121.

Rawls, John. (1971). *A Theory of Justice*. Cambridge, MA: Harvard University Press.

Raymond, Eric. (2006). "Homesteading the Noosphere." Available at http://www.catb .org/~esr/writings/cathedral-bazaar/ (accessed January 10, 2006).

Reichheld, Frederick F. (1996). *The Loyalty Effect: The Hidden Force behind Growth, Profits, and Lasting Value*. Boston: Harvard Business School Press.

Riesman, David. (1950). *The Lonely Crowd: A Study of the Changing American Character*. New Haven, CT: Yale University Press.

Roethlisberger, E. J., and Dickson, W. J. (1939). *Management and the Worker*. Cambridge, MA: Harvard University Press.

Rousseau, Denise M. (1997). "Organizational Behavior in the New Organizational Era." *Annual Review of Psychology* 48: 515–546.

Rubinstein, Saul A. (2006). "Collaborative Community and Employee Representation." In Charles Heckscher and Paul Adler (eds.), *The Firm as a Collaborative Community: Reconstructing Trust in the Knowledge Economy*. Oxford: Oxford University Press, chapter 8.

Rubinstein, Saul A., and Kochan, Thomas A. (2001). *Learning from Saturn: Possibilities for Corporate Governance and Employee Relations*. Ithaca, NY: Cornell University Press.

Ruhm, Christopher J. (1995). "Secular Changes in the Work and Retirement Patterns of Older Men." *Journal of Human Resources* 30, no. 2: 362–385.

Sabel, Charles. (1991). "Moebius-Strip Organizations and Open Labor Markets: Some Consequences of the Reintegration of Conception and Execution in a Volatile Economy." In James Coleman and Pierre Bourdieu (eds.), *Social Theory for a Changing Society*. Boulder, CO: Westview Press, pp. 23–54.

Sabel, Charles. (2006). "A Real-Time Revolution in Routines." In Charles Heckscher and Paul Adler (eds.), *The Firm as a Collaborative Community: Reconstructing Trust in the Knowledge Economy*. Oxford: Oxford University Press, chapter 2.

Sapienza, Massimo. (2003). "Do Real Options Perform Better than Net Present Value? Testing in an Artificial Financial Market." *Journal of Artificial Societies and Social Simulation* 6, no. 3, available at http://jasss.soc.surrey.ac.uk/6/3/4.html (accessed November 17, 2006).

Scheff, Thomas J. (1988). "Shame and Conformity: The Deference-Emotion System." *American Sociological Review* 53, no. 3: 395–406.

Scheff, Thomas J. (2000). "Shame and the Social Bond: A Sociological Theory." *Sociological Theory* 18, no. 1: 84–100.

Schein, Edgar H. (1985). *Organizational Culture and Leadership*. San Francisco: Jossey-Bass.

Schein, Edgar H. (1987). *Process Consultation: Lessons for Managers and Consultants*. Reading, MA: Addison-Wesley.

Scott, S. G., and Einstein, W. O. (2001). "Strategic Performance Appraisal in Team-Based Organizations: One Size Does Not Fit All." *Academy of Management Executive* 15: 107–116.

Senge, Peter. (1990). *The Fifth Discipline: The Art and Practice of the Learning Organization*. New York: Doubleday/Currency.

Sewell, Carl, and Brown, Paul B. (2002). *Customers for Life: How to Turn That One-Time Buyer into a Lifetime Customer*. New York: Doubleday.

Shorris, Earl. (1981). *Scenes from Corporate Life: The Politics of Middle Management*. New York: Penguin Books. (Originally published as *The Oppressed Middle*. New York: Anchor Press, Doubleday, 1981.)

Silverman, M, Kerrin, M., and Carter, A. (2005). "360 Degree Feedback: Beyond the Spin." Brighton, UK: University of Sussex, Institute for Employment Studies, IES Report no. 418.

Silverstein, Stuart. (1997). "Corporations Ally to Get a Handle on the Turbulent Labor Market." *Los Angeles Times*, March 9.

Simon, H. A. (1969). *The Sciences of the Artificial*. Cambridge, MA: MIT Press.

Simons, Robert (1991). "How New Top Managers Use Formal Systems as Levers of Strategic Renewal." Presented to the 11th Annual International Strategic Management Society Conference, Toronto, October.

Sloan, Alfred P. (1964). *My Years with General Motors*. Garden City, NY: Doubleday.

Smith, Adam. (1776). *An Inquiry into the Nature and Causes of the Wealth of Nations*. (many editions).

Srivastva, Suresh et al. (1975). *Job Satisfaction & Productivity*. Cleveland, OH: Case Western Reserve University.

Stephenson, Karen. (2001). "What Knowledge Tears Apart, Networks Make Whole." Zurich Insurance Group, Internal Communication Focus no. 36.

Stewart, Jay. (2002). "Recent Trends in Job Stability and Job Security: Evidence from the March CPS." Washington, DC: U.S. Department of Labor, Bureau of Labor Statistics, Office of Employment and Unemployment Statistics, BLS Working Papers, Working Paper 356 (March), available at http://www.bls.gov/ore/pdf/ec020050.pdf (accessed September 13, 2005).

Strathern, Marilyn. (1996). "Cutting the Network." *Journal of the Royal Anthropological Institute* 2, no. 3: 517–535.

Taylor, Charles. (1994). "The Politics of Recognition." In Amy Gutmann (ed.), *Multiculturalism: Examining the Politics of Recognition*. Princeton, NJ: Princeton University Press, pp. 25–74.

Taylor, Frederick Winslow. (1911). *The Principles of Scientific Management*. New York: W. W. Norton.

Taylor, Glen. (1993). "Parallel Processing: A Design Principle for System-Wide Total Quality Management." *Management International Review* 33 (First Quarter, Special Issue): 99–109.

Thompson, J. D. (1967). *Organizations in Action: Social Science Bases of Administrative Theory*. New York: McGraw-Hill.

Timmreck, C. W., and Bracken, D. W. (1997). "Multisource Feedback: A Study of Its Use for Decision Making." *Employment Relations Today* 24, no. 1: 21–27.

Urwick, Lyndall F. (1947). *The Elements of Administration*, 2nd ed. London: I. Pitman.

U.S. Department of Labor (1985). *Quality of Work Life: AT&T and CWA Examine the Process after Three Years*. Washington, DC: U.S. Department of Labor, Bureau of Labor-Management Relations.

Uzzi, Brian. (1996). "The Sources and Consequences of Embeddedness for the Economic Performance of Organizations: The Network Effect." *American Sociological Review* 61 (August): 674–698.

Vasconcelos, Isabella, and Vasconcelos, Flavio. (2002). "The Limits of ISO9000 Consulting Methods." In Anthony F. Buono (ed.), *Developing Knowledge and Value in Management Consulting*, vol. 2. Greenwich, CT: Information Age Publishing, pp. 50–67.

Vogel, Ezra F. (1979). *Japan as Number One: Lessons for America*. Cambridge, MA: Harvard University Press.

Waldman, D., Atwater, L., and Antonioni, D. (1998). "Has 360 Feedback Gone Amok?" *The Academy of Management Executive* 12, no. 2: 86–94.

Walter, A. G., and Smither, J. W. (1999). "A Five-Year Study of Upward Feedback: What Managers Do with Their Results." *Personnel Psychology* 52: 393–423.

Weber, Max. (1907/1948). *On the Methodology of the Social Sciences*. New York: The Free Press.

Weber, Max. (1919/1946a). "Politics as a Vocation." In H. H. Gerth and C. Wright Mills (trans. and eds.), *From Max Weber: Essays in Sociology*. New York: Oxford University Press, 1946, pp. 77–128. German edition: "Politik als Beruf." In *Gesammelte Politische Schriften* (Muenchen, 1921), pp. 396–450. Originally a speech at Munich University, 1918, published in 1919 by Duncker & Humblodt, Munich.

Weber, Max. (1919/1946b). "Science as a Vocation." In H. H. Gerth and C. Wright Mills (trans. and eds.), *From Max Weber: Essays in Sociology*. New York: Oxford University Press, 1946, pp. 129–156. German edition: "Wissenschaft als Beruf." In *Gesammelte Aufsaetze zur Wissenschaftslehre* (Tubingen, 1922), pp. 524–555. Originally a speech at Munich University, 1918, published in 1919 by Duncker & Humblodt, Munich.

Weber, Max. (1921/1968). *Economy and Society*. Guenther Roth and Claus Wittich, trans. and eds. New York: Bedminster Press. (Original edition 1921.)

Weisbord, Marvin R. (1987). *Productive Workplaces: Organizing and Managing for Meaning, Dignity, and Community*. San Francisco: Jossey-Bass.

Wenger, Etienne. (1998). *Communities of Practice: Learning, Meaning and Identity*. Cambridge: Cambridge University Press.

Wenger, Etienne C., and Snyder, William M. (2000). "Communities of Practice: The Organizational Frontier." *Harvard Business Review* (January–February): 139–145.

Wetlaufer, Suzy. (1999). "Driving Change: An Interview with Ford Motor Company's Jacques Nasser." *Harvard Business Review* (March–April): 77–88.

Whyte, William H., Jr. (1956). *The Organization Man*. New York: Simon and Schuster.

Womack, James P., Jones, Daniel T., and Roos, Daniel. (1991). *The Machine That Changed the World*. New York: HarperCollins.

Wright, Susan. (1998). "The Politicization of 'Culture.'" *The Journal of the Royal Anthropological Institute*, 14, no. 1: 7–15, available at http://www.therai.org.uk/pubs/at/editorial/wright.html (accessed February 7, 2006).

Yoshino, Michael Y., and Malnight, Thomas W. (1995). *Citibank: Global Customer Management*. Harvard Business School Case 395142 (January 20).

Yu, Julie, Farhoomand, Ali F., McCauley, Marissa, and Khan, Shamza. (2002). "Citibank's e-Business Strategy for Global Corporate Banking." University of Hong Kong Case HKU197 (June 7).

# Index

*Note*: Page numbers in *italics* refer to figures and tables.

ABACUS system, 149

ABB Group: accountability and, 175; collaborative infrastructure and, 143, 149, 159; collaborative vision and, 241; complexity and, 57; decentralization and, 221; outward focus and, 122, 233; research methods and, *283*; review processes, 165–66

accountability, 38, 40, 118, 170–72, *178*; extended collaboration and, 5, 249; hierarchies and, 99–101; infrastructure and, 136; obstacles to, 183–86; pay for performance, 172–77; reward for contribution, 177–83. *See also* performance management

acquaintanceships. *See* "weak ties"

adaptability (Denison), 133

adaptation, continuous, 2

adaptiveness, 75–77, 81, 82, *84*, 224, 247;

Citibank e-Solutions Group and, 88; corporate culture and, 110; corporate strategy and, 63, 75–77; decentralization and, 281; external relationships and, 157, 158; knowledge production and, 68–69; meta-structures and, 80–81; solutions strategies and, 58, 77–80; stages of business development and, 198; varieties of collaborative infrastructure and, *250–51*

adhocracy (Cameron and Quinn), 133

adult education, 190

Aegon Netherlands, *283*

Aegon-Spaarbeleg, 158, *283*

affirmative action, 264

Agassi, Shai, 273

Agilent, 156

agriculture, solutions strategies and, 61–62

airline industry, 62

alienation, 259

alliances, 109, 122, 150–51. *See also* cross-
　firm structures
Alliance team, Citibank e-Solutions
　Group, 89, 91, 95, 96, 102–4, 106
allocating resources. *See* resources, allo-
　cating
Amazon.com, 46
AMD, 75
anthropology, corporate culture and, 108,
　126, 131, 132, 278
anti-competitive practices, 78
anti-globalization movement, 16
AOL, 103
AOL/Time Warner, 14, 219, 220
Apple Computing, 238
appraisals. *See* performance appraisals
Argyris, Chris, 163
assembly lines, 9, 212, 213
assignment processes, for task teams, 91
associational relationships: in bureau-
　cratic organizations, 29–32, 33–34;
　Citibank e-Solutions Group and, 92–
　98; collaborative enterprise and, 199;
　corporate structures and, 26–28, *27*;
　formalization of, 34, 35, 37, 145–57;
　performance management and, 171–72;
　in professional and craft associations,
　28; types of, 53. *See also* relationships
AT&T, 70, 191, 213, 219, 268
audit functions, 105, 106
authority: corporate structures and, 25–
　26; deference to, 140; lines of, 102;
　linking mechanisms and, 147; personal
　control, 29. *See also* hierarchies
automotive industry, 4, 7–8; cross-firm
　structures and, 48; decentralization, of
　bureaucratic organizations, 30; difficul-
　ties of collaboration in, 14; evolution
　of work systems and, 213, 214; joint
　ventures, 62–63, 66–67; mass produc-
　tion and, 60; operational effectiveness
　and, 65; outward focus and, 122, 234,
　255–56; strategy and, 141–42. *See also*
　General Motors; Saturn

autonomous teams, 213
autonomy: bureaucratic organizations
　and, 111, 114–15, 238; collaboration and,
　118; cultural change and, 205, 206, 210.
　*See also* individualism
Avaya, 234, 235, 240

Baehr, Geoff, 146
Balanced Scorecard (BSC), 178–79, 183,
　237–38
balance of power, 271
banking industry, 61, 78. *See also*
　Citibank; Citibank e-Solutions Group
Barnard, Chester, 10, 17, 27
Barnevik, Percy, 221, 241, 265
Beer, Mike, 230
behavior modification, leadership as, 217,
　218–20
Bell, Daniel, 6
Bell Labs, 70
benchmarking, 122
benefits, employment, 138, 188, 190, 266,
　272
Bermudez, Jorge, 86, 88
Blau, Peter, 27
blue-collar workers, 114, 115, 142, 212–14,
　266
bonuses, determining, 100
bosses. *See* superiors, interactions with;
　supervisors, performance appraisal and
BSC. *See* Balanced Scorecard (BSC)
bureaucratic mentality, regression to, 6,
　205, 209–10
bureaucratic organizations, *250–51;* ac-
　countability in, 170–71, 172–73; at
　Citibank, 85–86, 104–5; Citibank
　e-Solutions Group and, 91, 106; corpo-
　rate culture and, 110, 111–17, 123–26,
　*127;* cultural change and, 201, 202–3,
　203–4; development of, 1, 2, 3–4; em-
　ployment in, 16, 140, 180, 187; evolu-
　tion of, 7–8, 29–35, 68, 212–14;
　infrastructure and, 137–40, 147–48,
　151–52, 167, 270; intellectual property

and, 273; leadership in, 229–30; learning and, 162–63; networks and, 52; openness to outside ideas, 122, 232; operational effectiveness and, 65; "politics" in, 31, 32, 72; process management in, 37–38; relationships in, 82, 83, 145, 154–55; reputational systems, 95, 182; strategy and, 141–42; structure of, 25–26, 49–50; teams and, 35, 46; utilization of knowledge and, 57–58; values and, 11–12, 254–56, 261, 263. *See also* paternalism

business consulting, solutions strategies and, 61, 64

business literacy, 167

business models, *21*

business plans, 47

business practices, 91–92

business schools, 167

business sponsors, 99, 102

business strategies. *See* strategy

Cameron, K. S., 133, 134

Canadian-Pacific, 78

capitalism, 274

capture teams, 175

careers. *See* employment

case studies, 18–19, *283–87*; Citibank e-Solutions Group, 85–107; research methods and, 277, 278, 281–82; strategy and, 63, 64

Castells, Manuel, 6

Center for Workplace Transformation (Rutgers University), 131

certification systems, 167

challenges, business: Citibank e-Solutions Group and, 104–7; collaboration as, 1–2, 270; performance management systems and, 176

Chandler, Alfred, 2, 3, 198

change: corporate culture and, 129, 130–31; corporate strategy and, 56; interactive change, 227–35; obstacles to, 201–10; performance management systems

and, 183; process of, 22, 195–96, 211–17, 235–40, *244*, 244–45, 249; role of leadership, 217–22, 226–45; social values and, 253; sociodynamic resistances, 204–10; speed of, 59; stages and, 197–201; study of, 131

change, incremental, 68, 195

change processes, 235–40, 244–45

chaos, 50, 199

choices, consumer, 59

Churchill, Winston, 211

Cisco Systems, 60, 64, 149, *283*

Citibank, 15, 19, *40*, *284*; "Compass" information system, 94, 107, 164; cross-firm structures and, 48; cultural change and, 205; customer relationships managers, 45, 75; evolution of work systems and, 215–17; high-complexity strategies, 63, 223; knowledge databases, 164; linking mechanisms and, 72; managing complexity and, 57, 71; meta-structures and, 80, 81; negotiation and, 152–53; outward focus and, 233; process management and, 155; shared mission and, 236; solutions strategies, 61, 64, 80

Citibank e-Solutions Group, 80, 85–86, 123, 175, *284*; Alliance team, 102–4; challenges for, 104–7; collaborative infrastructure, 92–98; corporate culture, 91–92, 119, 204, 268–69; employment, 139, 176, 181; formalization of processes and, 150–51, 154; hierarchy, 98–102, 153; linking mechanisms and, 147; review processes, 161–62; strategy, 86–88, 142; structure, 88–91; vision, 144–45, 242

clan, concept of, 133, 134

coding, of research data, 279, 280, 281–82

cognitive development, 198, 203, 228

collaboration, 2–4, 5, 53, 54–55, 89, 184; extended, 4–6, *6*, 6–9, 13–17, 66, 82–83, 246; local, 5–6, *6*; managed, 69–75, *84*, 247 (*see also* complexity); systemic, 77–80, *84*, 133, 134, 247–48, 281 collaboration, project. *See* adaptiveness

collaborative enterprise, 28, *84*, 247–49, *250–51, 257*; corporate culture and, 110, 117–23, 123–26, *127*; infrastructure and, 135–36, 137, 141–66; networks and, 52; precursors of, 211–25; societal values and, 252–75; stages of business development and, 199; structure of, 34–35, 37, 46–47, 49–50; transitions to, 195–210

collaborative infrastructure, 140–41, 168–69; external relationships and, 157–62; formalization and, 145–57; learning and, 162–66; strategic understanding, 141–45. *See also* infrastructure

collaborative vision, 240–44

collectivism, 130

commitments, following through on, 92

committees, 72. *See also* teams

commodity production, 2, 55–56

communication: assembling teams and, 157; associational relationships and, 199; in bureaucratic organizations, 13, 32, 33, 112; within Citibank Alliance team, 103–4; of collaborative vision, 241; between corporate units, 38, 65; cross-firm collaboration and, 89; diversity and, 264; forums for, 93–95, 154, 239; high-adaptiveness strategies and, 77; infrastructure and, 136, 147; strategy and, 142–43, 143–44; trust and, 95–96

communism, intellectual property and, 273–74

communities of practice, 140, 154, 162, 164, 239

compensation: in bureaucratic organizations, 171; change leadership and, 219; collective good and, 185–86; dualism and, 269; job mobility and, 188; pay for performance, 171, 172–77, 185, 278; pensions, 137, 190, 242; performance management and, 116–17; retention of employees and, 188; reward for contribution, 126, 177–83

competence, 92

*Competitive Strategy* (Porter), 56

competitors, 157, 232

complexity: adaptiveness and, 77–80, 224; Citibank e-Solutions Group and, 88; external relationships and, 157–58, 159; knowledge production and, 68–69; meta-structures and, 80–81; solutions strategies and, 58, 77–80; strategic challenges and, 247; strategy and, 57, 69–75, 81, 82; varieties of collaborative infrastructure and, *250–51*

complexity theory, 199

complication. *See* complexity

computer industry, 48–49, 60–61, 78, 168

computer technology, 136, 239

conference calls, 94, 147, 154

confidentiality, 149

conformity, traditional bureaucracy and, 113–14

consensus, building, 159, 160, 239

consulting industry, 46, 75, 76, 77, 158. *See also* business consulting

Consumer Bank, Citibank, 104–5

consumer groups, 168

consumers. *See* customers

contribution, culture of, 117, 126, 140, 185–86, 248, 263–64. *See also* collaborative vision

control, spans of, 65, 173–74, 215

cooperation. *See* collaboration, local

coordination, forms of, 92–98

core competencies, 57, 63, 75, 78, 87

core competencies group, Shell, 147

Corporate Bank, Citibank, 105

corporate culture. *See* culture, corporate

"Corporate Projects" group, ABB, 165

corporate structure. *See* structure, corporate

corporations, large, 3, 6, 10–11

corruption, 272, 273

cost, of products, 56, 59, 65, 75, 242

cost efficiency (strategy), 56

craft associations. *See* professional and craft associations creativity, managing performance and, 174

credit, sharing, 121

criticism, acceptance of, 120–21, 181

cross-firm structures, 48–49; Citibank e-Solutions Group and, 87, 88, 89, 102–4, 105; infrastructure and, 149, 166–68; for job mobility, 190–91; research methods and, 282; solutions strategies and, 58; trust and, 95, 96–97

culture: cultural expectations, 21–22, 108–9, 117–18, 201–2; infrastructure of, 135; research into, 126–34. See also culture, corporate

culture, corporate, 108–10, 251; bureaucratic organizations and, 31–32, 111–17; change and, 195, 196–97, 201–4, 207–8; Citibank e-Solutions Group and, 91–92; collaborative enterprise and, 117–23; collaborative vision and, 242; conflicts between differing, 109, 114–15, 123–26; culture of contribution, 117, 126, 140, 185–86, 248; free market ethic and, 267; IBM Values Jam, 228–30; infrastructure and, 136, 151; performance culture, 115–17; research on, 126–34; social values and, 253–54

Cummins India, 122, 220, 241, 284

customer loyalty, 178

customer relationships managers (CRMs), 45, 73, 75; Citibank and, 63, 152–53, 181–82, 216; Nokia and, 224

customers: Citibank e-Solutions Group and, 86, 87; collaborative vision and, 241; high-adaptiveness strategies and, 76; high-complexity strategies and, 63, 73; organizational charts and, 45; responding to, 88, 122, 157; solutions strategies and, 58, 59, 62, 152–53. See also outward focus

cynicism, 209, 267

Dalton, Melville, 27

Darwin, Charles, 252–53

data, gathering, 278, 279–80, 283–87

decentralization: adaptiveness and, 77, 281; of bureaucratic organizations, 30–32, 70; change leadership and, 217, 221–22

defense industry, 72–73

Degussa, 46, 47, 143

Dell Computers, 60

Delphi Corporation, 189

democracy, value of, 258, 259, 260. See also representation of employees

Denison, Daniel R., 133–34

design processes, automotive industry and, 7, 8

difference principle, 186

Digital Equipment Corporation, 14, 60

dimension adaptiveness, 56

dimensions of strategy. See strategic dimensions

distribution systems, 59, 60

diversity, 122–23, 153–54, 262–65

dominant firms, in cross-firm structures, 48–49

"dotted line" reporting relationships, 118

"double-loop" learning, 163, 165

dualism, 188–89, 269, 270

Dunlap, Al, 267

du Pont, Pierre, 17, 31

e-Business, Citibank. See Citibank e-Solutions Group

economy, the: global economy and, 15–16; twentieth-century, 2, 3–4; utilization of knowledge and, 6–7; value of collaborative enterprise and, 253

educational systems, 16–17; bureaucratic organizations and, 138, 140; collaboration and, 21; collaborative infrastructure and, 167, 168; job mobility and, 190; professional and craft associations and, 28

effectiveness-focused strategy. See operational effectiveness efficiency: of bureaucratic organizations, 33, 57–58; in collaborative enterprise, 50; cost efficiency, 56; networks and, 76; strategic challenges and, 63, 81–82, 247

egalitarianism, teamwork and, 66

Einstein, Albert, 198, 200, 252

Eisenhardt, Kathy, 151

e-mail distribution lists, 146, 156

emerging markets, infrastructure and, 167–68

emotional reactions, to change, 204–10

"empire-building," 102, 104, 155, 164, 209, 219

employees: blue-collar workers, 114, 115, 142; business literacy and, 167; Citibank e-Solutions Group and, 91; empowerment of, 258; evaluations of, 92, 178; insecurity of, 265–67; integrating new, 107; retaining, 141, 188, 190; value of participation and, 258–60; worker participation programs, 12. See also workforce, attitudes of

employment: in bureaucratic organizations, 34, 137–38; collaborative enterprise and, 139; extended collaboration and, 16–17, 249; infrastructure and, 136; mobility and, 188, 189–91, 266, 271–72, 281; trends in, 186–91. See also compensation; job security

enforcement: corporate culture and, 129; infrastructure of, 271, 272

"enterprise," 5, 21

environments, changing, 57, 58, 157, 158–59; adaptiveness and, 247; infrastructure and, 168; performance management and, 174–75; resistance to change, 201–10

e-Solutions Unit, Citibank. See Citibank e-Solutions Group

Europe, corporate culture in, 115

evaluations, employee. See performance appraisals

expectations: corporate culture and, 127–28, 130; cultural change and, 201–4; infrastructure and, 135; job security and, 139, 186–87

extended collaboration. See collaboration, extended

external relationships, collaborative infrastructure and, 157–66. See also outward focus

failure: of collaborative systems, 55, 211–12; personal, 220, 254–55

families: family styles, 16–17, 21; personal responsibilities and, 123; traditional bureaucracy as, 112–13

favors, exchange of, 33

feedback processes. See performance management

feudalism, traditional bureaucracy and, 112

Figgie, Harry, 116

Figgie International, 116

Fiorina, Carly, 222

flexibility, need for, 21; careers and, 187, 189–91; corporate culture and, 110, 128; infrastructure and, 136; process management and, 107. See also mobility

"focus." See core competencies

Foote, Nathaniel, 18

forced curves, performance management and, 172, 189

Ford Motor Company, 222, 243

formalization, 37, 52–53, 106–7, 145–57, 182–83

forums, for communication, 93–95, 154, 239

Freelancers' Union, 272

free market ethic, 254–56, 257, 267, 270, 273

friendships. See personal relationships

front–back structures, 43, 45, 53, 82, 247; linking mechanisms and, 73, 75; Nokia and, 224

functional organization stage, 198

Gage, John, 146, 156

Galbraith, Jay, 43, 73

Gates, Bill, 273

General Electric Company (GE), 57, 143, 254–55

General Motors: cultural change and, 203, 204, 205, 207–8; joint ventures, 62–63, 66–67; performance management and, 172; strategy and, 141–42; value of participation and, 268. *See also* Saturn

geographical divisions, corporate: at Citibank, 71, 86; Citibank e-Solutions Group and, 89, 103, 105; evolution of work systems and, 215–16; linking mechanisms and, 223; meta-structures and, 81

Gerstner, Lou: collaborative vision and, 241–42; corporate values and, 228; customers and, 233; shared mission and, 237; strategy and, 60, 223

GHX (Global Healthcare Exchange), 49, 149, 232, 235, 240

global economy: Citibank and, 71, 86, 216; decline of paternalism and, 115; extended collaboration and, 15–16; solutions strategies and, 59

global relationship managers, 155

Global Relationships Bank (GRB), 105

GM. *See* General Motors

goals: accountability and, 185–86; bureaucratic organizations and, 2–3; of collaborative enterprise, 117; corporate culture and, 119; individual, 99, 100, 174–75; setting, 87. *See also* mission, shared

Gordon, Fred, 186

governance systems, 28–29, 49

government regulation. *See* regulatory systems

Granovetter, Mark S., 146

group performance, pay for performance and, 173

hansei process. *See* Reflection Review process

Hawthorne studies, 26–27

health insurance, 188, 190, 266

Hewlett-Packard: decentralization and, 222; personal relationships and, 156; research methods and, *284, 285*; scanning teams, 158–59; solutions strategies and, 232; strategy and, 143

hierarchies, 2, 16–17, 53, 63, *250–51*; adaptiveness and, 76; Citibank e-Solutions Group and, 81, 98–102, 106; collaboration and, 3, 34–35; in collaborative enterprise, 55, 121–22; communication in, 13; corporate culture and, 133, 259; corporate structures and, 25–26, 27; evolution of, 29–35; "flattening," 187; learning and, 162; linking mechanisms, 54, 71, 72; network theory and, 51; operational effectiveness and, 65–66; organizational charts, 38, 43, *44, 45*; solutions strategies and, 79–80. *See also* bureaucratic organizations

hierarchy (Cameron and Quinn), 133

hierarchy (Denison), 134

high-adaptiveness strategies. *See* adaptiveness

high-complexity strategies. *See* complexity

high-performance work systems, 213–14

Hock, Dee, 151

Hofstede, Geert, 129–30, 132

homogeneity, in teams, 66

horizontal work relationships, 35, 51, 140, 145, 246

human development, 260–62

Human Genome Project, 15

Human Relations. *See* personnel management

human resources departments, 180

IBM Corporation: change and, 205, 217; collaborative vision and, 241–42; corporate culture and, 129–30, 220; corporate structures, 45, 73, *74*; extended collaboration and, 15; high-complexity

IBM Corporation (continued)
strategies, 63, 223–24; innovation
units, 218, 219; interactions with superiors and, 122; organizational learning
and, 166; organizational responsiveness
and, 8; outward focus and, 232, 233;
performance management and, 172; research methods and, 285; shared mission and, 236–37; solutions strategies
and, 60–61, 64; strategy and, 143, 144;
Values Jam, 228–30; vision and values
statements, 144
ideologies, 110, 116
incentives, for performance, 137–38, 219,
220. See also compensation
individualism, 11–12, 130, 183–84, 184–85,
256, 274
individual performance, 173
industrial democracy, 258, 260
industry trends, external relationships
and, 157
inequality. See diversity; dualism
influence, collaboration and, 75
informal organization. See associational
relationships
information systems. See communication
information transparency, 148–49
infrastructure, 20, 135–36, 251; building
networks and, 238–39; in bureaucratic
organizations, 137–40; change and,
195, 196–97; Citibank e-Solutions
Group and, 92–98; collaborative infrastructure, 140–66; cross-firm infrastructure, 166–68; for job mobility,
189–91, 266; pay for performance, 172–
77; shared mission and, 119; social infrastructure, 248, 270–75
in-groups, 33, 52, 137. See also outward focus
"initiatives," strategic, 47
initiative teams, 103
innovation: collaborative vision and, 245;
infrastructure and, 168; marginal

groups and, 51; operational effectiveness and, 65; product development
and, 224; solutions strategies and, 87;
strategy and, 56; task teams and, 46–
47; utilization of knowledge and, 6.
See also adaptiveness
innovation units, 218–19, 220
In Search of Excellence (Peters and Waterman), 277
insecurity, 265–67, 270, 274–75. See also
job security
integration: decentralization and, 222;
high-adaptiveness strategies and, 77;
IBM Corporation and, 60–61; solutions strategies and, 62, 87; strategy
and, 57, 70–71
Intel Corporation, 5, 49, 75, 78, 149
intellectual property, 273
intelligence, mobilizing, 2
interactive change, 227–35
interactive process management, 40, 41
interdependence: collaborative enterprise
and, 222; corporate units and, 104–6;
performance management systems
and, 186; social, 16–17
internal competition, 171–72, 189
international economy. See global economy
International Standards Organization
(ISO), 168
Internet, the, 52, 76, 86, 149. See also
Citibank e-Solutions Group
investment, technological advances and,
79
inward focus, 89. See also outward focus
ISO certification, 49
iterative codesign processes, 40
Iwata, John, 228–29, 242

James, William, 211
Japanese companies: paternalism and, 31–
32; production systems, 4, 7–8, 48, 65,
115; relationships with contractors, 255

Jensen, Michael, 188
job descriptions. *See* roles, defined
job enrichment programs, 12, 212
job hunting, 190
job security: bureaucratic organizations and, 16, 137, 138–39, 140; changing expectations, 186–87; in collaborative enterprise, 117–18; corporate values and, 256, 266–67; cultural change and, 208–9; job performance and, 188–89; layoffs, 114, 115, 187, 188, 204
John Deere Company, 61–62
Johnson & Johnson, *285*
joint ventures, 62–63, 66–67
judgment, research and, 279
jurisdictional areas, 111. *See also* roles, defined
just-in-time production systems, 213

Kafka, Franz, 186
Kairamo, Kari, 224
kaizen processes, 166
Kanter, Rosabeth Moss, 278
Kaplan, Robert S., 178, 179
Kaypro Computers, 60
Khalil, Elias, 228
Khosla, Vinod, 188, 269
knowledge: adaptiveness and, 63; associational relationships and, 26; bureaucratic organizations and, 57–58; communication of, 93–95; corporate values and, 259; information transparency, 121, 148–49; networks and, 52; ownership of, 273–74; review processes, 165–66; solutions strategies and, 56, 82–83; utilization of, 6–7, 154. *See also* learning, organizational
knowledge databases, 94, 107, 154, 162, 164, 166
knowledge management, 140
knowledge production, 68–69
Kodak (Eastman Kodak Company), 62
Kuhn, Thomas, 197–98, 200

labor markets, 167–68, 187, 189–90. *See also* employment
Langstaff, David, 243
lateral communication, 32, 33
layoffs. *See* job security
leadership: building networks, 238–40; in bureaucratic organizations, 2–3; change and, 208, 235–40; Citibank e-Solutions Group and, 89, 93, 99, 101–2, 104; collaborative vision, 240–44; corporate culture and, 108, 114, 115, 116; defining priorities and, 98–99, 159–60; defining value contributions and, 240; encouraging collaboration and, 226–45, 249; forced collaboration and, 72, 217–22; outward focus and, 232–35; performance management and, 100, 101, 183; public dialogue and, 281; solutions strategies and, 80; understanding of collaboration by, 18; visionary, 200
lean production systems, 4, 65, 68, 82
learning, models of, 198, 203
learning, organizational: in bureaucratic organizations, 8–9; collaboration and, 55, 226, 227; collaborative infrastructure and, 162–66; corporate values and, 241–43; efficiency and, 247; external relationships and, 157, 158; lean production systems and, 65; review processes, 66–67. *See also* knowledge
"level 4" organization. *See* collaborative enterprise
Lindahl, Goren, 165
linking mechanisms: collaborative structures, 53, 82; between corporate units, 105–6; creating, 238–39; formalization of, 146–48; IBM Corporation and, 223; linking teams, 46; managing complexity and, 71, 72, 73, 74, 75, 247; meta-structures as, 80–81
listening, importance of, 230, 231, 233–34
Locke, John, 260, 274
*Lonely Crowd, The* (Riesman), 4

loyalty: bureaucratic organizations and, 26, 31, 32, 112, 113, 114; corporate culture and, 124–25, 243; cultural expectations of, 202–3; to family, 123; human development and, 261; infrastructure supporting, 137; job security and, 138–39, 187; openness to outside ideas and, 122; performance culture and, 115; performance management and, 171; regression to, 208–9, 249; social relationships and, 9–11, 257; value of, 274

Lucent Technologies, 77, 78, 221, 232, 285, 286

Luther, Martin, 11

managed collaboration, 69–75, 84, 247. See also complexity

management: associational relationships and, 27; in bureaucratic organizations, 31; evolution of work systems and, 215–17; management styles, 104; managing performance and, 175; performance management and, 171–72, 173–74; review processes and, 80; strategic fitness process, 230–31; strategy and, 20, 143, 144. See also hierarchies; leadership; middle management

Management by Objectives (MBO), 100, 171, 249

management fads, 34, 212–14

manufacturing: manufacturing processes, 7, 8, 212–14; operational effectiveness and, 68; solutions strategies and, 61–62

marginal groups, 51

marketing, automotive industry and, 7, 8

markets: bureaucratic organization and, 29; common purposes and, 2; communication in, 13; expansion of, 58, 60; free market ethic, 254–56, 257, 267, 270, 273; networks and, 52; range of, 1

Martin, Carlos, 19, 279

mass production, 59, 60

matrix organization, 72–73

matrix organizational charts, 43

Mayo, Elton, 27

MBO systems. See Management by Objectives (MBO)

McGinn, Rich, 221

McGregor, Douglas, 132, 134

McKinsey and Company, 18, 63, 77, 121, 286

measurement, of performance. See performance management

meetings, purpose of, 96–97. See also forums, for communication

Men and Women of the Corporation (Kanter), 278

mergers and acquisitions, corporate culture and, 109, 219–20

meritocracy, 259

Merton, Robert, 11–12, 111–12, 273–74

meta-structures, 80–81

methodology, of collaboration research, 18–19

metrics, corporate culture and, 110

Michael, Boniface, 19, 279

micro-management, 111

Microsoft, 47, 72, 78, 223, 286

middle management: compensation and, 176; cultural change and, 203, 208, 209; evolution of work systems and, 213, 216; job security and, 266; strategic fitness process, 230–31; strategy and, 143–44

mindsets. See expectations

Mintzberg, Henry, 27

mission (Denison), 133

mission, shared: Citibank e-Solutions Group and, 92, 93; compensation and, 176–77, 184; corporate culture and, 119–20, 127; infrastructure and, 135, 141–45, 152, 153; leadership and, 236–38, 244; multisource appraisals and, 181; networks and, 52; outside groups and, 96

mobility, 188, 189–91, 266, 271–72, 281

Monsanto Global Product Management Group, 80–81, 146–47

moral autonomy, 184, 186

morality. *See* values, societal

movie industry, 269

multidivisional firm stage, 198, 199

multinational teams, 265

multi-skilling, 66

multisource appraisals, 179–83

mutual understanding, infrastructure of, 153–54

MyCiti.com, 103

NASDAQ, 49

Nasser, Jacques, 243

National Bank Online Financial Services (OFS), 238

NEC, 219

negotiation, 97–98, 150, 151–53, 160

"network orchestrators," 146

networks: building, 238–40, 244; exclusionary, 155; of linked roles, 45, 48–49; non-business organizations, 76; organizational learning and, 164–65; personal, 107, 155, 216

network theory, 50–53, 145–46

New Deal, the, 273

newsletters, 94

"NewTech" (pseudonym), 47, 64, 80, 182, *286*

Nokia, 63, 204, 223, 224, *287*

Norton, David P., 178, 179

NUMMI, 66–67

obstacles to change, 201–10

office design, 91

"old boy's network," 96, 263

"On Demand" concept (IBM), 60–61, 64, 224

open-source software, 12–13, 273, 274

operating committees, 72

operational effectiveness, 56, 58–59, 62–63, 64–68, 69, 81

Opportunity Evaluation Group, Shell, 161

"opportunity owners," 45

organizational charts, 38, 43, *44*, 45, *47*, *90*, 146

organizational charts, upside-down, 43

Organizational Culture Inventory, 132

organizational responsiveness, 8

organizational structure. *See* structure, corporate

organizational types, *248*

*Organization Man, The* (Whyte), 4, 185

Osborne Computer, 60

Oslo Airport project, 57

Ouchi, William, 132, 133, 134

outward focus, 68, 88–89, 149, 157–66, 232–35. *See also* customers

overlapping design, 66

overlapping responsibilities, task teams and, 88–89

ownership. *See* property, regulation and

Palmisano, Sam, 60, 62, 224, 228, 242, 243

paradigm shifts, 196, 197–98

Parsons, Talcott, 148, 228

participation: false, 267–69; value of, 258–60, 267–69, 270, 272

Pateman, Carole, 260

paternalism, 30–34, 184–85; in collaborative enterprise, 55; corporate culture and, 111–15; regression to, 208–9; research on collaboration and, 132–33. *See also* bureaucratic organizations

Pattee, Howard, 227, 228

pay for performance, 171, 172–77, 185, 278. *See also* compensation; performance management

peer reviews, publishing, 183

pensions, 137, 190, 242

performance: compensation and, 176; failure and, 254–55; personal relationships and, 156

performance appraisals: Balanced Scorecard (BSC), 178, 179; Citibank e-Solutions Group and, 92, 95–96, 99–101; measurement of performance, 174–75; multisource appraisals, 179–83; reward for contribution and, 177–78

performance culture, 96–97, 115–17, 126
performance improvement, 172–73
performance management: Citibank
  e-Solutions Group and, 96–97, 99,
  100; collaborative infrastructure and,
  140; effectiveness of, 183–86; expectations and, 127; formalization and, 107;
  hierarchies and, 99–101; job security
  and, 189; Management by Objectives
  (MBO), 100, 171, 249; measuring performance, 117, 174–75; peer-based relationships and, 120–21. See also
  accountability
personal control, of businesses, 29
personal growth, 260–61
personalities, of individuals, 16–17
personal relationships, 51, 76, 127; in bureaucratic organizations, 113, 138, 202;
  collaborative infrastructure and, 154–
  57; communication and, 33, 34; competition and, 183–84; corporate culture
  and, 110, 120–21; networks and, 52–53,
  238; performance management and,
  101, 107, 116, 179–83. See also associational relationships; relationships
personal responsibility, 261–62. See also
  trust
personnel management, 27, 31, 137. See
  also performance management
Piaget, Jean, 198, 203, 228
planning, organizational, 157, 158, 159–
  60, 160–62
politics: in bureaucratic organizations, 31,
  32, 72, 114; research studies and, 253;
  resistance to change and, 218
Porter, Michael, 56
power differences, enduring, 265, 267–
  69, 270
practices. See infrastructure
preconceptions, research studies and, 253
precursors, of collaborative enterprise,
  211–25
prices. See cost, of products
PricewaterhouseCoopers, 61, 64, 219, 224

primary labor markets, 139
principles, cultural, 110, 130–31. See also
  values, societal
priorities: balancing, 63, 105, 123; communicating, 93; complexity and, 247;
  defining, 98–99, 159–60; meta-
  structures and, 80, 81; solutions strategies and, 79–80
"prisoner's dilemma," 128, 155
problem solving: negotiation and, 152;
  problem-solving groups, 46, 55, 66,
  154, 212–13, 267; problem-solving techniques, 238, 239
procedures manuals, 106, 137
"process champions," 45
processes, change, 235–40
process improvement teams (PITs), 98,
  107, 214, 217, 239
process management, 37–45, 50; at
  Citibank, 86; Citibank e-Solutions
  Group and, 97–98; cultural change
  and, 203; formalization and, 106–7,
  150–51; infrastructure and, 135–36; for
  knowledge utilization, 154; learning
  and, 163–64; personal relationships
  and, 155; task teams, 46–47
"process managers," 45
process mapping diagrams, 38, 39, 40, 128
product development, 63, 65, 66, 102,
  224
product development groups, 80–81, 85
production companies, 75
production systems: commodity production, 55–56; global economy and, 15–
  16; solutions strategies and, 59; teams
  and, 4; utilization of knowledge and,
  7–8, 9
product managers, 45
professional and craft associations, 28–29
professionalism, 91–92, 96, 124, 125, 132,
  156
profit centers, 221
profits, commodity production and, 56
project approval, 99

project collaboration. *See* adaptiveness

project review processes, 182

project teams, 63, 79, 82, 107

promotions, 137–38, 140, 171, 188, 209.

See also performance management

property, regulation and, 272–73, 274

proprietary products, 60

public dialogue, leadership and, 228–32, 233, 281

purpose. *See* goals; mission, shared

purpose statements, 145

quality, of products, 4, 56, 63, 67

quality circle programs, 12, 213

quality management systems. *See* Total Quality Management (TQM)

"Quality of Work Life" efforts, 213

Quinn, R. E., 133, 134

railroad industry, 29

Rath Packing Company, 258

rational bureaucracy, 111–12, 114

Rawls, John, 186

Raymond, Eric, 274

Reed, John, 71, 86, 153, 215, 216, 233

Reflection Review process, 67, 82, 166

reflexiveness, of culture, 127–28

regression, cultural change and, 205–6

regulatory systems, 16, 138, 270, 272–74, 275

relationships: adaptiveness and, 75–76; in bureaucratic organizations, 33, 34; collaboration and, 3, 4; corporate structures and, 25–28; corporate values and, 9–13, 255–56; extended collaboration and, 5, 83; network theory and, 51–52; trust and, 95, 96, 97. See also associational relationships; personal relationships

reliability, of products, 65, 75

religious movements, 3, 11

representation of employees, 270, 271–72, 275

reputational systems, 95–97, 129, 177, 182–83, 190, 269

research: on associational relationships, 26–27; on collaboration, 17–19, 55, 246, 277–82, *283–87*; on corporate culture, 108, 110, 126–34; effect of values on, 252–53; on managing performance, 173, 185; methodology of, 18–19; on network theory, 50–53

research methods, 17–19, 277–282; disconfirming evidence, research and, 278, 279, 280; and corporate culture, 126–134; and response rates, 278

resistance to change, 204–10, 248–49; leadership and, 218, 231, 243; by outgroups, 235; power differences and, 270

resources, allocating: accountability and, 175; Citibank e-Solutions Group and, 89; defining priorities and, 160; defining value contributions and, 240; "empire-building" and, 102; hierarchies and, 99; negotiation and, 152–53; solutions strategies and, 79–80

response teams, 46–47

responsiveness. *See* organizational responsiveness

restriction of output, 31

restructuring, 9

retention, of employees, 188, 190

retirement planning, 16, 21

review processes: efficiency and, 247; infrastructure and, 66–67, 136, 160–61, *161*, 165–66; meta-structures and, 80; Total Quality Management (TQM) and, 67–68

reward for contribution, 177–83

reward systems. *See* compensation

roles, defined: bureaucratic organizations and, 3–4, 11–12, 111, 114–15; in collaborative enterprise, 5, 37; cultural change and, 201–2; infrastructure and, 137, 148; negotiation and, 97–98; performance appraisal and, 178; process management and, 45; shared mission and, 119–20; task teams and, 89, 91; worker attitudes and, 118

"roles and responsibility" sessions, 98, 150
Rousseau, Jean-Jacques, 260

Sabel, Charles, 40
salespeople, 8, 158, 221
Salomon, Smith, Barney, 105
Saturn, 122, 142, 149, 214, *287*
scanning. *See* sensing and scanning
scanning teams, 158–59
"Scenario Planning" process, Shell, 158
Scientific Management, 137
scientific research: adaptiveness and, 77;
    collaboration and, 6, 12, 15; effect of
    values on, 252–53; networks and, 52,
    76; paradigm shifts and, 197–98, 200
secondary labor markets, 139
self-interest, 253, 254
semi-autonomous teams, 4, 46, 65, 66,
    181, 247
seniority, 271
senior management teams, cross-firm
    structures and, 103
sensing and scanning, 158–59, 160–62
sequence, of change, 227
Shakespeare, William, 10
shared purpose. *See* mission, shared
Shell: Balanced Scorecard (BSC), 238;
    communities of practice, 164; defining
    priorities and, 159; experience-sharing
    forums, 154; information transparency
    and, 149; innovation units, 218; linking
    mechanisms and, 147, *148*; outward fo-
    cus and, 235; research methods and,
    *287*; "Scenario Planning" process, 158;
    Shell New Business Ventures, 160–61
Silicon Valley companies, 54
"simple rules" approach, 151, 158
simultaneous engineering, 65, 66, 68
"single-loop" learning, 163
Sloan, Alfred, 17, 31, 141
small groups, 1, 205, 206–8, 249
Smith, Adam, 2, 78
social capital, 136
social infrastructure. *See* infrastructure

socialism, 185
social values, 252–75
societal support, for job mobility, 189–91
society, global, effects of business on, 16–
    17
sociodynamics, change and, 204–10
software development, 12–13
"soldiering," 31
solutions strategies, 58–63, 63–64, 77–80,
    *250–51*; allocating resources and, 153;
    careers and, 187; Citibank e-Solutions
    Group and, 86–88; external relation-
    ships and, 158, 159, 160–62; implemen-
    tation, 230–31, 237; leadership and,
    230–32, 237; meta-structures and, 80–
    81; strategic challenges and, 247;
    strategic dimensions and, 81, 82; struc-
    tures and, 247–48; successful paths to,
    222–24. *See also* systemic collaboration
Southwest Airlines, 62
specialization, pay for performance and,
    173–74
spiral process model, 40, *42*
stability, of culture, 128
stages of organization development, 197–
    99, 199–201, 227–28
stakeholder groups, 232, 234, 235, 248
standardization, 48, 49, 136, 151; industry-
    wide, 168
"stovepipes." *See* units, corporate
strategic dialogue, 143–44
strategic dimensions, 63–64, *64*, 70, 71,
    77, 81, 159
strategic fitness process, 166, 230–32, 237,
    244, 259, 268
strategic partnerships. *See* cross-firm
    structures
strategy, *21*, 55–58, *250*; adaptiveness, 63,
    75–77; Citibank e-Solutions Group
    and, 86–88, 93, 102–3, 105; collabora-
    tive infrastructure and, 141–45; com-
    plexity and, 63, 69–75; cultural change
    and, 206; defined, 20; employee par-
    ticipation and, 268–69; knowledge

production, 68–69; meta-structures
and, 80–81; operational effectiveness
and, 63, 64–68; performance appraisal
and, 178–79; shared mission and, 236–
38; solutions strategies, 58–63, 63–64,
77–80; types of collaboration and, 54,
55, 247
structural change. See change
structure, corporate, 19–20, 21; change
and, 195, 196, 218; Citibank e-Solutions Group and, 88–91, 101–2; corporate culture and, 108, 228; cross-
firm structures, 48–49; evolution of,
28–35, 36; IBM Corporation and, 73,
74; infrastructure and, 46–47, 165, 250;
network theory, 50–53; process management, 37–45; relationships and, 25–
28; solutions strategies and, 247–48;
strategy and, 55–57
"successful failures," 211–12, 236
Sun Microsystems, 72, 146, 188, 196–97,
287
superiors, interactions with, 121–22, 127.
    See also leadership; management
supervisors, performance appraisal and,
173–74, 179, 180
supplier networks, 48, 67, 232, 234
supply chain management, 49, 149
surveys, validity of, 129, 130, 132
systemic collaboration, 77–80, 84, 133,
134, 247–48, 281. See also solutions
strategies

Talent Alliance, 191
task forces. See task teams
task teams, 5, 35, 46–47, 50; accountability and, 175, 182; building networks
and, 238–39; change and, 203–4, 218;
Citibank e-Solutions Group and, 88–
89, 91, 103; defining value contributions and, 240; diversity and, 264–65;
infrastructure and, 92, 135–36, 154, 155,
157, 163; operational effectiveness and,
65; strategic fitness processes, 230–31

Tavistock Institute, 258
Taylor, Frederick, 7, 8, 30, 212
teams, 4, 33, 35, 82; adaptiveness and, 76–
77; Alliance team, Citibank e-Solutions Group and, 102–4; autonomous
teams, 213; building networks and,
238; at Citibank, 86; evolution of work
systems and, 214; formal codes for,
150; hierarchies and, 63; multinational
teams, 265; operational effectiveness
and, 65, 66; personal growth and,
260–61; power differences and, 267–
68; process improvement teams
(PITs), 98, 107, 214, 217; scanning
teams, 158–59; semi-autonomous
teams, 4, 46, 65, 66, 181, 247; small
teams, 54. See also task teams
technological advances: business objectives and, 87, 88; change and, 59;
cross-firm structures and, 102–3; investment and, 79; solutions strategies
and, 61, 78. See also innovation
technology infrastructure, 136, 147–48,
151, 154, 164
telecommunications industry, 78, 79
templates, collaborative infrastructure
and, 151
theory of collaboration, evolution of,
281
"Theory X," 132
"Theory Y," 132
"Theory Z," 132, 133
360-degree feedback, 180–81, 183
"throwing over the wall" concept, 38, 70
tolerance, 263
tools, for collaborative enterprise, 92–98.
    See also infrastructure
top-down change initiatives, 217
Total Quality Management (TQM): cultural change and, 203; evolution of
work systems and, 214–15; operational
effectiveness and, 65; power differences
and, 267–68; problem-solving groups
and, 46; review processes and, 9, 67–68

town hall meetings, 154. *See also* forums, for communication

Toyota, 62–63, 66–67, 166

TQM. *See* Total Quality Management (TQM)

traditional bureaucracy, 112–15

training programs: infrastructure and, 136; job mobility and, 190; negotiation and, 152; in problem-solving techniques, 239; review processes and, 165; strategy and, 99, 142, 236. *See also* learning, organizational

transformative change, 195–96, 217–22, 226–45

transitional processes: to collaborative enterprise, 195–210; corporate culture and, 116, 124; for teaching collaboration, 227. *See also* change

*Trial, The* (Kafka), 186

trust: Citibank e-Solutions Group and, 95–97; corporate culture and, 109, 117, 119, 124–25, 126; corporate values and, 255, 262, 263; cultural change and, 202, 206; insecurity and, 267; job security and, 189; performance management and, 100, 101, 116; personal relationships and, 120, 156

uncertainty, defining priorities and, 99

unemployment, 189–90

unions: decline of, 140; evolution of work systems and, 213, 214; information transparency and, 149; job security and, 138–39; representation and, 271–72; teams and, 67; traditional bureaucracy and, 114; value of participation and, 268

unit firm stage, 198

units, corporate: at Citibank, 85–86; Citibank e-Solutions Group and, 88, 104–6; communication between, 38, 65, 66, 71; decentralization and, 70; linking mechanisms and, 72–73; shared mission and, 237

universal dimensions model, 129–30

validation, of research, 131–32, 280–81

value: adding, 147; communicating, 93–95; of contributions, 119; defining value contributions, 238, 239–40; of extended collaboration, 6–9; of knowledge, 56; of knowledge databases, 164; negotiation and, 97, 152

value orientations, of corporate types, 254–56, 257

values, corporate. *See* culture, corporate

values, societal, 184–85, 252–75

Values Jam, IBM, 228–30, 242, 243, 244, 259–60

values statements. *See* vision and values statements

Venkatesan, Ravi, 122, 220, 241, 243

Veridian, 143, 144, 166, 207, 230–31, 243, 287

Visa, 49, 151

vision: change and, 199–201, 217, 225; leadership and, 240–44; shared mission and, 236, 237

vision and values statements, 144–45, 241

voice, mechanisms of, 136, 140

wages, commodity production and, 56. *See also* compensation

Wal-Mart, 234

Wang Corporation, 14, 60

war for talent, 141, 188

weaknesses, of local collaboration, 6

"weak ties," 51, 146, 147

*Wealth of Nations, The* (Smith), 78

Weber, Max: on bureaucratic organizations, 3, 4, 11, 29–30; corporate structures and, 25; rational bureaucracy and, 111, 112

Web pages, 94, 103

Welch, Jack, 143, 254–55

Wenger, Etienne, 164

*White Collar Blues* (Heckscher), 18

Whyte, William, 185

"win–win" collaborations, 97, 152, 153

worker-owned companies, 258

worker participation programs, 12

workforce, attitudes of: in bureaucratic organizations, 30, 31; change and, 16, 196–97, 203, 205–10; collaborative enterprise and, 34–35; corporate culture and, 124–26; defined roles and, 118; IBM Values Jam, 228–29; job mobility and, 191; performance management systems and, 183–84; vision and values statements, 145. *See also* employees

Working Today, 272

"Work-Out" process, 143

work styles, traditional bureaucracy and, 113–14

World Bank, 164, 219

World Corporate Group (WCG), Citibank, 215–16, 218

Wriston, Walter, 215

"yellow pages," corporate, 147

9 780300 114645